NORMATIVE PATTERNS AND LEGAL DEVELOPMENTS IN THE SOCIAL DIMENSION OF THE EU

This book explores the normative and legal evolution of the social dimension of the European Union—in this case labour law, social security law and family law—in both the European Union and its Member States, during the last decade. It does this from a wide range of theoretical and legal-substantive perspectives. The past decade has witnessed the entering into force of the Lisbon Treaty and its emphasis on fundamental rights, a new Coordination Regulation (883/2004/EC) within the field of social security, and the case law of the Court of Justice of the European Union in the so-called *Laval* Quartet cases. Furthermore, structural changes affecting demographics and the family have also challenged solidarity in new ways. The book is organised by reference to distinct 'normative patterns' and their development in the fields of law covered, such as the protection of established groups, the position of market-functional values and the scope for just distribution. The book represents an innovative and important interdisciplinary approach to analysing EU law and Social Europe, and contributes a complex, yet thought-provoking, picture for the future. The contributors represent an interesting mix of well-known and distinguished, as well as upcoming and promising, researchers throughout Europe and beyond.

Volume 40 in the series Modern Studies in European Law

Modern Studies in European Law

Recent titles in this series:

The European Union and Global Emergencies: A Law and Policy Analysis
Edited by Antonis Antoniadis, Robert Schütze and Eleanor Spaventa

Public Liability in EU Law: *Brasserie, Bergaderm* and Beyond
Pekka Aalto

Professional Services in the EU Internal Market: Quality Regulation and Self-Regulation
Tinne Heremans

Environmental Integration in the EU's External Relations: Beyond Multilateral Dimensions
Gracia Marín Durán and Elisa Morgera

The Constitutional Dimension of European Criminal Law
Ester Herlin-Karnell

EU Counter-Terrorism Law: Pre-Emption and the Rule of Law
Cian Murphy

Children and the European Union: Rights, Welfare and Accountability
Helen Stalford

Federalism in the European Union
Edited by Elke Cloots, Geert De Baere and Stefan Sottiaux

Toward a Prosecutor for the European Union Volume 1: A Comparative Analysis
Edited by Katalin Ligeti

Empowerment and Disempowerment of the European Citizen
Edited by Michael Dougan, Niamh Nic Shuibhne and Eleanor Spaventa

Legal Reasoning and the European Court of Justice
Gunnar Beck

Lawyering Europe: European Law as a Transnational Social Field
Edited by Antoine Vauchez and Bruno de Witte

Services and the EU Citizen
Edited by Frank S Benyon

The Accession of the European Union to the European Convention on Human Rights
Paul Gragl

For the complete list of titles in this series, see 'Modern Studies in European Law' link at www.hartpub.co.uk/books/series.asp

Normative Patterns and Legal Developments in the Social Dimension of the EU

Edited by
Ann Numhauser-Henning
and
Mia Rönnmar

•HART•
PUBLISHING

OXFORD AND PORTLAND, OREGON
2013

Published in the United Kingdom by Hart Publishing Ltd
16C Worcester Place, Oxford, OX1 2JW
Telephone: +44 (0)1865 517530
Fax: +44 (0)1865 510710
E-mail: mail@hartpub.co.uk
Website: http://www.hartpub.co.uk

Published in North America (US and Canada) by
Hart Publishing
c/o International Specialized Book Services
920 NE 58th Avenue, Suite 300
Portland, OR 97213-3786
USA
Tel: +1 503 287 3093 or toll-free: (1) 800 944 6190
Fax: +1 503 280 8832
E-mail: orders@isbs.com
Website: http://www.isbs.com

British Library Cataloguing in Publication Data
Data Available

ISBN: 978-1-84946-435-2

Typeset by Compuscript Ltd, Shannon
Printed and bound in Great Britain by
TJ International Ltd, Padstow

MIX
Paper from responsible sources
FSC www.fsc.org FSC® C013056

Preface

This book aims to explore the normative and legal evolution within the social dimension—in this case labour law, social security law and family law—of the European Union and its Member States during the last decade or so from a multitude of theoretical and legal-substantive perspectives. It has its background in an international symposium on 'Normative Patterns and Legal Developments in Labour Law, Social Security Law and Family Law' which was held at the Faculty of Law at Lund University in May 2011 and funded by the Swedish Council for Working Life and Social Research. This symposium was arranged by the Norma Research Programme in memory of its former member Professor Anna Christensen (1936–2001), but also to mark the Norma Research Programme's first 15 years of activity (see *Fifteen Years with the Norma Research Programme, Anniversary Volume*, available at www.jur.lu.se/norma).

While the relation of this project to the Norma Research Programme and the late Anna Christensen mark the contents of this book, it is by no means to be viewed merely as a collection of conference proceedings. To elaborate on the complex issues of the EU social dimension from 'a broader than usual' perspective has proved to be an intellectually challenging exercise reflecting important overall developments within the social dimension in relation to innovations such as the coming into force of the Lisbon Treaty and the EU Charter of Fundamental Rights, as well as the Coordination Regulation 883/2004/EC, and also with respect to the case law of the Court of Justice of the European Union in the so-called *Laval* Quartet cases, and continual structural changes as regards demographics and families. It is our conviction that this book represents an innovative and important interdisciplinary approach to the analysis of European law, Social Europe and future social policy developments.

The contributors to this book represent an interesting mix of well-known and very prestigious researchers, as well as upcoming and promising young researchers. As editors we are, of course, deeply indebted to all the authors and to the effort and enthusiasm they have put into the project.

Ann Numhauser-Henning and Mia Rönnmar
Lund, December 2012

Contents

Notes on Contributors

Niklas Bruun is Professor of Private Law, University of Helsinki, Finland; director of the research programme Regulating Markets and Labour (ReMarkLab), Stockholm University; and member of the Centre of Excellence in the Foundations of European Law and Polity, University of Helsinki.

Simon Deakin is Professor of Law at the University of Cambridge, specialising in labour law, private law, company law, EU law, law and economics, law and development and empirical legal studies. He is a programme director in the Centre for Business Research and Editor-in-Chief of the *Industrial Law Journal*.

Thomas Erhag is Associate Professor of Public Law at the Department of Law, School of Business, Economics and Law, Göteborg University. He has written widely on issues of social security and EU law, and is on the editorial board of *Nordisk Socialrättslig Tidskrift*.

Judy Fudge is a Professor and Lansdowne Chair in Law at the University of Victoria, Canada, and a Fernand Braudel Fellow at the European University Institute in 2012, after which she will take up a Leverhulme Visiting Professorship at Kent Law School in 2013.

Titti Mattsson is Professor of Public Law at the Faculty of Law, Lund University, and a member of the Norma Research Programme. Her research primarily concerns child law issues, but also covers elder law, health law, social law and family law. She is an expert at the Swedish Children's Ombudsman and a Swedish member of the Nordic Council of Ministers' Committee on Bioethics.

Per Norberg is Assistant Professor of Private Law at the Faculty of Law, Lund University, and a member of the Norma Research Programme. His research interests are labour law, housing law, gender equality law and social security law. He is a member of the European Commission's Network of Legal Experts on Discrimination.

Ann Numhauser-Henning is Professor of Private Law at the Faculty of Law at Lund University. She is the former Pro-Vice Chancellor of Lund University and currently the coordinator of the Norma Research Programme and its research environment on elder law.

Eva Ryrstedt is Professor of Private Law at the Faculty of Law, Lund University, and a member of the Norma Research Programme. She often conducts her research in the interface between social welfare law and family law, and a current research theme is elder law. She is also writing a new Commentary to the Marriage Code in Sweden.

Mia Rönnmar is a Professor of Private Law at the Faculty of Law at Lund University, and a member of the Norma Research Programme and the ReMarkLab research programme. She is specialising in Swedish, comparative and EU labour law and industrial relations. She is the Editor-in-Chief of the *International and Comparative Labour Law and Industrial Relations Journal.*

Silvana Sciarra is Professor of Labour Law and European Social Law at the University of Florence. She is also a former Professor at the European University Institute in Florence and has been a Visiting Professor at, among others, Columbia Law School, Cambridge University, Stockholm University and Lund University.

Kaarlo Tuori is Professor of Jurisprudence at Helsinki University. At present he is Academy Professor and Director of the CoE Foundations of European Law and Polity. He is a specialist in both legal theory and public law, and in recent years he has increasingly focused on the legal and constitutional theory of European law.

Jenny Julén Votinius is Associate Senior Lecturer in Private Law at the Faculty of Law, Lund University, and a member of the Norma Research Programme. She conducts research within the fields of labour law, EU law and social security law. Her research has to a large extent been directed towards questions of discrimination and gender relations.

Abbreviations

CEFL	Commission on European Family Law
CJEU	Court of Justice of the European Union
CRC	Convention on the Rights of the Child
ECHR	European Convention on Human Rights
ECtHR	European Court of Human Rights
EFSF	European Financial Stability Facility
EFSM	European Financial Stability Mechanism
ESF	European Social Fund
EWC	European Works Council
ILO	International Labour Organization
MoU	Memorandum of Understanding
NGO	non-governmental organization
OMC	Open Method of Coordination
TEU	Treaty on European Union
TFEU	Treaty on the Functioning of the European Union

Part I

Introduction

1

Introduction

ANN NUMHAUSER-HENNING AND MIA RÖNNMAR

I. INTRODUCTORY REMARKS

THIS BOOK AIMS to explore the normative and legal evolution that has taken place in the last decade or so within the social dimension—in terms of labour law, social security law and family law—of the European Union and its Member States. The book analyses this development from a multitude of theoretical and legal-substantive perspectives. It represents an innovative and important interdisciplinary approach to the analysis of EU law, Social Europe, and future social policy developments linked to crucial societal and demographic changes in Europe as well as to EU law, policy and strategy.

A background factor of obvious importance from the overall perspective of this book is the coming into force of the Lisbon Treaty in 2009, implicating a new aim of creating a social market economy (Article 3(3) TEU), a legally binding EU Charter of Fundamental Rights, and a future accession to the European Convention on Human Rights (ECHR) (Article 6 TEU). Well before this, partial steps of great importance were taken, such as the introduction of EU Citizenship (already in the Maastricht Treaty, and now Articles 20–23 TFEU); the adoption of the EU Charter of Fundamental Rights as a soft law instrument in 2000; and the broadened competences as regards non-discrimination measures in the Amsterdam Treaty (now Article 19 TFEU). The Lisbon Treaty is in itself a basis for claiming that the former market hegemony is no longer indisputable, and that there is really no longer any basis for the 'decoupling' of the social and the economic forces within the Union.[1] On the other hand, the Court of Justice of the European Union (CJEU) case law in the so-called *Laval* Quartet[2] (and the

[1] Compare D Schiek, 'Transnational Collective Labour Agreements in Europe' in M Rönnmar (ed), *EU Industrial Relations v National Industrial Relations. Comparative and Interdisciplinary Perspectives* (Alphen aan den Rijn, Kluwer, 2008) and P Syrpis, 'The Treaty of Lisbon: Much Ado … But About What?' (2008) 37 *Industrial Law Journal* 235.

[2] Case C-341/05 *Laval* [2007] ECR I-11767, Case C-438/05 *Viking* [2007] ECR I-10779, Case C-346/06 *Rüffert* [2008] ECR I-1989 and Case C-319/06 *Commission v Luxembourg* [2008] ECR I-4323.

subsequent proposal for the Monti II Regulation,[3] later withdrawn, however) have formed the basis for a comprehensive discussion about the conflict between fundamental collective labour rights and fundamental Treaty freedoms, bringing the ECHR and the European Court of Human Rights (ECtHR) into the overall picture as well. EU Citizenship has broadened the fundamental freedoms of the European Union to encompass not only the economically active but also EU citizens generally, a feature reflected not only in important case law by the CJEU, but also by the broadened scope of Regulation (EC) 883/2004 on the coordination of social security systems ('Coordination Regulation'), which has replaced the old Regulation 1408/71. Since the substantive contents of social security law as well as family law are left to the Member States, basically, the developments concerning fundamental and basic social rights and the right to a family has evolved around the case law of the CJEU applying the Coordination Regulation, and the case law of the ECtHR. Finally, the new Treaty basis for non-discrimination initiatives and the EU Charter of Fundamental Rights have evolved into a new set of both primary and secondary law instruments, making EU equality law more comprehensive and transformative[4] than in the past.

A factual as well as political, institutional, legal and strategic change of the utmost importance during the last decade is, of course, the enlargement of the European Union to now include 27 Member States that possess considerable economic, political and legal differences. In combination with demographic developments such as unsustainable fertility rates and a rapidly ageing population, EU faces severe challenges–for societies and economies, culturally and organisationally, and from a legitimacy point of view. There are worries about how intergenerational solidarity and living standards will be affected, as each worker has to provide for the consumption needs of a growing number of elderly dependants in the form of pensions and health care.[5] Demographic projections have been made ever since the 2001 Stockholm European Council and now feed into EU strategies at all levels. In 2010, the Lisbon Strategy was replaced with the Europe 2020 Strategy for smart, sustainable and inclusive growth.[6] This overall strategy can be said to combine the concerns for a greener, more resource-efficient and more competitive economy based on knowledge and innovation, with social concerns of an inclusive growth fostering a high-employment economy delivering social and territorial cohesion. For some years EU social policy has been greatly influenced by a flexicurity discourse, also much debated. The European Council

[3] Proposal for a Council Regulation on the exercise of the right to take collective action within the context of the freedom of establishment and the freedom to provide services, COM(2012)130 final.

[4] Compare B Hepple, 'Equality at Work' in B Hepple and B Veneziani (eds), *The Transformation of Labour Law in Europe: A Comparative Study of 15 Countries 1945–2004* (Oxford, Hart Publishing, 2009), and the period 2000–04.

[5] Compare, for instance, the 2012 Ageing Report, Economic and Budgetary Projections for the 27 EU Member States (2010–2060), Joint Report prepared by the European Commission (DG ECFIN) and the Economic Policy Committee (AWG) (21 May 2012).

[6] COM(2010)2020 final.

has adopted Common Principles of Flexicurity, which are handled within the context of the European Employment Strategy and the Europe 2020 Strategy, and Directives on part-time work, fixed-term work and temporary agency work have been adopted. The aim of flexicurity is to reduce labour market segmentation, but also to increase economic growth and Europe's competitiveness in a global perspective. Flexicurity includes flexible and reliable contractual arrangements, effective and active labour market policies, reliable and adaptable systems for lifelong learning, and modern social security systems. Employment and economic growth are also dealt with in common Integrated Guidelines,[7] drawing attention to the interdependency between social issues, such as employment quality, social cohesion and economic growth, thus making us revisit the Treaty provision of the EU social market economy and 'the million-dollar question' regarding future market or social dimension hegemony within the European Union.

The question is all the more pressing as the European Union has experienced the deepest recession in decades, followed by the euro and sovereign debt crisis, putting an unprecedented stress on workers and enterprises and resulting in a major negative impact on public finances. The responses to the crisis have varied among the Member States, and have come in different phases. Many Member States first put crisis-related measures in place, such as internal flexibility, short-term working arrangements and wage concessions. The subsequent euro and sovereign debt crisis led not only to fundamental financial and governance reforms at EU level, but also to far-reaching austerity measures, deregulatory labour law and social security reforms in many Member States. These measures targeted, for example, employment protection regulation, collective bargaining, wage-setting and pension systems. Member States that were given 'bailout' packages by the 'Troika' were particularly affected. In several Member States these reforms were introduced hastily, without recourse to democratic and participatory procedures.[8]

In addition, changing family structures, the successive integration of women in paid work, and the need for reconciliation between economic activities and family and social life pose severe challenges for the EU social dimension.

The themes to explore are thus multifaceted and intertwined in complex ways. Both the book and this Introduction are structured to include different parts on Law as Normative Patterns and Other Theoretical Perspectives; Protection of Established Position and Normative Development; Market Functionalism and Normative Development; and Just Distribution and Normative Development, respectively. This way of organising the different issues at stake was inspired by the late Anna Christensen's theory of *law as normative patterns in a normative*

[7] Council Decision 2010/707/EU of 21 October 2010 (EUT L308/46, 24 November 2010), later extended to 2011 and 2012, compare Council Decision 2012/238/EU of 26 April 2012.

[8] See C Barnard, 'The Financial Crisis and the Euro Plus Pact: a Labour Lawyer's Perspective' (2012) 41 *Industrial Law Journal* 98; S Clauwaert and I Schömann, *The Crisis and National Labour Law Reforms: a Mapping Exercise*, ETUI Working Paper 2012:04 (Brussels, ETUI, 2012); and S Laulom *et al*, *How has the Crisis Affected Social Legislation in Europe?*, ETUI Policy Brief No 2/2012 (Brussels, ETUI, 2012).

field, and focuses on normative patterns that have proven to be crucial to legal development in the social dimension.[9]

The purpose of this Introduction is to link together the different chapters and issues in an attempt to highlight common traits, differences and thematic interrelations between the chapters, as well as normative and legal challenges for the future. This Introduction represents nothing more than our own understanding of the different topics and interrelated issues, and what is presented here can thus by no means be ascribed to the respective authors of the individual chapters.

II. LAW AS NORMATIVE PATTERNS AND OTHER THEORETICAL PERSPECTIVES

This initial part focuses on different theoretical perspectives on law and society. It begins with a chapter on Anna Christensen's theory of *law as normative patterns in a normative field*, written by Ann Numhauser-Henning. This is only natural, taking into consideration that this book has its origins in the Norma Research Programme, of which Christensen was a founder and Numhauser-Henning is now the coordinator.[10] The theory is by no means a common denominator for studies within the Norma Research Programme, but its application has proven to be very fruitful in various studies of the social dimension within this programme.

Christensen's theory is thus based on the thesis that different basic normative patterns can be distinguished in the multitude of legal norms—much like in a drawing by Escher—or as Hofstadter has described human thinking, attempting to distinguish and describe certain patterns. Christensen's analysis of law in the social dimension served to identify such crucial basic normative patterns within this area of law, and these patterns underlie every legal system; they are a part of those cultural values upon which society is built. Among the important basic patterns present in the normative field within the social dimension are, on the one hand, the Rights of Ownership and the Freedom of Contract, which together form the Market-Functional pattern; and on the other hand, Protection of Established Position (ie the right to one's possessions, or for instance, security of employment and the principle of replacement of lost earnings). A third basic normative pattern is Just Distribution, a distributive pattern related to social justice and solidarity. As social life is quite complex, these normative patterns do not make up the 'hierarchical legal system' we frequently imagine.[11] Instead, these patterns are put into play in a normative field as determined by different basic patterns, which also act

[9] See further Ann Numhauser-Henning, Chapter 2.

[10] See further www.jur.lu.se/norma.

[11] Compare Christensen who argues that '[l]egal theory … has been trapped in that Kelsean dream about a consistent, hierarchical system. This eternal arranging and rearranging of the different parts of the assembly of norms in order to make them fit into a system seldom brings about any new insight'. A Christensen, 'Polycentricity and Normative Patterns' in H Petersen and H Zahle (eds), *Legal Polycentricity: Consequences of Pluralism in Law* (Aldershot, Darthmouth, 1995).

as normative poles. The 'origin' of the patterns differs according to the values they are set to protect, and thus, typically speaking, there is tension between different patterns. Societal change is what effects the 'attraction' behind the poles over time, and thus also legal change. Changes in the underlying conditions of production provide explanations for the movements in the normative field. However, the basic normative patterns all represent enduring and legitimate normative conceptions in society, and it is the task of legislators and courts to balance these conceptions within the framework of law. Another crucial component of the theoretical framework is the *functional relationship between law and the structure of society.* The thesis that social structure (material conditions, principles of organisation, modes of production and societal conflicts) determines, inter alia, the content of the law underlies the writings of both Christensen and Numhauser-Henning. The basic normative patterns are thus held to reflect normative practices functional to society and human relationships. Changes in the conditions of production as well as other structures, institutions and conditions crucial to society are thus used to explain the movements in the normative field from time to time, and can also be pictured in a *functional field* in which these two components interact. Common for both of these components are also the possibilities to open up the national confines of legal science, as they both emphasise structures and patterns which are common to many different national legal systems, not least within the European Union.

This chapter by Numhauser-Henning thoroughly describes the evolution of Christensen's theory and also its application throughout the years (mainly within the Norma Research Programme) in the various legal fields of labour law, social security law and family law. The labour law studies deal, inter alia, with non-discrimination regulation and the flexibilisation of labour markets, whereas the social security studies tend to focus on pension issues—but also parental benefits—from both domestic and EU perspectives. In family law, we are acquainted with the normative patterns guiding marital property regimes, as well as their implications with regard to 'the right to a family' in social policy custody cases.

The theory of law as normative patterns in a normative field is a theory about normative perceptions within law and legal science itself, but it is also a theory addressing law as a societal—and basically functional—phenomenon. As Tuori puts it, Christensen's theory is not about legal solutions in the sense of being right or wrong from an internal legal interpretative perspective: 'the solutions can only be found at a political level'.[12] This underpins the theory's basically empirical character. Its theoretical framework provides for a basically *descriptive* theory/method of law as empirical facts. What is described, however, is the *normative* content of rules and regulations. In this regard, as is indicated throughout Numhauser-Henning's chapter, the theory of law as normative patterns in a normative field does of course relate to a vast theoretical background of classic

[12] See Kaarlo Tuori, Chapter 3.

works within sociology and other disciplines, such as those of Weber, Habermas and Durkheim.

There are, of course, also relations to a number of other legal theories and scientists. Some of these are briefly touched upon in the chapter itself. Here, we will also relate to the currently very influential *autopoiesis theory* of law, with Gunther Teubner and Niklas Luhmann as its most prominent representatives, and to Kaarlo Tuori and his theory of *critical legal positivism*.

The autopoiesis theory[13] is a theory of law and its limitations when considered as an agent of change. Perceiving law as an instrument of change or political steering has been accused of ignoring the problem of the law's integrity as a specific mode of reasoning, discourse or system of communication 'on its own'. The theory is a highly abstract theory providing a conception of law as a system confronted by its environment. Its central claim is that law is to be considered as an essentially self-referential system of communication. Law has its own understanding of things, such as efficiency or truth. Legal communication is essentially in terms of right and wrong, legality or illegality. This theory thus basically produces a binary output, and around this characteristic form of legal communication a whole apparatus of distinctive concepts and modes of reasoning develops. Law as a system is cognitively open but normatively closed. It can and does routinely recognise and respond to economic, scientific, political or other events or phenomena. However, it can only 'observe' its environment in relation to its own categories of evaluation and interpretation. It is thus normatively closed in the sense that it can, and does, operate only with its own imperatives as a system of communication.[14] Direct communications are possible only within communication systems and not between them. Different forms of communication (such as law, economics and science) are self-referential in the sense of being maintained not by inputs from their environment, but through the specific discursive criteria that they endlessly reproduce.

According to our understanding, the theory of law as normative patterns in a normative field is at least partly compatible with the autopoiesis theory as regards *normative reproduction*, in that it claims that law reacts to societal needs and perceptions. However, it transforms these influences in terms of normative patterns and other internal criteria inherent in the normative structure, and thus also limits the outcome. It is said that the autopoiesis theory encourages us to examine 'how law thinks'—and, that is precisely what we do when we identify and understand basic normative patterns in the multitude of legal norms(!) On the other hand, there is Christensen's conception of *basic* normative patterns as 'codifications' of social and also moral customs and practices in society. This may seem distant

[13] See, eg G Teubner, *Autopoietic Law: a New Approach to Law and Society* (Berlin, de Gruyter 1987) and N Luhmann, *A Sociological Theory of Law* (E King-Utz and M Albrow (trans), London, Routledge, 1985).

[14] 'Law's responses are not to an environment that in some way impacts directly on it, but to an environment that law itself constructs intellectually in its own terms, and understands in terms of its own communicative criteria', see R Cotterrell, *The Sociology of Law: An Introduction*, 2nd edn (London, Butterworths, 1992) 67.

from the view of law as a basically self-referential system of communication. However, the autopoiesis theory does hold the view that the autonomy of law arises from the character of the society in which law exists. The nature and limits of that autonomy cannot be understood except by analysing law as an aspect of society—in other words, in terms of a social theory of law.

To our understanding, there is also a kindred relationship to a considerable extent between Christensen's theory of law as normative patterns in a normative field and Kaarlo Tuori's way of analysing law in terms of its different layers.[15] In his chapter, Kaarlo Tuori places Christensen's theory in a broader context, analysing it in relation to the Norwegian legal philosopher David Doublet's theory on law's evaluation foundation as well as his own theory on *critical legal positivism*.[16] This is an analysis of 'law's hidden premises', or as this contribution is titled, 'law beyond law'. Tuori characterises Christensen's starting point of law as 'an assemblage of legal norms with a rather weak systems character', a consequence of the fact that legal norms have emerged in diverse manners and at diverse times. He then refers to Habermas' famous dichotomy between law as an institution and law as a medium, concluding that Christensen's basic normative patterns belong to the domain of law as an institution rather than that of law as a medium. Tuori then turns to a presentation of Doublet's thinking about law's evaluation foundation as a notion enabling us to overcome the dichotomy between legal positivism and natural law: the evaluation foundation is said to be an immanent normative yardstick of law implicit in law itself, an endeavour said to be 'a kind of synthesis of Habermas and Luhmann'. Crucial to Doublet is his distinction between positive and valid law. Positive law is law as it appears in traditional legal sources, whereas valid law is 'the end product of legal interpretation'. In the process of producing, reproducing and interpreting law 'the legal communicative community' is crucial; the evaluation foundation is said to offer normative criteria for assessing both positive and valid law (interrelated functions of criticism, boundary-drawing, legitimation and constitution) and seems to stem from the doctrine of legal sources, including both intra- and extra-positive values.

Tuori then turns to his own theory on critical legal positivism, describing the legal order as multi-layered: (1) the surface level, where modern law and its conscious aspiration to achieve social changes through legislation entails a tendency to disengage the past from the future; (2) the legal cultural level, which represents the memory of law and keeps alive the connection to the past of the law including the theory of legal sources as well as 'common law', but also typical juridical patterns of thought and argumentation, legal concepts and general legal principles of a certain field creating a 'tacit pre-understanding' of law; and (3) the deep structure of law (as a historical type of law). The question is how to combine the two

[15] Compare Christensen, 'Normative basic patterns are situated beyond the surface of legal-technical rules'. A Christensen, 'Anställningsskyddet och besittningsskyddet—en komparativ undersökning' in T Håstad *et al* (eds), *Festskrift till Anders Agell* (Uppsala, Iustus Förlag, 1994) 75. See further K Tuori, *Critical Legal Positivism* (Aldershot, Ashgate, 2002).

[16] See Tuori, *Critical Legal Positivism*, above n 15.

apparently incompatible features of the law: its positivity and its multi-layered nature. This is done in critical legal positivism by pointing to the relation of sedimentation prevailing between the law's multiple levels in legal practices.

Tuori thus concludes that there is 'law beyond law'—'law as a normative entity is not exhausted by surface level positive law'—thus also differentiating between law as a symbolic-normative phenomenon (legal order) and a social phenomenon (legal practices). Legal scholars participate in two communicative systems and are members in two communicative communities: legal and scientific practices. Both Tuori's own and Doublet's view of law are said to create a 'critical reflexive instance in law', 'replacing' (the function of) natural law in legal thinking. Tuori also understands Christensen's view on law as accepting the idea of legal cultural layers, and situates Christensen's normative patterns at his own 'second level'—legal culture representing the 'memory of law'.

An important conclusion by Tuori regarding Christensen's view on law is that despite her identification of normative patterns, 'the coherence they engender is not of total but merely local character. No internal hierarchy exists, among basic normative patterns, nor any higher-rank principle of definitive legislative resolution of conflicts'. Neither normative patterns nor principles should be 'understood in the sense of directly applicable'—instead, they are 'assigned a legal cultural sense, alluding to the sub-surface normative premises of various fields of law'. Here, there is said to be a difference as compared to both Tuori's own theory and Doublet's, emphasising the corrective rule of second or deep-culture level norms overcoming horizontal contradictions in law. Tuori states that, for Christensen, 'no *legal* [emphasis added] solution exists between divergent normative patterns. The solutions can only be found at a political level'. This is why her theory, despite studying the normative contents of different norms, represents a basically external view of law in society: 'a hidden social theory as it were'. Christensen's way of employing the term 'normative' implies a moral connotation, according to Tuori, who compares her normative patterns to Savigny's legal institutions combining a legal form and a social substratum of life relationships.

Tuori situates Christensen's theory in the social dimension, or at least states that she 'has developed her own proposal for bringing order into legal norm material with a view to what she calls the *social dimension*; legal norms regulating relationships which directly involve almost everyone in their daily life, and pursuing the function of protecting and developing this daily life'. Simon Deakin, in the debate at the international symposium preceding this book, also suggested that Christensen's theory was perhaps 'a theory on the nature of law in modern market democracies'. It is true that the studies Christensen carried out were situated in the social dimension. She did, however, claim her theory to be of general application. In our opinions, there is reason to believe that an exploration of basic normative patterns in other areas such as consumer law[17] but, for instance, also parts of

[17] Compare the works of Thomas Wilhelmsson.

public law and criminal law, would be very interesting for a better understanding of positive law. However, this is yet to be proven.[18]

As Christensen, and Tuori, rightly put it, 'different ways of ordering (legal norm material) illuminate different aspects of legal norms'. At least Christensen leaves it open to politicians and legislators to present solutions to societies' problems after analysing and revealing the conflicting patterns offered to us hitherto in legal culture.

There is also room for private actors, however, and this is precisely what Silvana Sciarra's chapter is about. She focuses on the developing role played by transnational law-making through the social partners at EU level as a result of the 'unprecedented economic and financial crisis [on the one hand], and on the other hand … an increasing mobility of companies and labour'. She starts out with Gino Giugni and the Italian example of recognition of 'autonomous' collective bargaining as a legitimate normative source as early as the 1960s, linking it to the current need to adapt such concepts of 'autonomy' of private governments—ie collective bargaining—to emerging transnational social spheres in the European Union. She presents us with the history of collective bargaining strengthened by 'structural coupling' of law and politics in the area of labour law, this specific 'social sphere', eventually ending up considerably 'juridified' (in the terms of Teubner). The challenges now faced by transnational labour law, Sciarra argues, recall the theoretical questions from the 1960s. She suggests that the transnationalisation of sources as 'a phenomenon affecting labour law as well as other legal disciplines, could be the effect of a lost centrality of nation states'. Developments emerging from transnational practices in collective bargaining give rise to new questions of the enforceability and legitimacy of bargaining agents, tending, she argues (after referring to Mireille Delmas-Marty's ideas on 'ordered pluralism' as well as Peter Lindseth's notion of/reasoning on 'constitutional legitimacy') to 're-nationalise' these issues in the hands of legitimate collective actors at national level. This is a process 'which should be accompanied by an impetus in re-building legitimacy of collective bargaining agents', ie of transnational collective labour law in action. She argues that 'a reflection on the search for new legal pluralism of sources should be enhanced within the EU' and that 'collective actors should be openly and transparently empowered, to facilitate processes of transnational standard setting and make them enforceable beyond nation states'.

Sciarra makes her inspirational and forward-looking argument concerning the social partners as a sort of integrative 'fore-runner' in EU collective labour law and practices in close relation to the ideas of legal pluralism and 'normative circles' or 'collective spheres' at the heart of not only Giugni's writings but also of Christensen's theory of law as normative patterns in a normative field; she

[18] See A Christensen, 'Protection of the Established Position: a Basic Normative Pattern' (2000) *Scandinavian Studies in Law* 285. Compare also HP Graver, 'Normative mønster i EF-retten' in C Henrichsen *et al* (eds), *Lovens Liv. Till Jørgen Dalberg-Larsen på 60-årsdagen 19. September 2000* (Copenhagen, Jurist- og Økonomforbundets forlag, 2000).

concludes that 'a widespread sense of "belonging" to transnational groups should be the outcome of current trends in the construction of new supranational bargaining agents'.

III. PROTECTION OF ESTABLISHED POSITION AND NORMATIVE DEVELOPMENT

This part focuses on normative development that reflects protective devices, and their strengthening or deterioration, for crucial societal players. This development can be in the form of employment protection for workers and its transformation in the flexicurity discourse, or the broadening of the concept of marriage to embrace same-sex partners. The normative pattern of Protection of Established Position can be said to be especially powerful in labour law due to its traditional character of protection for the weaker party. Through the years, it has also gained significant importance in social security law. Its status of a significant normative pattern in the whole of the social dimension (also in family law) is reflected in Titti Mattsson's contribution.

In his chapter, Niklas Bruun sets out to analyse the normative development of labour law in the new millennium, focusing on three strong features: the relationship between EU Treaty freedoms and fundamental collective labour rights following the *Laval* Quartet; the dominating general developments of EU labour law; and constitutional implications of the economic crisis. Bruun pictures the outcome of the *Laval* case as a battle between economic values/market functionalism and the social dimension in terms of the Protection of Established Position of Swedish trade unions. The legislative outcome—the Swedish *Lex Laval*—'clearly restricts the freedom of association or collective bargaining rights of the Swedish trade unions: they cannot demand more favourable terms and conditions than the minimum standards prescribed in Article 3.1 of the Posting of Workers Directive, they cannot raise demands concerning any other matter than those explicitly regulated in Article 3.1 and they cannot demand any collective agreement at all if the posted workers already enjoy terms and conditions that essentially are at least as favourable as those which apply in accordance with Swedish law and the applicable general collective agreement'.

Quite contrary to the general approach of discussing these situations in terms of the discrimination of transnational service providers, Bruun characterises the outcome as the introduction of 'a specific, strong protection for transnational service providers as employers'—'the requirement for equal treatment of employers has been turned upside down'. National employers can be forced to apply more favourable conditions (compared to the minimum standard in the Directive) and also conditions outside the hard nucleus of the Directive if they are not bound by a collective agreement. This can hardly be depicted as an expression of the Market-Functional pattern; rather, it can be seen as the Protection of Established Position of the transnational service provider. The rationale, however, is to strengthen internal market integration and efficiency. As regards general labour law developments, Bruun points to the fact that wage-setting is being decentralised by and even substituted with minimum wage legislation, implying a strong shift towards the Market-Functional pattern. He also points to the fact that developments are characterised by a 'fragmentation' within labour law, depriving it of its general character as a 'protection for the weaker party'. These developments are manifested in growing groups of flexible workers, such as part-time workers, fixed-term workers and temporary agency workers, but also contracted labour outside the scope of labour law. 'Rules are adapted to accommodate the need of employers in a dynamic and changing business environment.' To this we can add the economic crisis.

This change of perspective in labour law—from protection to a market-oriented focus considering different groups of workers' positions in the internal market—is even more accentuated when it comes to posted workers. They are not perceived as workers where they perform their work, but 'as a kind of institutional link of the service providers, taking advantage of the right to freely provide cross-border services'. Then there are third-country nationals linked or unlinked to the internal market, also labelled to an increasing extent in accordance with their position in the internal market: scientific workers, highly qualified workers, seasonal workers and intra-corporate transferees. Bruun depicts this order as an expression of a Market-Functional order, genuinely incongruous with the (general) labour law tradition. In the last part of his chapter Bruun describes in some detail the European Union's answer to the recent economic crisis in the cases of Greece, Ireland and Portugal, highlighting its far-reaching impact on social policy in the Member States at issue, as well as the incoherence of this development with international labour standards and the Lisbon Treaty itself.

Bruun's conclusions are quite pessimistic, claiming that labour—quite contrary to the fundamental principle of the ILO—is growing into a commodity on the internal market, as reflected in recent EU developments, and that the 'disruptive' features of this development do not really lend themselves to an evolutionary analysis in the normative field of labour law. Lack of political commitment has led us to a situation of an extreme Market-Functional pattern. As Christensen herself already suggested, Bruun acknowledges as an alternative the interpretation that what we are witnessing is a movement in the borders between different normative fields, or as he puts it, 'the borders between the field of labour law and social (security) law are being blurred'. Protection of Established Position is being replaced by a pattern of Basic Subsistence, be it in the form of (labour law) minimum wage regulations or (social security) basic benefits.

Mia Rönnmar focuses in her chapter on the legal situation of the elderly in terms of fundamental rights, age discrimination, mandatory retirement and employment protection. Her interest in the elderly originates in the demographic shift implied by an ageing population and she situates these aspects in the normative developments within EU law and policies. Important features are, of course, the Lisbon Treaty and the new status as primary law of the EU Charter on Fundamental Rights, as well as developments concerning non-discrimination law, including a ban on age discrimination. In addition to these legal developments are policy and strategy developments, such as the EU 2020 Strategy, multifaceted employment policies, and the social inclusion and pension processes within the open method of coordination. Added to this are the frequent release of Ageing Reports and the decision to make 2012 the 'Year of Active Ageing'. Following a broader introduction to the Treaty basis of the current legal and social protection of the elderly in the European Union, Rönnmar thus makes her analysis in terms of fundamental rights, age discrimination and mandatory retirement, and employment protection, respectively. Despite the fact that fundamental rights or human rights, on the one hand, and social protection in terms of social security (such as pension schemes), on the other, are said to belong to 'two different normative traditions', Rönnmar succeeds in relating the complex developments sketched here not only to the normative pattern of Protection of Established Position, but also to the hegemonic normative perceptions behind the poles of the Market-Functional pattern and Just Distribution.

The normative picture that evolves is as complex as the developments referred to in this chapter. The increased emphasis on fundamental rights, generally, Rönnmar interprets as a movement towards Just Distribution. Through pension reforms and austerity measures in the wake of the current economic crisis, pension developments are steering away from Protection of Established Position, making room for Just Distribution in the form of guaranteed or minimum pensions. Here, however, the battle is not clear-cut. Pension reform developments are also characterised by an increased importance of the Principle of Accumulated Entitlement, at the same time as the principle of accrued (pension) rights may be precisely what challenges the down-turn of the Protection of Established Position. In addition, the increase in minimum pension schemes does not necessarily reflect an up-turn of the normative perceptions behind the pattern of Just Distribution; rather, it is a 'necessary evil' in the wake of a stronger Market-Functional pattern. As regards employment protection, and as Rönnmar describes, stronger protection for the position of older workers in particular (and especially if we go so far as to prohibit mandatory retirement as an illegitimate, discriminatory practice) may threaten to hollow out employment protection, making way for using decreased working ability as just cause for dismissal.

In addition, when it comes to the elderly, the relation between the normative fields of labour law and social security law are complementary; normative developments may, as Bruun suggested, 'transfer' a labour law problem to be solved in the field of social security or vice versa. But in the elderly context, the tension is still 'on'. The major future social challenge is the high cost of pensions for an ageing population, but so far, neither EU law nor the CJEU has succeeded in strengthening the employment protection of workers of pensionable age to ease the pressure on pensions. Mandatory retirement is still accepted, despite extensive bans on age discrimination.

Under the heading 'Participation and Flexibility for All?', Titti Mattsson discusses modern family structures and children's rights. From these perspectives, the pattern of Protection of Established Position does not seem to have a significant impact. Nowadays, nothing about modern families seems to be very established. Despite family being 'the fundamental group of society and the natural environment for the growth and well-being of all its members and particularly children', according to the United Nation Convention of the Rights of the Child, changing family structures keep reconstructing this entity throughout people's lives. Giving us a brief presentation of the modern research conceptualisation of families, and also of recent case law on the subject by the ECtHR, Mattsson ends up with the Beck's and Beck-Gernsheim's definition of family as an individualisation process, a meeting place for individuals to fulfil their goals and interests. Given this high level of flexibility and negotiated relationships, children's participation rights are, of course, crucial when it comes to families. Despite the current stage of child care policy developments being identified as a paradigm of 'children's rights and child liberation', children's rights as they are currently applied are still characterised by a fairly weak position, whereas parental rights have long had a strong tradition. This was shown in Mattsson's study of custody claims following long-term foster placement in Sweden, where Mattsson interpreted the reluctance on the part of the courts to consider a formal change of custody to the foster parents whenever the biological parents disagreed; this was an expression of respect for the Protection of Established Position of such a parent in regard to his/her biological family. Quite contrary to socio-political ambitions revealed in the relevant *traveaux préparatoires*, there was also an unwillingness on behalf of social authorities even to initiate a custody case, should the biological parents not agree, seemingly casting aside the assessment of 'the best interest of the child'. However, recent developments related to the United Nations Convention on the Rights of the Child, implying the adoption of a new optional protocol that would introduce a complaint system for violations of child rights, are being put forward as a way to strengthen child participation and the implementation of children's rights.

IV. MARKET-FUNCTIONALISM AND NORMATIVE DEVELOPMENT

This part focuses on law as a well-known institution for 'constitutionalising', as well as restraining market concerns and expressions. The regulation of 'innovative' work contracts, and the balancing of markets and fundamental collective labour rights, as well as pension reforms, are but a few examples among recent developments, as is the issue of family and work reconciliation: balancing family concerns with the demands of working life. Simon Deakin's chapter focuses on the conceptual understanding of markets in economics and in law. It could just as well have been situated in the introductory part of the book concerning theoretical perspectives. It is, however, a wonderful example of how the market depends on the legal system (ie the market notion in the labour law discourse as balanced in the broader normative field of labour law) to instantiate certain social values essential for market operation. The analysis is founded on the premise that an inquiry into the nature of social institutions can be informed by studying the terms used by the legal system to describe those institutions, ie that the notion of the market in labour law discourse has 'wider potential applications'. Deakin's starting point is that 'in the social sciences, empirical data are mediated through theories and models which in many ways resemble the conceptual constructs which are used to shape legal reasoning … In both cases, fitting data to models, and adjusting the models in the light of the data, are among the techniques used to manage and process information drawn from an open-ended and complex social reality'. Like Christensen, Deakin is of the opinion that 'when mutations in … concepts [such as the market] are studied over time and in relation to the parallel experiences of other legal systems and their societies, the analysis is likely to be … revealing'. Starting out with a presentation (and a critique) of hegemonic market concepts in economics such as the 'Walrasian' model of a market as a mechanism of resource allocation, and as a spontaneous order for the coordination of private action, Deakin then turns to Hayek's model, recognising a role for the legal system in underpinning economic relations (however, founded on the principle of individual autonomy under abstract rules of just conduct in decision-making, resulting also in a 'spontaneous' order), and argues that these concepts or models 'are not intrinsically superior to conceptions of the market derived from within legal discourse itself'. Both the economic theories concerned are said, wrongly, to 'assume away entirely the role of institutions'. 'Legal scholarship can contribute to the formulation of a better (in the sense of more empirically grounded) set of models of the market … to inform policy choices'. Legal analysis is suggested to promote a better understanding of (i) a market having a normative base, (ii) not being self-equilibrating, and (iii) being institutionally bounded. Categorising a 'market' as not being a legal term of art, Deakin argues that an understanding of the nature, scope and limits of labour market relations is an intrinsic part of legal concepts such as *wage*, *employee* and *collective agreement*.

(i) The normative base of the (labour) market (not visible or adequately captured in the Walrasian and Hayekian models) is an understanding of the employment relationship as based on reciprocity and a basic trade-off between subordination and protection. 'As such, the legal concept is evidence for a model of the labour market in which "rational" economic behaviour is framed by conventional understandings of what is "fair" treatment in employment.' Moreover, Deakin argues that 'it would be equally plausible to see the duty of mutual trust and cooperation along with other legal expressions of fairness norms, as a device permitting more effective coordination, and thus more efficient contracting, in the context of the employment relationship'. (ii) Assuming that the idea of a perfectly competitive labour market is a contradiction in terms refuted by empirical evidence, labour law regulation is argued to be 'endogenous responses to market failures' of a much more complicated nature than mere external commands interfering with spontaneous private ordering. (iii) Legal doctrine is known to 'stress the limits of the market and its interdependence with societal institutions displaying a different logic' as there are 'other competing, and in some cases, superior values'. Thus, there are both state and civil society institutions there to limit as well as support the market.

Deakin's conclusion is that there is a pressing practical need, as well as an intellectual one, for a new theoretical synthesis in both economics and law. 'Labour law must be understood as a mode of market governance which provides the basis for sustainable economic development.' With a reference to the CJEU's judgments in the *Laval* Quartet, Deakin concludes that this cannot be done simply by subordinating 'social' values to 'economic' ones; rather, it requires the acknowledgement of the idea 'that as the labour market setting has a normative foundation, it cannot effectively operate in the absence of the "fairness norms" and values of solidarity to which labour law gives expression'. This is a view parallel to that of Anna Christensen, understanding labour law regulations as necessarily, and simultaneously, balancing market-functional concerns and other normative perceptions such as just distribution and protection of established positions.

If Deakin's chapter is a powerful argument for social values as a constitutive part of the market notion, Per Norberg demonstrates in his chapter how social normative perceptions can prove to be stronger than market incentives when it comes to both trade union behaviour and pension decisions. He presents us with two recent Swedish social security reforms, where the legislator has used market forces or mechanisms to stimulate certain behaviour on the part of the social partners or the general public. The first reform concerned the Swedish unemployment benefit scheme. In 2007–2008, there was a reform of the method of financing the income-related Swedish unemployment insurance, an insurance administrated by the specific trade unions' unemployment funds. To make the labour market work smoothly—and to keep costs down—the goal of the legislator was to steer unskilled unemployed workers towards accepting jobs with lower pay. As wage-setting is considered a task for the social partners, the legislator chose an indirect way to achieve the goal, by creating a system where high wages for unskilled workers would become so costly for the members of the unemployment funds that the trade unions would adapt by lowering wages in occupations with high unemployment. 'The unemployment insurance financing reform became like private insurance in the sense that the unemployment funds needed to take fees from their members reflecting the individual fund's costs for unemployment.'

The second reform concerned the Swedish public pension scheme, in which a major reform took place in 1997 to make pensions more sustainable in the long term. One important goal was to make people retire later. This was, however, not done by raising the pensionable age, but by introducing the life-time-earnings principle, making each additional year of work contribute to higher pensions, and giving people the right to delay retirement, thus making early retirement costly. In addition, part of the pension scheme was individually pre-funded, bearing a great resemblance to private 'bank savings'. Employment protection was also extended to 67 years. 'Using one's own money was supposed to make persons retire later.' However, this reliance on market mechanisms failed in both cases, in that they did not result in the intended behaviour. As regards unemployment insurance, trade unions continued their traditional 'solidarity wage-setting'—trade unions with low wages got above-normal wage increases, regardless of unemployment levels. The underlying logic is this: if employers provide work that has such low productivity that it can only be done at low wages, the jobs will disappear, the members will become unemployed, and later on they will be re-employed in another sector. Trade unions 'may well pay the market price to uphold their convictions (preferences)'. With regard to pensions the system was thus designed to make it a freedom—and financially rewarding—for the individual to choose more working years instead of a lower pension. Figures now show that people use the flexibility within the pension scheme to take early pension rather than to retire later, and most people still choose to take pension at the age of 65. This pattern of behaviour is not the result of individuals acting rationally in the market. Instead, Norberg finds the explanation in the following idea: by presenting people with a choice rather than a direct social norm on later retirement (that is, increasing the pensionable age), the individual 'is allowed to satisfy their preference as far as their financial resources admit … If the system provides them a pension that is exactly matched to their lifetime contribution and expected remaining lifetime, no one else should have any moral objection if their preference is to retire early rather than buying a new luxury car. Calculating lifetime earnings exactly creates a normative frame where taking pension early is a consumer decision like any other.'

Leaving active ageing (in the sense of longer working lives) to individual choice, backed up by economic incentives, has thus turned out to be less effective in the Swedish setting. This can be supposed to relate to the fact that the Swedish welfare system is still rather generous and pension levels still relatively high. One can afford to keep normative perceptions—'pension norms'—based on 'a right' to retire (even early) and have a long and satisfying life as a pensioner.[19] Then again, should conditions change, as they can be expected to do given the demographical trends towards a rapidly ageing society that will force the individual to work longer for a decent pension, behaviour can be expected to change. Intergenerational conflicts will grow stronger, and the importance of protection against (old) age discrimination will increase, as will the added need for employment protection at an advanced age. As Rönnmar argues in her chapter this can, however, be expected to be far from a linear process(!)

In her chapter, Jenny Julén Votinius addresses the normative conflict behind labour law intended to promote and support the reconciliation of family and working life, on the one hand, and on the other, modern labour law as an expression of market concerns. Julén Votinius argues that behind the protection of parenthood is the value of *work-family balance*, whereas the value of the employee's *work life commitment* is central for labour law in general. The study is carried out in a setting which provides for a comparative reflection over how the balance

[19] Cf A Numhauser-Henning, *Labour Law in a Greying Labour Market—in Need of a Reconceptualisation of Work and Pension Norms*, Keynote Paper on the occasion of the Fifth Annual Legal Seminar, European Labour Law Network, 11–12 October 2012.

is struck between the protection of parental needs and the interest of market efficiency, in EU and Swedish labour law, respectively. Julén Votinius' analysis is related to Christensen's theory of law as normative patterns in a normative field. It is a novel application of this theory, building on what Julén Votinius labels 'the heuristic aspects' of the theory, here allowing her to identify the missing gender dimension. The differences between EU law and Swedish domestic law are identified as being informed by two different value sets: that of the *uniqueness of motherhood* (EU) and that of *shared parental responsibility* (Sweden), respectively, in turn reflections of the 'missing' additional basic normative pattern Gender Difference, according to Julén Votinius.

This is a thought-provoking analysis. It reveals that Swedish law, with its fairly substantial period of paid parental leave, is far more powerful in supporting the value of work-family balance than EU law in general, notwithstanding the fact that EU law is more stringent (and thus powerful) when it comes to the protection of employment and employment conditions. This makes one recall Bruun's and Fudge's arguments in their chapters, on the 'amalgamation' of the two normative fields of labour law and social security law as a way to balance market-functional needs with a social dimension in our times. As for the normative pattern Gender Difference, Julén Votinius states that 'the further implications of this additional pattern remain to be explored'. In this context she is also pointing to the pressing issues of the flexibilisation of work and changing family structures, which are also touched upon by Fudge.

V. JUST DISTRIBUTION AND NORMATIVE DEVELOPMENT

This part focuses on distributive normative elements, at the heart of the Welfare State—and arguably at the heart of the European Social Model or Market. How, for example, do increasingly differentiated work relations, flexicurity, equal treatment principles and social cohesion aspirations, as well as 'the European Union integration project' as such, influence legal developments in terms of solidarity and social justice?

In recent years, the flexicurity strategy has been presented as a significant feature of EU social policy. In her chapter, Judy Fudge scrutinises the flexicurity strategy in relation to labour-market segmentation and precarious work. Fudge's chapter implies a novel application of the theory of law as normative patterns in a normative field, effectuating a kind of 'actors' analysis'. It is the discourse of flexicurity in an institutionalised EU setting that is being normatively analysed. According to Fudge, 'seeing flexicurity as a normative field constructed by actors and institutions through a range of processes allows us to appreciate the conflicts between normative patterns and differences in power relations that help to explain specific positions and understandings'. Flexicurity is found to have a deep affinity with the Market-Functional pattern, but 'nonetheless, Just Distribution is a strong competing norm since it is flexicurity's commitment to social protection that distinguishes it as a policy agenda from flexibility, which focuses exclusively on the market as the only legitimate norm of distribution'. These days, however, social justice is defined as 'employability', says Fudge, and as the key distributive conflict on the flexicurity agenda is labour market segmentation, the commitment to the Protection of Established Positions is minimized at this stage of development. To speak in terms of Deakin and Bruun, we are witnessing a shift from a conflict between labour and capital to a conflict between workers(!) Fudge pictures a rather unbalanced development, so far, favouring flexibility over the disadvantage of workers' security, since 'the OMC does not promote social protection and solidarity because the process is embedded in a specific economic agenda that emphasises deregulation and a governance structure at the EU that provides limited protection for social rights from downward harmonization'. She also refers in this context to the 'deregulatory bias' in the case law of the CJEU, manifested in the *Laval* Quartet (despite some more social rights-based case law concerning precisely the atypical work Directives), and EU enlargement 'creating conditions for a race to the bottom for wages and labour standards'. At best, it is an open question whether the extent to which precarious work in the forms of non-standard work has the potential to operate as bridges into the labour market and labour market participation, or whether it will rather function as a trap. 'The challenge for labour law is to develop a new standard employment contract, with new social rights and social obligations, and not simply to adapt atypical work arrangements to the old model', concludes Fudge. In the discussions following her conference presentation, she convincingly argued that flexicurity implies the actual amalgamation of the two normative fields of labour law and social security law, much in the same way as Bruun does.

Just as Norberg, Thomas Erhag refers in his chapter to the Swedish public pension scheme reform in the late 1990s. Now, however, focus is on pensions, EU Citizenship and the right to free movement. The Just Distribution pattern in the form of basic pension schemes becomes a centrepiece of social security, as flexible work increasingly becomes the rule; this is a real challenge for the internal market and free movement. Of course, this is especially true when it comes to 'free movement' of non-economically active EU citizens (and also resident third-country nationals), such as pensioners. The general trend in public pension schemes 'from emphasis on basic protection and hence Just Distribution towards acquired rights and the normative pole of Market Function' has proved 'to make the social situation for persons outside market labour increasingly difficult' and has also exacerbated the situation for those marginalised on a heavily segmented labour market. The chapter focuses on this normative shift, illustrating it with free movement examples. Traditionally, 'solidaristic community' and redistributive patterns such as basic pension schemes are framed by the nation-state: compare what was said above about 'normative circles' in relation to Sciarra's chapter. Through the principle of free movement for persons and not only workers, the European Union and its internal market are forcing the Member States 'to give up their old national right of refusing entry and residence to migrants'. This is, however, only partially true. Through EU Directive 2004/38, which lays down the conditions under which a Member State may deny an EU citizen the right to stay in the country, Member States have retained the right to proportional demands for sufficient economic means and sickness insurance coverage. It is in relation to these possibilities that crucial lacunae present themselves as regards the application of the Directive in relation to the Swedish systems of both pensions and health care.

As a consequence of EU requirements on the coordination of social security systems and the then-basic Swedish *folkpension*, Sweden introduced a reform which pro-rated this basic pension benefit, making 40 years of residence a requirement for the full pension. The (intended) consequence is that late-working-life immigrants may fall under the subsistence norm and find themselves in need of social assistance. In order to fill in this 'gap', the Maintenance Support for Elderly was introduced in line with Swedish Welfare State ambitions to provide minimum subsistence for all its residents. However, this benefit is not exportable, and thus requires residence in Sweden. A crucial issue discussed by Erhag is whether this Maintenance Support can be relied upon when claiming residence rights in Sweden under Directive 2004/38, since it is a national tax-financed solidarity benefit not traditionally regarded as 'social assistance' proper. Another problem occurs in relation to the Swedish model of organising health care, relying not on a right to care but on a duty for the authorities to provide such care for all locally resident persons, which makes it awkward for the Swedish administration to uphold sickness insurance as a requirement for residency. It is obvious that these issues imply a serious challenge, not only for Sweden but also in the bigger picture for social Europe, requiring a substantial degree of solidarity between the EU Member States and all EU citizens—and eventually requiring us to 'rethink the purpose and normative foundations of social security law' as a nationally restricted 'normative circle', instead giving way to a greater community, the European Union, where all who belong are treated in an equal manner.

The last chapter in this book reflects on normative patterns in the context of Swedish divorce law. Contrary to labour law, family law has not hitherto proved to lend itself to any more far-reaching harmonisation at EU level. There are still too many significant differences throughout Europe, which create a strong impact on the content of family law. These differences can be seen in family structures and culture and traditions, individualism or collectivism, gender equality and the development of the Welfare State. Even so, an independent group, the Commission on European Family Law (CEFL), is investigating whether a harmonisation of family law in Europe is possible. One additional important and difficult challenge in this respect is the development of a common conceptual framework. Against this background, Eva Ryrstedt has opted in this chapter for an in-depth presentation and analysis of the Swedish regulation surrounding divorce, and the principle of divorce as a 'clean break', but against a background regulation reflecting 'Community' as the dominant normative perception of ongoing marriage. The clean-break principle is characterised by free and unilateral access to divorce and total economic independence afterwards, exempting alimonies and making family reshaping a realistic option for any of the parties. The 'strange mix of rules' thus combines a perception of marriage as a 'free contract' when it comes to entrance and dissolution, but with a strong notion of Community during marriage reflected in the rules on maintenance during (but thus not after) marriage and the equal division of all the spouses' assets upon divorce as a primary rule. (And this division takes place despite individual ownership as the formally organising principle.)

The normative setting of Swedish divorce law can be said to confirm Deakin's suggestion that the more developed the Welfare State, the stronger the contract dimension can be allowed to be. (The impact of the notions of Community and the normative pattern of Protection of Established Position reflected in the equal division of the spouses' assets should not, however, be underestimated in this context.)

VI. CONCLUDING REMARKS

The social dimension of the European Union, Social Europe and European Welfare States are currently experiencing times of change and challenge. The general trend, depicted in basically all chapters of this book, is towards an increased influence of the Market–Functional pattern and a weakening of Protection of Established Position (though not coupled with a concomitant and robust strengthening of Just Distribution). The Lisbon Treaty of 2009, with its aim of achieving a social market economy and strengthening of fundamental rights through the legally binding EU Charter of Fundamental Rights and the future accession to the ECHR, implies increased *legal* possibilities for developing and strengthening the social dimension of the European Union and the rights of not only workers but also EU citizens more generally. However, economic, social and political realities, including the enlargement of the European Union and the current economic crisis, complicate and can even endanger such a development, and at the moment the outlook is rather bleak and pessimistic. The economic crisis, and the far-reaching austerity measures and deregulatory labour law and social security reform in its wake, affecting employment protection, collective bargaining, wage-setting and pension systems, etc, rather strengthen the Market-Functional trend. In addition, the case law of the CJEU in the *Laval* Quartet has already paved the way for market dominance and 'deregulation' in the labour law field, by placing free movement and economic freedoms first and fundamental trade union rights and social protection second. In recent years, not least after the 2004 and 2007 enlargements of the European Union, it has also become increasingly difficult to reach political agreement on 'hard law' solutions and EU legislation in the social dimension. Instead, there has been a continued emphasis on 'soft law' mechanisms and new modes of governance, such as the European social dialogue and the open method of coordination, and an increased importance of the courts and case law.

As was mentioned initially in this Introduction, and is touched upon in several chapters in the book, the demographic trend of a rapidly ageing population is one of the greatest future challenges for the European Union in terms of a sustainable society. It challenges both the functioning of labour markets as we know them, as well as pension and health care systems, and indeed all important parts of the social dimension. In this respect, a closer examination of the Japanese model would be interesting, as it represents an early example of an adaptation of existing lifelong employment and senior-wage-setting practices in terms of 'flexicurity', as a response to labour market flexibilisation and the need for active ageing. Whether it is an example to follow is, of course, quite another thing. Nevertheless, it should put developments in an interesting perspective.

A successful strategy to develop active ageing requires the adoption of a life-course perspective to many of the social issues of our interest. In addition, a future continued, and much needed, emphasis on work-life balance should focus not only on families with children and the caring obligations in relation to children, but also on the caring obligations in relation to elderly relatives. An adjustment of the working situation and working environment of elderly workers, enabling them to work longer, is also an important future element of work-life balance. All this relates in turn also to changing family structures and the need to accommodate the reconstruction of the 'nuclear' family and the formation of new and pluralistic families—the basic unit of Belonging—not only in different Member States, but also in an integrated European Union providing free movement across borders. The achievement of free movement across borders is, of course, a common challenge for labour law, social security law and family law, expressing itself in difficulties experienced in attaining, applying and interpreting a harmonisation and coordination regulation fit for a social market economy.

One important conclusion of this book is the fact that the boundaries between different normative fields—labour law, social security law and family law—are increasingly blurred or even 'amalgamated'. Thus, Christensen's thesis that the normative patterns are constant, but moving between different normative fields, is confirmed. For us, the 'amalgamation' of the normative fields depicted in the different chapters of this book is rather a reflection of the strengthening of Market-Functionalism and the weakening of Protection of Established Position, in terms of a restriction on the groups covered, and a minimum of solidarity rights in terms of Just Distribution to go with it. The problem with the elderly in this context is the need to move them *from* the complementary social security system and a reliance on pensions, *back* to the world of work, or, in other words, from the normative field of social security to the normative field of labour law. The (re-)integration of older workers in the labour market has proved a difficult task. At stake is the need for a strengthened Protection of Established Position in labour law by way of a ban on mandatory retirement, as well as the need for a weakened Protection of Established Position in social security law as benefits and accumulated entitlements are lowered or withdrawn.

All in all, these normative developments call for an interdisciplinary research approach, and the need to analyse labour law, social security law and family law together, which is precisely the aim of this book.

Part II

Law as Normative Patterns and Other Theoretical Perspectives

2

Understanding Law as Normative Patterns in a Normative Field

ANN NUMHAUSER-HENNING

I. INTRODUCTION

THIS BOOK IS about normative development within the social dimension during the last decade. The focus is on a deep concern and interest in the normative developments in the social dimension—or as it is in labour law, social security law and family law. This was and still is also the material scope of the Norma Research Programme at the Faculty of Law, Lund University, since its inception in 1996, a programme of which I am the coordinator.[1] Understanding law as normative patterns in a normative field has a key role in much of the Norma Research Programme's research, and certainly in mine. Here, the work of Anna Christensen plays a major role. This chapter is on her theory of Law as Normative Patterns in a Normative Field and its application within the social dimension, a theoretical perspective that throughout the years has proven very valuable, precisely in the studies of normative development within the social dimension.

Anna Christensen (1936–2001) created the theory of Law as Normative Patterns in a Normative Field in the early 1990s.[2] The theory developed during the process of writing her book *Hemrätt i hyreshuset*,[3] with a first sketch of the Normative Field on its back cover. This sketch in a later version was to become the logo of the Norma Research Programme.

In the late 1980s, I made a 'deconstruction' of landowners' rights from a normative functional perspective,[4] and just after Hofstadter's book *Gödel,*

[1] On the Norma Research Programme, see www.jur.lu.se/norma.

[2] See A Christensen, 'Skydd för etablerad position—ett normativt grundmönster' (1996) 4 *Tidsskrift for Rettsvitenskap* 519. For an English version, see A Christensen, 'Protection of Established Position, a Basic Normative Pattern' (2000) 40 *Scandinavian Studies in Law* 285.

[3] A Christensen, *Hemrätt i hyreshuset* (Stockholm, Juristförlaget, 1994).

[4] A Numhauser-Henning, *Rätten till fäderneslandet, Om jordförvärvslagen och dess funktioner mot bakgrund av jordbrukets utveckling i det svenska samhället* (Lund, Juristförlaget, 1988). For an English 'summary', see A Numhauser-Henning, 'Land Ownership: a Critical Study of the Swedish Land Acquisition Act and its Functions' (1990) 34 *Scandinavian Studies in Law* 181.

Escher, Bach[5] had become a global bestseller. Christensen referred to both these endeavours as sources of inspiration.[6] Another source of inspiration was Escher[7] and the way he illustrated the magic of depiction in his work—seeing 'patterns' in complex realities.

Hofstadter thus wrote the worldwide bestseller *Gödel, Escher, Bach* at the start of the 1980s. The more direct source of inspiration for Christensen's theory of Law as Normative Patterns in a Normative Field was, however, Hofstadter's second book, with his analysis of AI (Artificial Intelligence) programmes.[8] According to Hofstadter, there is something wrong with all AI programmes. They build on the idea that all cognition can be reproduced through 'a 100 percent top-down approach: functions calling subfunctions calling subfunctions and so on, until it all is bottomed out in some primitives'.[9] However, according to Hofstadter, the core of human intelligence is 'a general sensitivity to patterns, an ability to spot patterns of unanticipated types in unanticipated places at unanticipated times in unanticipated media … Any perceived situation seems to be surrounded by a cluster, a halo of alternative versions of itself, of variations suggested by slipping any of a vast number of features that characterise the situation'.[10] This way of thinking has close analogies in legal methodology. Hofstadter continues: 'There is no central manipulator, no central program. There is simply a vast collection of patterns … that trigger other patterns … the brain is the medium in which the symbols are floating and in which they trigger each other'.[11] This, says Christensen, is how she pictures the legal system: 'it is a medium where different moral and legal patterns appear and dissolve, float, clash and form new patterns'.[12]

In my own study on Swedish land ownership, I analysed the contents of the legal concept of 'ownership' and the tension between the conservative and the more dynamic elements in relation to its modern 'market-functional' understanding—a kind of deconstruction of the concept of property.[13] Understood as a concept in legal technique, 'ownership', 'title' or 'proprietary right' lacks any *a priori*

[5] D Hofstadter, *Gödel, Escher, Bach: An Eternal Golden Braid* (Hamondsworth, Penguin Books, 1980). For a Swedish version, see D Hofstadter, *Gödel, Escher, Bach—ett evigt gyllene band* (Stockholm, Brombergs, 1985).

[6] See Christensen, 'Skydd för etablerad position', above n 2, section 2 on 'Ownership' with n 18.

[7] Maurits Cornelis Escher (1898–1972) was born in the Netherlands and became widely known for, among other things, his symmetry drawings. See also Hofstadter, *Gödel, Escher, Bach*, above n 5.

[8] D Hofstadter, *Metamagical Themas: Questing for the Essence of Mind and Patterns* (New York, Basic Books, 1985). Compare the Introduction to Christensen, *Hemrätt i hyreshuset*, above n 3, and, later, the article 'Normative Patterns and the Normative Field: a Post-Liberal View on Law' in T Wilhelmsson and S Hurri (eds), *From Dissonance to Sense: Welfare State Expectations, Privatisation and Private Law* (Aldershot, Ashgate, 1999).

[9] Hofstadter, *Metamagical Themas*, above n 8, 648.

[10] Ibid 531 (652).

[11] Ibid 648.

[12] Christensen, *Hemrätt i hyreshuset*, above n 3, 6.

[13] See Numhauser-Henning, *Rätten till fäderneslandet*, above n 4, especially paras 1.3 and 8.2, but also A. Numhauser-Henning, 'Om äganderättens funktion'(1988) 1–2 *Tidsskrift for Rettsvitenskap* 29.

content.[14] The right to property is, however, also considered a general legal fundamental principle of our society,[15] and as such, also enjoys protection not only in constitutions, but in international law, later becoming protected as a human right. It is then only superficially a concept in legal technique: functionally speaking, it refers to values determined by factors fundamental to our current social order. The right to property has even been said to constitute the societal order or, more precisely, the economic order.[16] Changes concerning the content of the right to property reflect the material conditions of society at any given moment. In our society, it is production within a market economy that creates the framework for other social conditions. My study can be said to focus on how, in the shift from an agrarian to an industrial society, changing social and economic conditions related to land were reflected in the regulation of land ownership over time. I showed how the concept of ownership, being much older than the market economy, has different functions in different social systems (modes of production). Activities in the old farming community were not geared to change; on the contrary, preservation and farming use formed the focal point. Gradually, its changeability, ie the right to legally dispose of the property by selling or otherwise transferring it, became an increasingly essential dimension.

In *Hemrätt i hyreshuset*, Christensen applied and adapted this understanding of ownership to the area of tenancy law, and consequently developed her theory of Law as Normative Patterns in a Normative Field. The main object of study in this book is the tenant's residential rights or right to security (*hemrätt*), which Christensen traced as a transposition of the older, conservative element of property rights into a new sphere, rental dwellings, the transposition in itself a consequence of rented housing becoming a 'social good' of increasing societal importance—both rights being in competition with the landlord's/owner's right to sell a property. These competing interests, at any given time related to their own context and history, were also (with a little 'help' from Hofstadter) what led her to an understanding of law, not as an hierarchical system, but as competing normative patterns in a normative field. Despite having identified three main and competing normative basic patterns and including a first sketch of the Normative Field on the book's back cover, Christensen never actually mentions the concept of the Normative Field in this study. The concept first appears in an article in the Swedish daily newspaper *Dagens Nyheter* describing the results of her study,[17]

[14] However, the imagined legal-technical starting point with regard to ownership can still appear as a complete, unlimited, power over the property concerned; compare Bergström's concept 'latent' ownership right and Hedenius' 'ideal-typical' ownership concept, in S Bergström, 'Om begreppet äganderätt i fastighetsrätten' (1956) *Svensk Juristtidning* 145, and I Hedenius, 'Äganderättsbegreppet' (1977) *Filosofien i ett föränderligt samhälle* 143, respectively. We usually refer to the elasticity of the right of ownership, in that it automatically fills every empty space that is created when any previous limitations are withdrawn.

[15] Compare, eg, R Dworkin, *Taking Rights Seriously* (London, Gerald Duckworth & Co Ltd, 1978).

[16] Compare the Institutionalist school within economic science.

[17] Compare below n 22.

which according to Anna's notes, was actually intended to use that very title: *The Normative Field.*

In *Hemrätt i hyreshuset*, Christensen thus developed the disparate notions of ownership, in terms of the conservative and dynamic elements of ownership.[18] Labelling the conservative element its fundamental normative element, she stresses the functionality of the dynamic element in relation to modern market economy. Already in *Hemrätt i hyreshuset*, however, Christensen identified all three normative patterns—Protection of Established Position, the Market-Functional pattern, and Just Distribution—which were to become so important in studies of the social dimension.

Christensen thus first elaborated the theory's theoretical components in housing law (*Hemrätt i hyreshuset* 1994). She then applied them more broadly in her further studies of the social dimension, first in an article on the normative pattern of Protection of Established Position.[19] A general introduction to the theory as such, in a broader legal development context, can also be found in the essay *Normative Patterns and the Normative Field: A Post-Liberal View on Law* in 1999.[20]

Having described the background of the theory, I will now introduce its main components (section II), and also present some examples of its application within the social dimension (section III), and finish with some concluding remarks (section IV). It is only natural that this chapter depicts my own interpretation, not Christensen's or anyone else's, of the theory and its applications, ten years after Christensen passed away.

II. THEORY OF LAW AS NORMATIVE PATTERNS IN A NORMATIVE FIELD

The theory is thus based on the thesis that different basic normative patterns can be distinguished in the multitude of legal norms, much like in a drawing by Escher, or as Hofstadter has described human thinking, attempting to distinguish and describe certain patterns. Such patterns are taken to reflect and codify basic normative conceptions and practices in society, and thus the normativity beyond formal rules. Christensen's analysis of law in the social dimension served to identify such crucial basic normative patterns that lay beyond/beneath every legal system, and which are part of those cultural values society builds upon—formulated in the Theory of Law as Normative Patterns in a Normative Field. The pattern concept was chosen because of its capacity to reflect the relation, or tension, between what is and what ought to be, crucial to the legal tradition.

[18] Compare Numhauser-Henning, *Rätten till fäderneslandet*, above n 4, 31: 'The struggle was about freedom to change, not protection of the established order'.

[19] Christensen, 'Skydd för etablerad position', above n 2.

[20] Christensen, 'Normative Patterns and the Normative Field', above n 8, 83–98.

Because social life is rather complex, these normative patterns do not make up the 'hierarchical legal system' that we frequently imagine.[21] Instead, these patterns are put into play in a normative field as determined by different basic patterns, which also act as normative poles. The 'origin' of the patterns differ according to the values they are set to protect, and thus there is, typically, tension between different patterns. Societal change is what affects the 'attraction' behind the poles over time and thus also legal change. Changes in the underlying conditions of production provide explanations for the movements in the normative field. However, the basic normative patterns all represent enduring legitimate normative conceptions in society, and it is the task of legislators and courts to balance these conceptions within the framework of the law. In this endeavour, 'new' legal solutions may also profit from the legitimacy of older normative conceptions.

Amongst the most important basic patterns (or poles) present in the normative field within the social dimension are, on the one hand, the (dynamic) Rights of Ownership and the Freedom of Contract, which together form the *Market-Functional pattern*; and on the other hand, *Protection of Established Position* (ie the conservative right to one's possessions, or, as it were, the tenant's residential right/tenant security). A third basic normative pattern is *Just Distribution*, a distributive pattern related to social justice and solidarity. Whereas the pattern of Protection of Established Position is silent regarding how such a position is established, the pattern of Just Distribution deals with the distribution and redistribution of values, which consequently leads to the creation of new positions (see Figure 2.1).

Another crucial component of the theoretical framework is the *functional relationship between law and the structure of society.* The thesis that social structure (material conditions, principles of organisation, modes of production and societal conflicts) determines, inter alia, the content of the law underlies both my own writings and those of Anna Christensen. The basic normative patterns are thus held to reflect normative practices functional to society and human relationships. They reflect, and codify, social normative conceptions and practices aimed at making long-lasting human relationships and sustainable societies possible. Christensen herself often stressed this human-relational (social relations) base for the really *basic* normative patterns.[22] However, it is a basic characteristic of

[21] Compare A Christensen: 'Legal theory ... has been trapped in that Kelsean dream about a consistent, hierarchical system. This eternal arranging and rearranging of the different parts of the assembly of norms in order to make them fit into a system seldom brings about any new insight', A Christensen, 'Polycentricity and Normative Patterns' in H Petersen and H Zahle (eds), *Legal Polycentricity: Consequences of Pluralism in Law* (Aldershot, Ashgate, 1995) 239.

[22] Compare A Christensen, 'Äganderätten skyddar ditt säng och ditt vapen', article in the Swedish daily newspaper *Dagens Nyheter*, 23 September 1994, but also the prologue to her book *Hemrätt i hyreshuset*, above n 3. In this article, Christensen criticises the view of the legislator as 'inventing' the law and the view of 'the legal system' as an autonomous system with no relation to other social norms, and goes on to write: 'The basic normative patterns were there long before the modern legislator. They occur much like a lane in the woods ... Let us think of them as moral habits later to be elevated to laws and moral principles'. See also Christensen, 'Polycentricity and Normative Patterns', above n 21, and compare Kaarlo Tuori on Christensen in Chapter 3, relating Christensen's view on law to

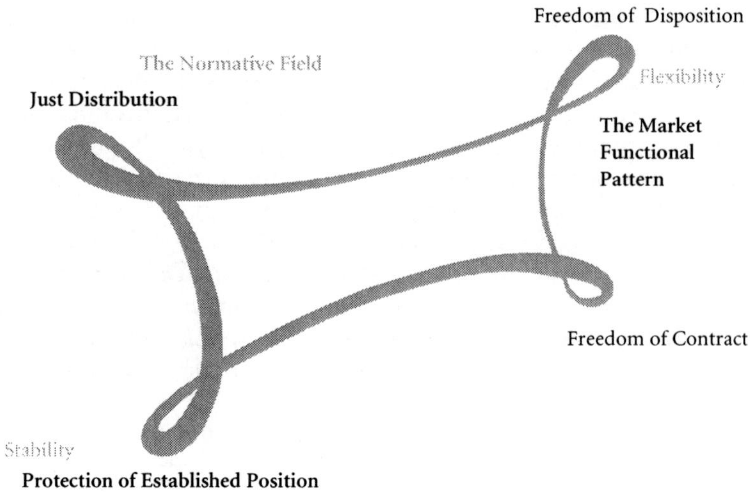

Figure 2.1: The Normative Field

the theory (and not only for my own work)[23] that law and normative solutions must also be functional in relation to fundamental societal conditions of a more materialistic nature, such as the mode of production and technology.[24] On this point, the theory is basically compatible with the ideas of historical materialism, as well as structuralist theories more generally.

The very concept of the Market-Functional pattern[25] is perhaps the strongest expression for the theory's view on the functional relationship between normative development and basic societal structure. One might even say that it is a misconception, 'mistaking' the underlying social organisational principle/logic itself

the Habermasian dichotomy between law as an institution and law as a medium, where Christensen's normative patterns adhere to the category of law as an institution. Compare also Durkheim on law as an integrative mechanism in modern society guaranteeing social cohesion in terms of organic solidarity, thus bridging the gap between morals and functionalism, Emile Durkheim, *De la division du travail social* (Paris, Presses Universitaires de France, 1930).

[23] See, eg, A Henning, *Tidsbegränsad anställning, Om anställningsformsregleringens samhälleliga funktioner* (Lund, Juristförlaget i Lund, 1984) and Numhauser-Henning, *Rätten till fäderneslandet*, above n 4.

[24] Compare the following quote from A Christensen: 'The moral norms are not there from the beginning ... They develop as a key part of the development of society' 'this view on the development of moral habits and state law is fully compatible with the view that law reflects the dominant mode of production in society. Also the daily moral habits are strongly influenced by the dominant mode of production': Christensen, 'Polycentricity and Normative Patterns', above n 21, 237. For a discussion of A Christensen's theory on normative patterns in relation to the employers' managerial prerogatives as 'a basic normative notion' (*en normative grunnforestilling*) in labour law from a functional perspective, see S Evju, 'Arbeidsrett og styringsrett—et perspektiv' (2003) 1 *Arbeidsrett og arbeidsliv* 3.

[25] I used the concept 'the market-functional ownership' in my 1988 study, *Rätten till fäderneslandet*, above n 4, 31 and 151; compare Christensen, *Hemrätt i hyreshuset*, above n 3, 22.

for the normative patterns that express it. These basic normative patterns are instead (dynamic) Ownership Rights, Freedom of Contract and Freedom of Trade.

As changes in the conditions of production, as well as in other structures, institutions and conditions crucial to society are thus used to explain the movements in the Normative Field from time to time, and can also be pictured in a *Functional Field*, these two components interact. Common to both components are also the possibilities for opening up the national confines of legal science, since these components both emphasise structures and patterns common to many different national legal systems, not least within the European Union.

The Theory of Law as Normative Patterns in a Normative Field is a theory about normative perceptions within law and legal science itself, but is also a theory addressing law as a societal (and basically functional) phenomenon. As Tuori puts it, Christensen's theory is not about legal solutions in the sense of being right or wrong from an internal legal interpretative perspective—'the solutions can only be found at a political level'.[26] This underpins the theory's basically empirical character. Its theoretical framework provides for a basically *descriptive* method of law as empirical facts. What have been described, however, are the *normative* contents of rules and regulations. In this regard, as indicated above, the Theory of Normative Patterns in a Normative Field does, of course, relate to a vast theoretical background based on a general understanding of a number of classics within sociology and other disciplines, some of which are addressed in the following discussion.

Already when introducing her theory, Christensen made it very clear that its approach was in sharp contrast with the legal theory dominant for decades in Sweden, *Uppsala-skolan* or Scandinavian legal realism.[27] To assume the existence of such a thing as *basic* normative patterns that reflected social or even moral, normative perceptions was, of course, provocative in the eyes of those who viewed law as nothing but the immediate expression of the will of the legislator.

Unique in her own generation of Swedish scholars, with her basically social science view of law, Christensen did, however, explicitly relate her own thinking on law to the writings of other Nordic scholars. Two of these are Torstein Eckhoff and Thomas Wilhelmsson, both of whom she considered had spotted 'normative patterns' in society.[28] According to Christensen, in his book *Retferdighet ved utveksling og fordelning av verdier*,[29] Eckhoff identified two important patterns, the one being that there should be balance between the performance of the various

[26] See Kaarlo Tuori, Chapter 3.

[27] See, eg, Christensen, 'Polycentricity and Normative Patterns', above n 21, and 'Normative Patterns and the Normative Field', above n 8, as well as in *Dagens nyheter*, above n 22. As the founders of Uppsala-skolan are normally mentioned Vilhelm Lundstedt (1882–1955), Karl Olivecrona (1897–1980) and also Axel Hägerström (1868–1939); see among others V Lundstedt, Samhället och rättsordningen, in: *Tiden*, fjortonde årgången, Nr 3 1922 129, and A Hägerström, *Stat och rätt, en rättsfilosofisk undersökning* (Stockholm, Almqvist & Wiksells,1904).

[28] Christensen, 'Protection of Established Position', above n 2.

[29] T Eckhoff, *Retferdighet ved utveksling og fordelning av verdier* (Oslo, Universitetsforlaget, 1971).

parties in various types of exchange and other situations, and the other relating to the varieties of a concept such as 'just distribution' or justice in value distribution. He distinguished various 'just' alternatives for distribution, such as equality of shares, distribution according to need, and queuing. As regards Wilhelmsson, Christensen referred to his work on social civil law,[30] where the method was described as 'to first take hold of a recurring pattern, and from this follows an attempt to establish a general principle of the normative kind'.

Christensen also wrote on the compatibility between the Theory of Law as Normative Patterns in a Normative Field and that of legal poly-centricity, indicating an understanding of law as being engendered in many centres, and not only within an hierarchical structure.[31] Legal pluralism has long been a well-known concept in legal sociology and legal anthropology,[32] and among Nordic scholars, Henrik Zahle is perhaps the most prominent representative of legal poly-centricity as a proper approach in legal science.[33] As Christensen herself put it: 'If you reject the idea of the law-maker and accept the idea of the legal order as a state codification of an already existing moral practice, it becomes obvious that law is and must be polycentric'.[34] We can thus say that the idea of polycentricity is inherent in the Theory of Law as Normative Patterns in a Normative Field.

Finally, this representation of Christensen's Theory of Law as Normative Patterns in a Normative Field would not be complete without a reference to the French scholar François Ewald and his writings on *L'Etat Providence*.[35] His analysis of the evolution of social insurance and the shortcomings of the liberal legal order in the wake of industrialism, where the old liberal doctrine of individual responsibility was replaced by the doctrine of assurance against collective social risks, has strongly inspired Christensen's writings on this important area of the social dimension.[36]

III. THEORY OF LAW AS NORMATIVE PATTERNS IN A NORMATIVE FIELD IN APPLICATION: ELABORATED EXAMPLES

A. Introduction

The development of the theory thus very much started with the concept of ownership and its competing conservative and dynamic elements, and their 'transposition'

[30] T Wilhelmsson, *Social civilrätt—Om behovsorienterade element i kontraktsrättens allmänna läror* (Helsingfors, Lakimiesliiton Kustannus, 1987).

[31] Christensen, 'Polycentricity and Normative Patterns', above n 21.

[32] Compare J Griffiths, 'Legal Pluralism and the Theory of Legislation, with Special Reference to the Regulation of Euthanasia' in H Petersen and Zahle (eds), *Legal Polycentricity: Consequences of Pluralism in Law* (Aldershot, Ashgate, 1995).

[33] H Zahle, 'Polycentri i Retskildelaeren' in A Bratholm (ed), *Samfunn, rett, rettferdighet* (Oslo, TANO, 1986).

[34] Christensen, 'Polycentricity and Normative Patterns', above n 21, 238.

[35] F Ewald, *Le'Etat providence* (Paris, B Grasset, 1986).

[36] Compare Christensen, 'Normative Patterns and the Normative Field', above n 8.

into tenancy law. Anna Christensen first elaborated the theory's theoretical components in housing law (*Hemrätt i hyreshuset* 1994). She then applied them more broadly in her further studies of the social dimension, first in an essay on the normative pattern Protection of Established Position.[37] There, she elaborated on how this (and other) basic normative patterns had been adapted into the legal areas of new social 'commodities/goods' such as labour and complementary social security benefits, and also, to some extent, family law.

It is, of course, no coincidence that the theory thus first and foremost has been applied to the legal areas of the social dimension regulations protecting the everyday life of the individual eventually came to be the main focus of Christensen's research, and are thus also central to the Norma Research Programme since its inception in 1996. One of the primary tasks of the Norma Research Programme within the given theoretical framework was, and still is, to identify the basic normative patterns present within the social dimension, and, through comparative studies both between different areas of law and between legal systems in different countries, to delineate how these patterns manifest themselves in the legal norms and articulate ever-changing societal conditions. The following paragraphs are an attempt to describe how the Theory of Law as Normative Patterns in a Normative Field has been applied and developed in the study of (and has contributed to a better understanding of the legal development of) labour law, social security law and family law, respectively, over the years.

B. Labour Law

It is obvious that the development of modern labour law has been closely related to the development of industrialism (and now post-industrialism) as well as the modern (and now post-modern) market economy. Christensen elaborated on the normative patterns put into play in labour law as early as in her 1996 article on Protection of Established Position, along the following lines.[38]

Christensen held Protection of Established Position to be a very influential pattern. This is the basic normative tenet of the Right to Property—the protection of an owner's rightful possession—and as such, an expression of the conservative element of ownership. However, the conservative structures emphasising stability and protection of the owner's established position were, to a large extent, gradually dissolved during the nineteenth century. Contract and Freedom of Contract are dominating normative patterns in market economy societies, as is Freedom of Trade and Services. The new Market-Functional pattern appeared and was recognised in statutes and other central documents. In tenancy law, the granting of

[37] Christensen, 'Skydd för etablerad position', above n 2.

[38] Ibid. See also A Christensen 'Anställningsskyddet och besittningsskyddet—en komparativ undersökning' in T Håstad, PH Lindblom and Å Saldeen (eds), *Festskrift till Anders Agell* (Uppsala, Iustus, 1994). The latter is a 'comparative' study of tenancy law and labour law.

perpetual tenures was already forbidden in the nineteenth century, and in Sweden, the New Land Code of 1905 was permeated with a strong belief in the dynamic effects of the owner's right to free disposition of his or her own property; rights of use were made subordinate to the new market-functional concept of ownership. Full freedom of contract prevailed. 'The new free contract of labour, which developed in the industrial sector, meant that work was released from the more comprehensive social relationship in pre-industrial society and transformed to a relationship of exchange. A market for labour was formed and wages paid in accordance with the value of work in this new market.'[39] At the dawn of modern labour law we have the doctrine of hire-and-fire at will. The Swedish December Compromise in 1906, between the social partners, and *the managerial prerogatives* contained therein, acknowledged the owner's right to dispose freely over his property and contracted 'goods' such as labour. The right to hire-and-fire at will was expressly included in the agreement itself. (Employees too, however, through this notion of the employment contract, were freed from their previous confinement to the contract.) Only gradually have these managerial prerogatives been restrained by compulsory labour legislation protecting the weaker party (which also, however, limited the freedom of employees by the imposition of periods of notice!). Christensen was eager to point out the fact that such protective rules were not there to create a balance between the parties (a contractual principle), but rather pointed to the asymmetrical character of the employment relationship and the aim to precisely protect the social position of the employee.[40]

Protection of Established Position was thus a very influential pattern. In tenancy law it found its parallel in the rules on *residential security or tenants' security*, as opposed to owners' rights to enter freely into and terminate tenancy contracts, and was, in Sweden, first introduced in connection with rent control during the First World War. (This was and is not a right to the flat as such, but simply a right to renewal of the lease.) This conservative pattern also eventually transferred into the area of labour law. Here, the strongest exponent is *employment security*, as developed mainly during the second part of the last century. There are, however, many exponents of this normative pattern, for instance in seniority principles regarding wage setting and other working conditions, reflecting how the position is gradually built up or 'established', as well as in rules on redundancy payments (eventually transforming into social security benefits; see below). However, the tension in relation to the Market-Functional pattern is reflected by the fact that redundancy, typically speaking, constitutes just cause for dismissal. It was also

[39] Christensen, 'Protection of Established Position', above n 2.

[40] Compare debates on employment protection and a segmented labour market, with an A-team in permanent positions, sometimes in the terms of 'work-owners', and a B-team of flexible workers. Compare also the Transfer of Undertakings Directive 2001/23/EC and the view that the rights under the employment contract are tied to the work/activity and are not affected by a change of owner/employer.

always possible to use more or less 'flexible' modes of employment that did not imply employment protection.[41]

As previously indicated, the pattern of Protection of Established Position is silent on how these positions are established. When property rights extend beyond the closest personal sphere, a conflict arises with normative perceptions concerning a 'fair' distribution of wealth—the normative pattern of Just Distribution. In labour law, the normative pattern of Just Distribution is not so dominant. It does, however, appear as the need-based rules for minimum wages in many systems, and as 'solidarity wage politics' in others, for example as in Sweden. It is, of course, possible to view seniority rules as such expressions (a variety of the queuing principle), but as already indicated they are obviously also strongly related to Protection of Established Position. The constitutional 'right to work' is another expression, but this rarely constitutes a proper right to employment; here, the managerial prerogative to 'hire at will' still has the upper hand. Already in the theme of Just Distribution, however, Christensen refers to the practice of compulsory retirement of the elderly (through legislation or collective agreements), as a 'fair distribution' among generations.[42] Christensen prefers to see these practices as a response to business needs, rather than as an exponent of normative fairness. Nevertheless, over the years debates have arisen regarding the rights of those with employment as opposed to those without, job-sharing, etc. Here, however, an important exponent in recent labour law is the principle of non-discrimination or equal opportunities.

The movement in the normative field of labour law over the last century is thus a movement from the free labour contract towards increased employment protection as an exponent of the normative pattern of Protection of Established Position. Lately, movement is once again in the other direction, with a broadening scope for *flexible work agreements*, and even the deregulation of employment protection.

Christensen touches upon the legal developments within the normative field of labour law in a Swedish perspective as early as the beginning of the 1990s.[43] I continued this analysis in a 1997 article on the conditions of future labour law, discussing the transition of industrial society into post-fordist society.[44] The article

[41] Somewhere in the process of developing employment protection, the (sometimes quite long) fixed-term contracts changed character, from being more secure than open-ended contracts to the opposite.

[42] Compare also the reasoning of the European Court of Justice, eg in the judgments in Case C-411/05 *Palacios de la Villa v Cortefiel Servicios SA* [2007] ECR I-08531; Case C-388/07 *Age Concern England v Secretary of State for Business, Enterprise and Regulatory Reform* [2009] ECR I-01569; Case C-45/09 *Rosenbladt v Oellerking Gebaudereinigungsges mbH*, [2010] ECR I-I-09391; Case C-341/08 *Petersen v Beerufungsausschuss fur Zahnärzte fur den Bezirk Westfalen-Lippe*, [2010] ECR I-00047; Cases C-250/09 and C-268/09 *Georgiev v Technicheski Universitet, Sofia* [2010] ECR I-11869; and Cases C-159/10 and C-160/10 *Fuchs och Köhler v Land Hessen* [2012] ECR I-0000.

[43] She also gives a rudimentary description of the legal developments within the public sector; see Christensen, 'Protection of Established Position', above n 2, 303.

[44] A Numhauser-Henning, 'Om den framtida arbetsrättens förutsättningar' (1997) 3 *Arbetsmarknad & Arbetsliv* 97.

sketches the move towards increased emphasis on social partners' cooperation in combination with individual fundamental rights and non-discrimination in relation to the movements in the normative field of labour law, but also in relation to flexibilisation theory. I argue that an increased acceptance of employment protection (and thus Protection of Established Position) has successively led to increased protection also against arbitrary—and, ultimately, discriminatory—conditions of employment, as the opposite of freedom of contract. It is also argued that the traditional manufacturing industry in industrialist society was more apt to bear restrictions such as a prohibition on arbitrary dismissal and collectively determined working conditions. The view that economic reasons always amounted to 'just cause' for dismissal made way for necessary structural reforms on the market, whereas seniority rules implied a 'balancing' of conflicting normative perceptions based on the protection of established position and social fairness.

Post-fordism is argued to change the preconditions and thus the normative balance within the normative field—the scope for flexibility—and thus change comes to the fore and typically strengthens the power behind the Market-Functional pole or pattern. However, the normative picture is not one-dimensional. Today's knowledge-based society makes a business increasingly dependent on a loyal and stable workforce, which corresponds to qualitative (or functional) flexibility strategies going hand-in-hand with employment protection—in combination with human resource strategies and lifelong learning taking us from job protection to employment protection with our current employer. In the era of 'flexicurity', the Protection of Established Position also finds a new expression in so-called *employability rights*.[45] Post-fordist work in the knowledge-based society implies a weakening of the notion of the employer prerogative as unlimited management rights—it is no longer really functional. I have already mentioned how employment protection eventually turned into collectively determined (and protected) working conditions. As diversification in production continues, it is only logical that such collective rules will be replaced by more individual (and thus flexible) conditions that are protected by bans on discrimination. Equal conditions are no longer market-functional, whereas formal equality for the equally situated is.

Arguably, the theoretical approach deepens the understanding of the normative values in play behind employment protection, and their transformation within the current EU flexicurity discourse. The flexicurity strategy can be understood as bridging the gaps between the three dominant patterns identified here: the Market-Functional pattern, Protection of Established Position, and Just

[45] With regard to the sometimes rather confusing terminology concerning the concepts of job protection/security, employment protection/security and employability rights, see further M Rönnmar and A Numhauser-Henning, 'Swedish Employment Protection in Times of Flexicurity Policies and Economic Crisis' (2012) 28(4) *International Journal of Comparative Labour Law and Industrial Relations* 443.

Distribution. Judy Fudge's chapter elsewhere in this book contains an elaboration on this issue.[46]

The issue of *discrimination* in relation to the theory was later followed up by me, in the book *Legal Perspectives on Equal Treatment and Non-Discrimination*.[47] There too, I refer to Equal Treatment as a pattern close to, or under the Market-Functional pattern, implying 'competition on equal terms' in the Aristotelian sense that what is alike shall be treated alike. Other normative patterns concerning distribution, such as need or equal distribution, which are clearly distributive patterns characterised by solidarity rather than market values, come closer to the pattern of Just Distribution. In a discrimination context, this is also where we find quota solutions and the like. Here, I also identify a pattern of *Belonging*. This pattern was placed as a sphere covering the pole of Protection of Established Position and the pole of Just Distribution.[48] This pattern is based on the profound willingness, but also the obligation, of the 'established group' to share with (but with only) those who are already in some way associated. This is a basically conservative pattern, although it is not hostile to a certain redistribution in relation to those who in some way 'belong'. It is of fundamental importance to note that it is the persons in the group behind the pole Protection of Established Position who, to a considerable extent, have been in the position to create the rules of the game—the reference rules[49]—setting the framework for equal competition, and that the Pattern of Belonging is by nature in conflict with the individual's right to equal treatment. It is a central function of discrimination law to help break up old structures of belonging, which for some reason are considered inadequate today, to the advantage and inclusion of hitherto marginalised groups and/or individuals. We can speak of the widening of established normative circles of belonging, to further inclusion and integration.[50] In this context, I chose to use the concept pattern of *Integration*, and placed it as a sphere covering not only the Market-Functional Pole, but also the pole of Just Distribution.[51] Here, it is all about change—the

[46] See ibid.

[47] A Numhauser-Henning, 'Introduction: Equal Treatment—a Normative Challenge' as well as the chapter 'On Equal Treatment, Positive Action and the Significance of a Person's Sex' in A Numhauser-Henning (ed), *Legal Perspectives on Equal Treatment and Non-Discrimination* (The Hague, Kluwer Law International, 2001).

[48] See also A Numhauser-Henning, 'Freedom of Movement and Transfer of Social Security Rights' in R Blanpain (ed), *Collective Bargaining, Discrimination, Social Security and European Integrations*, European Congress, Stockholm, September 2002, 48 *Bulletin of Comparative Labour Relations* (The Hague, Kluwer, 2003).

[49] The concept reference rule, referring to the actual rule/norm generally applied to the group of comparison (the reference group) in an alleged discriminatory situation, was introduced by Anna Christensen, see A Christensen, 'Structural Aspects of Anti-Discrimination Legislation and Processes of Normative Change' in A Numhauser-Henning (ed), *Legal Perspectives on Equal Treatment and Non-Discrimination* (The Hague, Kluwer, 2001).

[50] Compare the works mentioned below n 54.

[51] Compare also P Norberg, *Konkurrenslagstiftning och bostadspolitik, En studie av den svenska hyresregleringens förhållande till EG:s och Sveriges konkurrensrätt*, Norma 2 (Lund, Juristförlaget i Lund, 1999), as well as Numhauser-Henning, 'Freedom of Movement', above n 48.

change of attitudes and practices to destroy old patterns of belonging. Once the patterns of belonging are changed and those to be protected have entered the group of established positions, the era of non-discrimination regulation will have had its day. However, as I already stated back then, since basic normative patterns as such are fairly stable over time, and the structures and attitudes of belonging are shaped and reshaped on a daily basis, as are the ambitions of Integration, this situation is not likely to occur for a long time—if indeed ever.

Today, I would like to argue that the Pattern of Integration is not really a *normative* pattern, but rather the example of an external and more strategic rule, such as the principle of prevention, as according to Anna Christensen.[52] The particular pattern of Belonging as a basic normative pattern thus does not naturally include the integration of 'foreigners' or 'differing' groups, nor does it include the equal treatment of any individual. Moreover, the issue of belonging is considerably more complicated than hitherto described. Society is made up of various 'normative circles'. Traditionally, any legal scheme comprises an inherent principle of belonging as concerns the group of application. This can even be applied to the legal system as such. Originally, the notion of belonging/coverage was quite concrete, resulting in geographically limited social and legal units—compare the Swedish Landscape Acts, and before that, even the village. Eventually, these units grew into nation-states, based not only on ethnic and social conceptions of belonging, but also dependent on administrative and political powers. This evolution is taken a step further by a phenomenon such as the European Union. It is thus the goal of European integration policies to break the traditional conception of belonging present in the nation-state (Member State), widening the normative circle of inclusion (belonging).[53] Here we are taking Belonging to a mega-level, however. From this point of view, the mere existence of a social security system is an exponent for belonging and care obligations at system/state level. (And the lack of such an order at EU level (there are only coordinating rules) is but a reminder of the difficulties of such a project.) In fact, Mattias Malmstedt had already developed this line of reasoning in his licentiate thesis on social benefits with regard to the definition of belonging to this kind of social benefit system, be it citizenship, ethnicity, work or residency.[54] The strategy or principle of integration, on the other hand, has a more technical (not to say manipulative) character to it, and can

[52] Christensen, 'Protection of Established Position', above n 2, 289. Compare also Kaarlo Tuori, Chapter 3, including his discussion on Anna Christensen's theory on *basic* normative patterns and its relation to Habermas' dichotomy between law as an institution and law as a medium.

[53] Anna Christensen pointed to the Sovereignty of the Nation-state, reflecting the Pattern of Protection of Established Position as citizenship rights—as the most basic principle of International Law; Christensen, 'Protection of Established Position', above n 2, 323.

[54] See M Malmstedt, *Tillhörighet och sociala förmåner från 1600-talets Laws of Settlement till förordning nr 1408/71* (Lund, Juristförlaget i Lund, 2002). See also L Karlén, *Rätten till bostad, En komparativ undersökning av svensk och engelsk lagstiftning om rätt till bostad* (Lund, Jurisförlaget i Lund, 1998), as well as A Christensen and M Malmstedt, 'Lex Loci Laboris versus Lex Loci Domicilii: an Inquiry into the Normative Foundations of European Social Security Law' (2000) 2(1) *European Journal of Social Security* 69.

instead be seen as a tool for acquiring certain effects. It is designed to affect people 'externally' and does not really function as an internalised norm for interpersonal relationships; it is instead situated in the functional sphere.[55] Such a multi-layered analysis, however, may eventually be more confusing than clarifying. As Cotterell puts it,[56] 'no theory provides a magic key to understanding'—it is merely part of the 'continuous attempts to create knowledge that transcends partial perspectives'. The Theory of Law as Normative Patterns in a Normative Field is, of course, not an omnipotent theory on law in society that grasps it in its entirety, but it does lend itself to a partial and thorough (also comparative) analysis of the different areas of law, well in line with the idea of seeing 'patterns' and not 'systems'. This is especially true when we add functionality to the analysis.

The theory's functionality in *a comparative setting* was addressed by Christensen herself, both as a comparison between different areas of law, and in relation to cross-national comparisons, and has shown its efficiency through several doctoral theses within the Norma Research Programme. In his doctoral thesis, Andreas Inghammar made a complex comparison of the disabled and their right to work, in the legal terms of labour market measures, employment protection and non-discrimination regulation, respectively, comparing their regulation in Sweden, England and Germany.[57] There, the Theory of Law as Normative Patterns in a Normative Field is used to describe the respective regulations balancing competing normative interests in relation to an overall goal of social (or rather labour market) inclusion of disabled people. Labour market measures thus articulate facets of Just Distribution and seldom-implied individual rights, with the exception of Germany. The extent of Protection of Established Position or employment protection rights varied between the countries, not least when it came to seniority rules or social assessment in relation to redundancy situations. Discrimination law, it is argued, has the overall function of promoting competition on equal terms, or meritocratic principles, close to the Market-Functional pattern. The ban on indirect discrimination, however, may prove more challenging in relation to managerial prerogatives, in that it questions the very reference rules applied, ie the justification of certain requirements and/or qualities. The British system was found to promote equality through discrimination law and to demonstrate more reluctance towards positive measures and strong employment protection. Both the German and Swedish systems focused on employment protection, at the

[55] Compare Numhauser-Henning, 'Freedom of Movement', above n 48, 45, where I draw the conclusion that work and the Market-Functional Pattern are crucial to the process of creating the internal market, and thus one form of integration, whereas with regard to social cohesion other normative values such as solidarity and Just Distribution come to the fore when creating a Union. Compare, however, H-P Graver, 'Normative mønster i EF-retten' in C Henrichsen *et al* (eds), *Lovens Liv* (Copenhagen, Jurist- og Økonomforbundets Forlag, 2000), where Graver argues that Integration and Sovereignty are two opposite poles in the Normative Field of (then) Community Law.

[56] R Cotterell, *The Sociology of Law: An Introduction*, 2nd edn (London, Butterworths, 1992) 70.

[57] A Inghammar, *Funktionshindrad—med rätt till arbete? En komparativ studie av arbetsrättsliga regleringar kring arbete och funktionshinder*, Norma 9 (Lund, Juristförlaget i Lund, 2007).

same time providing more ambitious programmes for integration.[58] One overall conclusion was that the legislation concerning the issues at stake in all countries was inaccessible and difficult to categorise and analyse from a legal point of view. In this context, the use of the theory on normative patterns to bring order to the legal norm material not only served to improve the general understanding of the field, but also to make such a comparison possible.

In her doctoral thesis,[59] Mia Rönnmar made a comparative study of the managerial prerogative and the right to direct and allocate work (an element of the Market-Functional pattern) in relation to the employee's obligation to work, in terms of a flexibility study of Swedish, English and German labour law applying a social-legal functional approach. Strong similarities were found among the three countries when it came to the basic material content, and existence, of the employer's right to direct and allocate work, this however, being somewhat more restricted in Germany. As regarded the employee's obligation to work, basically a contractual perspective was applied, although working obligations were considerably more extensive in Sweden and England than in Germany. In Sweden and Germany, more extensive employment protection places a limit on contractual changes during employment; however, at the same time, in comparison with England, greater procedural flexibility in terms of the industrial relations system may nevertheless provide more functional flexibility. This study is less a literal application of the Theory of Law as Normative Patterns in a Normative Field than a study built on the basic notions of the theory of law as competing normative patterns put in play in a normative field, and constantly transforming, yet articulating a surprisingly stable system over time.

Per Norberg used what he called 'the Norma method' in his doctoral thesis in an attempt to predict legal application in the strands of labour law and competition law, within an otherwise broad and general description of the normative core of these two legal disciplines.[60] The normative analysis at structural level led the author to conclude that the principle of the open cartel within labour law puts a natural limit on the power of the unions, to be balanced against the principle of competition law immunity for trade union activity regarding key issues of collective bargaining, such as wages and working conditions. Arguably therefore, the principle of the open cartel is a key principle in delimiting permissible industrial actions from prohibited ones. A shorter study explores the Protection of

[58] Compare the thesis of M Ventegodt Liisberg, *Disability and Employment: a Contemporary Disability Human Rights Approach applied to Danish, Swedish and EU Law and Policy*, School of Human Rights Research Series no 43 (Intersentia, 2011), concluding that the labour market becomes more inclusive towards persons with disabilities if clear legal obligations are imposed on employers to be more inclusive, and that in particular, such obligations on employers in Swedish employment protection regulation made the Swedish labour market considerably more inclusive than the Danish.

[59] M Rönnmar, *Arbetsledningsrätt och arbetsskyldighet, En komparativ studie av kvalitativ flexiblitet i svensk, engelsk och tysk kontext*, Norma 8 (Lund, Juristförlaget i Lund, 2004).

[60] P Norberg, *Arbetsrätt och konkurrensrätt, En normativ studie av motsättningen mellan marknadsrättsliga värden och sociala värden*, Norma 6 (Lund, Juristförlaget i Lund, 2002).

Established Position in Japanese labour law and, more specifically, the so-called long-term employment system as compared to Swedish labour law.[61] Morozumi recognises (not surprisingly) that both the normative pattern of Protection of Established Position and the Market-Functional pattern are strong in the Japanese setting, making room, however, for a continuous weakening of lifelong employment, particularly in situations of farming-outs, etc. On the other hand, there is an extended scope of the Protection of Established Position in relation to newer groups, such as women and irregular workers.

Christensen's theory is also (outside the Norma Research Programme) used in the doctoral thesis of Carin Ulander-Wänman[62] on the Swedish employment protection rules concerning the priority right to re-employment following redundancy situations. Here, the theory was used in a context of analysing the construction of power relationships between employers, trade unions, and employees, concerning the priority right to re-employment, and the notions, values and other premises on which these power relations were based. The priority right to re-employment is an intervention in the employer's managerial prerogative or freedom to employ, in favour of employment protection, or, as it is, the Protection of Established Position. Nevertheless, the design of the regulation results in a fairly strong position for the employer, and while it invests some powers in trade unions and the rights to deviation through collective agreements, it leaves the employee fairly 'unprotected'. He or she is subordinate to both the employer's and the trade union's collective interests and powers, and such collective agreements normally emphasise the efficiency interests of the company rather than the security interests of the individual employee. The conclusion is that 'the priority right to re-employment mainly serves as a limit on the employer's right to employ rather than an accrued right of the employee'.[63] Recent developments regarding flexibility and competence requirements are predicted to reduce the protective potential of the rules even more, and imply even stronger emphasis on the Market-Functional pattern, as employees with established positions are increasingly found to have a reduced ability to be both flexible and qualified.

C. Social Security Law

Christensen had already elaborated on the normative patterns in social security law in her early article on Protection of Established Position,[64] but she did so

[61] M Morozumi, 'Protection of the Established Position in Japanese Labour Law: Basic Normative Patterns under the Long-Term Employment System' (1997) 4 *Norma*, also published in (1998) 14(1) *International Journal of Comparative Labour Law and Industrial Relations* 41.

[62] C Ulander-Wänman, *Företrädesrätt till återanställning* (Uppsala, Iustus Förlag, 2008).

[63] Ibid 365.

[64] Christensen, 'Skydd för etablerad position', above n 2.

again in an article a year later.[65] Later still, she also wrote an article on basic normative patterns in pension systems.[66]

Social security law developed as a necessary complement to the dominating modern *wage-work structure*—an important starting point for the normative analysis. As a system, social security entails a redistribution of resources at the collective level. Most people, during shorter or longer periods in their lives, will be unable to perform work that earns a salary, be this for structural or individual reasons. As work became detached from other parts of social life (such as the family), various social security schemes developed to fill these gaps. (This individualisation of maintenance is more developed in some countries than in others.) Such schemes must, however, at all times be designed so as not to threaten the dominant structure of waged work, and there is room not only for really redistributed patterns proper, but also for more conservative ones reflecting the individual's previous social position.

The Swedish system at least, with its emphasis on the lost income principle and thus protection of large groups of middle-class people, was early on marked by its character as an alternative Protection of Established Position. This pattern is characterised by providing protection only to those who have already achieved a certain position in society. Sickness benefits, as well as unemployment benefits, were always known to relate to previous income. Such benefits are thus related to earlier income and paid out over a limited period of time. This is basically functional: a worker cannot in the short term easily re-adapt to a radically lower 'income'. There are different requirements within the various branches of social security on how firmly established the economic position must be before these income-related benefits are granted. Normally, there is also a 'ceiling' on the benefits paid out, and the highest incomes are not protected by social security. Nevertheless, social security rights clearly distinguish themselves from social assistance based on the principle of basic needs.

Pensions, too, having started out as basic schemes in the spirit of solidarity, are nowadays, and to a great extent, income-related and thus built on Protection of Established Position. They are, however, also characterised by being long-term benefits. Such benefits are an even more evident exponent of ownership rights, as we talk about accrued pension rights being 'earned' throughout a working life, whereas occupational injury compensation is of a character similar to the so-called subtraction principle used in the calculation of damages in the law of tort and insurance. Christensen took the Earnings Principle pattern to constitute a special normative pattern closer to, but still distinguishable from, the Market-Functional pattern. A strictly actuarial pension meets the requirements of markets, whereas

[65] A Christensen, 'Normativa grundmönster i socialrätten' (1997) 78 *Retfaerd* 69.

[66] A Christensen, 'Normativa grundmönster i pensionssystemen' in *Lovens Liv, Festskrift till Jörgen Dalberg-Laarsen* (Copenhagen, Jurist- og Økonomforbundets forlag, 2000).

schemes built on the earnings principle refer to 'social earnings', such as years of work, study, child-rearing, etc, rather than mere economic calculations.[67]

Generally speaking, there is an obligation aspect to (short-term) social security benefits: the obligation to return to work as soon as possible. Nevertheless, depending on how benefit levels are balanced against lost income, the lost-income principle typically renders insured persons less willing to reconsider their situation and accept new and different positions offered by a new and changing labour market, and thus tends to burden 'production' with the costs for an ever-increasing part of the population that does not participate in that production. This was manageable as long as society was characterised by 'full' employment, but as the marginalisation of less productive or skilled groups increased, a structural problem arose. This is the logic behind a great deal of the changes that have taken place in social security schemes in recent years. The increased importance of actuarial factors when calculating benefits, as well as an increased dependency on contributions, are such expressions. So also are the changed criteria for 'suitable work', forcing individuals to change professions, as well as the increased qualification requirements for inclusion in the 'established' group. Generally speaking, the impact of these reforms has been less on core groups; instead they work to the detriment of those having difficulties in holding a job in the long term, or even getting onto the labour market in the first place. However, these reforms do not only imply negative consequences—pensions do not necessarily have to decrease; it is still possible to change jobs without negative consequences for pension rights already accrued, and a decrease in salary at the end of a career does not have the devastating effects as in a final salary scheme.

In pension schemes, we can thus identify the development from need-based minimum schemes to schemes built on an earnings principle, rather than on Protection of Established Position. Nevertheless, elements of the latter normally also have a role to play in most pension schemes. For instance, fixed-benefit schemes are closer to the Protection of Established Position than are fixed-contribution schemes, and closest of them all are final salary schemes, guaranteeing a pension at the final income level. Structural change, such as demographical change and considerably longer 'after-lives', have recently triggered pension reforms built on fixed contributions or, as is the case in Sweden, even lifelong average earnings. As was the case with short-term benefits, reforms will not necessarily have a very strong impact on core groups of workers, but they will be to the detriment of the growing groups of more marginalised and flexible workers. This (again) puts pressure on those parts of the social security system that are based on patterns of redistribution and solidarity, though not necessarily increasing the legitimacy of those patterns.

[67] For a presentation of a mainly actuarial and pre-funded pension system, the Chilean one, see A Numhauser-Henning, 'Premiepension för hela slanten, Det chilenska exemplet' (1997–98) 4 *Juridisk Tidskrift* 1266.

Swedish social security is dominated to a large extent by Protection of Established Position. There are, however, also important parts that express the pattern of Just Distribution, ie the guaranteed benefits level in many schemes, such as parental benefits and pensions. Nevertheless, these have not generally been construed as a radical redistribution of established positions, but have, as Christensen puts it, 'rather been constructed carefully and patiently by allocating new resources in such a way that larger and larger parts of the population have been able to obtain certain positions, which then are granted fairly strong protection'. Christensen thus held combinations of the normative patterns of Just Distribution and Protection of Established Position to be characteristic of the Swedish Welfare State. She also insisted that the system should be seen rather as a system of insurance covering everyone against certain risks (such as poor health or unemployment), rather than a system of redistribution among different groups (healthy and sick, etc). The principle of equal distribution, or distribution based on needs, is only a subsidiary principle in Swedish social security. Other systems, such as the one in the United Kingdom with its traditional flat-rate schemes, rely more heavily on the pattern of Just Distribution.

As regards pension schemes, there is no doubt that these (in response to demographical development and an increasingly older population) imply major transfers and thus redistribution, at societal level, both horizontally between groups of pensioners of the same generation, and between generations. These problems could not be solved by individual savings. An individual, being unable to predict his or her future, would need to have a level of savings that would hamper economic growth. Nor does the wage-work system, and thus level of earnings, permit appropriate private maintenance obligations at family level. There is a need for collective solutions, and a society must guarantee a decent level of living for all those who 'belong'. This is the basic question of legitimacy at the heart of the European Union and its policies for 'inclusion'.

In his doctoral thesis on pension scheme reforms, Nils Eliasson started out with the basic normative pattern of Protection of Established Position, and traced its 'status' in German, Norwegian and Swedish reform processes.[68] The focus was on the individual when various pension schemes were changed: did the pension position of the individual enjoy any protection, or did he or she have to accept without resistance that pensions were changing due to societal developments such as demographic change? The systems studied were reforms to statutory pension schemes (Germany, Norway and Sweden), and reforms to private collective pension schemes (Germany and Sweden). The protection offered by the legal systems was found to be based on property rights, but also legitimate expectations, the principle of non-retroactivity, a test of reasonableness (good faith) and contract. With regard to public pension schemes, Eliasson found a test against legitimate expectations to be more accurate than solutions based on the

[68] N Eliasson, *Protection of Accrued Pension Rights*, Norma 4 (Lund, Juristförlaget i Lund, 2001).

protection of accrued property rights as such—also when taking into account the possibly frustrated contract between generations underlying the pension system at issue. He also concluded that the rights the insured person had actually earned should be protected, unless it became necessary to change the scheme in order to secure a fair balance between the disposable income of the pensioners and the income of those insured currently financing their pensions (under so-called pay-as-you-go schemes) under the contract between generations. As regards actual protection, Sweden represented the two extremes: there was no formal legal protection of statutory pension rights, but there was absolute contractual protection (and thus Protection of Established Position) of pension rights earned under an occupational pension scheme. (De facto legal protection was, however, offered by means of transitional rules, etc, also concerning reforms of statutory pension schemes.) In Germany, on the other hand, there was protection in both cases, although it was not absolute in either: statutory social security rights were also formally protected as property rights, but this protection was 'complemented' by the legitimate expectations principle and also the principles on non-retroactivity and proportionality. This was also the case with changes to private occupational pension schemes, a solution taking into account the 'collective character' of the latter. The crucial question was whether a change in pensions was less favourable for the employees as a whole, not from the individual's point of view.

My own report, *Pension Rights and the EC Coordination Rules on Applicable Legislation in the Light of Migration and Labour-Market Developments*,[69] provides a normative and functional analysis of European social policy and the coordination of social security, and especially of pension rights. It thus examined the coverage, design and criteria of belonging within statutory pension schemes, as well as the adequacy of the rules on applicable legislation in the EU legislation on social security coordination from the viewpoint of current changes in the labour market and in society more generally. Demographic change and general attitudes, considering pension at a certain age both a right and an obligation, produce challenges to society, by putting pressure on statutory pension schemes. Developments were concluded to imply a change towards schemes based on longer earning periods, or lifelong average earnings with higher or no fixed pensionable age (and thus a shift towards the Market-Functional pattern) but also an increased pressure towards a need for guaranteed basic levels in statutory pension schemes, through less consistent pension schemes for more 'flexible' groups of workers. Flexible work and its reflection in statutory social security schemes implies that positions are no longer all that established, whereas social security solutions based on guaranteed levels represent a movement towards the pattern of Just Distribution.

These developments were then discussed from an EU integration perspective. In this context, nationality has long been a prohibited criterion for belonging. Instead, social security benefits at national level are generally based on work or

[69] Numhauser-Henning, 'Freedom of Movement', above n 48.

residence (or a mix of the two, based primarily on work, but with residence as an additional, auxiliary criterion for belonging). It is the function of the coordination regulations to break up the old solidarity circles of national social security schemes and the territoriality principle inherent therein. As regards the coordination of social security, applicable legislation is mainly decided according to the *lex loci laboris* principle. This is mostly adequate as regards social rights being mainly work-based and as a complement to wage-work structures. It is also (in the main) instrumentally effective as regards the goals of mobility and integration. For a long time, the internal market and free movement were for *workers*, in what can be described as a symbiosis between the Market-Functional pattern and that of Protection of Established Position: wages for wage-work and earnings-based pensions. A shift towards greater impact for basic-needs pensions at the minimum guaranteed level imply a new challenge to EU integration policies, as partly addressed in later years by European Union Citizenship, as a basis for free movement rights. Pensions based on need represent a solidarity-based redistributive benefit under the pattern of Just Distribution. In this case, improved integration requires a right to residence, also for the non-active. In the process of creating the internal market, work, and the Market-Functional pattern opening markets, have come a long way. With regard to social cohesion and genuine European integration, other normative values of solidarity/criteria of belonging also come to the fore, and EU Citizenship becomes the adequate category.

EU Citizenship as the basis for the coordination of social security rights at EU level was also addressed by Emma Holm in her doctoral thesis, using the Theory of Law as Normative Patterns in a Normative Field to dismantle the normative conflicts in a complex analysis of European Union primary law, the EU coordination regulation on social security benefits, and the Swedish regulation of parental benefits.[70] Many Europeans move for family reasons; for instance, when a spouse follows a partner starting work in another Member State. One important aspect of EU law is that this movement must not result in a loss of social security benefits, such as benefits relating to childbirth and family costs. In reality, however, there are many obstacles to free movement in this area. In her thesis, Holm shows how problems occur in relation to families moving to and from Sweden, as well as working and living in different states, due to the difficulties in reconciling the deviating normative structures of the Swedish rules on parental benefit as compared to the normative structure of the EU rules on free movement and coordination of social security. Maternity and paternity rights are work-based rights under the Market-Functional and Protection of Established Position patterns, and should pose no problems, whereas family rights according to the Coordination Regulation are solidarity-based, 'derived' rights, based on the patterns of Belonging and Just Distribution, and quite incompatible with the Swedish 'individualised' social

[70] E Holm, *Fri rörlighet för familjer, En normativ analys av föräldrapenningen och EU-rätten*, Norma 11 (Lund, Juristförlaget i Lund, 2010).

security system. Problems occur as the Court of Justice of the European Union has made a broad definition of family benefits, comprising not only basic allowances, but also income-based parental benefits such as the Swedish parental benefit. These 'problems' can also be seen as a reflection of the overall development within EU law (also as regards the coordination of social security), as a move from expressing the normative pattern of Protection of Established Position towards an increased expression of the normative pattern of Just Distribution.

D. Family Law

Christensen herself elaborated only briefly on the normative patterns put to work in family law.[71] One reason for this was said to be that 'many important social spaces have been left practically untouched by regulation through legal rules' and that such 'judicial voids' often represent feminine areas of life[72]—a challenge for feminist law.[73]

The family was the fundamental unit of society before industrialisation and the market-functional era. For Weber, the family is an exponent of status, and marriage was a lifelong union. Marriage regulation purported stability, and divorce was (if at all) only acceptable in extreme situations. Weber precisely depicts, however, how status relationships have been replaced by contracts in modern society, as the mode of production changes. In modern family law, the normative pattern of Protection of Established Position has been considerably weakened, if not abolished.

Formerly, there were rules for the protection of the marital state in adherence with Protection of Established Position,[74] and there were (and sometimes still are) rules on alimony and maintenance after the dissolution of a marriage.[75] (It is worth noting that such rules were introduced in Sweden only in 1915, when the dissolution of marriages had started to be a reality to be considered!) Within the complementary social security system, there were (and still are in some countries)

[71] Christensen, 'Skydd för etablerad position', above n 2 and 'Normativa grundmönster i pensionssystemen', above n 66.

[72] Christensen, 'Normativa grundmönster i pensionssystemen', above n 66, 286.

[73] In her 1995 article on legal polycentricity, Christensen made the following statement regarding feminist law: 'What is women's law or feministic law if not the discovery of a distinct normative pattern [of women as second to men] reappearing in a great number of norms and moral habits from very different parts of the entire normative field? This discovery sets the whole field in motion. Norms are changing and regrouping, perhaps forming a feministic cluster. But they will never form a feministic system, that will last forever'. See Christensen, 'Polycentricity and Normative Patterns', above n 21, 240.

[74] Rules designed to increase the stability of families in earlier days had another purpose than the basic normative pattern of protection of established position, however—they worked to increase the protection of family as a social institution, and not the protection of the individual, see Christensen, 'Skydd för etablerad position', above n 2, 571.

[75] On the normative patterns in today's Swedish divorce regulations, see Eva Ryrstedt, Chapter 13.

widow's (and even widower's) pensions. In Sweden, this expression of the Protection of Established Position was, however, abolished in principle in 1990.

In modern family law legislation, divorce is an exponent of a contractual conception of marriage, although more inclined towards the promotion of personal freedom and autonomy (or emancipation from an earlier status relationship) than market-functional.

Also within family law, there are rules reflecting the normative pattern of Just Distribution. Such rules can be seen as the result of the pattern of Belonging described earlier, implying obligations of maintenance within the family unit. At societal level, the (still) important family structure with its obligations is (as is wage-work) complemented or replaced (when family fails) by social security benefits.

Eva Ryrstedt's doctoral thesis 'Division of Property and the Joint Dwelling: Financial Independence or Community'[76] used the concept of normative patterns in relation to family law regulation of the division of property between married spouses and cohabitees, respectively. She elaborated on the tension between the normative concepts of *Community* (a pattern stronger than that of mere Belonging) and *Individual Ownership/Financial Independence*, as present in Swedish family law, and in particular in relation to the regulation of (the right to) the joint dwelling during and upon termination of the relationship. The Pattern of Community is found to be permitted to abrogate Individual Ownership at the moment of division of property, through the notion of marriage property, despite the fact that individual ownership is also the starting point between spouses. The same concept—division of (to a certain extent limited) property—is applied to the 'community' of cohabitees. This normative 'outcome' is arguably not only a result of the legitimacy behind the normative patterns at stake at this given moment in time, but also of more immediate political ambitions, such as achieving/furthering economic equality between men and women in an era of frustrated relationships.

Norma Research Programme member Titti Mattsson also applied the Theory of Law as Normative Patterns in a novel way. In her recent study on the legal understanding of the right to a family in relation to custody and guardianship cases before Swedish courts,[77] she concluded that the normative pattern Protection of Established Position did influence court practice, and did so in several ways. Courts did not seem willing to challenge the original family constellation (the parents' right to their biological child), and Social Welfare Committees did not even seem very willing to file petitions for such cases. Moreover, a greater willingness to accept the construction of new families occurred when the foster families selected to obtain not only substantive but also legal custody were relatives of the child; these families seem to obtain, as Mattsson says, an 'expanded established

[76] E Ryrstedt, *Division of Property and the Joint Dwelling: Financial Independence or Community* (Lund, Juristförlaget i Lund, 1998).

[77] T Mattsson, *Rätten till familj inom barn- och ungdomsvården* (Stockholm, Liber, 2010).

position' as original family of the child. The ultimate conclusion is that despite the fact that the best interest of the child is a principle that is supposed to inform any decision concerning a child, the biological parent's/original legal custodian's position is perceived to be strong.

From an EU law perspective, family law is still a void legal area; it is too deeply embedded in national and religious culture to be suitable for European Union regulation. However, as we have seen in, among others, Holm's doctoral thesis, the EU rules on free movement and social security coordination have important implications for families, as has the comprehensive EU regulation of women's rights, in the form of equal treatment. Until recently, the latter mainly concerned equal treatment in working life, an area of particular importance for families, since wage-work structures and families are competing institutions from (as it is) a woman's point of view.

IV. CONCLUDING REMARKS

There is no simple way to sum up recent normative developments in the EU social dimension. It can be said that recent movements in the normative field of the social dimension have frequently been towards the Market-Functional pole. To exemplify this we can mention the shift towards more flexible employment, non-discrimination and equal treatment, as well as earnings-related and contributions-based pensions. On the other hand, it is also true to say that, relatively speaking, the importance of guarantee levels within social security benefit schemes such as basic pensions have become more important. However, an increased actual importance does not necessarily mean that the normative values behind the pattern of Just Distribution really are strengthened. Such solutions are often seen as a necessary means of upholding societal legitimacy in the short term, at the same time as their relative importance is a reflection of market-functional flexibilisation of working life. Also, in relation to the pattern of Protection of Established Position, it might be said that flexible work and its reflection in statutory social security schemes implies that positions are no longer all that established. In any case, the aggregated result can, at any given point in time, be described as a socially and politically (more or less) legitimate balance between these conflicting normative patterns. Having said this, it is clear that in the wake of the recent economic crisis, this balancing act has become considerably more difficult and legitimacy harder to come by. Moreover, this is obviously truer for some European states than for others.

Christensen's Theory of Law as Normative Patterns in a Normative Field is, as Tuori says,[78] destined to reveal the law beyond the law. By distinguishing normative patterns in regulations and practice, the legal scientist can contribute to the

[78] Compare Kaarlo Tuori, Chapter 3.

identification of the substantial contents of (in this case) the EU social dimension and its articulation in legal-technical forms, and at the same time contribute to a broadened debate on democratic deficiency. The theory has the potential to contribute to the analysis of the accurate level of social inclusion, and therewith also to the public debate on these issues. It also helps reveal contradictions with other legitimate normative conceptions in society, thus avoiding excessive simplification of complex issues. We are not dealing with simple hierarchies of social values—normative conflicts have to be dealt with in a nuanced and subtle way. When we view law as an exponent of society and societal values, at a time when democracy and governance tend to leave the national state behind, a theory that has the potential to overcome national confines, as well as that of formal democracy, can contribute to situating public debate in the relevant 'room' of the EU Social Market Economy and substantial democracy.[79]

[79] For a further development of this line of argument, compare A Numhauser-Henning, 'Om rättens roll i en demokratisk samhällsutveckling' in *SOU 1999:76, Maktdelning* (Stockholm, Fakta Info Direkt, 1999).

3

*Law Beyond Law**

KAARLO TUORI

I. ANNA CHRISTENSEN'S BASIC NORMATIVE PATTERNS

ANNA CHRISTENSEN'S (1936–2001) main legal theoretical contribution is the idea of basic normative patterns (*normativa grundmönster*), which play an important role in law, primarily at what can be called a sub-surface level. In this chapter I shall first present Christensen's idea—or perhaps more accurately, my reading of Christensen's idea—and then try to locate it in a somewhat larger discursive context, among other Nordic suggestions for an analysis of the law's hidden premises. As reference points I shall use the Norwegian legal philosopher David Doublet's (1954–2000) notion of the law's evaluation foundation (*evalueringsgrunnlag*), as well as my own proposal for portraying the law's multi-layered nature; an approach I have termed 'critical legal positivism'.

So what does Christensen mean by basic normative patterns?[1] Christensen's starting point is law as consisting of an assemblage of legal norms with a rather weak systems character. The law's heterogeneity is a consequence of the fact that legal norms have emerged in diverse manners and at different times. Christensen alludes to a distinction that related to Jürgen Habermas'[2] famous dichotomy between law as an institution and law as a medium. Some legal norms have their basis in social norms that have developed within different fields of life and different types of human relationships. Other sets of legal norms are more technical in character; they have been drafted and adopted by a centralised governing body—by the legislator—and presuppose administrative arrangements that guarantee their maintenance.

* This chapter has been written within the research programme of the CoE in the Foundations of European Law and Polity, financed by the Academy of Finland.

[1] The most comprehensive presentation of Anna Christensen's legal theoretical views is A Christensen, 'Skydd för etablerad position—ett normativt grundmönster' (1996) 4 *Tidsskrift for Rettsvitenskap* 519. In English, she has exposed the notion of basic normative patterns in A Christensen, 'Normative Patterns and the Normative Field: a Post-Liberal View on Law' in T Wilhelmsson and S Hurri (eds), *From Dissonance to Sense: Welfare State Expectations, Privatisation and Private Law* (Aldershot, Ashgate, 1999).

[2] J Habermas, 'A Theory of Communicative Action' (1989) 2 *Cambridge: Polity Press* 356.

However, although the assemblage of legal norms seems to possess a rather weak systems character, there are various ways of ordering the norms. Christensen rejects striving for a master principle of systematisation; she calls the objective of arriving at a single system without overlaps or redundancies a dream, cherished by the codification movement. The intellectual movement today has adopted the opposite direction, that of deconstruction and polycentricism. In ordering legal norm material, different principles are used in different situations and contexts, and (this is Christensen's view) rightly so: different ways of ordering illuminate different aspects of legal norms.

Christensen has developed her own proposal for bringing order to legal norm material with a view to what she calls the *social dimension*; legal norms regulating relationships that directly involve almost everyone in their daily lives and pursuing the function of protecting and developing this daily life. At the Lund Faculty of Law, the subject Social Dimension includes family law, labour law, tenancy law and social welfare law. Christensen claims that the basic norms of the social dimension have emerged in a 'social manner' in social intercourse and have strong normative anchorage in society; to a great extent the social dimension is only a legal codification of society's moral customs and conceptions. It is here that we can discern basic normative patterns that are effective in different contexts and that possess a degree of constancy. Christensen's way of employing the term 'normative' implies a moral connotation. Basic normative patterns correspond to social patterns of action that are experienced as morally obligatory; they belong to the domain of law as an institution rather than that of law as a medium. Basic normative patterns may also be identical to what other authors have seen as legal principles. However, related to the Habermasian distinction, Christensen emphasises that not all legal principles are normative in the sense in which she uses the term. *Pacta sunt servanda* is because it has emerged from and corresponds to a social pattern of action that is experienced as morally obligatory. But the so-called prevention principle is not normative because it is of a more technical nature and is meant to influence behaviour from the outside and not as an internalised norm in human interaction. Christensen adds that in a legal culture not dominated by the tradition of legal realism, she could indeed have spoken of basic *moral* patterns.

As a previous example of an analysis of basic normative patterns, Christensen refers to Torstein Eckhoff's discussion of justice in value distribution. Eckhoff examines two basic normative patterns. The first of these requires a balance between the parties' performance in different types of exchange and even in other situations. The other pattern pertains to situations where different types of value should be distributed in a just way. This includes variations such as equality of shares, distribution according to need and the principle of queuing.

Christensen's special focus lies on a basic normative pattern that she calls 'protection of established position' (*skydd för etablerad position*). This normative pattern has applications in all the fields of law included in the social dimension: in labour law it protects the employee against dismissal, in tenancy law the tenant against eviction, and in social welfare law the recipient against loss of income. It has a different focus than the principles discussed by Eckhoff: it does not focus on distribution or redistribution of values (and positions) but protects already established positions (and distribution of values). In its conservatism it is in conflict with the dynamic market-functional normative pattern that consists of the right to property, freedom of contract and freedom of trade, and that is supposed to induce constant redistribution of values and shaking-up of positions.

In Christensen's view, the conflictual relationship between protection of established position and the market-functional normative pattern manifests a general feature of the law beyond law. Basic normative patterns have emerged at various times and in diverse relationships, and they fulfil diverse needs. They all possess a core area or area of origin, but they can be transferred beyond their domain of emergence. Herein lies the source of conflicts between basic normative patterns, as epitomised by the contestation between protection of established positions and the normative patterns pertaining to distribution and redistribution of values. Although basic normative patterns bring order to the assemblage of legal norms, they do not constitute a comprehensive system; in terms that Christensen did not employ, but which I think catch her point, the coherence they engender is not of total, but instead of merely local character. No internal hierarchy exists among basic normative patterns, nor does any principle of higher rank or definitive legislative resolution of conflicts.

Christensen elucidates the functioning of basic normative patterns through the notion of *normative field*. Normative field is equal to the social field where the law operates. Basic normative patterns are like poles that try to attract legal regulations, and where a regulation ends up depends on the respective attractive forces the poles exercise. Because a normative field is usually influenced by several normative patterns, these rarely appear in a pure form. Even if a regulation is dominated by a distinct normative pattern, other normative patterns will always give rise to modifications. Consequently, when studying a particular normative pattern in the context of a particular regulation, other normative patterns affecting the regulation must always also be taken into account. Furthermore, a normative field is never entirely stable, but is traversed by normative forces that pull towards opposite poles. Christensen seeks to prove her point by exploring both how protection of established position manifests itself in the social dimension and how the tension with market-functional normative patterns creates the underlying dynamics within this normative field.

II. DAVID DOUBLET'S EVALUATION FOUNDATION

David Doublet's main contribution to the discussion on law beyond law is his notion of evaluation foundation (*evalueringsgrunnlag*).[3] Doublet argues that this

[3] In my presentation of Doublet's views, I have relied on his doctoral thesis in legal philosophy. D Doublet, *Rett, vitenskap of fornuft* (Stavanger, Alma Mater, 1995).

notion allows him to overcome the dichotomy between legal positivism and natural law. Evaluation foundation is supposed to provide us with an immanent normative yardstick of law; a yardstick that is implicit in law itself. Substantively, Doublet's evaluation foundation of modern law is nearly identical with the fundamental principles of the democratic *Rechtsstaat*. But what interests us now is not so much Doublet's reading of the contents of the evaluation foundation as much as the way he claims to be able to reconstruct this foundation. He has dressed his reconstruction in systems-theoretical garb; actually what he tries to accomplish is a kind of synthesis of Habermas and Niklas Luhmann. Doing conscious injustice to Doublet's explicit intentions, I shall, however, remove the systems-theoretical embellishments; to my mind they are not necessary for catching the originality of his normative analysis.

Crucial to Doublet's understanding of law is the distinction he makes between positive and valid law (*gjeldende rett*) and the way he conceives of the road leading from the former to the latter. *Positive law* is law as it appears in such traditional legal sources as statutes and other regulations, *travaux préparatoires* and judicial precedents. Positive law is the object of legal interpretation that the legal communicative community exercises while employing the legal dogmatic method whose core Doublet (in a typically Norwegian manner) sees in the doctrine of legal sources. *Valid law* is the end product of legal interpretation. However, it is an ever-changing product to which members of the legal communicative community continuously contribute with ever-new readings of the positive law of legal sources.

In addition to 'positive law' and 'valid law', 'legal communicative community' is another central concept in Doublet's portrayal of modern law. In modern society, the production and reproduction of law falls mainly to the legal communicative community, whose principal members are judges, legislators and legal scholars. Thus, according to Doublet, 'in society, three main actors exist who all are members in the legal communicative community and who have a particular relation to valid law in comparison with other members of society: the judge, the legislator and the legal scholar'. However, it appears that for Doublet, the legislator's role is mainly to produce positive law as the object of legal interpretation, whereas judges and legal scholars play the primary role in the interpretation that produces valid law as a never-fixable normative entity. Both judges and scholars rely on the legal dogmatic method, and they share a similar perspective on law; although scholarly readings of law lack authoritative force, even when presented as descriptions they have (*pace* legal realism *à la* Ross) normative implications. Legal scholars' contribution to the argumentative process, where valid law is constantly being redefined, entails a peculiar dual role. Legal scholars participate in two communicative systems and are members of two communicative communities: legal and scientific. Legal scholarship's distinctive features as a branch of science are related to its practical orientation. Legal scholarship is a poietical science in the Aristotelian sense of the term.

Membership of the legal communicative community is open only to those in possession of a specific entrance ticket. Only those who master what Doublet calls the *qualification norm* of the legal communicative community are accepted. This qualification norm is the criterion by which the legal communicative community draws the line between law and non-law, or—to be more exact—between legal and non-legal argumentation. Doublet is not very precise in characterising the contents of the qualification norm. It appears to be nearly identical with the legal dogmatic method, with the doctrine of legal sources as a core component. The qualification norm is not a codified or positivised norm, but (and this is my reading) rather a cultural fact, something implicit in the legal culture of the legal communicative community.

Now, Doublet's conceptual apparatus provides us with the means to understand what the evaluation foundation is about, how it can be cognised, and which functions it fulfils in the legal system. Substantively, the evaluation foundation consists of values and principles that may function as evaluation norms with regard to law. But how is 'law' as the object of evaluation to be understood? Is positive law at issue, that is, the object of legal interpretation; or valid law, which is in turn the end product of legal interpretation? The answer would seem to be: both. The evaluation foundation offers us normative criteria for assessing both positive and valid law. In relation to positive law, the evaluation foundation contributes to the process of interpretation that leads from positive to valid law. The evaluation foundation finds its locus in the Norwegian doctrine of legal sources among the so-called real considerations (*reelle hensyn*). In legal interpretation, the evaluation foundation functions as a normative corrective with regard to the rules of positive law such as they appear in the traditional sources of law; that is, legislation, *travaux préparatoires* or precedents. Legal interpretation and the elaboration of valid law remain within the domain of *de lege lata* assessments. But the evaluative norms of the evaluation foundation can be applied to valid law as well, to justify singular *de lege ferenda* considerations or more comprehensive appraisals of valid law.

In Doublet's account, the evaluation foundation occupies a paradoxical position vis-à-vis valid law: it is part of valid law, the foundation of valid law, and a criterion for its assessment. How is this possible?

Doublet argues that the evaluation foundation includes two types of value: intra- and extra-positive values. The former consist of values that are expressly confirmed in positive law, or which rules of positive law expressly protect. But even the extra-positive values included in the evaluation are, as Doublet puts it, embodied (*nedfelt*) in valid law. They are implicit presuppositions on which valid law is based, even if they are not expressly articulated in positive law. This entails specific requirements for their cognition. They are only accessible to a hermeneutic or reflexive reconstruction that has its starting point in present (positive?) law, but which must be sensitive to the historical, *wirkungsgeschichtliche* development of the values basis of modern law; a development launched in the latter half of the eighteenth century and manifested, for example, in various conceptions of human rights and the *Rechtsstaat*.[4] Thus, the basics of the evaluation foundation were

[4] According to Doublet, 'the starting-point is given in present valid law and the objective is to find out what facilitates this law as the law of a *Rechtsstaat* defined as a communicative community,

laid more than 200 years ago, but have subsequently undergone transformations corresponding to the evolution of modern society. For the evaluation foundation Doublet claims a general validity covering the age of modern law, with its beginning in the constitutional and legislative projects of the late eighteenth century. However, this claim does not exclude transformations within the evaluation foundation—value transitions, as Doublet calls them.

What, then, are the functions the evaluation foundation accomplishes in the legal system? First, Doublet discusses the closely interrelated functions of criticism, boundary drawing and legitimation. In its critical task, the evaluation foundation establishes a normative corrective with regard to the rules of positive law and justifies legally relevant *de lege ferenda* standpoints. By the same token, it draws the boundary for legitimate law. Furthermore, Doublet also assigns the evaluation foundation a constitutive function with regard to the democratic *Rechtsstaat* and its law. The evaluation foundation includes the fundamental values that underpin the law of a democratic *Rechtsstaat*, and at least a potential if not actual awareness of these values among the citizenry is a prerequisite of such a state's character as a communicative community.

The evaluation foundation also plays a constitutive role in relation to the more restricted legal communicative community that occupies such an important position in Doublet's portrayal of modern law. As we may recall, membership in the legal communicative community requires mastering the qualification norm of that community. The qualification norm includes the evaluation foundation as its value dimension, which makes its entry into legal argumentation through the legal source factor called *reelle hensyn*. This means that arguments that express or invoke values contradicting them are not accepted as legally relevant by the legal communicative community. The qualification norm as an inter-subjective, legal-cultural structure is a constitutive presupposition of the legal communicative community, and the evaluation foundation is an integral part of it.

III. CRITICAL LEGAL POSITIVISM

In my own depiction of modern law, I argue in line with Anna Christensen and David Doublet that law as a normative entity is not exhausted by surface-level positive law as it appears in legal sources such as legislation and precedents; that there exists something that can be called law beyond law.[5]

I draw a distinction between two aspects of law, or (if you wish) two meanings of the concept of law. Law is at once a symbolic-normative and a social phenomenon: it consists both of a normative order—a *legal order*—and of specific social

mapping the value basis which creates the possibility for the emergence of the *Rechtsstaat* and the law which constitutes our reflexive starting-point'; D Doublet, *Rett, vitenskap of fornuft*, above n 3, 498.

[5] I have presented my view of modern law in K Tuori, *Critical Legal Positivism* (Aldershot, Ashgate, 2002) and *Ratio and Voluntas: the Tension between Reason and Will in Law* (Aldershot, Ashgate, 2011).

practices—*legal practices*, such as law-making, adjudication and legal scholarship. Legal practices are social practices that have specialised in production and reproduction of the law as a symbolic-normative phenomenon—as a legal order. Legal practices provide the framework for legal discourse and the individual speech acts making up this discourse. Various legal practices, such as law-making, adjudication, and legal scholarship—perform different tasks in the legal system. Yet they all participate in a common discourse, and it is this discourse that creates links between their particular contributions.

Legal scholarship's functioning as a legal practice is most evident in doctrinal research; in what is defined on the Continent as the province of *legal dogmatics*. Through its interpretive standpoints and systematisation proposals, doctrinal research contributes to production and reproduction of the legal order, and participates in ongoing legal discourse. But legal scholarship is not merely a legal practice. It is also a scientific practice and is subject to the limitations and commitments ensuing from this, such as the requirement of reflexivity. Both legal and social scientists are often at a loss when attempting to define the characteristic features of legal science and its relationship to social science. It is the peculiar dual citizenship of legal science that accounts for this embarrassment.

With regard to the symbolic-normative side of modern law, I emphasise its *multi-layered* nature. Law as a legal order does not consist merely of such explicit *surface-level* material as individual statutes and rulings or legal scholars' normative standpoints. The law also includes *legal-cultural* layers on which legal practices and legal discourse rely as indispensable presuppositions, but which largely unfold their effects unconsciously, through the tacit pre-understanding of legal actors. This legal-cultural infrastructure embraces normative, conceptual, and methodological ingredients: general legal principles, concepts and theories; doctrines of legal sources; and distinct patterns of legal argumentation. Within the law's sedimented layers we may discern a common core, something amounting to modern law's *deep structure*, and shared by different legal cultures. This common legal-cultural core (we could also call it modern law's *deep culture*) can be examined in terms of its normative, conceptual and methodological elements: modern law's fundamental principles and categories as well as its characteristic methods and patterns of argumentation.

These two aspects of law are constantly interacting. Law as a legal order is produced and reproduced by legal practices, which also provide the ontological support for law as a symbolic-normative phenomenon: without their backing we could not speak of the existence of a legal order. On the other hand, legal practices need support from legal norms. This is especially true for such institutionalised practices as law-making and adjudication, which receive their legal character from the legal norms of competence, organisation and procedure—secondary rules in the sense defined by HLA Hart.[6] But an even more profound dependence of legal practices on law as a symbolic-normative phenomenon exists.

[6] HLA Hart, *The Concept of Law* (Oxford, Oxford University Press, 1961).

The contribution of legal practices, especially of law-making and adjudication, lends modern law its positive character. However, the decisions on which law relies are not decisions 'out of nothing' (*aus Nichts*) but based on certain presuppositions. The legal-cultural layers of law stand in *constitutive* relation to events on the law's surface: they make up the normative, conceptual and methodological reservoir without which the legislator could not enact its laws, the judges issue their rulings, or the scholars write their articles and monographs. In legal practices, these layers mainly function in an unconscious, tacit way: they form an integral part of the hermeneutic pre-understanding through which legal actors approach their specific tasks. But the relationship between the law's surface and its legal-cultural infrastructure is of a recursive character: not only is the surface dependent on legal-cultural presuppositions, but these in turn originate from individual contributions from the legislator, judges or legal scholars, to mention the main actors of modern law. The cultural, sub-surface elements of law result from a process of *sedimentation*, starting from what transpires on the surface as a result of legal practices. The relation of sedimentation also extends the law's positivity from its surface to its legal-cultural underpinnings, bringing the idea of modern law's multi-layered nature into harmony with its positivity.

In my portrayal of a 'mature' modern legal system, legal practices are responsible not only for producing and reproducing law as legal order, but also for mediating the relations between the surface and the sub-surface cultural layers. This applies to the relations of constitution and sedimentation and also to the relations of criticism, limitation and justification I have analysed in my *Critical Legal Positivism*. In addition, legal practices also channel external influences into the legal system, such as those stemming from politics (legislation) or morals (legal principles as articulated by adjudication and legal scholarship).

IV. COMPARISONS

There are evident similarities between Doublet's depiction of modern law and the view I have termed 'critical legal positivism'. We both try to defend a position that lies beyond the dichotomy of natural law and (traditional) legal positivism. We both acknowledge the role of what Francois Ewald[7] has called the critical reflexive instance in law, something that Western legal thinking has traditionally defined as natural law, but which legal positivism tends to reject. I have posed the question in terms of what can fulfil the function of natural law when natural law itself has lost its cultural underpinnings. I venture to assume that Doublet could have accepted this way of formulating the problem. In Doublet's account, the solution to the problem lies in the law's evaluation foundation, in my own exposition in the law's sub-surface, cultural layers. Doublet's evaluation foundation is largely comparable

[7] F Ewald, *L'Etat providence* (Paris, Grasset, 1986).

to my legal cultural layers, especially to what I have termed the law's deep structure or culture. However, Doublet focuses only on the normative dimension of the law's legal-cultural foundation, whereas I emphasise the role of the conceptual and methodological dimension as well. But this difference between our accounts is at least partly effaced by Doublet's notion of the qualification norm that defines the boundary between legal and non-legal argumentation, and that also includes methodological (and conceptual?) elements, such as the legal dogmatic method with the doctrine of legal sources at its core. According to my understanding, the legal cultural layers primarily operate through the hermeneutical *Vorverständnis* of the legal actors. Doublet's emphasis on the mastering of the qualification norm as an entrance requirement to the legal communicative community can be understood in an analogical way.

I also see parallels between my analysis of the relations between the layers of the law and Doublet's account of the functions of evaluation foundation: we both draw attention to relations or functions of criticism, boundary-drawing and justification, as well as constitution. Doublet has not explicitly thematised the relation of sedimentation which in my scheme rescues the positivity of the sub-surface layers. But here, too, I dare to conclude that Doublet's emphasis on the evaluation foundation's being embodied (*nedfelt*) in valid law presupposes something corresponding to what I have termed a 'process of sedimentation'. Doublet does not discuss the law in terms of its two aspects. However, he does point to the central role of the legal communicative community (what I have called the legal community *in sensu stretto*) and identified judges, legislators and legal scholars as the main figures in the ongoing argumentative process (the legal discourse, as I would call it) where the valid law is constantly being defined and redefined. Moreover, he is aware of the peculiar dual position of legal scholarship (what I have characterised as the dual citizenship of legal scholarship) as belonging both to the legal and the scientific communicative community.

Doublet's focus is on the critical function of the law beyond law: on the normative censorship the evaluation foundation exercises in relation to both positive and valid law. This perhaps explains why he has largely ignored the conceptual and methodological dimensions in the sub-surface layers of law. But it is not only the normative aspect of principles and values, but also the conceptual and method logical dimensions that, through legal practices, accomplish both constitutive and limiting effects. In Doublet's terms, they form integral parts of the qualification norm of the legal communicative community and contribute to drawing the boundary between the legal and the non-legal.

I would like to point to yet another difference of emphasis between Doublet's view and my proposal for critical legal positivism. I have argued that even if different legal systems may well share a largely similar deep structure (deep culture), this is always modified and interpreted in a specific legal cultural context. It is in this culturally specified and interpreted guise that it is internalised in legal studies and practical legal work and informs the *Vorverständnis* of legal actors. Doublet presupposes such legal-cultural mediation and specification when discussing the evaluation foundation in terms of both its general validity during the modern era and its internal value transitions, but he does not elaborate further on this.

Let us return to where we started: Christensen's basic normative patterns. How does Christensen's proposal for analysing law beyond law relate to the other two Nordic suggestions?

I am not sure whether Christensen would have accepted the idea of the law's evaluation foundation or deep structure, which would have an extended validity in both geographical and temporal respects; perhaps she would have found the idea too speculative and still too tainted by the influences of natural law. I assume, however, that she would not have minded discussing her basic normative patterns in the context of a legal cultural layer in law. Christensen has compared her basic normative patterns with such fundamental legal principles as *pacta sunt servanda*. But what I think is important to stress is that in such a comparison, legal principles should not be understood in the sense of directly applicable, surface-level principles; this is the sense where the concept of principles is employed in the rules-principles debate initiated by Ronald Dworkin[8] and Robert Alexy.[9] Rather, legal principles should be assigned a legal cultural sense, alluding to the subsurface normative premises of various fields of law.

A parallel could also be drawn between Christensen's basic normative patterns and the legal theories, which, according to my understanding, constitute an integral element of the legal culture of the legal community in *sensu stretto* (or Doublet's evaluation foundation). In private law, these include theories of, for example, contract and property, and in public law, theories of, for example, the legal personality of the state and fundamental rights. Legal theories are not usually explicitly articulated in such surface-level legal material as statutes and precedents, but they still influence legal practices and legal discourse through the hermeneutical *Vorverständnis* of legal actors. The same way of functioning, I assume, is characteristic of Christensen's basic normative patterns as well. An important feature of her depiction of basic normative patterns is the way she relates these to the social relationships under regulation. Stripped of their legal attire, basic normative patterns are social patterns of action that are experienced as morally binding. In the above, I connected this view to Habermas' conception of law as an institution. Another point of comparison comes to mind as well: Savigny's notion of legal institutions as combining a legal form and a social substratum consisting of *Lebensverhältnisse,* or life relationships. Legal theories can now be argued to refer to legal institutions à la Savigny. I also claim that legal theories are related to society, through a conception (at least implicitly) of the social relationships under regulation; a hidden social theory, as it were.[10] Arguably, the same can be said of Christensen's basic normative patterns.

[8] R Dworkin, *Taking Rights Seriously* (London, Duckwoth, 1978).

[9] R Alexy, *A Theory of Legal Argumentation* (Oxford, Clarendon Press, 1989).

[10] Tuori, *Ratio and Voluntas*, above n 5, 196 ff.

So there are obvious similarities between Christensen's idea of basic normative patterns and Doublet's evaluation foundation, and my depiction of law in terms of the interplay between the surface level and legal-cultural, sub-surface layers. But there are differences too; at least differences of emphasis. These, I would argue, include our respective views of the role of contradictions in law and of the position a legal scholar should take vis-à-vis such contradictions.

Contradictions are an integral part of the picture Doublet or my proposal for critical positivism paints of law. Thus, Doublet's examination of the relationships the evaluation foundation maintains with positive and valid law implies a view of law as traversed by both vertical and horizontal contradictions. The vertical are contradictions between positive or valid law and the evaluation foundation; confronted with such contradictions, the evaluation foundation functions in its critical, corrective role. But Doublet's view of the reflexive (hermeneutic) reconstruction of the evaluation foundation, as well as his portrayal of its functions, presupposes horizontal contradictions as well, at least within positive and valid law. The reconstruction starts with an exploration of intra-positive values expressed or protected by positive law, and proceeds to extra-positive values that, although not expressly formulated in traditional legal sources, can still be said to be embodied by valid law. But choices are evidently made, within both intra- and extra-positive values: some values are included in the evaluation foundation, others are considered irrelevant or outright contradictory to it. Positive or valid law expressing such contradictory values constitutes the object of the evaluation foundation's critical and corrective operation. Correspondingly, my own view of reconstructing the law's cultural layers from the implications and presuppositions of surface-level legal material, as well as the critical function of the former in relation to the latter, is premised on the existence of both vertical and horizontal contradictions.

In her discussion of basic normative patterns, Christensen is not so much interested in vertical contradictions, which, according to Doublet and my own version of critical legal positivism, can be resolved through the corrective function of our versions of the law beyond law: the evaluation foundation or the legal-cultural layers of law. Indeed, it is rather doubtful whether she would in general have assigned the basic normative patterns a corrective function in relation to surface-level legal material. Be that as it may, Christensen's focus is clearly on what I have called horizontal contradictions within the law. The assemblage of norms constituting the starting point for legal analysis is traversed by contradictions, a result of, among other things, divergences in the time of issuance and the objectives of legal regulations. The primary function Christensen attaches to the basic normative patterns a legal scholar unearths and articulates, is simply to bring some order to the chaotic norm material; that is, a systematising or coherence-creating function. This is a function I have assigned to branch-specific general doctrines (*allgemeine Lehren*, *allmänna läror*) with legal concepts, principles and theories as their central elements. But the coherence that basic normative patterns are capable of bringing about is only of a local character; comprehensive or total conference is a dream from a bygone age. Christensen would perhaps have placed

Doublet and me in the camp of nostalgic dreamers: evaluation foundation and the law's deep culture involve a promise of a certain, albeit rather weak, comprehensive coherence.

Christensen's focus is on the tensions between opposing basic normative patterns. Normative patterns do not exercise their influence in isolation, but within a normative field where other, competing normative patterns wield a force of attraction as well. This implies that rival normative patterns, for example, protection of established positions and the market-functional normative patterns, propose rival orderings and systematisations of legal 'raw material'. What Christensen does not spell out is how a legal scholar should react to such horizontal contradictions in the law beyond law. Can they be resolved or reconciled by inter-subjective, legal criteria? Christensen's silence surrounding anything matching a deep culture that would underpin the level of basic normative patterns intimates a negative answer: the most we can achieve is local coherence established by mutually non-coherent normative patterns. No legal solution exists to conflicts between divergent normative patterns. The solutions can only be found at a political level. A legal scholar can, in the spirit of unmasking criticism, reveal internal contradictions in law by articulating rival normative patterns and thus define the issue for politics, but there her task and mandate end.

Is this the lesson Anna Christensen bequeathed to us?

4

The 'Autonomy' of Private Governments

Building on Italian Labour Law Scholarship in a Transnational Perspective

SILVANA SCIARRA*

I. INTRODUCTION: GINO GIUGNI AND THE THEORY OF 'AUTONOMY' IN COLLECTIVE LABOUR LAW

MY CHAPTER IN this book aims at linking the very special achievements of the Norma Research Programme with a stream of thought that started in Italy, mainly in the work of Gino Giugni, in the 1960s and that developed throughout the remainder of the previous century.[1] I argue that in an extraordinary way (considering that there were no formal interchanges between Italian scholars and the Norma Research Programme) a comparable way of looking at normative powers came to be developed. I then argue that a reflection on the search for a new legal pluralism of sources should be enhanced within the European Union, in consideration of a developing role played by transnational law.

The methodological option behind this chapter has to do with the observation of changes occurring in labour law, on the one hand as a reaction to an unprecedented economic and financial crisis, on the other hand as a consequence of an increasing mobility of companies and labour. The question relates to the position of collective bargaining, a safe and well-established normative source in the Western European tradition, even within national legal orders in which a 'voluntary' approach has traditionally been privileged.

* I am very grateful to Ann Numhauser-Henning and Mia Rönnmar for reading early drafts of this chapter, although I am solely responsible for its contents. The stimulating work of the Norma Research Programme has been one of the many intellectual discoveries during my visits to the Faculty of Law at Lund University. For this I am grateful, and for the enriching friendships created around a common research project.

[1] S Sciarra, 'Giugni, the Importance of Comparative Methodology and How Labour Law Developed in Italy: a Story from the Nineteen Sixties' in A Numhauser-Henning and M Rönnmar (eds), *Fifteen Years with the Norma Research Program* (Lund, Faculty of Law, 2010) 117 ff.

The notion of 'collective laissez faire', originally developed by Otto Kahn-Freund,[2] is well known to specialists in the field, and has to do with the proud acknowledgment of the 'autonomy' of private governments from the state, based on factual grounds, namely, the effectiveness of the normative function pursued by powerful private organisations in setting binding standards for the regulation of individual contracts of employment.

In Italy, the notion of the 'autonomy' of collective bargaining as a norm-setting mechanism became clear in the 1960s, essentially for historical reasons, and having to do with the choice not to give legal enforcement (via a constitutional law) to article 39, section 2 ff, of the 1948 Constitution, that would have granted an *erga omnes* enforceability to sector collective agreements. The choice of the legislature was supported by the most representative national unions of the time, for contingent and at times strategic reasons, added to an inborn mistrust towards the intervention of the legislature in trade unions' affairs.

It is interesting to note that all such pragmatic choices were supported by an extraordinarily innovative labour law scholarship, developed around a dynamic view of legal pluralism. Attention was focused on the role of private governments as norm-setting institutions of the labour market, active and powerful on the constitutional basis of freedom of association, dealt with in section 1 of the same article 39. Hence, the most innovative point was to recognise in all such institutions a spontaneous normative function, inherent in the exercise of a fundamental right.

Apart from establishing normative working conditions and wages applicable in individual employment contracts, autonomy meant enforcing a separate system of sanctions, independently of the state. This was possible under the enforcement of constitutional principles. The *erga omnes* enforceability of autonomous collective agreements developed over the years on a de facto basis, and for a long time remained unchallenged, due to a common understanding among the largest trade unions, both in negotiations and in the signing of collective agreements.

Legal pluralism here had to do with the diversification of sources, historically linked to the presence of pluralist unions, separate in their cultural identities, but nevertheless willing to find common solutions in the process of norm-setting and the establishment of social consensus. Pluralist actors were pursuing pluralist legal solutions. Gino Giugni interpreted the world of facts, in order to offer a theoretical framework that would strengthen social spheres, recognising them as normative patterns. In doing so, he was inspired by scholars such as Santi Romano and Ascarelli, arguing for legal pluralism as a methodology, while observing the expansion of social phenomena and of collective sources.[3] Hence, a heuristic function of legal theory was ascertained and proved illuminating both in describing new

[2] A critical appraisal of the theory in R Dukes, 'Otto Kahn-Freund and Collective Laissez-faire: an Edifice without a Keystone?' (2009) *MLR* 220.

[3] G Giugni, *Introduzione allo studio della autonomia collettiva* (Milan, Giuffrè, 1960).

foundations of norm-making and in promoting visibility in collective agreements within the hierarchy of sources.[4]

Over the years, case law filled (albeit only partially) the gap left by abstention of the law. The rather solid system of collective bargaining, built on the theory of the autonomy of private governments, became a point of reference for court decisions, especially in rulings on fair wages. No law on minimum wages was enacted, since the de facto enforceability of collective agreements was such as to expand the scope of voluntary sources, well beyond union membership.

Anna Christensen, and later, Ann Numhauser-Henning, have both devoted attention to normative patterns, in order to establish the expansion of law in its many facets and at different levels of the legal order as a whole. The pattern of 'belonging' is crucial in understanding how groups determine their own way of participating in the law-making process, including all those who enter the group in a 'normative circle'. Society in its entirety is composed of such 'circles', characterised, among other things, by territoriality.[5] One could even argue that a functional comparison can be drawn between Italy and Sweden, countries in which purely voluntary systems of collective bargaining developed efficiently, especially in times of high union membership. This scenario changes drastically in times of economic uncertainty and declining union membership, when the 'territory' of a normative instrument, such as a collective agreement, can change very rapidly.

Original developments in the work of the Norma Research Programme linked to the concept of territoriality prove very useful in developing one of the main arguments put forward in this chapter, namely, the need to adapt concepts of the 'autonomy' of private governments to transnational social spheres. This analysis is necessary when we observe current trends in the expansion of so-called international framework agreements signed by large multinational companies and international unions, often in coordination with the European Works Councils (EWCs).[6] Here, spontaneous 'normative circles' expand their influence beyond the state in

[4] Legal pluralism, or polycentricity, can be said to be inherent also in Anna Christensen's Theory of Law as Normative Patterns in a Normative Field. Compare A Christensen, 'Polycentricity and Normative Patterns' in H Petersen and H Zahle (eds), *Legal Polycentricity: Consequences of Pluralism in Law* (Aldershot, Dartmouth Publishing, 1995).

[5] A Christensen and M Malmstedt, 'Lex Loci Laboris versus Lex Loci Domicilii: an Inquiry into the Normative Foundations of European Social Security Law' (2000) 2 *European Journal of Social Security* 69. See also Ann Numhauser-Henning, Chapter 2.

[6] K Papadakis (ed), *Cross-Border Social Dialogue and Agreements: an Emerging Global Industrial Relations Framework?* (Geneva, International Institute for Labour Studies, 2008); I Schömann, A Sobczak, E Voss and P Wilke, *Codes of Conduct and International Framework Agreements. New Forms of Governance at Company Level* (Luxemburg, Eurofound, 2008); I Schömann, 'European Social Dialogue and Transnational Framework Agreements as a Response to the Crisis?' (2011) 4 *ETUI Policy Brief*, European Social Policy Issue. The European Commission's website gathers information on transnational framework agreements, see ec.europa.eu/social/main.jsp?catId=978&langId=en. The Commission has now opened a consultation among stakeholders. See European Commission Staff Working Document, *Transnational Company Agreements: Realising the Potential of Social Dialogue*, SWD(2012)264 final (Brussels, 10 September 2012).

an undefined territory, raising questions of enforceability and the legitimacy of the bargaining agents.

II. TRANSNATIONAL JURIDIFICATION IN LABOUR LAW: PLURALISM REVISITED

A. Introduction

Giugni's theory of the autonomy of collective spheres, like the theory of normative circles, was innovative and ground-breaking in Italian labour law at a time when the economic system was expanding and employment was increasing. At the end of the 1960s, Italy experienced widespread social unrest, as did many countries in and outside Europe. The theory needed to be adapted to the changing needs of representation at company level. The role of the unions had to be strengthened in the workplace, in order to limit managerial prerogatives.

Thus, the state as regulator was called upon in the 1970s to enact 'auxiliary' or 'supportive' legislation, in order to consolidate collective labour rights. This legislative option occurred in several European national systems, albeit with different characteristics.[7] It then developed into much more complicated regulatory schemes, where legal and collective agreements had to establish an internal equilibrium, acting as parallel sources, often on the grounds of an implied principle of subsidiarity. Giugni continued to be a protagonist for all of those years and was responsible for drafting the 'Workers' Statute', a piece of legislation enacted in 1970.[8]

It is no mere coincidence that many years later, in the late 1980s, we find Giugni among the labour lawyers (the others being leading figures such as Simitis, Wedderburn and Clark) engaged in Teubner's project on the juridification of social spheres.[9] Here, the intent is to foster legal reforms, as well as to describe changes occurring in the overall structure of labour law sources. The exercise in 'structural coupling', attempting to strengthen the links between law and politics, was proposed in the aftermath of the nation-states' regulatory crisis.

The decision to view the social players as the bearers of new regulatory tools was necessitated by the fact that national legislatures increasingly intervened, at times adopting controversial solutions. The law delegated certain functions to collective bargaining, thus creating uncertain situations as to the principle of subsidiarity. Who would the correct bargaining agents be, when dealing with falling standards (namely, *in pejus*, as in reduction of working hours) or with redistributive measures, whenever economic difficulties were put forward and objective managerial strategies became a priority? Under these circumstances, autonomy could not

[7] O Kahn-Freund, *Labour and the Law* (London, Stevens, 1972).
[8] G Giugni, *Il sindacato fra contratti e riforme 1969–1973* (Bari, De Donato, 1973).
[9] G Teubner (ed), *Juridification of Social Spheres* (Berlin/New York, de Gruyter, 1987).

remain a dogmatic assumption. It was instead caught in an inextricable web of rules. One might go so far as to say that autonomy was, at least partly, juridified.

There is no straightforward comparison that can be suggested for the situation in the 1960s, when European national legal orders were still consolidating their own post-war identities. In 1957, six of these national legal orders started a 'common market', to enhance economic efficiency and to found a *sui generis* supranational legal order. However, some of the challenges now faced by transnational labour law recall the theoretical questions that were formulated in the 1960s and partially revised in the 1980s. National legal identities are shaken by the ever-increasing evidence of supranational law in its many facets, similar to what happened in the past, when the post-war settlement required robust responses from national administrations, in order to defend national constitutional traditions.

Looking at Teubner's research on the juridification of social spheres, we observe that inasmuch as welfare states contributed to the shaping of modern labour law, the crisis of the same created new ideas about the changing role of law-makers. However, theoretical analysis can be contingent in all such matters, due to the volatility of legal solutions and to the constantly changing number and nature of private and public actors playing a role in the process of law-making.

This is the reason why, when taking into account historical developments, there is an urgent need in scholarship to re-organise theoretical assumptions in labour law around new concepts. The aim is to evaluate the current crisis of nation-states, aggravated by a global economic and financial crisis and influenced by an increased interdependence of markets. Transnationalisation of sources, a phenomenon affecting labour law as well as other legal disciplines, might be the effect of a lost centrality of nation-states.

B. Transnational Bargaining: the Search for Legitimacy

Labour lawyers are currently facing the challenges of transferring their discourse into a transnational scheme. Transnational collective interests and transnational implications of industrial action are forcing them to reconsider the hierarchy of sources regulating employment contracts. In previous experience, this meant empowering social sub-systems of norms, so that they would become functionally comparable to law. Energy was devoted to developing solid organisations representing employers and labour and in acknowledging them as actors in the law-making process, in order to overcome legal positivism in its most conventional form.[10]

This choice was also the consequence of an increasing specialisation of labour law as a legal discipline, and of its centrality in all economic strategies developed by national governments. Frequent adjustments to legislation, required by the

[10] For comparative remarks, see K Tuori, *Critical Legal Positivism* (London, Ashgate, 2002).

need to expand flexibility in labour markets as well as in employment contracts, have progressively put at serious risk the overall coherence of labour law, and in some cases, its compliance with fundamental social rights.

In Mireille Delmas-Marty's proposal of an 'ordered pluralism', it is acknowledged that notions of 'indeterminacy, inconsistency and instability that accompany the internationalisation of law'[11] are characterised by, among other factors, the proliferation of international organisations, multinational corporations and other private organisations. In integration processes, interactions among different legal systems become normative interactions, since they deal with the 'ought to be' rather than the 'is'.[12]

Thus, Delmas-Marty observes interactions as an alternative to hierarchy and as a way of approaching legal pluralism, via coordination and judicial dialogue. This leads her towards a flexible hierarchy of sources and, one could add, a more open and variable one. This analysis is not totally convincing if applied to European labour law developments, particularly if we take into account the failures of the Open Method of Coordination (OMC), as applied to employment policies.[13]

Searching for the origin of normative powers, away from the nation-states, we find a similarly concerned approach in the historical investigation conducted by Peter Lindseth. He adopts the notion of 'constitutional legitimacy', in order to explain how constitutional principles allow a delegated agency relationship among Member States and EU supranational institutions. Historically constituted bodies of the Member States serve as the principals in the integration process and the EU institutions ultimately serve as agents.[14]

Lindseth puts forward a critique of experimentalism, arguing that there are serious doubts about an autonomous legitimacy of European governance regulatory powers. There is nothing more to take into account than a system of supranationalised regulatory powers, with no constitutional grounding. Thus, we need to return to states as the only sources of constitutional democracy. This analysis is relevant in the reconstruction of the discussion that took place in academic circles at the end of the 1990s and in the first years of the 2000s.

Governance in the European Union, one of the '*cahiers*' produced by the Forward Studies Unit,[15] almost symbolically marks the change of leadership in the European Commission. Following the tempestuous end of Santer's presidency,

[11] M Delmas-Marty, *Ordering Pluralism: a Conceptual Framework for Understanding the Transnational Legal World* (Oxford, Hart Publishing, 2009) 14.

[12] Ibid 15.

[13] S Sciarra, 'Experiments in the Open Method of Coordination: Measuring the Impact of EU Employment Policies' (2011) *Rivista italiana di diritto del lavoro* 475; C Barnard, 'The Shaky Legal Foundations for Institutional Action under the Employment, Lisbon and EU2020 Strategies' in C Barnard and O Odudu (eds), *Cambridge Year Book of European Legal Studies 2009–2010* (Oxford, Hart Publishing, 2010) 12, 16.

[14] P Lindseth, *Power and Legitimacy: Reconciling Europe and the Nation-State* (Oxford, Oxford University Press, 2010) 257.

[15] O De Schutter, N Lebessis and J Paterson (eds), *Governance in the European Union* (Luxembourg, Office for Official Publications of the European Communities, 2001).

there was a need felt for highlighting transparency and accountability. Academic research followed a similar line of thinking. In reviewing that literature, one can detect a slight marginalisation of traditional labour law regulatory techniques, and speculate why such a marginalisation happened.

It is not always direct—nor is it very useful—to establish an almost mechanical interrelationship between scholarly contributions and institutional changes. However, the theoretical framework elaborated at the turn of the millennium at the Catholic University of Louvain, as well as the active contributions emerging from similarly intense and thought-provoking discussions throughout Europe, ran parallel to the issuing of *A White Paper on European Governance*.[16] Soon after, the Commission issued several Communications, aimed at reinforcing the climate of openness and consultation that needed to be built. It also indicated recourse to external expertise, following highly transparent and rigorous criteria.[17] This seemingly technocratic approach needed to be confronted with the intellectual broadness in which theories on European governance had been cultivated within academic groups.

Governance, both in intellectual and political circles, carried with it several meanings, all related to notions of openness and efficiency in pursuing the aim of European integration. The European legal order needed closer links with civil society. What is most relevant to underline is whether and how governance techniques influenced law-making processes. There is a need to verify whether governance caused, in the long run, a weakening of 'internal' authoritative legal points of view and an underlying, if not latent, de-legitimisation of law-makers.

Procedural law, advocated in sophisticated ways and with different disciplinary intuitions, became a communicative tool, besides being a methodological option. It attempted to overcome black letter law interpretations and to ascribe less relevance to case law. It reviewed traditional hierarchies among sources, implying that different deliberative techniques take place and remain independent from law-making.

It could be argued that the alleged shift in emphasis towards deliberations that differ from legal commands was hiding the crisis of 'law in books' behind a nebulous 'law in action'. Unlike the aforementioned research on juridification, this exercise did not fully acknowledge the (by then increased) crisis of welfare states. Emphasis on 'soft law' built expectations on undefined and scattered notions of civil society, as well as on single-issue organisations, at times lacking the strength and legitimacy to act as makers of 'law in action'. It relied on national governments for 'mutual learning' and 'peer review', thus impoverishing the language of rights and decreasing the visibility of parliaments as law-makers. Furthermore, the visibility of NGOs or similar private actors was very uneven in different European

[16] COM(2001)428 final.

[17] S Sciarra, 'The "Making" of EU Labour Law and the "Future" of Labour Lawyers' in C Barnard, S Deakin and G Morris (eds), *The Future of Labour Law, Liber amicorum Bob Hepple* (Oxford, Hart Publishing, 2004).

countries. This element of diversity and differentiation in private law-making should be better underlined and examined in comparative terms.

From the observatory of transnational labour law, I submit that transnational juridification is slowly emerging in the practice of transnational collective bargaining. Transnationality enshrines old and new notions of norm setting. Inasmuch as transnationality originates from national legal systems, it then deviates from them, in the attempt to develop new non-national legal boundaries.

Transnational private governments, and large associations representing employers and labour, operate as makers of a new 'law in action', namely, law emerging from transnational autonomous practices in collective bargaining. The question to be asked is whether they are formally empowered to set transnational standards, and whether the latter are normative standards *stricto sensu*.

Can transnational private governments operate without interacting with the state as regulator, when the transnationalisation of law forces nation-states to reconsider their own powers and rethink enforcement mechanisms? Does this new limited sovereignty affect the 'autonomy' of private governments and does it question their normative function in setting standards?

In recent research based at the University of Bremen, the origin of such transformative processes has been found in the transformation of the state[18] and in changing policies in the governance of welfare.[19] Globalisation and transnational norm building are also under observation by research teams based at the University of Hamburg,[20] as confirmation of the centrality in interdisciplinary research of changes taking place in national legal orders, as a consequence of transnational developments.

Transformative processes in labour law, this chapter argues, are in an extraordinary line of continuity with experiments performed in Italy in the 1960s, when new light was thrown on legal pluralism and on normative patterns emerging from voluntary collective bargaining. These processes can also ideally be connected with the concerted attempts of the Norma Research Programme to reconfigure regulations shaped within normative orders.

A new theoretical framework should now be built, in order to prove a renewed authority of a legal point of view, while acknowledging the immense strength of social systems in which processes of norm setting are taking place. Within transnational social systems, business and labour organisations are very active, together with European and Global Works Councils. They are attempting to introduce new forms of collective representation and new procedural norms, which should be able to capture new expectations of business and labour.

[18] P Genschel and B Zangl, 'Transformations of the State: From Monopolist to Manager of Political Authority' (2008) 76 *TranState WP*; M Zamboni, 'Globalization and Law-making: Time to Shift a Legal Theory's Paradigm' (2007) 1 *Legisprudence* 125.

[19] I Dingeldey and H Rothgang (eds), *Governance of Welfare State Reform* (Cheltenham, Edward Elgar Publishing, 2009).

[20] See www.giga-hamburg.de.

The transnationalisation of law, labour law in particular, coincides with the opening up of spaces in which processes of standard setting are taking place. The point of equilibrium is not to be found in reconciling national collective interests, but in constant adaptation and change due to external factors. In a sense, one might argue that denationalised and open processes of negotiation are part of transnational collective labour law 'in action', which is slowly changing the structure of bargaining agents and signifying new notions of representativeness.

However, the transnationalisation of collective labour law does not imply the abandonment of the national field. On the contrary, parallel levels of negotiation are still put in place, especially when answers to the crisis must be found. Renationalisation becomes yet another resource and an interesting one at that, when it comes to searching for alternative solutions, for example, in mass dismissals or when dealing with the consequences of restructuring. Territorial pacts are invoked as a return to sub-national levels of negotiations[21] and measures to support access to financing for medium and small enterprises are held as legitimate by EU institutions, as an indirect way of protecting employment.[22]

Nation-states reappear as guarantors of redistributive actions. When collective interests are at stake, no such actions can be started without the intervention of legitimate bargaining agents. The rules on 'legitimacy' thus become a crucial point to address, when labour lawyers observe the functioning of transnational private orders, constantly interacting with national ones and constantly seeking a point of equilibrium among autonomous regulatory processes. A new principle of 'belonging' develops out of new quasi-normative circles.

The hybridisation of legal and non-legal sources, emblematic of governance techniques, acquires specific relevance when discussing processes of transnational standard setting. The autonomy of private governments could be weakened by the lack of clear powers in establishing and enforcing sanctions. Even sanctions of a different nature (for example, in making alternative dispute resolution compulsory before recourse to industrial action, or in seeking financial incentives in support of social rights) should return to the hands of the legitimate collective actors. This often implies a renationalisation of bargaining, which should be accompanied by an impetus in seeking or re-establishing or rebuilding legitimacy of collective bargaining agents.

The notion of 'legitimacy' can be used as a key concept, useful in developing transnational labour law theories, based on the observation of collective actors

[21] Commission Staff Working Document, *The Partnership Principle in the Implementation of the Common Strategic Framework Funds: Elements for a European Code of Conduct on Partnership*, SWD(2012)106 final (Brussels, 24 April 2012); C Panara and A De Becker (eds), *The Role of the Regions in EU Governance* (Heidelberg, Springer, 2011).

[22] Commission Communication, Temporary framework for State aid measures to support access to finance in the current financial and economic crisis [2009] OJ C83/1). See also European Commission Communication. Working together to create new growth: Single Market Act: twelve levers to boost growth and strengthen confidence, COM(2011)206 final, para 2.1 with references to the Small Business Act.

and on notions of cross-border collective interests. All such evolutionary trends in collective labour law mark a distancing from previously experienced governance regulatory techniques, inasmuch as they represent new expressions of transnational collective labour law 'in action'.

'Legitimacy' has to do with the democratic accountability of collective bargaining agents, to be measured against transnational collective interests. Therefore, collective actors should be openly and transparently empowered, to facilitate processes of transnational standard setting and to make them enforceable beyond nation-states.

It can be said, as an indication of the open process of transnational juridification in transition, that international unions impose a requirement on their affiliated associations to add their signature (in conjunction with European or Global Works Councils) to international framework agreements or other transnational texts that might result from the practice of informal negotiations with large multinational companies. In this regard, European secondary law, namely, the 2009 Recast Directive 2009/38EC on EWCs, is producing effects well beyond its scope and its enforceability.[23]

Another sign to take into account supporting the notion of 'legitimacy' is that transnational agreements are relied upon as binding sources within supply chains or chains of sub-contractors. The interesting point here is that organisational and economic links between different segments of production are combined with the enforceability of collectively agreed standards. Bargaining agents should be fully empowered when the aim is to keep the supply chain together, while enforcing labour standards.

Bearing in mind all these examples (and there are many more), my search for legitimacy becomes the search for solid ground on which to build social sub-systems whenever these systems are asked to perform a quasi-institutional function, such as when addressing widely diffused collective interests. As previously suggested, this implies a critique of governance techniques, arguing that particularly in the current situation, collective bargaining addresses unique issues, all necessitated by the inevitable interconnection between economic policies and social and employment policies.

III. CONCLUDING REMARKS: A NEW SENSE OF 'BELONGING'

In globalised processes of law-making beyond the state, it is not contradictory to see a return to the state as the originator of powers to be conferred upon private organisations. This needs to be said for labour law, a legal discipline in which the need is felt for a renewed authority of law over policies and for new legal mechanisms of empowerment whenever private governments deal with collective interests.

[23] F Dorssemont and T Blanke (eds), *The Recast of the European Works Council Directive* (Antwerp, Intersentia, 2010).

In line with Anna Christensen's intuition, a widespread sense of 'belonging' to transnational groups should be the outcome of current trends in the construction of new supranational bargaining agents.

My purpose in this chapter has been to offer a few examples of legal and voluntary sources currently characterising the transnationalisation of labour law. In order to do so, I built my observations on Italian scholarships in labour law, linking these efforts with the work of the Norma Research Programme.

'Structural coupling' among legal and social systems now occurs in a transnational framework, where most actors are potentially mobile across frontiers and thus exposed to more than one system of norms. In particular, collective labour law is a field in which deep transformations are taking place. These have to do with the exercise of collective rights beyond national legal systems, despite the fact that such rights have traditionally been, and still are, embedded in national constitutional traditions, as well as in consolidated customs and practices.

The aim of my contribution in this book has been to highlight the point of view of labour law and to do so by looking at transnational developments. The geographical metaphor I have used in describing renationalisation as a response to transnational developments supports my main argument, namely, the need to revisit legal and voluntary sources within a new transnational legal pluralism.[24]

If Anna Christensen had been here, I am sure she would have helped me immensely on the research path I am following.

[24] P Grossi, *A History of European Law* (English trans, Oxford/Chichester, Wiley-Blackwell, 2010).

Part III

Protection of Established Position and Normative Development

5

Protection of Established Position, Normative Incoherence and the Changing Normative Field of Labour Law

NIKLAS BRUUN

I. INTRODUCTION

ANNA CHRISTENSEN DEVELOPED her theory on law as normative patterns in a normative field in a period when the European and European Union influence on the national legal system was becoming evident. She discussed the social dimension extensively and was, in fact, the driving force behind the establishment of a subject to become known as 'the Social Dimension' at the Faculty of Law at Lund University. In this subject, she and her colleagues dealt with family law, labour law, housing law and social security law. Legal regulation in these fields shares the common feature of regulating the everyday life of ordinary people and is deeply rooted in the normative culture of a particular society.[1]

Christensen was interested in the normative structures' process of development, and she saw this development as taking place in a normative field containing various poles, such as the Market-Functional pattern (the right to ownership and freedom of contract), the Protection of Established Position and the third pole of Just Distribution. Christensen described these different patterns as 'magnetic poles seeking to attract the legal rules', and argued that legal change and development can be described as movements within the normative field.[2]

One of the normative fields studied by Christensen was the one constituted by working life and labour law. In my chapter of this anthology, I intend to apply

[1] See A Christensen, 'Protection of the Established Position: a Basic Normative Pattern' (1998) 42 *Scandinavian Studies of Law* 286.

[2] See A Christensen 'Normative Patterns and the Normative Field: a Post-Liberal View on Law' in T Wilhelmsson and S Hurri (eds), *From Dissonance to Sense: Welfare State Expectations, Privatisation and Private Law* (Aldershot, Ashgate, 1999).

Christensen's theory in analysing the normative development of labour law in the new millennium. This is a period that is not examined by Christensen herself, since she passed away in 2001. I will attempt to reflect on this development from the point of view of Christensen's theoretical starting points, and especially, as indicated by my title, the protection of established position.

As my starting point, I wish to emphasise that Christensen stressed that there are always conflicts between the different normative patterns within a normative field. These patterns do not make up a system, they cannot be ordered in a hierarchy, and there are no principles of superior dignity determining which pattern dominates or gets the upper hand.[3] This fact already shows that the theory does not address the normative content and interpretations of individual norms, but rather how the normative content can be placed in the normative field, and how legal changes and developments can be understood as movements within the normative field.

In order to analyse how these changes can be positioned within the normative field of labour law, I will deal with three strong developmental features in European and EU labour law. These are:

(1) the tension between the EU economic freedoms and fundamental labour rights (the right to collective action) after the *Viking* and *Laval* judgments;
(2) the dominating general developments in European and EU labour law, as I see them;
(3) the latest developments in the economic constitution of the European Union after the economic and financial crisis.

I will try to evaluate these developments in light of Christensen's theory, and will also reflect on the limits and prospects for applying the theory to these legal changes within labour law.

II. TENSION BETWEEN EU ECONOMIC FREEDOMS AND FUNDAMENTAL LABOUR RIGHTS

The *Viking* and *Laval* story[4] is taken from the battlefield of normative patterns as Christensen described them. Internal market freedoms representing the Market-Functional pattern are in conflict with the social dimension, especially as regards the maintenance of established positions achieved by the trade union movement when it comes to control of the national labour market in a certain aspect of wage competition. These judgments have been heavily criticised, not only

[3] Ibid.

[4] See Case C-438/05 *International Transport Workers' Federation* [2007] ECR I-10779 ('*Viking*') and Case C-341/05 *Laval un Partneri* [2007] ECR I-11767 ('*Laval*'), and the 2008 decisions in Case C-346/06 *Rüffert* [2008] ECR I-1989 and Case C-319/06 *European Commission v Luxembourg* [2008] ECR I-4323.

by labour lawyers, but also generally in Sweden, as endangering the traditional Swedish model for the regulation of the labour market. The right-wing government therefore wanted to protect the Swedish trade unions' established positions as far as possible within the scope allowed by the case law of the Court of Justice of the European Union (CJEU). Consequently, the Swedish legislation Lex Laval was adopted as a response and a defence for the established position of Swedish trade unions.

Through Lex Laval, Sweden has attempted to link and integrate the granting of minimum protection for posted workers with the Swedish system of collective bargaining. In combination with the interpretation by the CJEU of the provisions in the Posting of Workers Directive, the requirement in the Directive[5] for equal treatment of employers has made it rather complicated to achieve this integration.[6]

The first problem in this context is that the formulation of the requirement that employers must be treated equally seems to be in contradiction with the explicit acceptance in the Directive to use the wage levels in collective agreements (which do not have an *erga omnes* effect) as the basis for setting a minimum standard, especially on wages.

The Directive (Article 3(8)) explicitly prescribes that in the absence of a system for declaring collective agreements to be of universal application or having an *erga omnes* effect, Member States may, if they so decide, base themselves on:

— collective agreements or arbitration awards that are generally applicable to all similar undertakings in the geographical area, and in the profession or industry concerned; and/or
— collective agreements concluded by the most representative employers and labour organisations at national level, as applied throughout the national territory.

The Swedish Lex Laval is based on the first of these two. The problem with both of these situations, however, is that by definition there is no legally binding general application of the agreement (and this is the starting point for the need for these two paragraphs), nor can there be 100 per cent coverage of the collective agreement. There may well be some employers at national level who, for various reasons, fall outside the scope of the application of these general agreements.

The preparatory works for the Lex Laval quite rightly underline that this conflict cannot mean that the principle of equal treatment must be given such a strict interpretation as to make the use of the two alternatives in Article 3(8)

[5] Directive 96/71/EC of the European Parliament and of the Council of 16 December 1996 concerning the posting of workers in the framework of the provision of services.

[6] The following analysis of the Lex Laval draws heavily on the reasoning in N Bruun and J Malmberg, 'Lex Laval: Collective Actions and Posted Work in Sweden' in R Blainpain and F Hendrickx (eds), *Labour Law Between Change and Tradition: Liber Amicorum Antoine Jacobs* (Dordrecht, Kluwer, 2011).

impossible.[7] The reasonable interpretation put forward in the Swedish *travaux préparatoires* is that the principle of equal treatment must be understood to mean that these applicable collective agreements and their terms on minimum wages must be applied to and enforced in the same manner for both foreign and Swedish service providers.

The Swedish interpretation, therefore, makes a distinction between the requirements or conditions on which an existing collective agreement can be given the normative effect of indicating a mandatory minimum standard and the criteria for equal treatment. Only a national branch-level collective agreement can qualify for setting such a standard, and in the absence of such an agreement, no minimum wage is to be found. In accordance with this, the requirement on equal treatment does not imply that all employers at national level must be bound by the agreement, but only that the terms and conditions in the agreement are equally applied and enforced for all national and foreign employers.[8]

By opening up the possibility for Swedish trade unions to demand to enter a collective agreement with the foreign service provider in order to grant posted workers minimum protection, Lex Laval links the posting situation to the Swedish model for collective bargaining. By restricting the demands that Swedish trade unions can make on the foreign employer, in accordance with the *Laval* ruling, the legislation clearly restricts the freedom of association or collective bargaining rights of the Swedish trade unions: they cannot demand more favourable terms and conditions than the minimum standard prescribed in Article 3(1) of the Posting of Workers Directive;[9] they cannot make demands concerning any other matter than that explicitly regulated in Article 3(1); and they cannot demand any collective agreement at all if the posted workers already enjoy terms and conditions that essentially are at least as favourable as those that apply in accordance with Swedish law and the applicable general collective agreement.

The consequence of these restrictions is that the legislator has introduced specific and strong protection for transnational service providers as employers. This protection does not apply to national employers. Trade unions can still demand more favourable collective agreements (compared to the minimum standard in the Directive) as regards both the scope of terms and conditions, and the level of protection against national employers not bound by the agreement. Those bound by the nationwide agreement must also apply a wide range of terms and conditions regarding issues outside the scope of the hard nucleus. The requirement

[7] This interpretation is also supported by the *Laval* judgment, above n 4, where the CJEU indicates that Sweden has not made use of the possibilities offered by Art 3(8) (see paras 62–72). This reasoning would be meaningless if the criteria for using Art 3(8) are interpreted in such a manner that Sweden does not qualify.

[8] See Government Bill Proposal 2009/10:48, 31.

[9] The CJEU explicitly underlined that the provisions included in the trade union's demand for a collective agreement in the *Laval* case went beyond what the transnational service provider was required to observe in terms of mandatory rules for minimum protection in accordance with the Directive. See *Laval*, above n 4, para 108 and paras 81 and 83, referred to in para 108.

for equal treatment of employers has been turned upside down: we find here a situation of so-called *reverse discrimination*, to the disadvantage of national Swedish companies (and Swedish employers' associations) that compete with foreign service providers.

The only case in which it can be argued (at least theoretically) that Swedish employers are in a better position than a foreign service provider, is in the fact that a Swedish collective agreement made at a lower level than the minimum defined by the hard nucleus will bring about an obligation to settle, while a foreign collective agreement that does not fulfil the minimum criteria can be set aside by trade unions that resort to collective action.

The new legislation restricts some of the fundamental principles of free collective bargaining and freedom of association, as has been applied in the Nordic countries, but also as interpreted by international bodies protecting fundamental rights in the field of collective labour law, especially ILO Conventions 87 and 98.[10] The problems relate to several elements concerning free collective bargaining: demands are usually to be decided by the trade union, and not set by law. In particular, restrictions on the material scope of what trade unions can demand are very difficult to justify in the light of ILO Conventions 87 and 98. Furthermore, the outcome of the bargaining process and possible collective action should not be defined beforehand. The new Swedish legislation introduces all these elements and restricts wage competition at the transnational level.

III. GENERAL DEVELOPMENTS IN EUROPEAN AND EU LABOUR LAW

The development regarding transnational labour law also has its counterpart in national labour law. Here we can see a gradual transformation of collective bargaining at branch level in the whole of Europe.[11] In this context, I will not document the development in detail, but my argument is that a transformation has gradually taken place, with the end result being that wages are no longer settled through branch-level collective bargaining, but increasingly through company-level collective bargaining, and also by minimum wage legislation.

The old principle that branch-level collective bargaining sets a general minimum wage level that cannot be undermined by companies is no longer a valid description of the general situation. In the old post-war days, this branch-level minimum was seen as the great achievement that forced companies to compete in

[10] The ILO Freedom of Association Committee (CFA) has interpreted ILO Conventions 87 and 98 very strictly when it comes to allowing different types of restrictions on the principle of free and voluntary bargaining that the legislator and the authorities might create. See ILO, *Freedom of Association: Digest of Decisions and Principles of the Freedom of Association Committee of the Governing Body of the ILO*, 5th (revised) edn (Geneva, 2006).

[11] See D Vaughan-Whitehead (ed), *Work Inequalities in the Crises: Evidence from Europe* (Geneva, ILO, 2011) (reports on separate countries).

productivity, and not in low wages.[12] In present-day Europe, even the economically strong Member States such as Germany and Austria have introduced concession bargaining that makes it possible to agree on standards below the branch minimum at local level. In countries where the principle of the minimum is still upheld, the practical implications of this principle are significantly limited by the far-reaching possibilities for introducing local deviations—but only when the parties have agreed on such measures. From Christensen's point of view, this development indicates a strong shift towards the Market-Functional pattern, and both the normative patterns of Protection of Established Position and Just Distribution are undermined.

Christensen was a sharp observer of this development in labour law. She emphasised that labour law had become a kind of organisational principle for Swedish society—everyone should be a paid employee, in Swedish a '*lönearbetare*'. The result of this was a generalisation of labour law, which was constructed around the existence of the employment relationship: a weaker party who deserved protection by legislation and trade unions. This trend towards a general labour law, from a more specific and narrower version, is a general trend all over Europe, but has been exceptionally strong in the Nordic countries. In fact, this trend is still ongoing, for example in Finland, where in 2010 university professors and other staff were transformed from public servants into employees under the Employment Contracts Act, in the context of a change in the legal position of the universities.[13] This trend towards an all-encompassing labour law has been clear, although a certain fragmentation within labour law has also occurred: the groups of fixed-term employees, part-timers and employees working for temporary agencies and on contract have, for instance, been growing.

The starting point and logic for this development in labour law has been the need to protect the employee, and the rules have been adapted also to accommodate the needs of employers in a dynamic and changing business environment.

It is interesting to contrast this development within national labour law in most European states against the development currently taking place in EU law.

Within the European Union, the starting point for the economic constitution was a general broad concept of the worker or employee who was entitled to move around freely in the entire internal market. This concept has been interpreted rather broadly and has been considered as being in line with the national perception in most Member States of who is regarded as a worker.

The evolution of EU law has gradually led to a radical fragmentation of the category of employees. Within the regime of the posting of workers, the CJEU has succeeded in creating a category of workers not deemed to be on the labour market of the country in which they perform their work. Instead, these workers are simply regarded as a kind of institutional link to the service providers taking

[12] This was the central content of the old Rehn-Meidner doctrine in Sweden.

[13] See N Bruun, 'Universitetsstyrning och autonomi i ett Corporate Governance-perspektiv' in *Festskrift till Boel Flodgren* (Lund, Juristförlaget i Lund, 2011) 32.

advantage of the right to freely provide services across borders. The position of these employees is not determined by their need for social protection; rather, the decisive factor is their position on the internal market. Again, this approach has been difficult to fully uphold regarding temporary agency workers, who actually can move across borders and are employed by service providers. This dilemma has been tackled by a specific Directive on temporary agency work,[14] creating some problems for Member States in upholding normative coherence between different forms of exploiting labour.[15]

The position of employees on the internal market can also be dependent on their citizenship and country of origin. There are illegal workers (third-country nationals) who are in very weak positions, and there are third-country nationals who are long-term residents, and who can even be regarded as EU citizens. This again gives them a fairly strong position as employees on the internal market.

In 2005, a specific Directive was adopted concerning working conditions for third-country nationals in the field of scientific research.[16] In 2011, a Directive was adopted regarding a single application procedure for a single permit for third-country nationals to reside and work in the territory of a Member State, and on a common set of rights for third-country workers residing legally in a Member State.[17]

So, for some time now, we have had pending proposals for Directives on:

— highly qualified workers;[18]
— seasonal workers;[19]
— intra-corporate transferees.[20]

The common feature of all this adopted and pending 'labour law regulation' of different groups of workers is the starting point that these employees perform some kind of useful function from an economic point of view. The primary aim is not to protect them, but to create a legal form in which employers who need to do so can recruit employees, and where these employees can gain access to the EU labour market. In an ongoing study, Petra Herzfeld Olsson has shown just how inconsistent these regulations are from a traditional labour law point of view.[21]

[14] Directive 2008/104/EC [2008] OJ L327.

[15] See K Ahlberg *et al*, *Transnational Labour Regulation: a Case Study of Temporary Agency Work* (Brussels, PIE Peter Lang, 2008).

[16] Council Directive 2005/71/EC of 12 October 2005 on a specific procedure for admitting third-country nationals for the purposes of scientific research [2005] OJ L289.

[17] Directive 2011/98/EU of 13 December 2011 [2011] OJ L343.

[18] This Directive was adopted in 2009: Council Directive 2009/50/EC of May 2009 on the conditions of entry and residence of third-country nationals for the purposes of highly qualified employment [2009] OJ L155.

[19] COM(2010)379.

[20] COM(2010)378.

[21] See P Herzfeld Olsson, *Giving to Those Who Have and Taking from Those Who Have Not: the Development of an EU Policy on Workers from Third Countries*, Formula Working Paper 34 (2012).

From a normative pattern of labour law, these regulations lack all coherence and the principle of equal treatment is applied differently in different instruments.

From Christensen's perspective, these developments can perhaps be seen as an illustration of how the Market-Functional pattern takes over labour law normative patterns such as Just Distribution. To some extent, the pattern of Protection of the Established Position applies, since those with the strongest position on the labour market are also given the strongest protection by the law. However, the main problem here is the normative incoherence that national labour law faces and will continue to face as a result of these new approaches. One can foresee a clash between national labour law and European instruments during the years to come, as a result of the fact that the regulatory patterns the European Union introduces are based on a different regulatory approach than traditional national labour law.

IV. ECONOMIC CONSTITUTION OF THE EUROPEAN UNION AND THE ECONOMIC AND FINANCIAL CRISIS

A. Background

The current developments in European labour law cannot be adequately described without examining the economic governance of the economic crisis and its impact on labour and social law, especially in those countries that have been forced to seek economic assistance from the European Union.

The background for the crisis is well known. In the aftermath of the global 2008 financial crisis, the situation in Greece (which has long had a weak public economy with severe structural problems) reached a state of alarm in April 2010. Potential Greek bankruptcy was a matter for serious concern, especially for the European Union's Euro Group, to which Greece belongs. This situation prompted the Group to fulfil the promise they had given at the European Council meeting: to take necessary determined and coordinated action as required to safeguard the financial stability of the euro.[22]

As a result, negotiations were started between the Greek government, on the one hand, and a group consisting of the European Commission, the European Central Bank (ECB) and the International Monetary Fund (IMF), on the other. Within a few weeks, a complicated contractual and legal structure was devised: one key document is the detailed Memorandum of Understanding (MoU), signed by Greece and by the European Commission on behalf of the Member States belonging to the Euro Group.[23] Other agreements are the Intercreditor Agreement, and a Loan Facility Agreement that settles the availability of credits

[22] See European Council, Conclusions (25 March 2010), available at ww.consilium.europa.eu.

[23] The MoU comprises a Memorandum of Economic and Financial Policies, Memorandum of Understanding on Specific Economic Policy Conditionality and Technical Memorandum of Understanding; available at www.imf.org/external/pubs/ft/scr/2010/cr10111.pdf.

in the form of pooled bilateral loans for Greece, as well as an agreement between Greece and the IMF in the form of an Exchange of Letters.[24] In the latter, the Greek government undertook to fully implement the agreed measures, including the MoU. These agreements have also been ratified separately by the Euro Group Member States.[25]

On 10 May 2010, the Council took a decision on certain measures that Greece must undertake before the end of June 2010. Furthermore, the decision listed measures that had to be undertaken by the end of September 2010, or by the end of December 2010. The measures listed in the Council's decision were the same as those listed in the MoU.

The Greek bailout package was an alarm call for the European Commission, which in the first half of May 2010 had already made proposals for measures to preserve financial stability in Europe, consisting of a European Financial Stability Mechanism (EFSM) and a European Financial Stability Facility (EFSF). The EFSM was established by a Council Regulation on 11 May 2010.[26] The EFSF was established by an intergovernmental agreement (Framework Agreement) of the Euro Group Member States, in the form of a registered limited liability company under Luxembourg law. These Member States own shares in the company in proportion to their participation in the arrangement with guarantee commitments. Altogether, the commitments formed a total guarantee of 440 billion euros.

In September 2010, the government of Ireland revealed that the full cost of the January 2009 bailout to the Irish taxpayer was estimated at 50 billion euros, or about 32 per cent of Ireland's GDP. This sparked a crisis that led to a dialogue between Ireland, on the one hand, and the IMF and the European Union, on the other, similar to the one that had taken place concerning Greece.[27] A National Recovery Plan for 2011–14 was drawn up in cooperation with the IMF and the European Union. This plan was published on 24 November 2010 after a formal request from the Irish government for financial assistance from the European Union and the IMF on 21 November 2010. The Joint Commission-ECB-IMF mission team negotiated the conditions of the programme, and agreement at the technical level was reached on 28 November 2010 on a comprehensive policy package for the period 2010–13, supported by financing at a total of 85 billion euros.

On 11 March 2011, the Portuguese authorities requested financial assistance. The Euro Group and ECOFIN ministers invited the Commission, the ECB, the IMF and Portugal to set up a programme and take appropriate action to safeguard financial stability. At the same time, they issued a statement according to which, in the context of a joint EU/IMF programme, the financial assistance package to

[24] See A Antoniadis, 'Debt Crisis as a Global Emergency: the European Economic Constitution and other Greek Fables' (1 September 2010), available at http://ssrn.com/abstract=1699082.

[25] An exception was Slovakia, which refused to ratify the agreements.

[26] Council Regulation (EU) 407/2010 of 11 May 2010 [2010] OJ L118.

[27] As late as December 2009, the European Council had concluded that Irish authorities had taken effective action to correct the excessive deficit and had moved the deadline for correcting it to 2014.

Portugal would be financed on the European side within the framework provided by the EFSM and the EFSF.[28] It was furthermore stated that the euro zone and EU financial support will be provided on the basis of a policy programme that will be supported by strict conditionality and be negotiated with the Portuguese authorities.[29] Both Spain and Italy have subsequently been forced to adopt strong economic programmes.

B. Reform Programme

The European Commission reacted without delay to the Greek crisis also at a general level of norm setting. As early as 8 May 2010, the Commission announced that it would present to the Council a concrete proposal for a European Stabilisation Mechanism to preserve financial stability in Europe, as indicated above. On 12 May, the European Commission issued a Communication entitled 'Reinforcing economic policy coordination'.[30] Here, we find already the main elements in the reform programme that have subsequently been further elaborated on.

On the same day, 12 May 2010, the Council also adopted a Regulation establishing a European financial stabilisation mechanism.[31] Following a general discussion in the European Council in June, the Commission issued a new Communication.[32] This document contained an annex with a roadmap, where seven concrete legislative proposals were envisaged during the period September 2010 to January 2011.

The European Commission followed the roadmap quite closely, and presented a number of proposals[33] aimed at increased and improved control of economic

[28] Statement on 8 April 2011, Memo 11/227.

[29] In accordance with the statement, the programme will be based on three pillars: (1) ambitious fiscal adjustment to restore fiscal sustainability; (2) growth and competitiveness-enhancing reforms designed to remove rigidities in the product and labour markets, and encourage entrepreneurship and innovation, allowing for sustainable and balanced growth and the mitigation of internal and external macro-economic imbalances, while safeguarding the economic and social position of its citizens; this should include an ambitious privatisation programme; and (3) measures to maintain the liquidity and solvency of the financial sector.

[30] Communication from the Commission to the European Parliament, the European Council, the Council, the European Central Bank, the Economic and Social Committee and the Committee of the Regions. 'Reinforcing economic policy coordination', COM(2010)250 final (Brussels, 12 May 2010).

[31] Council Regulation (EU) 407/2010 of 11 May 2010 establishing a European financial stabilisation mechanism [2010] OJ L118/1–4.

[32] Communication from the Commission to the European Parliament, the European Council, the Council, the European Central Bank, the Economic and Social Committee and the Committee of the Regions, 'Enhancing economic policy coordination for stability, growth and jobs: tools for stronger EU economic governance', COM(2010)367 final (Brussels, 30 June 2010).

[33] (1) Proposal for a Regulation of the European Parliament and of the Council on the prevention and correction of macro-economic imbalances, COM(2010)527 final; (2) Proposal for a Regulation of the European Parliament and of the Council amending Regulation (EC) 1466/97 of 7 July 1997 on the strengthening of the surveillance of budgetary positions and the surveillance and coordination of economic policies, COM(2010)526 final; (3) Proposal for a Regulation of the European Parliament and of the Council on enforcement measures to correct excessive macro-economic imbalances in the

governance within the European Union. In general terms, these proposals can be divided into three types of instruments. The first instrument attempts to introduce new procedures for national economic policy and budgetary prudence, and to also strengthen surveillance. Here also, sanctions can be introduced against a state that does not follow economic policy recommendations from the Council, and the Member State in question may be deemed liable to fines that may amount to 0.2 per cent of its GDP. The second type of instrument has its focus on the prevention and correction of so-called macro-economic imbalances, and also on the enforcement mechanism to correct them. Here, the Commission also proposes that economic sanctions can be introduced at up to 0.1 per cent of the GDP of a Member State.[34] The third type of instrument attempts to harmonise and coordinate national budgetary structures and content, in order to increase transparency and possibilities, among other things, to compare accounting systems and perform statistical reporting.

These proposals have now been adopted as amended, especially by the European Parliament. At the same time, preparations for the introduction of a permanent European Stability Mechanism (ESM) have been initiated, mostly in the form of a codification of current practice, and the guiding political decisions were taken at the European Council meeting in March 2011.

C. Social Policy Implications

I am not, in this context, interested in a detailed study of the mechanisms of the stability instruments of the European Union, but wish to study their impact on social policy in the Member States experiencing economic difficulties, and also how these measures fit into the Lisbon Treaty's description (Article 4 TEU) of the European Union as a social market economy and other Treaty Articles regarding the European Union and its relationship to its Member States.

If we briefly map the measures undertaken in Greece and Ireland, we can note the following: in Greece, the report from the Prime Minister and the Governor of the Bank of Greece gives a picture of what had taken place from the period of the Spring of 2010 up until 6 August 2010.[35] The government reports that the fiscal programme is making good progress, but makes no mention of reactions to the measures undertaken: massive nationwide and per-sector collective action

euro area, COM(2010)525 final; (4) Proposal for a Regulation of the European Parliament and of the Council on the effective enforcement of budgetary surveillance in the euro area, COM(2010)524 final; (5) Proposal for a Council Directive on requirements for the budgetary frameworks of the Member States, COM(2010)523 final; (6) Proposal for a Council Regulation (EU) amending Regulation (EC) 1467/97 of 7 July 1997 on speeding up and clarifying the implementation of the excessive deficit procedure, COM(2010)522 final.

[34] See COM(2010)525 final.

[35] Greece, Memorandum of Economic and Financial Politics, Athens, 6 August 2010, available at www.imf.org/external/pubs/ft/scr/2010.

during the period, as well as mass demonstrations and street protests. In the report, significant reductions are reported in health care and public administration, which will lead to a significant reduction in employment. From the point of social policy, the most contested reforms were related to pensions and the labour market. For these sectors the following reports were given.

Parliament approved a substantial pension reform ahead of schedule. This introduces a new system consisting of a contributory pension for topping up a non-contributory, means-tested, basic pension, and aiming to control the increase in pension spending. These assessments will determine whether further adjustments to pension system parameters will be required, to contain the increase in pension spending to 2.5 ppts of GDP in the period 2009–60. Any further adjustments required will be completed by the end of June 2011, in consultation with pension experts, as foreseen in Law 3863.

Labour market reform is almost completed. Substantial legislative changes were introduced in July, with relaxations on employment protection legislation and collective dismissals, reforming minimum wages, reducing overtime premia, and allowing company-level agreements to take precedence over other levels. Alongside reforms in public employment to reduce labour market distortions, these measures will increase the adjustment capacity of businesses, ultimately boosting employment. Further measures will be taken to reform collective bargaining, including the elimination of the automatic extension of per-sector agreements to those not represented in the negotiations. Finally, the government will adopt legislation to introduce symmetry in the arbitration system, while strengthening its independence and transparency.

The Greek trade unions complained to the ILO concerning the policy in Greece.[36] In its 2011 Annual Report,[37] the CEACR (Report of the Committee of Experts on the Application of Conventions and Recommendations) reiterated its established positions on the relationship between economic crisis, public interference in collective bargaining, and ILO Convention 98 on collective bargaining,

[36] The critical voices from the trade union side described the situation quite dramatically: 'The GSEE concludes that Acts Nos 3833/2010, 3845/2010 and 3863/2010 lead to workers' disempowerment in the face of the combined spill-over effect of lay-offs, wage freezes and the abolition of the minimum standards of wages, negate the State's fundamental obligation to provide and protect decent work, violate the very essence of individual and social rights, and endanger social peace and cohesion. The GSEE emphasises that the measures in question are permanent and irreversible, notwithstanding the specific time frame and limited duration of the loan mechanism; are disproportionate, socially unjust and discriminatory vis-à-vis workers, especially the most vulnerable; have been adopted without examining sufficiently other well-weighed and more appropriate alternatives; are not quantifiable and their scope has no perceivable causal relationship with the pursued aim of implementing the stability programme; are not accompanied by adequate and concrete safeguards to protect the living standard of workers and support vulnerable groups in addressing the combined effect of economic austerity measures and the economic crisis; have had a serious and direct impact in weakening the position of GSEE during the collective negotiations that began in January 2010 for the conclusion of the new national general collective agreement'. See Report III (1A) 84, available at www.ilo.org/global/standards/WCMS_151490/lang--en/index.htm.

[37] See ibid.

on the occasion of its preliminary comments on Greece in the framework of the mechanism to support the Greek economy with the involvement of the IMF and European Union:

> The CEACR emphasised the importance of holding full and frank consultations with the employers' and workers' organisations on the revision of collective bargaining machinery, in accordance with the principle of the autonomy of the parties to the collective bargaining process, and in light of the long-ranging implications of such revision for the standard of living of workers. Furthermore, it considers that as a general matter, if, as part of its stabilisation policy a government considers that wage rates cannot be settled freely through collective bargaining, such a restriction should only be imposed as an exceptional measure and only to the extent necessary, without exceeding a reasonable period, and should be accompanied by adequate safeguards to protect workers' living standards.[38]

The principle of the autonomy of the parties to the collective bargaining process, as well as the right to collective bargaining, are both enshrined in Convention 98. During an economic crisis, the Freedom of Association Committee (CFA) has further specified the principle:

> In cases of government intervention to restrict collective bargaining, the CFA has considered that it is not its role to express a view on the soundness of the economic arguments used by the Government to justify its position or on the measures it has adopted. However, it is for the CFA to express its views on whether, in taking such action, the Government has gone beyond what the CFA considers acceptable restrictions that may be temporarily imposed on free collective bargaining.
>
> While the CFA appreciates that the introduction of wage restraint measures must be timed in order to obtain the maximum impact on the economic situation, it nevertheless considers that the interruption of already negotiated contracts is not in conformity with the principles of free collective bargaining; as such contracts should be respected.
>
> If, as part of its stabilisation policy, a government considers that wage rates cannot be settled freely through collective bargaining, such a restriction should be imposed as an exceptional measure, and only to the extent necessary and without exceeding a reasonable period, and should be accompanied by adequate safeguards to protect workers' living standards.
>
> A three-year period of limited collective bargaining on remuneration within the context of a policy of economic stabilisation constitutes a substantial restriction.
>
> In any case, any limitation on collective bargaining on the part of the authorities should be preceded by consultations with workers' and employers' organisations, in an effort to obtain their agreement.[39]

[38] See ibid 83.

[39] *Digest of Decisions and Principles of CFA* (2006) paras 992–1045, available at www.ilo.org/global/standards/information-resources-and-publications/publications/WCMS_090632/lang--en/index.htm.

The Committee concluded that it should be highlighted that all 27 EU Member States have ratified Convention 98 on the promotion of collective bargaining and Convention 87 on freedom of association. These are part of the eight core labour standards Conventions. Over 90 per cent of all 183 ILO member states have ratified these Conventions. Conventions 87 and 98 have also strongly influenced other regional fundamental rights instruments, such as the European Social Charter, the European Convention on Human Rights (freedom of association is included here) and the EU Charter on Fundamental Rights.

These strong conclusions by ILO seem clearly to indicate that the Greek bailout has not conformed to ILO standards. From the government positions above, we can also see that there are concerted efforts to change the structural features of the Greek industrial relations system in the context of crisis management.

In September 2011, the ILO sent a high-level Mission of Inquiry to Greece. Its extensive report is publicly available.[40] In the Spring of 2012, the Committee of Experts in their report dealt extensively with Greece, and again serious violations of the principle of freedom of association were discovered. In fact, it seems that the entire institutional labour market system of Greece is being destroyed as a consequence of the crisis, as public promotion of the national trade unions in the form of public funds has also been withdrawn.

In Ireland, the crisis has had a series of negative impacts on the labour market. Apart from the general increase in unemployment and emigration, cutbacks in public services (especially in health care), increased taxes, the introduction of new forms of taxes affecting the lowest paid, increase in prices (especially of food prices) and the serious mortgage debts incurred by families are some of the measures and events related to the labour market we can mention. The Minister for Finance used 'emergency' legislation to:

- cut public servants' pay and pensions;
- restrict collective bargaining for certain categories of workers;
- cut minimum wages (ignoring the established minimum wage-setting mechanism) by 1 euro per hour;
- reduce social welfare payments, including unemployment benefit, sickness benefits and maternity payments in both amounts and the duration of payment;
- remove tax relief for trade union subscriptions.

These drastic measures were undertaken by a government that lost office in the elections of early Spring 2011. There is now a new programme for government, and while this holds some prospects for improving the situation, the strong MoU is still in place. The new majority partner, Fine Gael Party, is reported not to be very supportive of labour and trade union rights. One of the main areas this

[40] See *Report on the High Level Mission to Greece, Athens, 19–23 September 2011*, available at www.ILO.org.

party has criticised is universally applicable collective agreements. Therefore, the outcome remains to be seen in this regard.

The conclusion is that what we are observing is an extremely strong impact on social policy and social policy legislation caused by the bailout mechanism. Formally speaking, the final decisions in both Greece and Ireland were in the hands of the Parliaments of these states, but the content of the MoUs were clearly a result of negotiations, or even of negotiations 'in the shadow of bankruptcy', in which the borderline between negotiations and dictates becomes very blurred. In Spain and Italy, the same types of measures are being introduced, partly on a voluntary national basis, and partly under pressure from international financial institutions and the European Union.

The timeframe and procedures for reducing costs do not respect established national or international requirements for making changes (eg mutually agreed wage agreements or pension schemes). It is of interest to investigate how this new economic policy and constitutional practice fit into the framework of the Lisbon Treaty, especially whether this governance and practice are in conformity with the requirements of a social market economy (Article 4 TEU), but this discussion cannot take place here.

V. BACK TO CHRISTENSEN AND THE THEORY OF LAW AS NORMATIVE PATTERNS IN A NORMATIVE FIELD

The legal developments sketched above do not easily fit into the theory introduced by Christensen. The problem seems to be that Christensen's theory uses the perspective of legal evolution within the normative field, which she describes as working life and labour law.

The problem with the disruptive features the development of the European Union represents is that it does not actually—as a starting point—accept the basic international standard for modern labour law: 'Labour is not a commodity'. On the contrary, it might be argued that the starting point here is that labour is a market commodity on the internal market and that wage competition is a relevant and even necessary factor for gaining competitive advantages for Member States. All restrictions in this regard seem to be viewed as being incompatible with the economic constitution of the European Union. The consequence of this is a clash between the EU Charter of Fundamental Rights and international labour standards, on the one hand, and EU law and governance, on the other.

From the point of view of Christensen's theory, one could argue that we have moved on to an extreme Market-Functional pattern. Within this new pattern, however, questions of the implications of the normative patterns of Just Distribution and Protection of Established Position will still be relevant.

I argue here that Christensen's theoretical thinking actually offers two plausible solutions when attempting to apply her theory to the current development. The first solution would argue that the normative field, so well described by

Christensen, can exist only if there is some basic acknowledgement of the various poles or cornerstones. The new disruptive EU practice does not seem to recognise any Protection for Established Positions within the social dimension, and thus the present development actually goes beyond Christensen's theory of normative development—which is perhaps better suited to describing legal evolution in a local or nation-state context. However, there is another alternative that I think Christensen herself would have favoured, and which she actually hinted at when she stated that normative patterns can move between different social spheres.[41] In actuality, the present development is shifting the borders between different normative fields. What is happening is that the borders between the fields of labour law and social (security) law are being blurred. We actually get a new kind of pole or normative pattern in the labour law field, a pole that could be termed Basic Subsistence.[42] When the traditional tools for protecting established positions are seriously undermined, the legislator must still ensure that workers can survive. Suddenly, schemes for minimum wage legislation become necessary, in order to compensate for the lack of collective bargaining, and the debate will centre on how to decide on a proper minimum wage level, in order to place at least some restrictions on the 'race to the bottom' in wage competition.

[41] See Christensen, 'Normative Patterns and the Normative Field', above n 2, 16.
[42] The term was used by Anna Christensen in her article, ibid, in 1999.

6

Protection of Established Position, Social Protection and the Legal Situation of the Elderly in the European Union[*]

MIA RÖNNMAR

I. INTRODUCTION

TODAY, AN AGEING population and an increased number of elderly people represent an important global and European demographic trend that implies crucial economic and societal challenges, in need of political, normative and legal solutions. The aim of this chapter is to explore and analyse the legal situation and social protection of the elderly in the European Union, most specifically in some aspects related to older workers and working life, in relation to the theory of law as normative patterns in a normative field and the normative pattern of Protection of Established Position. Social protection is perceived here in a broad sense, encompassing, inter alia, social security law, labour law, social and labour market policy and fundamental rights. Labour law and social security law have close links. Social security has developed as part of the industrial society, and can be understood as a system that is complementary to and dependent on wage work. At an aggregated societal level, social security supplements wage-work and its distribution of resources. Social security provides protection against risks and maintenance in situations in which a person is unable to earn a living through wage-work, owing to, for instance, old age, sickness, unemployment or childbirth.[1]

At EU level, the concept of the social dimension also reflects this notion of social protection and the complementarity of labour law and social security law. The

[*] This chapter was written within the Elder Law Project (www.jur.lu.se/elderlaw), carried out within the Norma Research Programme at the Faculty of Law at Lund University, and funded by Ragnar Söderberg's Foundation and the Marianne and Marcus Wallenberg's Foundation.

[1] See A Christensen, 'Normativa grundmönster i socialrätten' (1997) 78 *Retfaerd* 69; A Christensen, 'Normative Patterns and the Normative Field: a Post-Liberal View on Law' in T Wilhelmsson and S Hurri (eds), *From Dissonance to Sense: Welfare State Expectations, Privatisation and Private Law* (Aldershot, Ashgate, 1999); and E Holm, *Fri rörlighet för familjer. En normativ analys av föräldrapenningen och EU-rätten* (Lund, Juristförlaget i Lund, 2010).

social dimension refers precisely to the part of EU politics and legal regulations connected to the citizen's social needs, social protection and social integration. The labour market, social security and families are central areas of regulation in the social dimension, forming the legal structures of 'everyday life'. Labour law at the EU level is only partly harmonised due to the principle of subsidiarity and the limited legislative competence of the European Union. In principle, the content of social security law is a matter for the individual Member States and national legislation. However, the coordination of social security in the European Union and between the Member States was implemented early on as a way to facilitate the free movement of workers. Through the open method of coordination not only employment policy (through the European Employment Strategy, the Integrated Guidelines and the Europe 2020 Strategy), but also aspects linked to social security, such as old-age pensions, social inclusion and social protection, have been further developed. Thus, through the 'pension process' pension systems in the Member States are being coordinated, with an aim to achieve sustainable pension systems.

The outline of the chapter is as follows. Section II provides a brief description of the theory of law as normative patterns in a normative field and the normative pattern of Protection of Established Position. Section III discusses the legal situation of the elderly in the European Union, especially in terms of the fundamental rights of the elderly, age discrimination and mandatory retirement and employment protection. Lastly, section IV contains an analysis and some concluding remarks in relation to the theory of law as normative patterns in a normative field and the normative pattern of Protection of Established Position.

II. PROTECTION OF ESTABLISHED POSITION

The starting point of the theory of law as normative patterns in a normative field, first created by Anna Christensen and subsequently developed by Ann Numhauser-Henning, is the insight that the law comprises a multitude of often conflicting legal norms, and therefore forms anything but a consistent and hierarchical legal 'system'. Within this multitude of legal norms a number of basic normative patterns can be distinguished. These normative patterns—showing both significance and a high degree of constancy—reflect social and normative practices and moral conceptions central to human relations and society. Such basic normative patterns can be said to make up magnetic poles in a normative field of law. The contents of legal regulation, and their position in the normative field, are determined by the attraction of the poles, and this attraction in turn changes with time and economic and societal conditions. Thus, legal developments are represented by movements in the normative field. Even though a certain normative pattern can appear dominant in a particular area of law, in principle the legal regulation is always influenced by several different normative patterns.[2]

[2] See, eg, A Christensen, 'Skydd för etablerad position. Ett normativt grundmönster' (1996) *Tidsskrift for Rettsvitenskap* 519; Christensen, 'Normative Patterns and the Normative Field', above n 1;

Studies of the law of the social dimension reveal the existence of three particularly influential normative patterns, Protection of Established Position, the Market-Functional pattern and Just Distribution. Protection of Established Position, in focus in this chapter, is a conservative, protective normative pattern, with origins in property law and the protection of an owner's rightful possessions. Protection of Established Position is manifested in labour law as employment protection, securing the continued employment of those already employed; in social security law, as the principle of replacement of lost earnings; and in tenancy law as tenants' security.[3] Protection of Established Position is conservative, in the way that it preserves the positions and social constellations which have been achieved.[4] At the same time the pattern is 'silent on *how* these positions are established and who will be able to achieve these establishments'.[5] Christensen emphasises that the pattern of Protection of Established Position has historical constancy and broad application, and is forceful and persistent in the way that it puts a clear mark on the legal rules.[6]

Protection of Established Position is in obvious conflict with the Market-Functional pattern, which is a composite pattern representing normative conceptions central to the functioning of the market economy, such as dynamic ownership rights, freedom of contract and freedom of trade. In labour law, for example, the Market-Functional pattern manifests itself as the managerial prerogative and freedom of contract. The Market-Functional pattern aims to promote new activities and businesses and a constant redistribution of wealth, and results in a continuous shift in achieved positions.[7]

Protection of Established Position can also conflict with another protective normative pattern, Just Distribution. Just Distribution is based on the idea that resources should be distributed according to different material principles of justice, and is thus a distributive pattern related to social justice, solidarity and the 'distribution and re-distribution of values, which as a consequence, leads to the creation of new positions'.[8]

In non-discrimination law the normative pattern of Equal Treatment, which is close to or part of the Market-Functional pattern, implies competition on equal terms. Here, a protective normative pattern of Belonging is also found as a sphere in the normative field, covering both Protection of Established Position and Just Distribution. According to Numhauser-Henning, this normative pattern is 'based on the profound willingness, but also the obligation, of the "established group" to

A Christensen, 'Protection of the Established Position: a Basic Normative Pattern' (2000) *Scandinavian Studies in Law* 285; and A Numhauser-Henning, 'Den framtida arbetsrättens förutsättningar' (1997) 3 *Arbetsmarknad and Arbetsliv* 97. For a more detailed description and analysis of the theory of law as normative patterns in a normative field, see Ann Numhauser-Hennning, Chapter 2.

[3] On expressions of the Protection of Established Position in family law, see Titti Mattsson, Chapter 7 and Eva Ryrstedt, Chapter 13.

[4] See Christensen, 'Protection of the Established Position', above n 2, 291.

[5] See ibid 290. However, the positions must have been achieved by lawful means.

[6] See ibid 317 ff.

[7] See ibid 219.

[8] Ibid 290. Cf also Ann Numhauser-Henning, Chapter 2.

share with (but with only) those who are already in some way associated. This is a basically conservative pattern, although it is not hostile to a certain redistribution in relation to those who in some way "belong".[9] Non-discrimination law thus aims at breaking up old structures of belonging, and at the inclusion and advantage of marginalised groups and individuals.[10]

III. LEGAL SITUATION OF THE ELDERLY IN THE EUROPEAN UNION

A. Introduction

The rapidly ageing population in the European Union and an increased number of elderly people challenge social and economic sustainability in terms of employment, pension systems and health care systems, as well as social cohesion and intergenerational solidarity. Even though life expectancy has risen, and continues to rise quite dramatically, workers are still leaving the labour market prematurely. Apart from the need to provide the elderly with adequate social protection, there is also a need to make people work beyond their pensionable age, ensure that they continue to work until they reach pensionable age and to facilitate access to employment for older workers.[11]

The elderly as a group are not easy to define, at least not in a coherent way. The concept of age can refer to chronological age, biological age, social age and functional age. In discussions related to working life, the elderly (older workers) are often workers 55 years or older (55+).[12] In her research on social security law and pension systems and their reform and development in Europe, Christensen referred to different phases of life, where the 'after life' followed upon, and referred to, the years following retirement.[13] In a European Union with a rapidly ageing population, working life must be extended, and the 'after life', or normative perceptions about the 'after life', must be transformed (see below).[14]

[9] See Ann Numhauser-Henning, Chapter 2. See also A Numhauser-Henning, 'Introduction: Equal Treatment—a Normative Challenge' in A Numhauser-Henning (ed), *Legal Perspectives on Equal Treatment and Non-Discrimination* (The Hague, Kluwer Law International, 2001).

[10] See Numhauser-Henning, 'Introduction: Equal Treatment', above n 9.

[11] See A Numhauser-Henning, 'Labour Law in a Greying Labour Market: in Need of a Reconceptualisation of Work and Pension Norms', Keynote Paper on the occasion of the Fifth Annual Legal Seminar, European Labour Law Network, 11–12 October 2012.

[12] Compare Art 2 of the Commission's Proposal regarding a European Year of Active Ageing, COM(2012)462 final.

[13] See Christensen, 'Normative Patterns and the Normative Field', above n 1.

[14] Similarly, in his analysis of the social human rights of the elderly in Europe Mikkola refers to the third and fourth lives. He explains that '[e]xit from the labour market opens up a so-called third life which will be longer than before for those generations that have enjoyed the general welfare during the last decade. How a person conceives that part of life is both a social and individual matter. Fourth life resembles the first one. Dependency on other members of the family, close relatives or society's care becomes paramount in the last years of a person's earthly toil', see M Mikkola, *Social Human Rights of Europe* (Porvoo, Karelactio, 2010) 526.

The 2012 Ageing Report reports that by 2060 '[t]hose aged 65 and above will represent a much larger share of the population (rising from 17% to 30%). The number of persons aged 80 and above will come close to the group of 0–14 years olds (rising from 5% to 12%). The economic dependency ratio (persons aged 65 or above relative to those aged 15–64) will thus double, shifting from four working age persons for every person over 65 to only two working age persons'.[15] The average age for leaving working life in the Member States generally differs from the 'normal' pensionable age. According to the 2012 Ageing Report, in 2009 the average labour market exit age in EU-27 was 61.4 years.[16]

2012 has been named the Year of Active Ageing in the European Union, with an overall purpose to 'promote active ageing and to better mobilize the potential of the rapidly growing population in their late 50s and above'. Active ageing implies generating better opportunities and working conditions for the participation of older workers in the labour market, combating social exclusion through fostering active participation in society, and encouraging healthy ageing.[17] The policy strategy of active ageing contains different target areas. One important target area, of specific interest for this chapter, is increased labour market participation of 55+ persons. Other target areas include dignity, independence and influence, social integration and health-related activities and independent living for the elderly.[18] Similar ambitions are part of the Europe 2020 Strategy and the 2010 Employment Guidelines.[19] The Europe 2020 Strategy is generally aimed at smart growth, sustainable growth and inclusive growth, and also aims, inter alia, at meeting the challenge of promoting a healthy and active ageing population to achieve social cohesion and higher productivity. According to Employment Guidelines 7 and 8, Member States are urged to increase labour market participation of individuals 50 and older by introducing policies of active ageing. Employment Guideline 10 emphasises the importance of effective social security and integration policies to empower individuals and prevent social exclusion.

Many elderly people are marginalised in the European Union. For example, in 2008, 19 per cent of all persons in the European Union aged 65 and over lived at risk of poverty, with elderly women being particularly vulnerable. Today, an important general issue is the segmented labour market in Europe, and the increasing numbers of *vulnerable* workers, such as flexible workers, *older workers*, younger workers, disabled workers, and immigrants. Developments such as

[15] See European Commission, *Active Ageing Report 2012*.

[16] See ibid.

[17] See Decision 940/2011/EU of 14 September 2011 by the European Parliament and the Council, EUT L246.

[18] See European Commission, *Active Ageing Report* 2012 and Decision 940/2011/EU of 14 September 2011 by the European Parliament and the Council, EUT L246.

[19] See Communication from the Commission, 'Europe 2020: a strategy for smart, sustainable and inclusive growth', COM(2010)2020, Employment Guidelines 2010 and Council Decision of 26 April 2012 on guidelines for the employment policies of the Member States, which states that the 2010 Employment Guidelines are maintained for 2012.

the flexibilisation of work, changing demographics, and the current economic crisis, form an important background. The EU law flexicurity discourse is in itself a response to an increasingly segmented labour market. For some years, EU employment policy and labour law have been greatly influenced by a flexicurity discourse, inspired, for example, by the Dutch and Danish labour market strategies and experiences. The Council has adopted Common Principles of Flexicurity, which are handled within the context of the European Employment Strategy and the Europe 2020 Strategy. The aim of flexicurity is to reduce labour market segmentation, but also to increase economic growth and Europe's competitiveness in a global perspective. Flexicurity at EU level includes flexible and reliable contractual arrangements, effective active labour market policies, reliable and adaptable systems for lifelong learning, and modern social security systems.[20] The EU law flexicurity discourse has been criticised for focusing predominately on labour market flexibility and deregulation. Thus, flexicurity is partly about a deregulation of permanent employment, combined with the equal treatment of various forms of employment, as well as a 'tenure track approach' and a 'ladder' of legal protection. The EU law flexicurity discourse and its emphasis on flexible and contractual arrangements pose a risk of increasing the number and groups of vulnerable workers. Inclusion of these vulnerable workers, including older workers, is fundamental, not only to increase employment and growth, but also to achieve overall stability and legitimacy for the European Union.[21] Here, equal treatment and non-discrimination has proved to be an important legal technique. Consequently, the Part-Time Work Directive,[22] Fixed-Term Work Directive[23] and Temporary Agency Work Directive[24] all incorporate principles of non-discrimination and equal treatment.[25]

[20] See Communication from the Commission to the European Parliament, the Council, the European Economic and Social Committee and the Committee of the Regions, 'Towards common principles of flexicurity: more and better jobs through flexibility and security', COM(2007)359 final.

[21] Cf Fineman on the vulnerability theory, who argues that vulnerability is a basic human condition that characterises the relationship that must exist between the state and the individual—the state and the legal system must in some sense guarantee the equal opportunities arising from the principle that all human beings are equal, see M Fineman, 'The Vulnerable Subject and the Responsive State' (2010) 60 *Emory Law Journal* 251.

[22] Council Directive 97/81/EC of 15 December 1997 concerning the Framework Agreement on part-time working concluded by UNICE, CEEP and the ETUC.

[23] Council Directive 1999/70/EC of 28 June 1999 concerning the Framework Agreement on fixed-term work concluded by ETUC, UNICE and CEEP.

[24] Directive 2008/104/EC of the European Parliament and of the Council of 19 November 2008 on temporary agency work.

[25] The equal treatment and inclusion of vulnerable workers also relate to the boundaries and personal scope of labour law, the subject of an influential and lively scholarly debate in recent years, see, eg, A Supiot (general rapporteur), *Transformation of Labour and Future of Labour Law in Europe, Final Report* (Luxembourg, European Commission, 1999); G Davidov and B Langille (eds), *Boundaries and Frontiers of Labour Law* (Oxford, Hart Publishing, 2006); and M Freedland and N Kountouris, *The Legal Construction of Personal Work Relations* (Oxford, Oxford University Press, 2011). A related issue is the promotion of core labour rights, which in turn is linked to the fundamental work by the ILO in recent years on Core Labour Standards, a Decent Work Agenda and Fair Globalisation.

Recent Treaty developments confirm this increased emphasis on the legal situation and social protection of the elderly. The Lisbon Treaty of 2009 introduced a social market economy and solidarity between generations as main aims of the European Union. Thus, Article 3(3) TEU states that the:

> Union shall establish an internal market. It shall work for the sustainable development of Europe based on balanced economic growth and price stability, a highly competitive social market economy, aiming at full employment and social progress … It shall combat social exclusion and discrimination, and shall promote social justice and protection, equality between women and men, solidarity between generations.

According to Article 2 TEU, the European Union is founded, inter alia, on the values of respect for human dignity and human rights, and these values are said to be common to the Member States in a society in which, for example, pluralism, non-discrimination, tolerance and solidarity prevail. In defining and implementing its policies and activities, the European Union shall, according to Article 9 TFEU, 'take into account requirements linked to the promotion of a high level of employment, the guarantee of adequate social protection, the fight against social exclusion'; and according to Article 10 TFEU, 'aim to combat discrimination based on sex, racial or ethnic origin, religion or belief, disability, *age* [emphasis added] or sexual orientation'. Article 153 TFEU states that the European Union shall support and complement the activities of the Member States as regards, for example, improvement of the working environment to protect workers' health and safety, working conditions, social security and social protection of workers, the integration of persons excluded from the labour market, the combating of social exclusion, and the modernisation of social protection systems.[26]

B. Fundamental Rights of the Elderly in the European Union

At an early stage, respect for fundamental rights and freedoms became part of EU law.[27] The Court of Justice of the European Union (CJEU) jurisprudence on fundamental rights and general principles of EU law developed with reference, inter alia, to constitutional traditions common to the Member States and from international conventions, most especially the European Convention on Human Rights (ECHR). The Lisbon Treaty implies a new emphasis on fundamental rights. According to Article 6 TEU, the EU Charter of Fundamental Rights is made

[26] However, according to Art 153(4) TFEU the 'provisions adopted pursuant to this Article: shall not affect the right of Member States to define the fundamental principles of their social security systems and must not significantly affect the financial equilibrium thereof'.

[27] Due to the limited space here I refrain from discussing fundamental rights of the elderly established by way of ILO and UN Conventions, etc.

legally binding[28] and part of primary law.[29] Even before the entry into force of the Lisbon Treaty and the changed legal status of the EU Charter of Fundamental Rights, the CJEU (both in Opinions by Advocate-Generals and in judgments) has referred to the Charter and used it as a source of fundamental rights.[30] Another important legal implication of the Lisbon Treaty in the area of fundamental rights is the future accession of the European Union to the ECHR (Article 6 TEU).[31] One aspect of the future accession relates to the relationship between the CJEU and the European Court of Human Rights (ECtHR), and the way in which possible conflicts between case law from these courts need to be addressed.[32]

The EU Charter of Fundamental Rights encompasses rights, freedoms and principles, such as respect for private and family life, freedom of expression, freedom of assembly and of association, right to property, non-discrimination, right of collective bargaining and action, social security and social assistance and health care; the Charter thereby transcends the traditional division of rights into civil and political rights and social and economic rights, respectively (or first and second generation rights, respectively). Instead, the indivisibility of human and fundamental rights is emphasised.[33] At present, as the case law of the CJEU on the EU Charter of Fundamental Rights, and accompanying legal doctrine, develop, attention is drawn to the importance and interpretation of the Charter when it

[28] See, eg, S Fredman, 'Transformation or Dilution: Fundamental Rights in the EU Social Space' (2006) 12 *European Law Journal* 41; G de Búrca and B de Witte (eds), *Social Rights in Europe* (Oxford, Oxford University Press, 2005); TK Hervey and J Kenner (eds), *Economic and Social Rights under the EU Charter of Fundamental Rights: A Legal Perspective* (Oxford, Hart Publishing, 2003) and X Groussot *et al*, *The Scope of Application of Fundamental Rights on Member States' Action: In Search of Certainty in EU Adjudication*, Eric Stein Working Paper No 1/2011 (2011).

[29] The Amsterdam Treaty had also highlighted fundamental rights. The protection of fundamental social rights in working life was strengthened, for instance through express references in the Treaty to the European Social Charter from 1961 and the 1989 Community Charter of the Fundamental Social Rights of Workers, cf Art 136 EC. In December 2000 at the Nice summit, the Council, the European Commission and the European Parliament made a joint proclamation of the EU Charter of Fundamental Rights.

[30] See, eg, Case C-540/03 *European Parliament v Council* [2006] ECR I-05769.

[31] See, eg, P Syrpis, 'The Treaty of Lisbon: Much Ado … But About What?' (2008) 37 *Industrial Law Journal* 235.

[32] The ILO *acquis* and its role as regards labour law and social protection within EU law have also been discussed more intensely in recent years. ILO Conventions have been used as inspirational sources when developing EU fundamental rights and have served as interpretative guidance for the CJEU. This development relates also to the important work by the ILO in recent years on Core Labour Standards, a Decent Work Agenda and Fair Globalisation. This work by the ILO is endorsed by the European Commission, inter alia, through different policy statements and through their encouragement to all Member States to ratify all up-to-date ILO Conventions. However, it is worth noting that the ILO Core Labour Standards are not mentioned in Art 6 TEU or in the explanatory document related to the EU Charter of Fundamental Rights, reflecting an incongruent stance towards the ILO *acquis*, see P Herzfeld Olsson, 'The ILO Acquis and EU Labour Law' in M Rönnmar (ed), *Labour Law, Fundamental Rights and Social Europe*, Swedish Studies in European Law vol 4 (Oxford, Hart Publishing, 2011), with further references.

[33] Cf Mikkola, who applies the term 'social human rights': Mikkola, *Social Human Rights of Europe*, above n 14.

comes to issues of substantive fundamental rights and scope and (vertical and horizontal) application of the Charter.[34]

Article 51 of the EU Charter of Fundamental Rights states that the provisions of the Charter are 'addressed to the institutions, bodies, offices and agencies of the Union with due regard for the principle of subsidiarity and to the Member States only when they are implementing Union law'. The Charter does not extend the field of application of EU law beyond the powers of the Union or establish any new power or task for the European Union (Article 51(2)). According to Article 52 of the EU Charter of Fundamental Rights, a distinction is to be made between rights and principles when it comes to interpretation and application. According to Article 52(1), '[a]ny limitation on the exercise of the rights and freedoms recognised by this Charter must be provided for by law, and respect the essence of those rights and freedoms. Subject to the principle of proportionality limitation may be made only if they are necessary and genuinely meet objectives of general interest recognised by the Union or the need to protect the rights and freedoms of other'. And according to Article 52(5), '[t]he provisions of this Charter which contain principles may be implemented by legislative and executive acts taken by institutions, bodies, offices and agencies of the Union, and by acts of the Member States when they are implementing Union law, in the exercise of their respective powers. They shall be judicially cognisable only in the interpretation of such acts and in the ruling on their legality'. However, the CJEU has not always adhered strictly to this distinction.[35]

Article 25 of the EU Charter of Fundamental Rights establishes the rights of the elderly and states that '[t]he Union recognises and respects the rights of the elderly to lead a life of dignity and independence and to participate in social and cultural life'. The Explanations relating to the EU Charter of Fundamental Rights (which do not have the status of law, but are a valuable tool of interpretation, intended to clarify the provisions of the Charter) emphasise that this Article draws on Article 23 of the European Social Charter, and Articles 24 and 25 of the Community Charter of the Fundamental Social Rights of Workers. Participation in social and cultural life is also said to cover participation in political life.[36]

[34] See, eg, Groussot *et al*, *The Scope of Application of Fundamental Rights*, above n 28; C. Barnard, *EU Employment Law*, 4th edn (Oxford, Oxford University Press, 2012) 27; Case C-555/07 *Seda Kücükdeveci v Swedex GmBH & Co* [2010] ECR I-00365; Case C-282/10 *Maribel Dominguez v Centre informatique du Centre Quest Atlantique and Préfet de la region Centre* [2012] not yet reported, and Case C-108/10 *Ivana Scattolon v Ministero dell'Istruzione, dell'Università e della Ricerca* [2011] not yet reported.

[35] For example, in the *Viking* and *Laval* cases, when interpreting the right to collective action in Art 28 of the EU Charter of Fundamental Rights (which forms part of the Solidarity Chapter, encompassing *principles*), the CJEU said that 'the right to take collective action must therefore be recognised as a fundamental *right* [emphasis added] which forms an integral part of the general principles of Community law'.

[36] See *Explanations relating to the Charter of Fundamental Rights*, 2007/C303/02.

Article 23 of the European Social Charter, establishing rights of elderly persons to social protection, is more elaborate and states that:

> With a view to ensuring the effective exercise of the right of elderly persons to social protection, the Parties undertake to adopt or encourage, either directly or in co-operation with public or private organisations, appropriate measures designed in particular:
>
> to enable elderly persons to remain full members of society for as long as possible, by means of:
> a) adequate resources enabling them to lead a decent life and play an active part in public, social and cultural life;
> b) provision of information about services and facilities available for elderly persons and their opportunities to make use of them;
>
> to enable elderly persons to choose their life-style freely and to lead independent lives in their familiar surroundings for as long as they wish and are able, by means of:
> c) provision of housing suited to their needs and their state of health or of adequate support for adapting their housing;
> d) the health care and services necessitated by their state;
>
> to guarantee elderly persons living in institutions appropriate support, while respecting their privacy, and participation in decisions concerning living conditions in the institution.

Furthermore, Articles 24 and 25 of the Community Charter of the Fundamental Social Rights of Workers, gathered under a common headline of 'Elderly persons', state that: 'Every worker of the European Community must, at the time of retirement, be able to enjoy resources affording him or her a decent standard of living', and 'Every person who has reached retirement age but who is not entitled to a pension or who does not have other means of subsistence, must be entitled to sufficient resources and to medical and social assistance specifically suited to his needs'.

In addition to these specific fundamental rights of the elderly, the EU Charter of Fundamental Rights, the European Social Charter and the ECHR encompass other, general, fundamental rights, of great importance to the legal situation and social protection of the elderly, such as a right to social security and social assistance, a right to health care, a right to property (including accrued pension rights).[37] In the following, the fundamental right to non-discrimination and the fundamental right to protection against unjustified dismissal will be further discussed in relation to older workers, age discrimination and mandatory retirement and employment protection, respectively.

C. Age Discrimination, Mandatory Retirement and the Elderly

Non-discrimination law is a particularly prominent feature of law in the social dimension, and here we have seen important interventions and innovations by the

[37] See further Mikkola, *Social Human Rights of Europe*, above n 14, 526.

CJEU. The principle of non-discrimination on the basis of nationality is essential to European integration and the European Union, and EU regulation in the area of sex and gender discrimination is also comprehensive and has strong traditions. In 1999, through the Amsterdam Treaty, the European Union's competence in the non-discrimination field widened, and in 2000 two new Directives were adopted: the Race Directive[38] and the Framework Directive.[39] The latter covers discrimination on grounds of religion or belief, disability, *age* and sexual orientation. Article 21(1) of the EU Charter of Fundamental Rights, with an 'open list of discrimination grounds', states that '[a]ny discrimination based on any ground such as sex, race, colour, ethnic or social origin, genetic features, language, religion or belief, political or any other opinion, membership of a national minority, property, birth, disability, *age* [emphasis added] or sexual orientation shall be prohibited'. The purpose of the Framework Directive is to 'lay down a general framework for combating discrimination on the grounds of religion or belief, disability, age or sexual orientation as regards employment and occupation, with a view to putting into effect in the Member States the principle of equal treatment' (Article 1). The Framework Directive encompasses prohibitions on direct and indirect discrimination, harassment and instruction to discriminate, and provisions on positive action and active measures (Article 2).[40] According to Preamble, paragraph 25, 'prohibition of age discrimination is an essential part of meeting the aims set out in the Employment Guidelines and encouraging diversity in the workforce'. Ageism—beliefs, attitudes, norms and values to justify age-based prejudice, discrimination and subordination—has been put forward as the most important reason why older workers are prevented from working longer. Thus, the prohibition of (old-)age discrimination helps to reduce ageism, and is also an important part of the EU strategy for active ageing.[41] Age, as grounds for discrimination, and the legal regulation of age discrimination stand out in some respects. The protection against age discrimination covers all chronological ages; thus, both old people and young people are protected.[42] Discrimination on grounds of age (even

[38] Council Directive 2000/43/EC of 29 June 2000 implementing the principle of equal treatment between persons irrespective of racial or ethnic origin.

[39] Council Directive 2000/78/EC of 17 November 2000 establishing a general framework for equal treatment in employment and occupation.

[40] According to Framework Directive, Art 2(2)(a) 'direct discrimination shall be taken to occur where one person is treated less favourably than another is, has been or would be treated in a comparable situation, on any of the grounds referred to in Article 1', and according to Article 2(2)(b) 'indirect discrimination shall be taken to occur where an apparently neutral provision, criterion or practice would put persons having a particular religion or belief, a particular disability, a particular age, or a particular sexual orientation at a particular disadvantage compared with other persons unless: (i) that provision, criterion or practice is objectively justified by a legitimate aim and the means of achieving that aim are appropriate and necessary'.

[41] See Numhauser-Henning, *Labour Law in a Greying Labour Market*, above n 11.

[42] According to Art 3 of the Framework Directive, the Directive does not apply to payments of any kind made by state schemes or similar, including state social security or social protection schemes; and according to Art 4, the Member States may provide that the Directive, insofar as it relates to discrimination on the grounds of disability and age, shall not apply to the armed forces. In addition, the Framework Directive provides for further exceptions from the prohibition on age discrimination, such as Art 4 on occupational requirements, which states that '1. Notwithstanding Article 2(1) and (2),

direct discrimination) can be justified to a greater extent than discrimination on other grounds. This is related to the traditional role given to age in the labour market and in labour law. Article 6 of the Framework Directive on justification of differences of treatment on grounds of age states that:

> 1. Notwithstanding Article 2(2), Member States may provide that differences of treatment on grounds of age shall not constitute discrimination, if, within the context of national law, they are objectively and reasonably justified by a legitimate aim, including legitimate employment policy, labour market and vocational training objectives, and if the means of achieving that aim are appropriate and necessary.
>
> Such differences of treatment may include, among others:
>
> (a) the setting of special conditions on access to employment and vocational training, employment and occupation, including dismissal and remuneration conditions, for young people, older workers and persons with caring responsibilities in order to promote their vocational integration or ensure their protection;
>
> (b) the fixing of minimum conditions of age, professional experience or seniority in service for access to employment or to certain advantages linked to employment;
>
> (c) the fixing of a maximum age for recruitment which is based on the training requirements of the post in question or the need for a reasonable period of employment before retirement.[43]

An ageing population, and the resultant increasing costs for future pensions, have resulted in reforms of pension systems in many Member States in the European Union in recent years. Through the 'pension process', pension systems in the Member States are also being coordinated, with an aim to achieve sustainable pension systems. Pension systems in Europe generally started out as basic schemes, which in time have become income-related to a large degree. In recent years there has been a change towards pension systems based on longer earning periods or lifelong average earnings combined with a higher pensionable age or not fixed-pensionable age.[44] Statutory pension systems often also provide for rules on

Member States may provide that a difference of treatment which is based on a characteristic related to any of the grounds referred to in Article 1 shall not constitute discrimination where, by reason of the nature of the particular occupational activities concerned or of the context in which they are carried out, such a characteristic constitutes a genuine and determining occupational requirement, provided that the objective is legitimate and the requirement is proportionate'.

[43] In addition, Art 6(2) provides that 'Notwithstanding Article 2(2), Member States may provide that the fixing for occupational social security schemes of ages for admission or entitlement to retirement or invalidity benefits, including the fixing under those schemes of different ages for employees or groups or categories of employees, and the use, in the context of such schemes, of age criteria in actuarial calculations, does not constitute discrimination on the grounds of age, provided this does not result in discrimination on the grounds of sex'.

[44] The notion of pensionable age generally refers to the age for retirement benefits within the public pension scheme, see further Numhauser-Henning, *Labour Law in a Greying Labour Market*, above n 11; cf also D O'Dempsey and A Beale (supervised by M Freedland), *Age and Employment*, European Network of Legal Experts in the Non-discrimination Field (European Commission, 2011).

guaranteed basic levels.[45] Rules on mandatory retirement are found in some Member States of the European Union. Numhauser-Henning describes how rules on mandatory retirement form part of the prevailing 'pension norm', which implies that there is 'a right and a duty to retire at a certain age'.[46] This 'pension norm' and rules on mandatory retirement contravene the promotion of active ageing, and complicate the efforts to make older workers work to, and beyond, pensionable age. There is also a need to increase the pensionable age.

In recent years, since the Framework Directive was adopted, much of the case law from the CJEU in the non-discrimination field has evolved around age discrimination, and particularly old-age discrimination. The first case was *Mangold* in 2005, which created a lot of attention and controversy.[47] In this case the CJEU unexpectedly declared that not only was age discrimination covered by the Framework Directive, but that EU law encompassed an (independent) general principle of non-discrimination on grounds of age. This was reaffirmed in 2010 in *Kücükdevici* (despite academic debate 'post-*Mangold*' and strong national opposition and even constitutional challenge in Germany, where the case originated).[48]

Several of the cases have dealt with mandatory retirement rules, and whether or not these are age-discriminatory.[49] Mandatory retirement, in contrast with the general welfare question of pensionable age, is covered by the Framework Directive, and the CJEU basically deems rules on mandatory retirement to be age-discriminatory. The CJEU (for example, in *Palacios de la Villa*, *Age Concern England*, *Rosenbladt*, *Georgiev*, *Fuchs and Köhler* and *Hörnfeldt*) has in many cases accepted such mandatory retirement rules and found them justifiable. The Member States have been given a large margin of appreciation, and when applying Article 6 of the Framework Directive, the CJEU has found the differences of treatment on grounds of age to be objectively and reasonably justified by legitimate aims, such as intergenerational fairness in terms of access to employment, prevention of humiliating forms of termination of employment and a reasonable balance between labour market and budgetary concerns.[50] In addition, the means for achieving these aims have frequently been found appropriate and necessary. The CJEU has also, in some instances, taken into account whether or not the

[45] See Ann Numhauser-Henning, Chapter 2, Per Norberg, Chapter 9 and Thomas Erhag, Chapter 12 for initiated discussions on pension systems and their reform and normative development.

[46] Numhauser-Henning, *Labour Law in a Greying Labour Market*, above n 11, 13.

[47] See Case C-144/04 *Werner Mangold v Rudiger Helm* [2005] ECR I-9981.

[48] See Case C-555/07 *Seda Kücükdeveci v Swedex GmBH & Co* [2010] ECR I-00365.

[49] See Case 411/05 *Palacios de la Villa v Cortefiel Servicios SA* [2007] ECR I-8531; Case C-388/07 *Age Concern England v Secretary of State for Business, Enterprise and Regulatory Reform* [2009] ECR I-01569; Case C-45/09 *Rosenbladt v Oellerking Gebaudereinigungsges mbH* [2010] ECR I-09391; Cases C-250/09 and C-268/09 *Georgiev v Technicheski Universitet, Sofia* [2010] ECR I-11869; Cases C-159/10 and C-160/10 *Fuchs and Köhler v Land Hessen* [2011] ECR not yet reported; Case C-341/08 *Petersen v Beerufungsausschuss fur Zahnärzte fur den Bezirk Westfalen-Lippe* [2010] ECR I-00047; Case C-499/08 *Ole Andersen v Region Syddanmark* [2010] ECR I-09343; Case C- C-447/09 *Prigge v Deutsche Lufthansa AB* [2011] not yet reported; and Case C-141/11 *Hörnfeldt v Posten Meddelande AB* [2012] not yet reported.

[50] See Numhauser-Henning, *Labour Law in a Greying Labour Market*, above n 11, 9.

employee is receiving a reasonable compensation, by way of an old-age pension.[51] Numhauser-Henning argues, however, that '*Palacios de la Villa* seems to make the case that the legitimacy of compulsory retirement should be dependent on the existence of a "reasonable" pension for individuals. The later case *Rosenbladt*, however, demonstrates that there really is no room to scrutinise the actual level of pension benefits—the case concerned a part-time cleaner who received a fairly inadequate pension in absolute terms—but rather at system level. That the amount of retirement pension at stake cannot be taken into account at the individual level becomes even clearer in the *Hörnfeldt* case'.[52]

In Sweden, mandatory retirement is regulated through the '67 year-rule', in sections 32a and 33 of the Employment Protection Act (1982:80).[53] An employee has a right to stay in employment up until the age of 67, when the employer may terminate the employment relationship after one month's notice and without having to provide objective grounds for dismissal. If the employer does not make use of this possibility, the permanent employment relationship continues; however, it does so with limited employment protection (the employee has, for example, one month's notice, and is given no right of priority in accordance with seniority rules or rules on re-employment in redundancy situations).[54] This Swedish system has now, in the recent *Hörnfeldt*[55] judgment, been tried and found acceptable according to EU law. The CJEU found that the Swedish rule, which allows an employer to terminate an employee's employment contract on the sole ground that the employee has reached the age of 67, and which does not take account of the level of the retirement pension which the person concerned will receive, is permissible under Article 6(1) of the Framework Directive, since that measure is objectively and reasonably justified by a legitimate aim relating to employment policy and labour-market policy and constitutes an appropriate and necessary means by which to achieve that aim.

D. Employment Protection and the Elderly

In general, employment protection as such is only partly regulated at EU level (cf Article 153(1) TFEU). Article 30 of the EU Charter of Fundamental Rights states

[51] However, in *Ole Andersen* the CJEU found the Danish rule and practice not to pay severance payment to the employee in case of redundancy dismissal when the employee was eligible for old-age pension, to be disproportionate, unjustifiable and age discriminatory, since the rule did not take into consideration whether or not the employee in question actually received old-age pension or continued to work; see Case C-499/08 *Ole Andersen v Region Syddanmark* [2010] ECR I-09343.

[52] See Numhauser-Henning, *Labour Law in a Greying Labour Market*, above n 11, 9.

[53] Cf, however, the first Governmental Inquiry Report (SOU 2012:38) from the Swedish Pensionable Age Inquiry, which is likely to propose a rise in the pensionable age in Sweden. Cf also B Nyström, 'Active Ageing and Labour Law in Sweden' in F Hendrickx (ed), *Active Ageing and Labour Law. Contributions in Honour of Professor Roger Blanpain* (Antwerp, Intersentia, 2012).

[54] Coupled with this is also an unlimited access to fixed-term employment contracts after 67 years (see further below).

[55] Case C-141/11 *Hörnfeldt v Posten Meddelande AB* [2012] not yet reported.

that '[e]very worker has the right to protection against unjustified dismissal, in accordance with Union law and national laws and practices'. The Explanations relating to the EU Charter of Fundamental Rights clarify that Article 30 draws on Article 24 of the European Social Charter, which in turn states that all workers have the right not to have their employment terminated without valid reasons for such termination connected with their capacity or conduct, or based on the operational requirements of the undertaking, establishment or service, and that all workers whose employment is terminated without a valid reason have the right to adequate compensation or other appropriate relief.[56] In addition, the Fixed-Term Work Directive, the 'restructuring' Directives on Transfers of Undertakings[57] and Collective Dismissals,[58] and different Directives on non-discrimination regulate different aspects of employment protection. Thus, employment protection regulation may, and does, differ in the Member States.

In the wake of the economic crisis, especially the euro and sovereign debt crisis, we have seen far-reaching austerity measures and deregulatory labour law reforms in many Member States. These measures targeted employment protection regulation, but also collective bargaining and wage-setting and industrial relations processes. The Member States that were given 'bailout' packages by the 'Troika' were particularly affected. This development has been harshly criticised, inter alia, by the ILO and trade unions, for example, as regards the disrespect for fundamental rights and the strong move towards labour market flexibilisation. Furthermore, there are signs that some governments may be using the economic crisis as a 'cover' for introducing further deregulation.[59] Thus, deregulatory reforms affecting employment protection regulation can now be found in countries such as Greece, Portugal, Spain, and Italy—but also in countries such as the United Kingdom, Hungary and Poland.[60] In addition, as was mentioned above, the EU law flexicurity discourse is partly about a deregulation of permanent employment,

[56] Cf *Explanations relating to the Charter of Fundamental Rights*, 2007/C303/02. Note should also be taken of ILO Convention 158 on Termination on Employment (1982).

[57] Council Directive 2001/23/EC of 12 March 2001 on the approximation of the laws of the Member States relating to the safeguarding of employees' rights in the event of transfers of undertakings, businesses or parts of undertakings or businesses.

[58] Council Directive 98/59/EC of 20 July 1998 on the approximation of the laws of the Member States relating to collective redundancies.

[59] See, eg, C Barnard, 'The Financial Crisis and the Euro Plus Pact: a Labour Lawyer's Perspective' (2012) 41 *Industrial Law Journal* 98; S Clauwaert and I Schömann, *The Crisis and National Labour Law Reforms: a Mapping Exercise*, ETUI Working Paper 2012:04 (Brussels, ETUI, 2012); S Laulom et al, *How has the Crisis Affected Social Legislation in Europe?*, ETUI Policy Brief 2/2012 (Brussels, ETUI, 2012); and ILO, *Report on the High Level Mission to Greece, Athens, 19–23 September 2011* (Geneva, 2011).

[60] See M Rönnmar and A Numhauser-Henning, 'Swedish Employment Protection in Times of Flexicurity Policies and Economic Crisis' (2012) 28 *International Journal of Comparative Labour Law and Industrial Relations* 443 for an analysis of Swedish employment protection regulation in light of the EU law flexicurity discourse, and recent developments in legislation, collective bargaining and case law.

combined with the equal treatment of various forms of employment, as well as a 'tenure track approach' and a 'ladder' of legal protection.

The vulnerability of older workers has characterised the formation of employment protection regulation in many Member States. In Sweden, for example, an important background to the first Employment Protection Act from 1974 was the need for social protection of especially vulnerable workers due to old age or sickness, and the need to counteract a segmented labour market, with a division between young and well-educated employees, on the one hand, and old, disabled and less educated employees, on the other.[61] Thus, employment protection regulation may provide for various kinds of special protection for older workers. A general rule, as in Sweden, that sickness or old age does not constitute objective grounds for dismissal is, of course, very important as a starting point. The employer in Sweden has extensive obligations to rehabilitate the employee and to adjust the working environment and the job duties or tasks. An employee can be dismissed only after such measures have been taken, and the employee can no longer perform work of any importance for the employer. The extent to which sickness or reduced working capacity constitutes objective grounds for dismissal differs in the Member States.[62]

In addition, seniority rules offer protection for older workers in redundancy situations and make them less vulnerable. In Sweden, the statutory seniority rules imply that the priority and selection of employees is to be made according to the last in first out principle, ie according to each employee's total period of employment with the employer (and in the event of equal periods of employment giving priority to senior age (section 22 of the Employment Protection Act (1982:80)). In principle, the order of dismissals encompasses all employees of the same production unit and covered by the same collective agreement (redundancy unit). However, the seniority rules are 'semi-compelling' and the employer and the trade union may, in virtually all respects, deviate from the statutory rules when determining the order of dismissals. The principal restriction is that the decided order of dismissals must not go against so-called good labour market practice,[63] and be blatantly discriminatory or offensive.[64] Seniority principles can also be influential when it comes to wage-setting and working conditions, such as periods of notice and length of annual leave.

[61] See Governmental Bill prop. 1973:129, 126 and Nyström, 'Active Ageing and Labour Law in Sweden', above n 53.

[62] Cf Numhauser-Henning, *Labour Law in a Greying Labour Market*, above n 11.

[63] See Labour Court judgments AD 1983:107, AD 1996:114 and AD 2002:37. An employer with at most 10 employees may, before the order of dismissals is determined, exempt at most two employees who in the opinion of the employer are of particular importance for the future activities: Employment Protection Act (1982:80), s 22(2). See Government Bill Prop. 1999/2000:144 and Labour Court judgment AD 2005:32.

[64] Important to note, however, is that recent and controversial case law (Labour Court judgments AD 2009:50 and AD 2011:30) shows that an employer has considerable opportunities to reorganise and set aside the seniority rules, and thereby undermine the employment protection of older workers. See further Rönnmar and Numhauser-Henning, 'Swedish Employment Protection', above n 60.

The Swedish seniority rules, and the last in first out principle, are potentially indirectly age-discriminatory (with a directly age-discriminatory element, in the way in which the employee's age is decisive in situations when the period of employment of two or several employees is the same).[65] Perhaps surprisingly, the age-discriminatory character of the rules has not been the subject of much discussion in Sweden. Instead the discussion, which at times has been, and today is, a lively one, has revolved around the need for protection against arbitrary dismissals and the need for increased labour market flexibilisation and a right for the employer to choose which employees to maintain in a redundancy situation, based on the needs of the business and the qualifications of the employee. The debate regarding the seniority rules has also touched upon the current problem of high youth unemployment in Sweden, and the disputed links between seniority rules and the last in first out principle and youth unemployment. There are, however, signs that seniority rules such as these may be found acceptable according to EU law.[66]

If the employee is actually dismissed, this employee has a priority right to re-employment, a rule that facilitates access to employment for older workers. Any employment opening within nine months from the expiry of the former employment should be offered to employees dismissed by redundancy, on the condition that the employees are sufficiently qualified and have been employed in total for more than 12 months during the last three years with the employer (section 25 of the Employment Protection Act (1982:80)).[67] The order of

[65] Some directly age discriminatory elements, for example, providing extra protection for employees above the age of 45, were removed from the Employment Protection Act in 2007.

[66] The Advocate-General argued in *Kücückdevici* that 'The purpose of the extended period of notice is clearly to protect workers whose capacity to adapt, and the possibility of their being retrained, was regarded by the German legislature as reduced when they have been employed for a long time in an undertaking. If an employer decides to dismiss a worker who has been in his undertaking for a long time, an extended period of notice certainly facilitates the movement of that worker to a new employment situation, in particular, the search for a new job. That strengthened protection of dismissed workers on the basis of the time they have spent in the undertaking can, to my mind, be regarded as seeking to achieve an employment policy and labour market objective within the meaning of Article 6(1) of Directive 2000/78'; Opinion of Advocate-General Bot in Case C-555/078 *Seda Kücükdeveci v Swedex GmBH & Co KG*, para 43, C-555/078 *Seda Kücükdeveci v Swedex GmBH & Co KG* [2010] ECR I-00365. Similarly, O'Conneide argues that 'it is also worth noting that many other relevant factors in redundancy decision-making may have an indirectly discriminatory effect … Granting older workers greater protection during redundancies can be seen as a positive action strategy, especially in particular member states where specific historical and economic factors may cause older workers may [sic] be in a much more vulnerable position than younger workers. Therefore, provided it is proportional, such preferential treatment might be treated as reasonably justified. Article 6(1)(a) again supports this interpretation, with its reference to "dismissal and remuneration conditions" as an example of appropriate measures to protect older workers. However, shifting social conditions, similar to those highlighted in the UK consultation paper, may call into question the proportionality of such measures and leave them over time more exposed to legal challenges', see C O'Conneide, *Age Discrimination and European Law* (European Commission, 2005) 40. See also A Numhauser-Henning, 'Åldersdiskriminering och några anställningsskyddsrelaterade frågor' in K Ahlberg (ed), *Vänbok till Ronnie Eklund* (Uppsala, Iustus, 2010) 469 ff and Governmental Bill Prop. 2007/08:95, 183.

[67] See Numhauser-Henning, *Labour Law in a Greying Labour Market*, above n 11, and Rönnmar and Numhauser-Henning, 'Swedish Employment Protection', above n 60. On the issue of the potentially age-discriminatory character of these rules, see above in relation to the seniority rules.

employees being offered employment is decided in accordance with the last in first out principle.[68]

There is also regulation providing for a broader scope for fixed-term work (or other forms of flexible work) for older workers (older workers above a certain age or older workers after mandatory retirement or 'normal' pensionable age). Such regulation aims at facilitating access to employment for older workers and at prolonging working life. In Sweden, short fixed-term employment was 'normalised' in a 2007 reform through the introduction of general fixed-term employment. The employer is free to enter into general fixed-term employment contracts, and there is no requirement for objective reasons. However, when an employee has been employed (on a general fixed-term employment or as a temporary substitute) by one employer for a total of two years during the last five years, the contract is automatically converted into an indefinite permanent employment contract (section 5(2) of the Employment Protection Act (1982:80)). A long 'catalogue' of fixed-term contracts has been replaced by general fixed-term employment, supplemented only by temporary substitute employment, seasonal employment, fixed-term contracts for employees above the age of 67 years, and probationary employment.[69] When an employee turns 67, fixed-term contracts may be freely entered into.[70] This rule can also be challenged as potentially age-discriminatory, and the question is here if the CJEU would find arguments linked to intergenerational fairness and the need to keep older workers in work longer to be legitimate aims, and the means of achieving those aims appropriate and necessary according to Article 6(1) of the Framework Directive.

IV. CONCLUDING REMARKS

Recent normative developments, and movements in the normative field, in the social dimension of the European Union have frequently been moves away

[68] Numhauser-Henning depicts how other rules linked to employment protection, such as occupational pension schemes, collectively bargained pre-retirement schemes and seniority wage-setting practices, may well work to the detriment of active ageing; see Numhauser-Henning, *Labour Law in a Greying Labour Market*, above n 11. Cf similarly Nyström, 'Active Ageing and Labour Law in Sweden', above n 53.

[69] For further details and a more in-depth analysis of the regulation of fixed-term work, see M Rönnmar, 'Labour Policy on Fixed-Term Work: Sweden' in T Araki and H Nakakubo (guest eds), R Blanpain (ed), *Bulletin of Comparative Labour Relations* (Alphen aan den Rijn, Kluwer Law International, 2010) 157–73. See also Governmental Bill Prop. 2006/07:111.

[70] The 2007 reform was challenged by Swedish trade unions that made a complaint to the European Commission, which in turn in a formal notification declared that Sweden had failed to correctly implement the Fixed-Term Work Directive and did not adequately prohibit the abuse of successive fixed-term employment contracts. The Government initially opposed the view of the Commission, but subsequently put forward two different reform proposals in order to clarify and strengthen the prohibition of abuse of successive fixed-term employment contracts and to bring Swedish law more in line with the Fixed-Term Work Directive and EU law. The first proposal was much criticised and therefore set aside, the second one has been sent out for remit, but no Governmental Bill has been presented.

from Protection of the Established Position and towards the Market-Functional pattern.[71] This normative development is discernible also with regard to the legal situation and social protection of the elderly. However, the normative 'picture' is complex. The elderly are also viewed as a vulnerable and marginalised group in need of special social protection—an expression of social justice and Just Distribution. At the same time, affording special social protection to the elderly (merely) on grounds of their achieved chronological age is an expression of Protection of Established Position.

An increased emphasis on fundamental rights in general, and fundamental rights of the elderly in particular, within the European Union is an expression of social justice and solidarity, and thus a reflection of the normative pattern Just Distribution. The protection offered by fundamental rights is often universal, unconditional and not related to a previously established position—apart from that as a human being. Generally, some of the fundamental rights of the elderly, such as the right to be included in social life, to be provided with adequate housing and to receive health care and other forms of care, have a more distinct redistributive element, and relate even more clearly to Just Distribution and more specifically to the normative pattern of Basic Subsistence.[72] Of relevance for a discussion on the social protection of the elderly, is Christensen's argument that fundamental rights (human rights) and social security are two different normative traditions. According to Christensen, the 'core of the human rights tradition is the individual and especially her freedom, dignity and integrity. The core of the social security tradition is the individual's economic and material security'.[73] Equality is a basic value in both traditions, however, and one aim of modern social security systems was to liberate the elderly and the disabled from the humiliating aspects of the poor law, and to protect the dignity and integrity of the individual. It is important to remember, though, that in social security systems, not all human beings are treated alike.[74]

Sustainable pension systems are crucial not only for the future social protection of the elderly as individuals, but also for economic and societal stability and the political legitimacy of the European Union as a whole. Pension systems in Europe started out as basic schemes and expressions of solidarity and Just Distribution. In time, they have become income-related to a large degree, and built on Protection of Established Position. This is true for Sweden, where the basic principle of the social security system is the principle of replacement of lost earnings, an expression of Protection of Established Position.[75] In Sweden, however, the new

[71] Cf Ann Numhauser-Henning and Mia Rönnmar, Introduction, Chapter 1.

[72] Cf Christensen, 'Normativa grundmönster i socialrätten', above n 1.

[73] A Christensen, *Human Rights and Social Security in Sweden*, Swedish National Report to the 15th World Congress of the International Society of Labour Law and Social Security, Buenos Aires, 1997, Norma 1997:1 (Lund, 1997) 1 ff.

[74] Ibid 2.

[75] However, the requirements on how firmly the economic position must be established before an earnings-related benefit is granted vary among the different parts of the social security system, see Christensen, 'Protection of the Established Position', above n 2.

old-age pension system, introduced in the late 1990s, represents a movement away from Protection of Established Position and the principle of replacement of lost earnings and towards another normative pattern, the Principle of Accumulated Entitlement, which is much closer to the principle of private insurance and the Market-Functional pattern.[76] Just Distribution in the new old-age pension system is still present as guarantee pension.[77] Numhauser-Henning emphasises that the development towards a rapidly ageing population in the European Union requires major transfers and redistribution within the pension systems, at societal level and 'horizontally between groups of pensioners of the same generation, and between generations', also a manifestation of the normative pattern of Just Distribution.[78] However, particularly forceful accrued pension rights, 'earned' over time in working life, have been afforded fundamental rights protection, inter alia, by the ECtHR in relation to the ECHR, and national courts in different Member States by way of property rights and principles of legitimate expectations—an expression of Protection of Established Position.[79] The far-reaching pension reforms in the Member States in the wake of the economic crisis are likely to be legally challenged in similar ways.

The right not to be discriminated against is a fundamental right. Non-discrimination law, and the prohibition of (old-)age discrimination, is also an important part of the EU strategy for active ageing, and aims at the inclusion and advantage of the elderly as a vulnerable group. In non-discrimination law the normative patterns of Equal Treatment, close to the Market-Functional pattern, and Belonging, interact and influence the legal regulation. At the same time, the fact that mandatory retirement is seen in principle as an age-discriminatory practice, makes Equal Treatment in this case 'collaborate' with the Protection of Established Position of the older workers. Article 6 of the Framework Directive offers rather extensive possibilities to justify differences of treatment on grounds of age, and the case law of the CJEU (with the *Hörnfeldt* case related to the Swedish situation as one of its most recent examples) has to a large extent found mandatory retirement regulation justifiable with reference to employment policy and labour market objectives; these objectives include practices such as promotion of employment of younger workers and a fair distribution of work between generations and avoidance of a practice where the exit from working life, as a general rule, is based on the 'disqualification' of the older worker. These arguments

[76] See Christensen, 'Protection of the Established Position', above n 2, 308 ff; Christensen, 'Normativa grundmönster i socialrätten', above n 1; and A Christensen, 'Normativa grundmönster i pensionssystemen' in C Henrichsen *et al* (eds), *Lovens Liv. Till Jørgen Dalberg-Larsen på 60-årsdagen 19. September 2000* (København, Jurist- og Økonomforbundets forlag, 2000).

[77] Compare Per Norberg, Chapter 9 and Thomas Erhag, Chapter 12.

[78] See Ann Numhauser-Henning, Chapter 2.

[79] See, eg, N Eliasson, *Protection of Accrued Pension Rights: an Inquiry into Reforms of Statutory and Occupational Pension Schemes in a German, Norwegian and Swedish Context* (Lund, Juristförlaget i Lund, 2001); N Eliasson, 'Towards a New Property?' (2002) 4 *European Journal of Social Security* 55. Cf also Ann Numhauser-Henning, Chapter 2.

are linked to notions of intergenerational solidarity, fairness and social justice, and are expressions of the normative pattern of Just Distribution. However, some of these arguments can also be said to represent the Market-Functional pattern, such as the need for an appropriate and balanced age composition of the workforce at the workplace. At present, European labour markets and societies are (not least considering the economic crisis and its implications) marked by a conflict between two different economic and societal needs, to make the elderly work longer and to get young people into work. This is so despite the fact that existing research shows no clear link between retiring older workers and creating employment for younger workers.[80]

Employment protection is a clear expression of Protection of Established Position. The vulnerability of older workers, and their need for special protection, have characterised the formation of employment protection regulation in many Member States. In relation to older workers, Protection of Established Position is reflected in basic principles, for example that sickness or old age does not constitute objective grounds for dismissal, and in the application of seniority rules in the case of redundancy dismissals (both principles characteristic of Swedish employment protection regulation). The seniority rules imply that the employee gradually builds up an increasingly secure (Established) Position at the workplace.[81] Seniority principles can also be influential when it comes to wage-setting and working conditions, such as periods of notice and length of annual leave. In addition, nowadays when the EU law flexicurity discourse is influential, Numhauser-Henning argues that 'the Protection of Established Position also finds a new expression in so-called *employability rights*'.[82] But, following the economic crisis, and as employment protection is increasingly deregulated in the Member States of the European Union, older workers run a special risk.

Regulation providing for a wider scope for fixed-term work (or other forms of flexible work) for the elderly, as in older workers above a certain age or older workers after mandatory retirement or 'normal' pensionable age, is an expression of both managerial prerogative and the Market-Functional pattern, and an expression of active ageing and as such a continued (though clearly weakened) Protection of Established Position. Here, non-discrimination law and the prohibition of age discrimination form a restriction, but differences of treatment on grounds of age can thus be found not to constitute discrimination if they are objectively and reasonably justified by a legitimate aim (including legitimate employment policy, labour market and vocational training objectives, and if the means of achieving that aim are appropriate and necessary). Similarly,

[80] See Numhauser-Henning, *Labour Law in a Greying Labour Market*, above n 11, with further references.

[81] Numhauser-Henning argues that it is also possible to view seniority rules as an expression of Just Distribution, in the form of a variety of the queuing principle, see Ann Numhauser-Henning, Chapter 2.

[82] See Ann Numhauser-Henning, Chapter 2.

seniority rules in redundancy situations (and seniority principles when it comes to wage-setting and working conditions) can also be challenged by the prohibition on age discrimination. (At the same time, an employment protection regulation like the Swedish one also reveals a great respect for the managerial prerogative, and influence of the Market-Functional pattern, in the way that redundancy is decided by the employer, and redundancy per se always constitutes objective grounds for dismissal.)[83]

If the scope for mandatory retirement were limited in the future, for example, through a stricter interpretation by the CJEU of Article 6 of the Framework Directive, or if economic and societal necessity made it more urgent for the elderly to continue to work longer in order to receive decent pensions, employment protection would have to be reconstructed.[84] There would be an added need for employment protection at an advanced age, thus doing away with mandatory retirement.

The achievement of equal treatment and inclusion of vulnerable workers, such as the elderly, of course implies increased protection for these workers, but also entails reforms and deregulation of labour law, and the risk of weakening and 'hollowing out' employment protection and employment rights *for all*. Numhauser-Henning has held that an abolition of mandatory retirement risks weakening employment protection before actual retirement age is reached. She argues that '[i]f retirement practices are to become more diffuse or individualised, there is no possibility to uphold a practice such as that in Sweden where, as a general rule, "normal ageing" does not compensate for just-cause dismissal, and incentives for age management may weaken. There may thus be a risk that setting no upper limit to employment will cause a decrease in the number of people aged 55+ who work, hence undermining both employment protection from within and "good quality work"'.[85]

[83] Cf Christensen, 'Protection of the Established Position', above n 2 305 ff.
[84] See Numhauser-Henning, *Labour Law in a Greying Labour Market*, above n 11.
[85] Ibid 16.

7

Participation and Flexibility for All? A Study of Modern Family Structures and Children's Rights

TITTI MATTSSON

I. INTRODUCTION

THE FAMILY IS considered to be the basic foundation for the child all over the world. According to the Preamble of the United Nations Convention on the Rights of the Child (CRC), the family is 'the fundamental group of society and the natural environment for the growth and well-being of all its members and particularly children'. The family is supposed to be the adequate environment for children as well as for adults, and is even pronounced to be a human right in several international documents. For example, Article 8 in the European Convention on Human Rights (ECHR), as well as Article 7 in the Charter of Fundamental Rights of the European Union, state a right to respect for the family life of individuals.[1]

The reliance on the family in promoting the welfare of children also dominates the agenda of national family law. This legislation mainly focuses on creating certain legal obligations between individuals with biological or partnership bonds within the family, such as custodianship and guardianship of the children of biological parents. The rest of the form and management of the family unit are left to be decided and practised within the private sphere of each family. It is generally assumed in law that the child's rights will be continuously promoted in the family. In this chapter, two current societal developments that appear relevant to this framework for family life are highlighted and discussed. One of these developments involves changing family structures, creating 'new' kinds of families and different

[1] Article 8 ECHR states: '1. Everyone has the right to respect for private and family life, his home and his correspondence. 2. There shall be no interference by a public authority with the exercise of this right except such as is in accordance with the law and is necessary in a democratic society in the interests of national security, public safety or the economic well-being of the country, for the prevention of disorder or crime, for the protection of health or morals, or for the protection of the rights and freedoms of others'.

reconstructions during people's lives. The other is the legal implementation of a rights-based approach to children in many areas of the law.

According to modern sociology research, the characteristics of the modern family unit are the individual and the procedural traits of the family.[2] The family is focused on the individuals in the family and how family life is constructed, and reconstructed, according to the needs of the individuals. These needs are continuously formed and shaped through negotiations between the individuals in the family.[3] How then do these characteristics affect the position of the child in the family? The aim here is to analyse this question with the help of the normative pattern of Protection of Established Position, in Anna Christensen's theory of law as normative patterns in a normative field.[4] This pattern, which forms asymmetric relations between those who have some sort of power and those who have not, may serve as a fitting point of departure for investigating the position of the child in the family. First, the two developments briefly mentioned above will be described in more detail. This will be followed by a discussion of the problems that may arise for children's rights policy due to the pattern of Protection of Established Position. Finally, there will be some remarks made on the importance of an active child participatory policy in family law to balance the strong impact of this pattern. The third Protocol to the CRC is put forward as a promising example of such development.

II. CHANGING FORMS AND FUNCTIONS OF THE FAMILY

A. Relationship between Family and Social Change

The family has been portrayed in different forms and functions in research over the last century. During the first half of the twentieth century, the family's stabilising role in society was in focus. At the time, the nuclear family seemed to be a good adjustment to the new industrialised society.[5] This family form was not dependent on other family bonds, and it was flexible as a work force, both in economic and geographical terms. Without strong family connections, it was possible to make geographical changes, as well as changes in social status. Later on, this patriotic family structure came to be questioned. Family research turned away, in much, from the traditional idea of the family's stabilising role in society, and, instead focused issues relating to the changing forms and functions of the family.[6] More and more, family research came to include concepts such as equality of the sexes, equality of opportunity and equal treatment. The nuclear family was questioned as the 'perfect' family form, and instead sometimes criticised as functioning

[2] For a discussion on this research, see below.

[3] U Beck and E Beck-Gernsheim, *The Normal Chaos of Love* (Cambridge, Polity Press, 1995).

[4] See Ann Numhauser-Henning, Chapter 2.

[5] C Roman, 'Sociologiska perspektiv på "familjen"' in M Bäck-Wiklund and T Johansson (eds), *Nätverksfamiljen* (Stockholm, Natur och Kultur, 2003) 44.

[6] T Johansson, *Familjeliv* (Stockholm, Liber, 2009) 26.

as an arena for injustice and imbalance in power between the partners.[7] Later on, the position of the child in the family and society's role (school, pre-school, social services) became integrated in the study of the family. The family has become increasingly pluralistic and diversified over time, and research has followed this development. Nowadays, family research paints many different pictures of family and family life. New concepts in research reflect the development towards pluralistic family life, such as network families, four-leaf clover families, transnational families and serial families.

Many researchers today would argue that the forms and functions of the family are related to societal and historical changes, and are therefore not static. In an article describing the normative pattern of Protection of Established Position from 1996, Christensen highlights the changing forms and functions of the family in modern society, where she is particularly interested in these changes as a consequence of the changing structures in the labour market.[8] She portrays how the function of the family changed and became weaker when society developed from an agricultural to an industrialised and urban society. This change made the family weaker as a social unit, and it was also the starting point for the development of new and changing forms of the family. As a result of this development, legislative changes opened up for increased individualisation, new family forms, and additional possibilities for changing the individual's family membership. For example, divorce became easier to obtain and the economic burdens for the ex-wife or ex-husband diminished. Later on, further legislative changes in the direction of increased individualisation have taken place, regarding, for example, cohabitation and same-sex partnerships in different forms.

Christensen's conclusion on the relevance of societal changes to changes in the family is relevant to understanding the changing role of the family today. Modern family issues in legislation and in the media (gender-neutral relations, diminishing birth rates, children through *in vitro* fertilisation or surrogacy, children's competence and parental relations to children, etc) all reflect this changing focus towards issues concerning the forms and functions of families. We live in a time when our understanding of the family as a stable core construction in our lives is being challenged. The so-called nuclear family in its traditional form, with stable family members for as long as they live, is no longer the only formation (or even the most frequent one) for adults and children in many countries. For example, in Sweden, more than one-third of the population lives in other family forms than the typical nuclear family.[9] Additionally, a family construction may well be remodelled one or even several times during a person's lifetime, and in new and different constellations. For a child, his or her family may therefore consist of a mixture of biological,

[7] Roman, 'Sociologiska perspektiv på "familjen"', above n 5, 44, with further reference to C. Roman, *Familjen I det moderna. Sociologiska sanningar och feministisk kritik* (Stockholm, Liber, 2004).

[8] A Christensen, 'Skydd för etablerad position—ett normativt grundmönster' (1996) 4 *Tidskrift for Rettsvitenskap* 519.

[9] T Johansson, *Familjeliv*, above n 6, 87.

legal and social family members during the child's upbringing. Furthermore, the child may be part of more than one household during childhood.

B. Case Law at the European Court of Human Rights

Sweden is one of the countries at the fore, in both practical and legal terms, of adjusting to new family forms. However, in the rest of Europe too, a diversity of families exists and develops. This development sometimes requires changes to existing domestic legislation, and sometimes completely new legislation. The European courts seem to be gradually adjusting to the development of new family forms, for example, by stating that the constitutional principles of equality and non-discrimination should wield influence in matters concerning alternative family structures. This development of adapting court rulings to an acceptance of new family forms can, for example, be seen in two cases from the European Court of Human Rights (ECtHR) from 2010, *Schalk and Kopf v Austria* and *JS v Austria*, where the Court concluded that the right to family in Article 8 ECHR may comprise a same-sex partner relationship.[10] In the first case, the applicants, two men, complained about the Austrian authorities' refusal to allow them to enter into a contract of marriage, referring to Article 12 (the right to marry and build a family). Also, referring to Articles 14 and 8, they complained that they were discriminated against because of their sexual orientation, in that they were not allowed the right to marry. The ECtHR concluded that there was no consensus regarding same-sex marriage in Europe. Furthermore, the Court noted that the Article 12 references 'men and women'. As all other substantive Articles of the Convention grant rights to 'everyone', the wording in Article 12 must be deliberate. The ECtHR thus concluded that the Convention only granted right to marry for opposite-sex couples. The decision on whether or not to allow same-sex marriages was seen as being within the countries' margin of appreciation. According to the Court, the Member States were the best placed to decide on this issue, since marriage is deeply rooted in society and differs greatly from one society to another. In conclusion, the ECtHR found that Article 12 did not impose an obligation on Austria to grant a same-sex couple access to marriage, and that there had been no violation ofArticle 12. The Court also found (by four votes to three) that there had been no violation of Article 14 in conjunction with Article 8. However, the ECtHR also concluded that the relationship of the applicants, a cohabiting same-sex couple living in a stable partnership, also fell within the notion of family life in Article 8, as does

[10] *Schalk and Kopf v Austria* (Application no 30141/04), Judgment of 24 June 2010; and *PB and JS v Austria* (Application no 18984/02), Judgment of 22 July 2010. For further reading, see L Hodson, 'A Marriage by Any Other Name? *Schalk and Kopf v Austria*' (2011) 1 *Human Rights Law Review* 171; C Sörgjerd, *Reconstructing Marriage in a Changing Legal and Societal Landscape: Challenges of New Cohabitation Models in Sweden* (Uppsala, Uppsala University Press, 2011); and P De Cruz, *Family Law, Sex and Society: A Comparative Study of Family Law* (London, Routledge, 2010).

the relationship between a couple of different sexes in the same situation. The argument was that there had been a rapid evolution of social attitudes towards same-sex couples in many Member States, and that a considerable number of states had recognised them in legislation. It was assumed that same-sex couples were in a similar situation as regards their need for legal recognition of their relationship. However, because the Convention is to be read as a whole, thus including the fact that Article 12 did not impose an obligation on Austria to grant same-sex couples access to marriage, the Court concluded that there was no violation of Articles 14 and 8.

In the second case, *JS v Austria*, the ECtHR ruled that Austria had violated Article 14 (prohibition of discrimination) in conjunction with Article 8 when a certain health and accident insurance policy for civil servants was extended, but only to cohabiting partners of the opposite sex. In addition, even after legislative changes in 2006, when Austria amended its Insurance Act, so that same-sex couples could qualify for the extension of one partner's insurance to the other partner only if they were raising children together, the Court unanimously found that there had still been a breach of Articles 14 and 8, because same-sex partners could only partially benefit from the insurance cover. Referring to earlier court decisions, the Court emphasised that a difference in treatment according to Article 14 is discriminatory if it has no objective or reasonable justification; that is, if it does not pursue a legitimate aim or if there is no reasonable relationship of proportionality between the means employed and the aim intended to be realised. Just as for differences based on gender, differences based on sexual orientation require particularly serious reasons by way of justification. In this case, the difference in treatment had no such objective and reasonable justification.

Other recent cases that deal with issues of the right to family life concern the use of artificial insemination in order to have children. One such case is *Dickson v United Kingdom* from 2007, where a prisoner's wife was denied access to artificial insemination.[11] Here, the ECtHR ruled in favour of the right to create a family by artificial insemination. According to the Court, the refusal of the United Kingdom to exercise its discretion in allowing a prisoner to have facilities for artificial insemination breached the prisoner's and his wife's rights under Article 8 of the ECHR. In 1994, a man was convicted of murder and sentenced to life imprisonment with a tariff of 15 years. In 1999, he met a woman, while she too was imprisoned, and who was later released. Two years later, the couple married. They wished to have a child and therefore applied for facilities for artificial insemination. They argued that due to the one partner's earliest release date and the second partner's age, it was unlikely that they would be able to have a child together without the use of artificial insemination facilities. However, the Secretary of State refused their application. The couple complained about this refusal, arguing that that it breached their right to respect for private and family life guaranteed by Article 8.

[11] *Dickson v United Kingdom* (Application no. 44362/04), Judgment of 4 December 2007.

The ECtHR based its decision on the dispute between the state and the couple on the breadth of the margin of appreciation to be accorded to the authorities. The Court discussed how the breadth of the country's margin of appreciation varies, and depends on the nature of the activities restricted and the aims pursued by the restrictions. On the one hand, in a situation where an important circumstance of a person's identity is at stake (for example, in the form of the choice to become a genetic parent) the margin of appreciation accorded to the state ought to be restricted. On the other hand, when there is no consensus within the state as to the importance of the interest at stake, or as to how best to protect it, the margin will be wider. Referring to earlier court cases, the Court argued that there will also usually be a wide margin accorded if the state is required to strike a balance between competing private and public interests, or Convention rights. In this case, artificial insemination remained the only realistic hope of the couple for having a child together, given the second applicant's age and the first applicant's release date. The Court considered it evident that the matter was of vital importance to the couple. Based on this, the ECtHR found that the absence of an assessment as regards a matter of significant importance for the applicants must be seen as falling *outside* an acceptable margin of appreciation. A fair balance was not struck between the competing public and private interests involved. Therefore, there had been a violation of Article 8 of the ECHR.

The question of whether or not the possibility to build a family through *in vitro* fertilisation as a right under Article 8 is a recent example of changing family structures. There is a development in legislation within Europe towards allowing medically induced conception. According to a ruling by the ECtHR in November 2011, this emerging consensus may still be limited by the state's margin of appreciation. Thus, the question of whether Article 8 also encompasses the right of couples to all possible means of medically induced conception is not yet completely settled. In *SH and others v Austria*,[12] two married couples suffering infertility were denied having biological children through *in vitro* fertilisation using donor sperm and ova. As Austria bans the kind of *in vitro* fertilisation required by these couples (conception outside the woman's body) the couples took the case to court, arguing that their right to a family according to Article 8 was being breached.[13] In a decision on the merits, a Chamber of the First Section of the ECtHR found that the domestic law violated Article 8, and the Court also found a violation of Article 14, ie prohibition of discrimination, by not allowing those unable to conceive access to that right. However, Austria appealed the decision to the higher Grand Chamber, which ruled otherwise. The state argued that the right to conceive does not include all kinds of artificial conception. In the final judgment, the lower Chamber's ruling was struck down. The Court found no violation of Articles 8 and 14. According to the Court, the domestic law was within the state's margin

[12] *SH and others v Austria* (Application no. 57813/00), Judgment of 3 November 2011.

[13] Four judges gave a jointly dissenting opinion to the judgment.

of appreciation, under the circumstances that the issue gives rise to sensitive moral and ethical issues for which there are as yet no common ground among the Member States. The Court found that Austria's laws struck a balance between public and private concerns. The issue of the extent to which the use of artificial conception is a right according to Article 8 will most probably be tried again in the ECtHR in the near future. Other issues also concerning family form and function will continue to reach the ECtHR, and challenge domestic law for being in violation of human rights. A common trait seems to be a slow but steady acceptance of an increasing flexibility on the part of the courts, on issues relating to family forms and the right to family.

C. Participation and Flexibility: Central Ingredients

As mentioned in the introduction to this chapter, family research over the last century has gradually switched from focusing on the family's stabilising role in society to a focus on the changing forms and functions of family in today's society. Contemporary family research portrays the family and family life as a variety of constellations. Thomas Johansson has analysed what constitutes the typical characteristics for the modern family according to this research.[14] Johansson puts forth two characteristics: on the one hand, the individual, and on the other, the procedural trait of the family. He refers to Ulrich Beck and Elisabeth Beck-Gernsheim, who describe the development of the family as an individualisation process. Instead of being a stable unit, the family is more of a meeting place for individuals to fulfil their goals and interests.[15] The family gives the individual a social context, and becomes a platform for existential and emotional needs.[16] Family life is constructed, and reconstructed, around these needs, being continuously formed and shaped through negotiations between the individuals in the family—instead of as in the traditional form of the nuclear family, in which certain fixed and established norms decided who would do what. The basis of the family is the individuals' common goals and feelings. This creates a certain fragile structure in the family, as the goals and needs of the individual most often change over time. The children become the link that remains between the adults after a separation. Other adults, such as step-parents, may also enter the child's life.

Another influential researcher, Anthony Giddens, presented similar ideas of the fragile family, concentrating on the relationship between the partners in the family. In short, according to Giddens, the family is often based on a relationship between two individuals who are not dependent on each other, but who instead

[14] Johansson, *Familjeliv*, above n 6.

[15] Ibid 14, with further reference to Beck and Beck-Gernsheim, *The Normal of Chaos of Love*, above n 3.

[16] Johansson, *Familjeliv*, above n 6, 19 ff, with further reference to C Smart, 'From Children's Shoes to Children's Voices' (2002) 40(3) *Family Court Review* 307.

choose this 'pure relationship' based on communication and mutual respect, for the fulfilment it gives each partner. Such a relationship is dependent on reciprocal exchange and the fulfilment of each partner, and is thus very fragile; it may be demolished if one partner acquires more satisfaction than the other.[17] Giddens' depiction of the modern relationship is put forward by Johansson as a possible explanation for the increasing number of divorces and reconstructed families.[18] Another family researcher, Manuel Castells, agrees on the fragility of the family and describes the new partnership and family structure as demanding a variety of family forms. He describes children as the losers in this development, arguing that a child's need for stability during its upbringing is contrary to the exposition of different and changing family forms.[19]

In summing up, a common trait of modern family research is the emphasis on the individualisation process and the fragility of the family. The family becomes an arena for negotiations, with many participants and interests. In research, this development towards increased participation and flexibility is described as both the strength and the weakness of the modern family.[20] From a children's rights perspective, the question arises as to what are the strengths and weaknesses in this development for children.

III. CHILDREN'S RIGHTS ON THE AGENDA

A. Four Legislative Approaches to Child Issues

Parallel to the changes in the family concept, the claim to individual rights has become the dominating legal agenda for groups and individuals. This development includes children and the claim for children's rights. However, historically speaking, this is a new view of child legislation and policy. Lorraine Fox Harding has identified four main value positions in child care policy in Europe over the last centuries.[21] They all reflect different attitudes towards the role and rights of parents, children and families. Although some date back in time, they are, to some extent, still existent in many countries in some way, for example, due to the continuing in force of old but still valid legislation, or due to local customs and traditions. The first paradigm is based on the family as a private sphere with a superior role in society. This paradigm, called *laissez-faire and patriarchy*, takes

[17] A Giddens, *The Transformation of Intimacy: Sexuality, Love and Eroticism in Modern Societies* (Cambridge, Polity Press, 1992) 136 ff.

[18] Johansson, *Familjeliv*, above n 6, 13.

[19] M Castells, *Informationsåldern. Ekonomi, samhälle och kultur. Identitetens makt* (Göteborg, Daidalos, 2000) vol II.

[20] See, eg, K Larsson Sjöberg, 'Mamma, pappa, styvbarn—barn' in M Bäck-Wiklund and T Johansson (eds), *Nätverksfamiljen*, (Stockholm, Natur och kultur, 2003).

[21] L Fox Harding, *Perspectives in Child Care Policy*, 2nd edn (Boston, Addison Wesley Longman Ltd, 1997).

the view that the family should not be disturbed by the state, except in extreme circumstances. Instead, the role of the state in family life should be minimal. According to Fox Harding, this strong emphasis on the value of non-intervention in family life entails the consequence that family power continues according to practice and customs, which in practice means that it remains in the hands of adults, and particularly men in their roles as husbands and fathers.[22] This perspective has its origins in the late nineteenth and early twentieth centuries.

In the second paradigm, the role of the family and society is contrary to the *laissez-faire* paradigm. Here, the liberties of the family and the parents are given a low priority. This policy approach is primarily associated with the growth of state intervention in welfare issues during the first half of the twentieth century. The family has a fairly minor role at the expense of the state. According to this position, which Fox Harding calls *state paternalism and child protection*, the legitimate need for extensive state protection and child protection is not only accepted, but also promoted and favoured, even before biological bonds in cases where the care of a child is found to be inadequate. The child is of paramount consideration in state actions. At the same time, this intervention is based on a paternalistic attitude and is not formulated in terms of individual rights. In other words, it focuses on the child's dependency and need for nurture and care, as judged by professionals and experts. The state is construed as being the neutral and the wise party, adopting the best course of action for the child, sometimes rescuing it in rather heavy-handed state action. In this policy-making position, there is a belief that sometimes the state can provide a better future for the child than can the parent.[23]

The third paradigm stands for (as the term implies) *the modern defence of the birth family and the parents' rights*. This is a critique of the former positions, in that it holds that state intervention may be legitimate, but only in order to preserve and assist biological families. The viewpoint is that birth families should be supported in their caring role, and that, at times, extensive state intervention may be required to support birth families, for example when responding to poverty and deprivation.[24] This position, entailing preventive policies, became increasingly favoured in child care policy in several European countries during the 1950s and 1960s. According to Fox Harding, the atmosphere in child care policy in the early post-Second World War period exhibited a greater awareness than before of the importance of families, and a greater interest in the psychological condition of childhood.[25] Later on, the 'parents' rights' position has often been used by different parental pressure groups.

Finally, the fourth paradigm promotes the child as the subject and as a holder of rights, thus distinguishing this concept from the other positions, which view the child more as an object for protection and guidance, and a part of the family.

22 Ibid 11.
23 Ibid 53.
24 Ibid 73.
25 Ibid 100.

Fox Harding calls this value paradigm *children's rights and child liberation*, because it is based on the acceptance of individual human rights for children. The role of the parents, as well as of the state, is to promote these rights, such as the rights to family, health care and education. The general principle of the best interests of the child is supposed to balance the protective aspects of the rights of the child with the participatory aspects. The basic idea is that all decisions made by public authorities and courts regarding children should aim to be in the best interests of the child itself. The CRC is a document produced from the belief of fundamental child rights. Established in 1989, the CRC was the first legally binding international instrument incorporating a full range of human rights for children. The Convention has today been signed and ratified by almost all the countries of the world,[26] and has even been incorporated into the national legislation of some countries, such as in Norway and Finland. The document reflects a significant change, both in the conceptualisation of childhood and in the treatment of children. The children's rights paradigm has the shortest history. The point at which the CRC was established is for many countries the starting point in time when the values were introduced in national policy and legislation.

Fox Harding's analysis of the main value positions concerning the child and the family in Europe during the last century is valuable when we want to understand how such issues may have been, and still are, handled as regards the making of policy. It becomes clear that the approaches are quite different in these four policy-making positions. For example, the issue of a child's own participation is treated in very disparate ways. In the first approach, the child's own viewpoint is not present at all, instead its interests are put forward solely by the parents. The second approach sees children as having fundamental needs, but at the same time emphasises adult/state protection and guidance, and does not promote the child's participation in any decision-making. According to the third position, the parents make all decisions for the child, so here too the child is not a party to the process. Thus, child participation has a low profile in all three positions. Only the fourth approach holds the child's participation as central. This observation is relevant to the issue of strengths and weaknesses in the development of changing family forms and functions for children today. In a family where participation is a central ingredient, participation for all seems relevant, including participation for the children.

B. Children's Rights Policy Today

The children's rights paradigm is influencing national legislation in many European countries, thus recognising children as individual holders of rights in law. Thus, gradually, children are acquiring rights that in many respects bring them

[26] Except the United States and Somalia.

close to adults.[27] In some countries, children have even received constitutionally, specially protected rights. This may include the right of respect for personal integrity, the right to equal treatment, the right to be provided for and protected, and the right to participation. For example, on the matter of participation, according to the Finnish Constitution from 1999, 'Children shall be treated equally and as individuals and they shall be allowed to influence matters pertaining to them to a degree corresponding to their level of development'.[28] Since 2008, the Belgian Constitution also includes a provision on the right of children to participate. In article 22, it is stated that every child has the right to express his or her opinion in all matters affecting him or her; and that his or her opinion is to be taken into consideration in accordance with his or her power of judgement.[29] In Norway, a revision of the Constitution in order to strengthen the position of human rights includes a proposal for specific children's rights.[30] In addition to protection afforded by the national legislation of some countries, children's rights are also protected in the Charter of Fundamental Rights of the European Union. According to Article 24, children should have the right to protection and care, and they may express their views freely. In addition, the child has a right to maintain a personal relationship and direct contact with its parents, unless this is contrary to the best interests of the child.

Parallel to the implementation process of children's rights in Europe, there is a steady critique of the gap between principles and practice regarding children's rights issues. For example, research indicates that it is difficult to implement child participatory rights in practice.[31] Although children themselves find it important to be viewed as individuals with feelings and opinions, as well as subjects capable of participating in different decisions, their voices and views are still excluded from a variety of decisions.[32] Thus, it seems difficult to implement some children's

[27] H Cunningham, *Children and Childhood in Western Society since 1500* (London, Longman Group Ltd, 1995) 186 ff.

[28] Finnish Constitution 1999, s 6.

[29] See K Sandberg, 'Children's Rights in the Norwegian Constitution' in F Malekian and K Nordlöf (eds), *The Soverignty of Children in Law* (Cambridge, Cambridge Scholars Publishing, 2012) 98.

[30] Ibid 87.

[31] See, eg, M Hill *et al*, 'Moving the Participation Agenda Forward' (2004) 18(2) *Children and Society* 77; L Dahlstrand, *Barns deltagande i familjerättsliga processer* (Uppsala, Uppsala University Press, 2004); JM Davis and M Hill, 'Introduction' in KM Tisdale *et al* (eds), *Children, Young People and Social Inclusion: Participation for What?* (Bristol, Policy Press, 2006); R Stern, *The Child's Right to Participation: Reality or Rhetoric?* (Uppsala, Uppsala University Press, 2006); A James, 'Giving Voice to Children's Voices: Practices and Problems, Pitfalls and Potentials' (2007) 109(2) *American Anthropologist* 261; E Ryrstedt, 'Samarbetssamtal—leder de till en sann överenskommelse för barnets bästa, eller bara en förhandlingslösning?' (2009) *Svensk juristtidning* 821; T Mattsson, 'Foster Children's Right to Family: a Description and Analysis of the Legislative Approach in Sweden' (2012) 7(7) *US-China Law Review* 29.

[32] See, eg, C Smart, 'From Children's Shoes to Children's Voices' (above n 16); AB Smith, 'Interpreting and Supporting Participation Rights: Contributions from Sociocultural Theory' (2002) 10 *International Journal of Children's Rights* 73; P Parkinson *et al*, '"Parents" and Children's Views on Talking to Judges in Parenting Disputes in Australia' (2007) 21(1) *International Journal of Law, Policy and the Family* 1.

rights. Kirsten Sandberg, Professor of Law, is of the opinion that there is a long way to go before children's rights are taken as seriously as the rights of adults. In practice, it is adults that set the limits for children's opportunities to influence decisions concerning themselves, both in their own lives and in society.[33] According to Sandberg, children's rights ought to be constitutionally protected, and strengthening children's participation in society should be a paramount issue as regards children's rights. For her, it is important to include children in processes where important decisions are made.[34]

Sandberg's argument may be easily transferred to the family arena. Several studies in Swedish research demonstrate that new family or social welfare legislation does not always have the expected effect from a child rights perspective.[35] One possible explanation put forward for this is that parental rights traditionally have a strong tradition in Swedish legislative practice. Those with custody of the child have great influence on many decisions concerning the child, regardless of whether or not the custodian resides with the child.[36] In this perspective, it becomes an important task to study the implementation of new legislation that aims to protect children's rights and interests, and which might collide with parental rights and interests.

IV. PARALLEL OR CONFLICTING DEVELOPMENTS? USE OF A THEORY

A. Theory of Law as Normative Patterns in a Normative Field in Family Law

In the following, I wish to discuss the two lines of development—changing family structures and children's rights—using the theory of law as normative patterns in a normative field, by Anna Christensen. This theory makes it possible to view the legal system from a structural perspective, and it opens up for studies of colliding interests in questions relating to everyday human life.[37] The discussion focuses primarily on the normative pattern of Protection of Established Position. According to Christensen's theory, this pattern is central to many legal areas.[38] In brief, the pattern is a basic, old and conservative pattern that can be found in

[33] K. Sandberg, 'Children's Rights', above n 29, 90.

[34] Ibid 91.

[35] See, eg, T Mattsson, *Barnet och rättsprocessen—Rättssäkerhet, integritetsskydd och autonomi vid beslut om tvångsvård* (Lund, Juristförlaget i Lund, 2002); Dahlstrand, *Barns deltagande i familjerättsliga processer*, above n 31; R Stern, *The Child's Right to Participation*, above n 31; J Schiratzki, *Mamma och pappa inför rätta* (Uppsala, Iustus, 2008); E Ryrstedt, 'Samarbetssamtal—leder de till en sann överenskommelse för barnets bästa, eller bara en förhandlingslösning?' (2009) *Svensk juristtidning* 821.

[36] In addition, as a main rule the consent of both parents/custodians is necessary for decisions concerning the child. This gives each parent/custodian great authority to oppose changes, or to disagree on actions for the child, which the other parent/custodian or an authority wishes to implement for the child.

[37] A Hollander and K Alexius Borgström, *Juridik och rättsvetenskap i socialt arbete* (Lund, Studentlitteratur, 2009) 31 ff.

[38] See Ann Numhauser-Henning, Chapter 2.

many areas of the law having to do with the daily life of people. Typical for this pattern is that it upholds social positions obtained by law, inheritance, etc, and it forms asymmetric relationships between those with power and those without, whatever the form of that power.[39]

The focus of my interest in using this theory is on the problems of implementation of children's rights in Swedish family law. Over the last two decades, in accordance with the international developments described above, Swedish law has undergone many changes to enhance children's rights. In family law, these changes include a greater acceptance of the fact that custodians' interests can sometimes collide with the material rights of the child. For example, according to a legislative change in the Social Services Act in 2010, a child will be permitted to speak to the Social Welfare Committee in the course of an inquiry conducted by the social services, irrespective of the opinion of those in custody of the child.[40] As a result of a recent change to the Child and Parents Code in 2012, the Committee may also decide to award a child certain social welfare assistance or health care, even if one of those with custody disagrees, as long as the other person with custody (and the child) agrees to the treatment or the benefit.[41] Yet another example is legislation that allows a transfer of custody and guardianship for children in foster care to the foster family, without the consent of the person(s) with custody of the child.[42] These legislative changes imply the fact that children's rights might not always be in accordance with the parents' rights and wishes. In such situations, the legislation suggests an assessment based on the best interests of the child as the guiding principle. The legislation affects both children and adults; this is an unavoidable consequence, as legislative changes concerning a child often affect the position of the person with custody of the child in some way. From the perspective of the theory of law as normative patterns in a normative field, this raises the issue of two colliding patterns, ie the pattern of Just Distribution and the pattern of Protection of Established Position. The basic normative pattern of Just Distribution is a distributive pattern related to social justice and solidarity, encompassing codifications of children's rights and interests.[43]

B. An Empirical Study

It has been argued that the long-term foster placement system is used too widely for children in Sweden, and that Swedish legislation does not take sufficient

[39] Christensen, 'Skydd för etablerad position', above n 8.

[40] Social Services Act, ch 11, s 10. Before this change, only children over the age of 15 were allowed to speak to the Committee without the consent of both parents/custodians.

[41] Prop 2011/12:53 *Barns möjlighet att få vård*, the Child and Parents Code, ch 6 s 13a.

[42] Social Services Act, ch. 6, s 8, Child and Parents Code, ch 6, s 8.

[43] See Ann Numhauser-Henning, Chapter 2.

account of children's rights as required by the CRC.[44] As a result, Swedish legislation made a switch in the 2000s from the idea of reuniting the child and its biological parents as an upholding principle, towards a more flexible advocacy for different solutions aiming for the best interests of the child. As a consequence, new legislation was amended, with the aim of reducing the large number of children in long-term foster care. The new amendment to the Social Services Act of 2001 implies that Social Services Committees should regularly evaluate the possibility of applying to the District Court for a transfer of custody and guardianship to the foster parents,[45] the aim of which is to promote the best interests of the child, in particular the child's right to continuous upbringing and family life. This is clearly stated in the legislative works that preceded the amendment.[46] Accordingly, such a court decision does not involve an assessment of the wishes or current fitness of the persons formerly having custody, who most often are the biological parents. Instead, the main goal of the rule is to promote the child's right to family, irrespective of the custodians' interests and wishes of those with custody of the child. Thus, the goal of the legislative changes is to promote the interests of the child.

I will refer to an empirical study of Swedish District Court cases concerning the transfer of custody and guardianship during 2005–2009, where this theory is used.[47] The cases were collected from eight different courts, from various parts of Sweden, and included a total of 77 cases from 2005–2009. The purpose of the study was to examine the District Courts' arguments for their decisions in custody and guardianship cases in relation to the instructions in the Children and Parents Code of 1949.[48] My intention was to investigate the practice of legislation concerning the responsibility of the Social Welfare Committee to initiate custody and guardianship cases for children in long-term foster care.

According to the Swedish Child and Parents Code, chapter 6 section 8, in conjunction with the Social Services Act, chapter 6, section 8, the Social Welfare Committee may apply for a transfer of custody and guardianship for some children who have resided in foster homes. Such a decision means that the foster parents take on the role as the child's day-to-day carer as before, but also

[44] Prop 2002/03:53.

[45] Social Services Act, ch 6, s 8.

[46] Prop 2002/03:53.

[47] The study is published in *Rätten till familj inom sociala barn- och ungdomsvården (The Right to Family in the Child Care System)* (2010) 133–70. See also Mattsson, 'Foster Children's Right to Family', above n 31.

[48] The terms custody and guardianship are used in slightly different ways in different countries. In Sweden, the term 'custody' is often used to include the role of guardianship, and as such, is described as encompassing both 'factual custody' and 'legal custody'. In this chapter, I take into consideration the legal terminology that often exists in Anglo-Saxon countries; ie 'custody' is defined as the right to daily care for a child or young person, and 'guardianship' the right of the legal connection with the child (ie the legal duties, powers and rights and responsibilities for the child). In addition, in order to adjust to the Swedish translation of the words in official documents, I will add the word 'custody' when discussing these decisions. Thus, I refer to this alternative of changing the legal connection between the foster parents and the child as a court decision of custody *and* guardianship.

receive the legal duties and rights of care for the child. The regulation states the following:

> If a child is permanently cared for and brought up in a private home other than that of his or her parents, and it is obvious that it is best for the child that the current relationship continues, and that custody be transferred to the person or persons who have cared for the child, the Court may decide to appoint him or them specially appointed custodians of the child. A case for the transfer of custody under the first paragraph may be initiated by the Social Welfare Committee.[49]

This regulation focuses on the child's rights and best interests, not on the fitness or willingness of those with custody to have the child return home (or alternatively to continue to keep the child in public foster care). As a consequence, the consent of those with custody is not a necessary prerequisite. Instead, the assessment should be based solely on the rights and interests of the child. The purpose of the study was to examine the District Courts' arguments for their decisions in relation to the instructions in the Child and Parents Code of 1949. I wanted to investigate the practice of this legislation, with the main question being how the District Courts argued for the best interests of the child in relation to the child's right to family. The method used to discover how the practice of this child rights legislation functioned was to study which normative positions appear and stand out in an analysis of the empirical material.

C. Results

One result of the study is that the position of those with custody of the child dominates the cases, although the assessment should focus solely on the child. This can be seen in several ways. One way is simply to study the low number of cases and the many years that must pass before a custody/guardianship case actually occurs. The expressed intention by the legislator was to increase the number of custody and guardianship cases and decrease the number of children in long-term care.[50] There is a slight increase each year in the number of foster care cases taken to the District Courts. So far, however, these are far fewer than expected by the government. One explanation is that some Social Welfare Committees do not routinely apply for custody/guardianship changes for long-term foster children. Another explanation is that the Committees seem unwilling to apply in cases where the parents disagree on such changes. According to my study, in only one of 10 cases did those with custody disagree on a change of custody and guardianship. The Committees did not seem to take the case to court when those with custody disagreed on the measure in general. Further reasons for not going to court may also

[49] Author's translation.
[50] Prop 2002/03:53.

be that the Committee assessed that a change of custody was not in the individual child's best interests, or that the foster parents did not agree to take custody.

The study also demonstrates that when custody cases do actually occur, they often occur very late in the childhood. Of the 76 children in the study, 46 of those moving into the custody of others, and/or receiving new guardians through a court decision, had lived in foster homes for their entire lives (with the exception of the first six months, which I do not include because this period was often when the family was being assessed, or when the baby was in a temporary living arrangement). This most often involved long-term foster placements, as the average time of placement for children in the study was 11 years. Contact with the persons with custody of the child was at this time often very rare, or even non-existent. Even in those 'clear' cases where the child's relationship with those with custody would not run the risk of deteriorating after a transfer of custody, the child remained in foster care for the same extended period. In some cases in the study, the passivity of the Social Welfare Committee finally prompted the children to act themselves. Several custody cases were initiated informally by children and young people who wanted to have their foster parents recognised as their 'real' parents, and therefore they contacted the Committee. Thus, the initiative of the proper institution, the Social Welfare Committee, was sometimes called forth by the children themselves.

The interests of those with custody tend to dominate in the custody and guardianship case, although this is not the intention of the legislation. This can be seen in the analysis of the court arguments. In the group of cases where those with custody disagreed on a transfer of custody, the petition for custody/guardianship was turned down by the courts in half of the cases. In all the other cases in the study, the petition was approved. The reasoning in these cases focuses mainly on the fitness and willingness of those with custody to continue as the child's custodian. The court discussion then becomes legal-technical, leaving the overall assessment of what is in the best interests of the child as questions of proof of fact, and lack of evidence arguments. Although these cases are no different from the other cases in the study (ie long-term foster placements; poor, non-existent or detrimental contact with those with custody; children expressing that they want the change), the court's conclusion is that those with custody should get 'one more chance' from the court. Thus, the concurring opinion of those with custody seems to make the court focus on the issue, whereas a dissenting opinion has the reverse result of focusing on those with custody.

D. Relevance for Family Law in General

Using Christensen's theory, it is shown that the interest of those with custody may unintentionally take precedence over the interests of the child. Expressed in other terms, the best interests of the child principle may be interpreted in a way that upholds the parents' rights and interests. Thus, here there is a risk that rights-based legislative efforts, such as in the Child and Parents Code, will not be as successful as planned, due to the impact of the normative pattern of Protection of Established Position. In more general terms, another result is the risk that legislation that is supposed to promote children's interests might not have the desired effect, due to the dominating pattern of Protection of Established Position. This normative pattern upholds the interests of those with custody, and, in regulations where the interests of the child and those with custody may occasionally collide, in the worst case the result will not be fully in accordance with the original intentions. In other words, the normative pattern of Protection of Established Position will dominate before the pattern of Just Distribution. This ought to be seen as a risk, particularly in areas where no specific participation rights are given to children. In such situations, the child will have no chance of gaining a position of his or her own. If the child, or his/her representative, may not put forward his or her opinion before a decision on a matter concerning the child, there is a risk that the interests of those with custody will take precedence over the interests of the child. In this matter, using Christensen's theory opens up general and central conclusions applicable to other parts of family law relating to the relationship between children and adults.

V. CHILD PARTICIPATION IN THE DECISION-MAKING PROCESS

Research demonstrates that children seem to be especially vulnerable in cases where there are no clear procedural tools for child participation.[51] In the study mentioned above, the children's voices were often not visible in the documents preceding the judgments or the judgments themselves, making it difficult to trace the child's opinions and feelings in the relevant cases. The legislation in question encourages the social welfare investigator, as well as the decision-maker, to speak to the child, but it does not demand it unconditionally. The child has no formal standing in the court and no legal representative in these cases. The lack of procedural tools is one explanation why children's voices and influence have not clearly emerged in the legal process. The poor inclusion of children's voices demonstrates the difficulties in balancing child and parent interests without clear procedural tools for each party, at least where there is a risk of imbalance in the assessment of the child's best interests.[52] In other words, the imbalance of power between the adult and the child in the process is most probably not compensated procedurally. The child will have no way of gaining a position equal to the adult in the decision-making process.

[51] See, eg, Mattsson, *Barnet och rättsprocessen*, above n 35; and T. Mattsson, *Barnet som subjekt och aktör. En rättslig studie om barn i familjehem* (Uppsala, Iustus förlag, 2006); Dahlstrand, *Barns deltagande i familjerättsliga processer*, above n 31; Schiratzki, *Mamma och pappa inför rätta*, above n 35.

[52] Compare E Ryrstedt and T Mattsson, 'Children's Rights to Representation: a Comparison between Sweden and England' (2008) 1 *International Journal of Law, Policy and the Family, Oxford Journals* 135.

The problem of children's lack of procedural tools in custody cases was highlighted in a case from the Court of Justice of the European Union (CJEU), Case C-491/10PPu *Aguirre Zarraga v Pelz*[53] in December 2010. This case dealt with the issue that a child had not been able to speak in a custody case in a Spanish court. A Spanish-German couple who had resided in Spain separated in 2007, and their eight-year-old daughter stayed with the mother. The spouses applied for divorce at the Spanish court and each parent sought sole parental responsibility for their daughter. In May 2008, the Spanish court transferred custody temporarily to the father. The daughter moved to live with the father and the mother returned to Germany. However, in the summer of the same year, the girl did not return to Spain after a holiday with her mother in Germany. A Spanish court order that requested the return of the girl was not recognised under the Hague Child Abduction Convention in Germany, the reason being that the girl had been heard by the German family court and she did not want to return to her father. In December 2009, the Spanish court decided to transfer custody to the father, without personally hearing the mother and daughter. The mother also went to the German family court, seeking a statement that the Spanish decision was unenforceable in Germany because the girl (and her mother) had not been personally heard by the Spanish judge. According to the court, the Spanish court had not sufficiently respected the child's right to be heard. The Spanish court issued a certificate under Article 42 of the Brussels II a Regulation (Council Regulation (EC) No 2201/2003 of 27 November 2003 ordering the immediate return of the girl to her father. According to Article 11(8) of the same Regulation, a national family court must immediately enforce the return order of another family court, with no recognition proceedings. Nevertheless, the mother filed a new action in the German family court, seeking a declaration that the Spanish decision was unenforceable in Germany because the girl and her mother had not been personally heard by the Spanish judge.

As a result, the German court asked the CJEU whether a serious violation of human rights makes it possible to review a judgment of another Member State, even in the context of mutual recognition: in this case Article 24 of the Charter of Fundamental Rights of the European Union. Unfortunately, the CJEU did not try the question of the child's procedural rights, finding that the issue fell within the jurisdiction of the Member State's courts. The Court ruled that a court with jurisdiction in the Member State of enforcement cannot oppose the enforcement of the national judgment, since the assessment of whether there is such an infringement fell exclusively within the jurisdiction of the courts of the Member State of origin. Still, the case demonstrates that child participation in the decision-making process in family matters has become a legal issue in an EU context, due to Article 24 of the Charter.

[53] Case C-491/10PPu *Aguirre Zarraga v Pelz*, CJEU, Judgment of 10 December 2010.

VI. GRADUAL ALLOWANCE OF PROCEDURAL TOOLS FOR CHILDREN: THE OPTIONAL PROTOCOL IN CRC—A RECENT EXAMPLE

Traditionally, the promotion of children's rights has been more-or-less based either on arguments resting on the human rights discourse, involving a claim for equal treatment with other humans, *or* on a claim for the need for special treatment owing to vulnerable childhood status.[54] A problem with these types of justifying child rights is that both are roughly based on the idea of human beings as self-determining individuals able to claim their own rights. This problem is reflected in legislation and in the practice of children's rights. Children are seldom assigned legal capacity themselves, their rights instead being assumed to be taken care of by adults in different ways. For example, it is often those with custody in the home, or the teacher at school who assists the child in claiming his or her rights. In some cases, other adults, such as judges, welfare officers, or health personnel take on this role temporarily. Thus, children's rights are most often claimed by adults, sometimes through the guidance of legal documents instructing the adults about a certain child right and its implementation, such as the right to education or health care. However, without legal guidance on children's rights and without adults with the knowledge and willingness to implement these rights, it is very difficult to realise them. In this sense, claiming a child's rights is dependent on the surroundings of the child. An expression of this in legislation is the principle that the best interests of the child shall be the primary consideration. This principle exists mainly to compensate for the child's inexperience, immaturity and inability to make independent decisions. The idea is that an assessment of the child's best interests should be possible, without considering the wishes of the child in cases where the decision-maker finds it most appropriate or practical.

However, as discussed in this chapter, there is a risk that the interests of the adults may sometimes precede the interests of the child in this assessment, and do so in situations where the legislation promotes the interests of the child. One example is the custody case study, which demonstrates that children's participation or children's interests may not always be given priority in the decision-making in the search for a decision in the best interests of the individual child. In the light of the established position of those with custody of the child, the imbalance between the possible counter-interests of the parties becomes a problem from a child rights perspective. The underlying idea of equal treatment with other individuals, or special treatment owing to vulnerable childhood status, will not then be fulfilled in practice.

New procedural tools for allowing child participation will probably become an issue for increasing discussion in law in the years to come.[55] The new Optional Protocol to the CRC is a sign pointing in that direction. The Protocol was adopted

[54] R Fitzgerald *et al*, 'A Struggle of Recognition' in B Percy-Smith and N Thomas (eds), *A Handbook of Children and Young People's Participation* (London, Routledge 2010) 298 ff.

[55] Compare Mattsson, 'Foster Children's Right to Family', above n 31.

in December 2011 by the General Assembly, and opened for signature in February 2012. This Optional Protocol is a new complaints mechanism for violations of children's rights. Before this change, there were no such mechanisms for filing individual complaints. Instead, states that are parties to the Convention must submit regular reports describing the situation for children in their state, to the Committee on the Rights of the Child. This new Protocol reinforces these already existing methods by adding a complaints mechanism, enabling children to complain about rights violations. The protocol also introduces interstate communication and an inquiry procedure, in addition to an international mechanism of individual complaints.

Children or their representatives may bring their complaints about human rights violations before the Committee on the Rights of the Child once all domestic legal procedures have been exhausted. According to Article 5 of the CRC, complaints (communications) that a country has violated any of the rights in the CRC (to which that country is a party) may be submitted on behalf of an individual, or group of individuals, to the Committee on the Rights of the Child. The Committee will bring the country's attention to the issue at hand and will request written explanations or statements clarifying the matter, as well as the solution, if there exists one (Article 8). The aim is a quick, transparent and smooth process, with the goal to reach an amicable settlement that will promote the present and future interests of the child or children. In case of indications of grave or systematic violations by a state party, there is an independent inquiry procedure, complete with follow-up system (Articles 13–14).

VII. FINAL REMARKS

In this chapter I have described two parallel developments related to family: modern family forms and child rights. In short, sociologists describe our society as one where the family has become an arena for negotiations, with many participants and interests, among those being children and children's interests. These are current developments, which can easily be seen in legal practice and in legislation. In some cases, developments will correspond and harmonise for both the adults and children involved in the family process. In other cases there may be conflicting interests between the parties. For these latter situations, it is relevant to pay attention to the risk of the automatic lead of the adults, often those with custody of the child, resulting from the normative pattern of Protection of Established Position. Flexible procedural tools, also suitable for participation on the part of less advantaged parties, may be one way to reduce this lead and create conditions for lasting and appropriate decisions for all individuals involved in the decision-making process. The new Optional Protocol to the CRC is a recent example of such development. Irrespective of the success and practical implications of this new complaints system for violations of children's rights, this is a signal that child participation issues are relevant and central to the implementation of children's rights. The aim of this chapter has been to discuss the two developments of modern family structures and the promotion of children's rights. The result is that there ought to be an increasing awareness of the potential vulnerability of the child in the family, and of the need for state resilience, such as procedural tools and state intervention mechanisms in future child policy and legislation.

Part IV

Market-Functionalism and Normative Development

8

Conceptions of the Market in Labour Law

SIMON DEAKIN

I. INTRODUCTION: MODEL BUILDING AND NORMATIVE ANALYSIS IN ECONOMICS AND LAW

ONE OF THE foundations of Anna Christensen's methodology is the idea that legal research can help to identify the values underpinning social institutions, including those of the market.[1] What she called the 'Market-Functional' pattern is as much a part of the normative field of labour law as are the patterns of 'Just Distribution' and 'Protection of Established Position' which speak more directly to the social policy objectives of labour regulation. Conversely, the market depends on the legal system to instantiate certain social values, which are essential for its operation. The market is not a free-standing institution, and attempts to treat it as such risk misdescribing its nature and effects.

The aim of this chapter is to build on Anna Christensen's insights in exploring how the notion of the market is constructed through legal discourse, with the focus on the labour market and labour law discourse as an illustrative case with wider potential applications. The analysis is founded on the premise that an inquiry into the nature of social institutions can be informed by a study of the terms used by the legal system to describe those institutions. This is not to assume that legal thought provides descriptions of social forms and relations which are inherently more accurate than those derived from alternative perspectives, including, most pertinently for current purposes, those of the social sciences, in particular economics. Legal theory and scholarship long ago came round to the view that terms used in legal doctrine, such as 'contract', 'property' and 'employment', are not some kind of higher-order expression of concepts to which social relations either do or should conform,[2] but are, at best, uncertain approximations of phenomena

[1] A Christensen, 'Normative Patterns and the Normative Field: a Post-Liberal View on Law' in T Wilhelmsson and S Hurri (eds), *From Dissonance to Sense: Welfare State Expectations, Privatisation, and Private Law* (Aldershot, Ashgate, 2000).

[2] Mark van Hoecke refers to 'a belief in a kind of "natural law" which could be retrieved empirically', which 'used to be quite popular in Europe and in the United States in the nineteenth century, but seems to have almost completely disappeared today': 'Legal Doctrine: Which Method(s) for What Kind of Discipline?' in M van Hoecke (ed), *Methodologies of Legal Research: Which Kind of Method for What Kind of Discipline?* (Oxford, Hart Publishing, 2011) 7.

which exist in a realm of interactions which take place, by definition, beyond the law, and which it can only incompletely grasp. These phenomena should be studied according to the methods of the social sciences, using techniques of empirical observation and testing which are not only qualitatively different from those used in the analysis of legal doctrine, but generally superior to it in the sense of providing a systematic basis for data collection and analysis, which legal analysis lacks. Yet, while a compelling case can be made for such empirical approaches to the study of legal systems, it may be important, at the same time, to avoid a naive form of realism, which associates empirical methodologies with a direct line to 'social facts'.[3] In the social sciences, empirical data are mediated through theories and models which in many ways resemble the conceptual constructs which are used to shape legal reasoning. Nor is it always possible to draw a sharp distinction in practice between 'descriptive' or 'positive' social science methods, on the one hand, and 'normative' or value-orientated legal analysis, on the other. In both cases, fitting data to models, and adjusting the models in the light of the data, are among the techniques used to manage and process information drawn from an open-ended and complex social reality.

The study of the 'models' or concepts which are in use in a given legal system at a particular point in time may tell us relatively little about the 'external reality' of the society to which that legal system relates. When, however, mutations in those concepts are studied over time and in relation to the parallel experiences of other legal systems and their societies, the analysis is likely to be more revealing. Far from describing some kind of 'higher reality' which abstracts from social practice (and which, in some traditions of legal thought, has a claim to articulate a higher set of values), legal concepts are (indirect and incomplete) expressions of social practice, and change as it changes. Even if the process is far from linear, and a precise fit between legal categories and social relations cannot be assumed, legal evolution involves the adjustment of legal modes of thought in the light of the information received by the legal system through litigation and legislation, and evolutionary processes are at work, ensuring that certain rules are retained for inclusion in the corpus of the positive law while others are selected out. The historical and comparative study of labour law regimes thus has much to tell us about the evolution of the wider economic and political structures in which those labour law regimes are embedded.[4]

The analysis of models, whether legal or economic, inescapably has normative implications. Models of the social world inform and shape evaluative judgements and thereby enter into the realm of public policy. The legal system is not at all

[3] See Alf Ross's far from naive view of the relationship between doctrinal legal analysis and empirical (sociological and economic) legal research, in *On Law and Justice* (Berkeley/Los Angeles, LA, University of California Press, 1959) 19, arguing that 'law in action and the norms of law are not two independent spheres of existence, but different sides of one and the same reality'.

[4] For further articulation of this methodological position, see S Deakin and F Wilkinson, *The Law of the Labour Market: Industrialization, Employment and Legal Evolution* (Oxford, Oxford University Press, 2005) ch 1.

immune from the influence of models of the market, drawn from the social sciences, which have the potential to reshape the content of the legal rules themselves. The growing influence worldwide of neoclassical economic thinking in labour law discourse in recent years is testament to this process.[5] However, economic models such as the neoclassical one are not intrinsically superior to conceptions of the market derived from within legal discourse itself. Indeed, there is a case for saying that they are deficient precisely because they neglect features of 'real life' markets which the legal system has recognised and incorporated into its mode of thinking. Rather than uncritically receiving what the social sciences have to teach it, legal scholarship should be actively contributing to the formulation of a better (in the sense of more empirically grounded) set of models of the market, which can be used, with appropriate adjustments, in economics and law alike, to inform policy choices.[6]

There are numerous models of the market within economics. Two of the most influential, as outlined in section II below, stress its nature as a mechanism of resource allocation and as a spontaneous order for the coordination of private action. In differing degrees, these accounts assume away, or treat as invisible, what Anna Christensen referred to as the values underpinning the Market-Functional pattern, or what Alain Supiot, in a similar vein, has called the dogmatic or conceptual foundations of the market, which can become visible again when we look at the market through the lens of the law.[7] Section III argues that a legally focused analysis, by contrast, helps to throw light on three linked propositions concerning the institutional underpinnings of the market. First, *the market has a normative*

[5] The influence is sporadic but tangible. For example, Gordon Anderson (*Reconstructing New Zealand's Labour Law: Consensus or Divergence?* (Wellington, Victoria University Press, 2011)) discusses the 'repositioning' undertaken by the New Zealand Court of Appeal in the 1990s along the lines of a 'neoliberal right to manage ideology' (at 131). In France, the first President of the Court of Cassation, Guy Canivet, has argued for the more extensive use of neoclassical law and economics reasoning in legal education and practice, including judicial decision-making (G Canivet, 'Préface' in B Deffains (ed), *L'analyse économique du droit dans les pays de droit civil* (Paris, edition Cujas, 2000), a stance arguably reflected in the Court of Cassation's recent case law; for discussion, see A Supiot, 'Les salariés ne sont pas à vendre (en finir avec l'envers de l'article L.122-12 alinéa2)' (2006) *Droit Social* 264. On the US case, see the critique of economic reasoning to justify the employment-at-will rule by Ellen Dannin, 'Why At-Will Employment is Bad for Employers and Just Cause is Good for Them' (2007) 58 *Labor Law Journal* 5. The (questionable) use of economic concepts by the European Court of Justice in the so-called *Laval* Quartet of cases on the relationship between labour law and the law of the EU internal market is discussed in S Deakin, 'Regulatory Competition After *Laval*' (2008–9) 10 *Cambridge Yearbook of European Legal Studies* 581.

[6] The use of empirically grounded legal research to inform policy is entirely defensible and does not constitute a reversion to 'natural law' theories which violate the fact/value distinction. See Ross, *On Law and Justice*, above n 3, 315–25, discussing 'science and policy making'. In economics, similarly, the modern tradition of positivistic research methods in no sense denies a place for 'normative' reasoning about economic policy; on the contrary, the predictions which positive economic analysis aims to achieve should, according to Milton Friedman, inform the choices made by policy-makers: M Friedman, 'The Methodology of Positive Economics' in *Essays on Positive Economics* (Chicago, IL, University of Chicago Press, 1950) 4–5.

[7] A Supiot, 'The Dogmatic Foundations of the Market (Comments Illustrated by Some Examples from Labour Law and Social Security Law' (2000) 30 *Industrial Law Journal* 321.

base. 'Rational' economic behaviour in a market setting turns out to be founded on conventional understandings of the limits to self-interest, and hence on certain social values. Secondly, *the market is not self-equilibrating*. Insofar as the operation of the market results in socially stable states or equilibria, these equilibria reflect the role of non-market mechanisms in coordinating expectations. Thirdly, *the market is institutionally bounded*. The principles of market-based exchange do not govern all social relations, nor does the market extend into all other social domains. Section IV offers some concluding reflections on the need for new models of the law-economy relation.

II. THE MARKET IN ECONOMICS: EQUILIBRIUM AND SPONTANEOUS ORDER

In economics, the principal conception of the market is as a mechanism of resource allocation, the operation of which ensures efficiency in the production and distribution of goods and services. The elements of a market include autonomous decision-making agents (individuals, households and firms) and publicly known prices. Agents decide to trade with one another on the basis of a schedule of prices which none of them, individually, can control. Competition between buyers and sellers ensures that prices fully reflect information on the preferences of agents, which are based on their subjective wants and are taken as given. At the point where supply and demand intersect, there is a 'unique' or single price for the good or service in question, which ensures that the market 'clears' in the sense of exhausting all opportunities for trade. The clearing of the market implies that it has reached an equilibrium in which supply and demand are equalised. This 'equality' also implies a state of affairs in which the aggregate value of the wants or preferences of all agents has been maximised, value here being synonymous with the exchange value of goods and services. A market in equilibrium is therefore a stable state in which resources are allocated to their most efficient use, and the aggregate 'welfare' (measured in exchange-value terms) of society is maximised.

The model of market equilibrium holds such an important place in contemporary economic theory in large part because of the success of attempts, going back more than a century, to give it a precise mathematical formalisation. The equilibrium-based model of the market is generally referred to as 'Walrasian' after the mathematical model initially developed by Léon Walras in the late nineteenth century.[8] In a Walrasian economy, households supply labour and capital to firms which combine them to produce goods and services which households then consume. Firms are assumed to maximise profits and households to maximise their utility subject to income constraints. All agents are price takers, meaning that they

[8] L Walras, *Éléments d'économie politique pure, ou théorie de la richesse sociale* (Lausanne, Corbaz et cie, 1874), later published as *Elements of Pure Economics, or The Theory of Social Wealth* (W Jaffe trans, Homewood, IL, Irwin, 1954).

decide to trade on the basis of public prices which they cannot individually affect. The mathematical expression of the Walrasian model takes the form of a series of equations which describe the relationships between prices and quantities in a decentralised market setting.[9] An equilibrium, in the mathematical sense, consists of a solution to these equations which describes a fundamental equality between supply and demand. The various 'proofs' of the existence of equilibria under different assumptions concerning the structure of supply and demand which were developed in the course of the twentieth century[10] are mathematical solutions of this kind.

With this more complete mathematical formalisation, a market economy could be said to be characterised by the idea of 'general equilibrium', that is, a state of affairs in which all markets clear. Thus, the models apparently demonstrate that a societally welfare-maximising equilibrium can be arrived at through decentralised exchange, that is, on the basis of the trading decisions of individual agents alone. There is no need for the 'invisible hand' of the market to be supplemented by conscious, centralised direction; indeed, centralised price fixing (or wage regulation in the case of labour) is more likely to introduce an element of distortion into the resource allocation process.

The demonstration of equilibrium is, however, only apparent within the terms of the Walrasian model, because the process by which prices are adjusted over time to reflect changes in quantities is not explained. Walras posited a process of adjustment (*tâtonnement*) conducted by an 'auctioneer' who had the function of calling out the prices and adjusting them up and down to reflect the different 'bids' made by buyers and sellers. More recent studies of the dynamics of Walrasian equilibria suggest that the knowledge that the auctioneer would need to carry out this task is such that the conditions for achieving stability by this route are extremely strict.[11]

A possible interpretation of the Walrasian model is that, for a market-based equilibrium to be achieved, there must be in place, alongside the process of exchange, a series of institutions or mechanisms which perform the role of the 'auctioneer' in receiving and transmitting information on prices. For prices to be public and hence available to all actors, institutions ranging from trade associations to stock exchanges, and in the case of the labour market collective bargaining arrangements, would all have a role. However, these institutions are not explained by the Walrasian model; they are only present in it in the sense of being

[9] Prices reflect the respective *marginal* utilities of buyers and sellers, that is, the costs and benefit of exchanging an additional unit of the commodity in question. 'Marginalism' played a significant part in justifying the use of mathematical methods to explain competitive market equilibrium.

[10] K Arrow and G Debreu 'The Existence of an Equilibrium for a Competitive Economy' (1954) 22 *Econometrica* 265; K Arrow and F Hahn, *General Competitive Analysis* (San Francisco, Holden Day, 1971).

[11] See the discussion of this point in H Gintis, *Agent-Based Models as Markov Processes: Theory and Application to the Dynamics of Market Exchange*, Working Paper (March 2012), available at http://people.umass.edu/gintis/.

posited or assumed, rather than being the subject of a formal demonstration or mathematical proof as is the case with the process of market clearing. It would therefore seem untenable to argue that the Walrasian model *demonstrates* the possibility of stability through decentralised exchange alone.

The price-setting process is not the only feature of Walrasian equilibrium that is not explained by the model's mathematical formulation. The model assumes that the subject matter of exchange is clearly defined and that contracts can be enforced by some means. It assumes that there are no externalities (unbargained for, and hence unpriced, third-party effects of exchange) or, that if there are, there are means of correcting for them, so that prices more fully 'internalise' the relevant costs and benefits. In general, then, the Walrasian model posits the existence of, but does not itself explain, the wider 'infrastructure' of a market economy, including property rights and mechanisms of contract enforcement supplied by the legal system, as well as public goods of various kinds to address externalities, and a system of taxation for supporting those public goods.

If the relationship between the market mechanism and the surrounding infrastructure of a market economy is left unspecified in equilibrium-based models, this is not the case with certain other economic theories of the market, which have explicitly addressed the role of the legal system and other forms of governance in underpinning economic relations. In FA Hayek's account, both the market and the legal system possess the qualities of 'spontaneous orders' founded on the principle of individual autonomy in decision-making.[12] The legal system provides the underpinning for a system of market-based exchange by identifying and protecting a space for individual action. This is done through the 'abstract rules of just conduct', which are essentially the rules of private law in its classical, nineteenth-century incarnation. Property law identifies the subject matter of exchange, contract law enforces voluntary agreements, and tort law ensures protection of the person and of property. The abstract rules of just conduct are the outcome of a process of trial and error in the evolution of legal rules, which works best in systems which prioritise judge-made law as a source of law. The 'spontaneous order' of the common law is thereby contrasted with the 'constructivist' interventions characteristic of civil law codes and regulatory legislation. The latter are unlikely to produce efficient rules, Hayek suggests, because it is impossible to collate, at a central level, the information needed to match legal rules to intended outcomes.

Hayek's conception of decentralised decision-making in a common law legal system producing, through a process of social learning, workable rules of just conduct, is at one with his conception of decentralised market exchange.[13] There is no

[12] Hayek's writings on law and the economy received their most explicit and elaborated form in his three-volume study, *Law Legislation and Liberty: A New Statement of the Liberal Principles of Justice and Political Economy* (London, Routledge and Kegan Paul, 1983). The three volumes had earlier been published separately as *Rules and Order* (1973), *The Mirage of Social Justice* (1976) and *The Political Order of a Free People* (1980).

[13] FA Hayek, 'The Use of Knowledge in Society' (1945) 35 *American Economic Review* 519.

need, in Hayek's model of the market, for a central 'auctioneer'. The information embodied in prices cannot be collated centrally; it is too dispersed, and subject to change, for this to be possible. Hayek accordingly rejects economic models which assume the existence of a public pricing mechanism. Rather, prices are private, and only become public through the process of exchange itself. Insofar as it is possible to speak of public prices at all, this is possible only by virtue of learning on the part of private actors, who adjust their behaviour by raising or lowering their prices on the basis of their own experience and their observation of others.

Equilibrium is present in Hayek's account, but it has a different meaning from the sense it has in the context of the Walrasian model. In the Hayekian model, the alignment of quantities through the operation of the price system is likely to be contingent and temporary. Thus, prices do not represent a unique intersection point of supply and demand, and a general equilibrium, which maximises the respective utilities of buyers and sellers across markets, is not achievable. However, the price system can still perform a coordinating function, which is superior to that achieved through central direction. Prices are, at one and the same time, the expression of agents' adaptive expectations, and a feature of the exchange environment which permits individual trading strategies to be mutually adjusted and hence coordinated over time. The equilibrium represented by this process is a dynamic one, in which what matters is the quality of the feedback between publicly expressed prices and private exchange relations. Decentralised trading, supported by the abstract rules of just conduct, supports a rich information base as the foundation for the coordination of expectations. The equilibrium which arises from the interplay between the lower-level interaction of economic agents and the higher-order properties of the system, which are expressed in the formulation of prices, is what matters here. This equilibrium can be upset by conscious or deliberate regulation, which, Hayek argued, would interfere with the signals through which private action is translated into public knowledge.[14]

Stability is not absent in the Hayekian approach. Herbert Gintis presents a mathematical account of market dynamics using agent-based simulation techniques, in which prices are initially entirely private, but where, through social learning on the part of market actors, a set of 'quasi-public' prices emerges.[15] His model predicts reduced variance of prices over time leading to an equilibrium which approximates to the Walrasian notion of market clearing. In models

[14] Hayek thereby distinguished between a 'spontaneous order' or *cosmos* and a 'made order' or *taxis*. The latter, as it depended for its operation on hierarchical control, was less able to mobilise private information. The imposition of a 'made order' in a realm characterised by 'spontaneous order' would lead to a loss of efficiency as well as to a restriction on liberty. This is the context in which Hayek was especially critical of what he called the 'transformation of private law into public law by "social" legislation' (see *Rules and Order*, above n 12, 142), although he also accepted that labour law was required 'in such fields as the law on relations between master and servant' in which 'the rules have been shaped largely by the views of one of the parties and their particular interests' (*Rules and Order*, above n 12, 89).

[15] Gintis, *Agent-Based Models*, above n 11.

which assume entirely public prices, there is *less* stability because agents respond by shifting their exchange strategies in a synchronised way. Public prices may, paradoxically, make market systems more prone to the destabilising effects of exogenous shocks.

Both the Walrasian and Hayekian models of the market represent attempts to explain the properties of decentralised exchange as a mechanism of resource allocation which does not depend upon conscious direction on the part of collective or governmental agencies. The Walrasian account assumes the existence of a set of non-market institutions which are a precondition for the operation of the market, but which are not part of the model itself and cannot be explained by it. Hayek's model, by contrast, argues for continuity between the market and the legal system, and uses the same notion of 'spontaneous order' to explain them both. An implication of his approach is that the market and the legal system are mutually complementary, in the sense that an economic order based on decentralised exchange both supports, and is supported by, a legal system which protects property and contract rights.

Hayek's approach marks an improvement on the Walrasian one at least from the point of view of integrating legal and other institutional mechanisms of coordination into the analysis and of treating them as endogenous to the process of price formation. His model has not been mathematically formalised in the same way that the model of general competitive equilibrium has been. Whether it will be possible to produce formal models of co-evolution between law and the economy is an open question at present, but the absence of such models does not in itself invalidate the wider significance, in particular for legal scholars, of Hayek's insights on the law-economy relation. Hayek's theory of law as a spontaneous order faces other difficulties, however, in particular the sharp distinction he draws between judge-made law and legislation as sources of law, and his characterisation of the civil law codes as instances of 'constructivist' regulation. This is not well grounded empirically. Hayek's vision of law is akin to the nineteenth century model of a 'private law society'[16] in which the concepts of property and contract are deemed sufficient to explain social institutions ranging from the family to the business firm and the work relationship, without reference to the specific laws which were emerging even then to govern these relations. Hayek cannot accommodate the modern expansion of regulation in these areas without (mostly) condemning it as an 'interference' with an idealised (and most likely fictitious)[17] private economic order. Unable to explain more than a small portion

[16] Or *privatrechtsgesellschaft*: see W Steinmetz, 'Introduction: Towards a Comparative History of Legal Cultures' in W Steinmetz (ed), *Private Law and Social Inequality in the Industrial Age: Comparing Legal Cultures in Britain, France, Germany and the United States* (Oxford, Oxford University Press, 2000) 9.

[17] It is fictitious because there never was a stage in the historical evolution of labour and other markets in Western Europe and North America when legislation did not play a central role in shaping the legal conception of the market and in regulating emerging exchange relations. See D Hay and P Craven (eds), *Masters, Servants and Magistrates in Britain and the Empire, 1562–1955* (Chapel Hill, NC,

of the regulatory framework of modern economies except in these uncompromisingly normative terms, at the end of the day Hayek offers only a limited advance on more orthodox theories of market equilibrium, which assume away entirely the role of institutions.

III. THE MARKET IN LAW: JURIDICAL CONSTRUCTION OF LABOUR MARKET RELATIONS

A. A Conceptual Model of Labour Law Regulation

It is not straightforward to search for a notion or notions of the market in legal discourse, because, at least in the context of labour law, the 'market' is not a legal term of art in the sense that is true of 'employment' or 'contract'. The argument, then, is not that the 'labour market' is straightforwardly identified or defined in legal texts, but that an understanding of the nature of the labour market can be inferred from an analysis of legal rules and concepts. The rules of labour law operate in a functional relationship to the labour market phenomena they purport to regulate, while legal concepts or terms of art including 'wage', 'employee', collective agreement', and so on, disclose understandings of the nature, scope and limits of labour market relations. Not surprisingly, given the context, it is within legal discourse that we find a series of attempts to express the nature of the relationship between the legal and economic systems that economics has, as we have seen, such profound difficulty in formulating.

Abstracting from the detail of case law and legislation which makes up the content of labour law systems, a number of structural features of those systems can be identified.[18] Labour law is a form of regulation which is specific to work relations in modern market economies, in which labour capacity or the 'power' to work is exchanged for wages or salary. Labour law defines the nature of this exchange by granting the employer inherent powers of coordination in return for imposing obligations to have regard to the physical, economic and psychological wellbeing of the employee.

The precise extent of the employer's powers of coordination, on the one hand, and the correlative duties to have regard to the wellbeing of the employee, on the other, vary across sectoral and national contexts, but cannot be entirely eliminated

University of North Carolina Press, 2004); Deakin and Wilkinson, *The Law of the Labour Market*, above n 4, chs 2 and 3; Steinmetz, 'Towards a Comparative History', above n 16, 10–12.

[18] The account which follows draws on a number of recent attempts to infer the ontological status or nature of labour law systems from a study of their operations in a comparative and economic context, namely, A Supiot, *Critique du droit de travail* (Paris, PUF, 1994, new edition 2007); A Hyde, 'What is Labour Law?' in G Davidov and B Langille (eds), *Boundaries and Frontiers of Labour Law* (Oxford, Hart Publishing, 2006); and G Davidov, 'The (Changing?) Idea of Labour Law' (2007) 146 *International Labour Review* 311; as well as Deakin and Wilkinson, *The Law of the Labour Market*, above n 4.

in any relationship that is properly characterised as 'employment'. Labour law systems differ too in how far the regulatory operations are performed by legislation or by forms of collective self-regulation, including collective bargaining and variants of workplace-based co-determination. The precise mix of regulatory methods at country level is often a result of local political and industrial factors rather than any inbuilt tendency for labour law to favour one mode over another.

By contrast, the basic trade-off between 'subordination' and 'protection' is not contingent on local factors. It is a universal feature of labour law systems and is a function of their common response to the conditions of industrialisation in modern market economies. Thus, it is a response to the organisational requirements of the business enterprise and its public-bureaucratic equivalents, on the one hand, and to the nature of the risks to which wage-dependent workers are inevitably exposed in a market economy, on the other. These include the risks of workplace injury in a context where the pace and content of the work obligation is, to a certain degree, for the employer to define, as well as the risks of loss or non-availability of waged income, through unemployment, sickness or old age. The legal status of the 'employee' denotes a worker who, by virtue of being at the disposal of another, can thereby access forms of protection which are in some cases built into the wage itself and in other instances depend on co-insurance across a group of employers and workers, as expressed through systems of social security.

Labour law regulation involves an adjustment of the basic private law forms of contract and property, but does not entail their complete displacement. The employment relationship remains a contract, founded on reciprocal obligations, and is not especially unusual in containing certain implied terms which can only with difficulty be modified or avoided, or may, in some systems, take the form of imperative norms or *ius cogens*; other distinct contract types have these features. In this context, it may not be helpful to refer to the 'decommodification' of the employment relationship through labour law rules.[19] On the contrary, labour and social security law together commodify labour power, in the dual sense of identifying the capacity to work subject to the coordinating power of the employer as the essential subject matter of the contract of employment, and in putting in place the mechanisms of protection and co-insurance which form the basis for the reproduction of labour capacity or the power to labour over time. For a market economy to be sustainable, a means must be found for the reproduction of commodities on a sustainable basis.[20] In the case of labour law, the reproduction of labour power on a continuing basis is a function of, among other things, rules on training and skills acquisition which in many national contexts were carried over and adapted from pre-modern apprenticeship regulation; health and safety and working time regulation which limit the exposure of workers to physical and

[19] On the complexities inherent in the use of this term, see G Esping-Andersen, *The Three Worlds of Welfare Capitalism* (Princeton, NJ, Princeton University Press, 1990) ch 2.

[20] A Picchio del Mercato, *Social Reproduction: the Political Economy of the Labour Market* (Cambridge, Cambridge University Press, 1992).

psychological harms; minimum wage laws and collective agreements which seek to guarantee access to a 'living wage' which reflects at least subsistence needs; laws which permit active labour market participation to be combined with family commitments, including pregnancy and parenthood more generally; and legislation aiming at the elimination of discrimination on grounds unrelated to individual capabilities and, in some cases, requiring the accommodation of particular forms of disadvantage.[21]

Labour law rules are contested terrain. This observation applies both to the coordinating rules which empower employers and serve to protect their claims to property in the enterprise (including rules limiting collective industrial action by workers), and to the risk allocation rules which protect employees against labour market hazards. These rules inevitably have distributional consequences in addition to serving wider goals which in principle are in all relevant parties' interests. It is thus not surprising that employers lobby against labour law rules and describe them as an 'imposition' or 'burden', any more than trade unions can be expected to stand quietly by when laws limiting strike action or restricting the scope of freedom of association are enacted and applied. In neither case does the intensely political character of labour law regulation amount to a negation of its role as a form of economic governance.

The above brief description of the essential features of labour law regulation can be thought of as a conceptual model which draws on (inevitably somewhat reductively) the rich institutional detail of individual systems. Certain salient features of the operation of the market which are implied by this legal model can now be identified.

B. The Market has a Normative Base

From the viewpoint of labour law, labour market relations are not free-standing, in the sense of simply representing the outcomes of exchanges agreed between rational, utility-maximising agents. The 'rationality' displayed by the actors in the context of the contract of employment is conditioned by shared understandings of what the employment relationship entails in terms of reciprocal obligations, which are articulated at the level of the legal system. In this sense, the labour market rests on a normative foundation which is invisible in the Walrasian conception of the market and inadequately captured by the Hayekian one.

Nearly all labour law systems express norms of reciprocity, either at the level of the individual employment relationship, where they may be termed mutual duties of cooperation or care, and/or at the collective level, in particular in systems which recognise the institutions of workplace-level co-determination or joint decision-making between representatives of management and labour.

[21] See Deakin and Wilkinson, *The Law of the Labour Market*, above n 4, ch 5.

In the English common law, the evolution of mutual duties of cooperation, expressed as implied terms of the contract of employment, has been one of the most striking features of the past three decades.[22] It is perhaps not a coincidence that this tendency towards the legal formalisation of a duty of 'mutual trust and confidence' was gaining ground during a period of deregulation, when collective labour law protections were being removed in the name of market efficiency; the common law expanded to fill a gap left by the growing absence of trade unions in the workplace. Whether it has done so effectively is another question. Arguably, British workers were better protected against abuse of power by employers when collective agreements and other wage-fixing arrangements covered over 80 per cent of the workforce, as they did up to the late 1970s, as opposed to less than 30 per cent today. What is of interest for current purposes is the way in which the law of contract was able to accommodate the logic of cooperation, inserting diffuse obligations into the contract of employment for the protection of the physical, economic and psychological interests of the employee, as the equivalent to the open-ended duty of obedience which it has long recognised as a foundation of the employer's 'managerial prerogative'. This was a development which aligned British labour law with a continental European model of the employment relation which had already recognised inherent limitations on the power of the employer through the civil law notions of 'good faith' in the middle decades of the twentieth century, mostly before the rise of modern employment protection legislation.[23]

The US case offers a potential counter-example and a refutation of the hypothesis of labour law's recognition of the reciprocal character of the employment relationship, in its adherence to the rule of 'employment at will' and related resistance to the logic of inherent obligations of cooperation or good faith within the employment relationship. In the British case, too, something of the logic of the common law model of the contract at will also remains in the refusal of the judiciary to extend the effects of the term of mutual trust and confidence to the employer's decision to terminate the contract. The position of the UK courts on this point can be explained, in part, by the (questionable) policy of giving priority to statutory rules on dismissal over those of the common law, and the wish to avoid creating a dual jurisdiction, with common law claims running alongside statutory ones.[24] No such explanation is available for the US case, which remains an outlier in this regard as it adheres to the common law rule of employment at will in a context where employment protection legislation, along European lines,

[22] D Brodie, 'The Heart of the Matter: Mutual Trust and Confidence' (1996) 25 *Industrial Law Journal* 121, and 'Beyond Exchange: the New Contract of Employment' (1998) 27 *Industrial Law Journal* 79; M Freedland, *The Personal Employment Contract* (Oxford, Oxford University Press, 2003) 154–70. On the equivalent development in the New Zealand context, see Anderson, *New Zealand's Labour Law*, above n 5, ch 9.

[23] M Freedland and N Kountouris, *The Legal Construction of Personal Work Relations* (Oxford, Oxford University Press, 2011)180–87.

[24] H Collins, 'Compensation for Dismissal: In Search of Principle' (2012) 42 *Industrial Law Journal* 208.

is almost entirely absent.[25] The reluctance of the US courts to modify the rule of employment at will owes much to a strong ideological framing of the issue of employment regulation, which until the middle decades of the twentieth century saw legal intervention in the employment contract as an unjustified interference with the employer's property rights,[26] and has more recently relied on instrumental economic reasoning characterising dismissal protection as 'inefficient'.[27]

Support for the view that the US position on employment at will is ideological rather than functional comes from survey evidence suggesting that US workers believe that an employer cannot lawfully dismiss an employee for arbitrary reasons or without just cause.[28] This view is mistaken because, cases of discrimination law and unionised workplaces aside, the employment at will rule enables the employer to do precisely this. It would seem that US law on this point is out of step with the expectations of one side to the contract, at least. A common response to this point is to argue that if arbitrary dismissal, while lawful, is widely perceived as a breach of social norms, a non-legal sanction is available in the form of the resulting reputational damage to the employer. This argument is a slightly reformulated version of the idea that the 'rationality' of the contracting parties, defined as their propensity for self-interested behaviour, is sufficient to ensure the emergence of self-enforcing, cooperative equilibria.[29]

The conditions under which parties engaged in repeated exchange will gravitate spontaneously towards a mutually welfare-enhancing stable state or 'Nash equilibrium' are, however, unlikely to be satisfied through self-interested action alone. In evolutionary and epistemic game theory, concepts of 'correlated equilibrium' increasingly stress the role of shared understandings of fair behaviour in framing contractual interactions.[30] Fairness norms, such as versions of the Rawslian 'maximin' principle (according to which parties contracting behind a veil of ignorance would agree to a distribution of resources which minimised the disadvantages of the least well off), turn out to provide a good, formal description of stable states in which the gains from cooperation between parties engaged in long-term trade are maximised.[31]

[25] S Deakin, P Lele and M Siems, 'The Evolution of Labour Law: Comparing and Calibrating Regulatory Régimes' (2007) *International Labour Review* 133.

[26] C Sunstein, 'Lochner's Legacy' (1987) 87 *Columbia Law Review* 873.

[27] R Epstein, 'In Defense of the Contract at Will' (1984) 51 *University of Chicago Law Review* 947.

[28] P Kim, 'Bargaining with Imperfect Information: a Study of Worker Perceptions of Legal Protection in an At-Will World' (1997) 83 *Cornell Law Review* 105.

[29] Epstein, 'In Defense', above n 27.

[30] H Gintis, *The Bounds of Reason: Game Theory and the Unification of the Behavioral Sciences* (Princeton, NJ, Princeton University Press, 2009), discussed in a legal-theoretical context by S Deakin 'Legal Evolution: Integrating Economic and Systemic Approaches' (2011) 7 *Review of Law and Economics* 659.

[31] L Sacconi, *A Rawlsian View of CSR and the Game Theory of its Implementation (Part I): the Multi-Stakeholder Model of Corporate Governance*, Econometica Working Paper No 22 (August 2010), available at http://econometica.it/wp/wp22.pdf.

These theories may provide a justification for the labour law technique of inserting norms of reciprocity and fairness into the contract of employment, a technique often denounced as an 'interference' with freedom of contract and as a potential distorting factor in the operation of the market. It would be equally plausible to see the duty of mutual trust and cooperation, along with other legal expressions of fairness norms, as a device permitting more effective coordination, and thus more efficient contracting, in the context of the employment relationship. Of most interest for present purposes, however, is the significance of the emergence of the model of mutual trust within legal discourse on employment. The legal concept may be understood as a refracted version of an element in the practice of employment, which has emerged within juridical discourse via the selective pressures placed on the law through a combination of legislation and litigation. As such, the legal concept is evidence for a model of the labour market in which 'rational' economic behaviour is framed by conventional understandings of what is 'fair' treatment in employment. Put slightly differently, rationality itself is defined by reference to widely-held beliefs concerning limits to self-interest. This is the sense in which the labour market has a 'normative base'.

C. The Market is Not Self-equilibrating

In the Walrasian model of competitive equilibrium, the forces of supply and demand tend towards equality and hence towards an efficient distribution of resources without the need for an external agency, such as the legal system or social norms, to correct or redirect market allocations. In the Hayekian model, the legal system and social norms are at least visible, but the role of the abstract rules of just conduct is to provide the building blocks of exchange, not to alter outcomes. Direct intervention to reverse or modify the results of autonomous contracting will disrupt the 'spontaneous order' of the market and prevent it from operating to align expectations.

At first sight, it would seem that reversing market outcomes is precisely what most labour law rules aim to achieve. Setting legally-binding minimum rates of pay, limits to working time and controls over termination of employment imply a legal alteration of the distributions that would have been arrived had the contracting parties been left to make their own agreements. To take this view, however, is to confuse the legal formality of the principle of freedom of contract with the empirical existence of an efficient market allocation. A market may be said to be in equilibrium if society's resources are being well used, or, if the equilibrium is complete, as well used as possible in the circumstances. Individual exchanges may sum to a perfect market allocation only if very specific conditions are met, including complete specification of property rights and optimal contract enforcement, both of which imply zero transaction costs. Information asymmetries and 'natural' distortions arising from inequalities of power and resources can similarly prevent a spontaneous movement to equilibrium. Theoretically, the idea of a perfectly competitive labour market is a contradiction in terms, and it is refuted by empirical evidence as well.[32]

It does not follow from the inherent implausibility of a perfectly competitive labour market that labour law has the aim or effect of 'perfecting' market outcomes. To make this the benchmark for the legitimacy of labour market interventions it to set an impossible standard. A common objection to minimum wage laws, even on the part of those who accept that there may be a monopsony-based case for regarding wages in low-paying occupations as an incomplete or inaccurate signal of value, is that it is not possible, though legal intervention, to calibrate in a precise way the level of wages that would restore the market to equilibrium.[33] This is a sound objection as far as it goes, since it is almost certainly the case that a central wage-fixing body cannot collate the information needed to identify a market clearing wage. But it does not follow that it would be preferable to leave low-paying labour markets entirely unregulated. Low pay is not solely, or even predominantly, a consequence of a lack of skill on the part of workers. It is, mostly, an institutional phenomenon, associated with structural barriers to autonomous worker organisation and with firms' reluctance to invest in training and skills formation.[34] The solutions to low pay are, consequently, institutional in nature; they include proactive state support for training as well as incentives for firms to invest in productivity-improving techniques and modes of organisation, as well as legally mandated wage floors.[35] Institutional solutions of this sort may not exactly replicate perfectly competitive equilibria, but they may have the effect of shifting the *equilibrium path* of a given industry or sector, away from dependence on low pay as a source of competitive advantage, in favour of a productive system based on the upgrading of labour and capital stocks.

Labour law regulation, then, does not displace the operation of the labour market, so much as compensate for the absence, in practice, of the general self-equilibrating mechanism assumed by the Walrasian model. Labour law rules should be thought of, not as external interferences with the market, but as endogenous responses to market failures, triggered by self-regulatory mechanisms and, in turn, supporting their operation.[36] This is how labour law discourse itself mostly views the functioning of labour law rules. Direct displacement of contractual relations by mandatory regulation is, in practice, the exception; labour laws much

[32] See B Kaufman, 'The Impossibility of a Perfectly Competitive Labour Market' (2007) 31 *Cambridge Journal of Economics* 775.

[33] See the discussion of this point by Bruce Kaufman, 'Labor Law and Employment Regulation: Institutional and Neoclassical Perspectives' in K Dau-Schmidt, S Harris and O Lobel (eds), *Labor and Employment Law and Economics* (Cheltenham, Edward Elgar, 2009) 17–20.

[34] C Craig, J Rubery, R Tarling and F Wilkinson, *Labour Market Structure, Industrial Organisation and Low Pay* (Cambridge, Cambridge University Press, 1982).

[35] S Deakin and F Wilkinson, 'Minimum Wage Legislation' in K Dau-Schmidt, S Harris and O Lobel (eds), *Labor and Employment Law and Economics* (Cheltenham, Edward Elgar, 2009).

[36] S Deakin and P Sarkar, 'Assessing the Long-Run Economic Impact of Labour Law Systems: a Theoretical Reappraisal and Analysis of New Time Series Data' (2008) 39 *Industrial Relations Journal* 453, 455–57.

more often take effect by supplementing or extending the scope of industry- or firm-level self-regulation, or by opening up spaces for self-regulation through the operation of default rules of various kinds. The repertoire of such 'reflexive' regulatory techniques is now very extensive.[37] To speak, as the Hayekian model does, of social legislation as a series of external 'commands' interfering with spontaneous private ordering, is to set up a false dichotomy.

D. The Market is Institutionally Bounded

In *The Economic Approach to Human Behaviour*,[38] Gary Becker influentially argued that the fundamental axioms underlying the Walrasian model of competitive equilibrium (consistent preferences and maximising behaviour, together constituting the core of rational actor concept, and the notion of the self-equilibrating market mechanism), if 'relentlessly and unflinchingly applied', were capable of explaining all societal phenomena. The implication of this view is that institutions which might appear to have a role in underpinning economic exchange, including the legal system, can best be understood using a market logic. Thus, it becomes pointless to try to explain the institutional origins of the market since, in a reversal of perspective, it is in the market that the origins of institutions are to be found. Conversely, the logic of market exchange can be seen to extend into all spheres of social life. Individuals always and everywhere act according to the postulates of rationality, and their interactions are universally guided by the invisible hand of the market, even in contexts apparently far removed from commercial or business relations, such as the family. Richard Posner's *Economic Analysis of Law*[39] took this idea and applied it to the study of legal rules and institutions in the unrelenting way that Becker envisaged.

By contrast, a view from within legal doctrine, in this case referring not just to labour law discourse but also to that of contract law more generally, would stress the limits of the market, and its interdependence with societal institutions displaying a different logic. The private law of the nineteenth century, notwithstanding its general orientation towards the value of freedom of contract, imposed limits on that principle which derived from an understanding that there were other competing and, in some cases, superior values. Thus, contracts with a tendency to undermine the legal system and the family were regarded as void and hence unenforceable even in the liberally-minded English common law, as were agreements for slavery or bonded labour. In this way, even in the nineteenth century heyday

[37] See R Rogowski and T Wilthagen (eds), *Reflexive Labour Law* (Deventer, Kluwer, 1994); C Arup, P Gahan, J Howe, R Johnstone, R Mitchell and A O'Donnell (eds), *Labour Law and Labour Market Regulation* (Sydney, Federation Press, 2006).

[38] Chicago, IL, University of Chicago Press, 1976.

[39] Boston, NJ, Little, Brown, 1972, mostly recently published in its eighth edn, New York, Aspen Publishers, 2011.

of *laissez-faire*, the common law rejected the idea that a market logic had universal application.[40] In the civil law systems, ideas of *ordre public* and abuse of rights played a somewhat more extensive role in subordinating contractual freedom to values of social solidarity. These were all doctrines initially developed within the core of private law, and not simply extra-contractual impositions derived from social legislation. As the pace of social reform increased from the final quarter of the nineteenth century onwards, these private law limits on freedom of contract were overtaken by legislation enacted on a more systematic basis and on a far greater scale than the private law of contract, property and tort had ever admitted. But the Hayekian idea of a sharp break between a market-orientated private law of the nineteenth century and the constructivist regulatory programme of the twentieth masks a more fundamental continuity of institutional design across the two periods. The market did not have the priority over other societal institutions that more recent theories, in both economics and law, have sought to give it.

The idea that the market is institutionally bounded has a dual sense: the market is both limited by, but also supported by, the state and the institutions of civil society. The market, if left purely to its own devices, is not self-sustaining. In the long evolution of the English law of contract, a continuous running thread is the idea that the law will not enforce contracts 'in restraint of trade', that is, agreements which, while in all other respects conforming to the requirements of valid contracts, seek to suppress the competitive mechanism.[41] The same idea of a market which, through 'free' or unregulated contracting, tends towards its own destruction, is found in modern economic theories of the market-limiting effects of asymmetric information (the 'market for lemons').[42] It is also present in the modern continental European ordoliberal school of economic thought, which insists on the need for an active state to support the system of competition through, among other things, controls on cartels and the maintenance of stable prices.[43]

IV. CONCLUSION: THE NEED FOR NEW MODELS IN LAW AND ECONOMICS

Whatever its value as a heuristic device, the model of competitive equilibrium cannot serve as a basis for a society-wide institutional design. Attempts to make it

[40] S Deakin, '*Capacitas*: Contract Law, Capabilities, and the Legal Foundations of the Market' in S Deakin and A Supiot (eds), *Capacitas: Contract Law and the Institutional Foundations of a Market Economy* (Oxford, Hart Publishing, 2009).

[41] See Deakin, '*Capacitas*', above n 40.

[42] G Akerlof, 'The Market for "Lemons": Quality Uncertainty and the Market Mechanism' (1970) 84 *Quarterly Journal of Economics* 488.

[43] On the ordoliberal conception of the law-economy relation, see generally V Vanberg, *The Constitution of Markets: Essays in Political Economy* (London, Routledge, 2001), and on its relevance to the methodology of the Norma research programme building on Anna Christensen's work, see P Norberg, 'Market Forces, Market Prices and the Market Functional Pattern' in A Numhauser-Henning and M Rönnmar (eds), *Fifteen Years with the Norma Research Programme* (Lund, Faculty of Law, Lund University, 2010).

do so inevitably run up against severe practical difficulties which sooner or later lead to a reappraisal of the limits of market ordering. Thus, efforts to 'deregulate' the labour market, of the kind which have been pursued in varying degrees in developed market economies since the late 1970s, have most often succeeded only in adding to the extent and complexity of labour legislation. The result has been a contradictory division of labour, between, on the one hand, the domain of economic 'science', within which the adapted Walrasian model of general equilibrium holds sway, and the realm of 'political economy' or practical politics, in which the application of that model is attenuated by the need for workable forms of governance. But because models matter, the persistence of the Walrasian model in the domain of economic theory represents a continuing constraint on policy-making.[44] There is a pressing practical need, as well as an intellectual one, for a new theoretical synthesis in both economics and law.

In economics, the inadequacy of models which abstract from the real-world conditions of markets is increasingly being recognised. In theory, market interactions take place between agents whose behaviour can be predicted using axioms of rationality and expected utility, on the basis of stable prices which incorporate all relevant information. In practice, agents have unequal access to information and resources and prices are at best imperfectly expressed. For the market to operate effectively as a mechanism of resource allocation, non-market institutions for overcoming asymmetries of knowledge and resources are required. These include mechanisms of governance arising from self-regulation but also the public and governmental apparatus of the legal system. Legal and regulatory norms often cannot be straightforwardly mandated or imposed, but they may share with the mechanisms of market exchange certain properties of adaptive adjustment to a changing environment, properties which need to be identified and modelled if they are to be better understood. This points to a research agenda that would seek to identify both the shared evolutionary properties of the market and the legal system, and also the boundaries between the two.

Legal models of the law-economy relation too are in need of adjustment. Under the influence of a highly formalistic analysis, legal rules are increasingly assumed to have an invariant relationship to economic outcomes. Thus, labour law regulations, according to a view which has even been endorsed by the European Court of Justice,[45] inevitably produce distortions in the operation of the market, which can only be justified if a non-economic goal or aim, generally described in terms of the protection of social or other non-economic interests, can be weighed in the balance against the value of market efficiency. Such an analysis, while leaving open a space for the articulation of social rights within the discourse of European law, ultimately reinforces the view that labour legislation is a fetter on the operation of

[44] See D Colander, H Föllmer, A Haas, M Goldberg, K Juselius, A Kirman, T Lux and B Sloth, 'The Financial Crisis and the Systemic Failure of the Economic Profession' (2009) 2–3 *Critical Review* 249.

[45] In the '*Laval* Quartet': see Deakin, 'Regulatory Competition', above n 5.

the economy. It is not surprising, then, that the balancing exercise undertaken by the courts ends up privileging 'economic freedoms' over 'social rights'.

The alternative to the mode of analysis just described is to understand labour law as a mode of market governance which provides the basis for sustainable economic development. As Anna Christensen recognised,[46] this alternative does not imply subordinating 'social' values to 'economic' ones. Rather, it involves a systematic articulation and defence of the idea that, as the labour market setting has a normative foundation, it cannot effectively operate in the absence of the 'fairness norms' and values of solidarity to which labour law gives expression. Just as there can be no market without law,[47] so there can be no economic sphere without the social one.

[46] Christensen, 'Normative Patterns', above n 1.
[47] Supiot, 'Dogmatic Foundations', above n 7.

9

The Use of Market Forces in Social Security: How Insurance-like Should Social Insurance Be?

PER NORBERG

I. INTRODUCTION

THERE ARE MANY different ways of considering social security. Anna Christensen often chose to analyse it using the Theory of Law as Normative Patterns in a Normative Field,[1] which I will also apply in this chapter. Each normative pattern can be seen as a 'magnetic pole' that more or less successfully attracts the solution to a legal problem. The three normative patterns relevant to most social security problems are: Just Distribution, Protection of Established Position and the Market-Functional pattern.

Just Distribution is a pattern covering a number of regulatory outcomes that are considered 'just'. This might be a benefit that pays all recipients an equal amount, such as the Swedish child benefit, or it might be a benefit awarded according to needs, such as a housing benefit.

Protection of Established Position is based on a hierarchical view of justice. Its aim is to protect citizens from moving too far down the societal ladder. Two examples are the protection of tenants, and social security built on the income replacement principle. If an unemployed person is to be able to keep the house he or she has built with borrowed money, the person must receive benefit payments in relation to previous income. If a person is accustomed to a high income, he or she needs more money to maintain a usual standard of living.

[1] On the theory, see A Christensen, 'Skydd för etablerad position—Ett normativt grundmönster' (1996) 4 *Tidskrift for rettsvitenskap* 519; A Christensen, 'Protection of Established Position, a Basic Normative Pattern' (2000) 40 *Scandinavian Studies in Law* 285; A Christensen, 'Polycentricity and Normative Patterns' in H Petersen and H Zahle (eds), *Legal Polycentricity: Consequences of Pluralism in Law* (Aldershot, Ashgate, 1995). See also *Normative Development within the Social Dimension*, Norma 1996:1 (Lund, 1996). The interaction between the legal system and basic societal structures began to be developed in A Numhauser-Henning, *Rätten till fäderneslandet, Om jordförvärvslagen och dess funktioner mot bakgrund av jordbrukets utveckling i det svenska samhället* (Lund, Juristförlaget,1988).

The Market-Functional pattern consists of freedom of contract, freedom of trade, and the part of proprietary rights that deals with an owner's right to use, change the use of, or dispose of a property. The Market-Functional pattern espouses all changes that increase economic efficiency and, because such changes often involve changes in a person's established position, the Market-Functional pattern very often contradicts the Protection of Established Position.

In the marketplace, people use their resources to buy the things that give them most utility. When social security is constructed along the same market-functional principles as private insurance, people are sometimes given the same power to choose, as long as they pay for what they have chosen.

The balancing of the Market-Functional pattern against other normative patterns can be done in at least two different ways:

(1) directly, with the aim of upholding or changing the social norms inherent in the social security system; if so, people are not given a choice in how to act in relation to a social norm–the state continues to decide on the social norms involved;
(2) indirectly, as a way for the state to avoid making a normative choice directly, and instead to use market mechanisms with the aim of achieving the same goal indirectly. When the state avoids making a normative choice directly and instead creates a market in this way, people are given the opportunity to act against the social norm if they pay the market price for it.

Section II contains a short description of the discussion about a ceiling for the benefits in the Swedish unemployment insurance system created in 1997. This is an example of the balancing of market-functional concerns and the concern for protection of established position, and is also an example of a direct conflict between two normative patterns. If the benefit ceiling is high, there is strong protection of established position, but there is an economic incentive not to seek new work with low pay. The lower the ceiling, the less protection there is, but also less incentive to refuse new work at low wages. In this example, the state sets the norm, and the balance of the normative patterns occurs in relation to that norm. The salient feature of this example is that the unemployed person was *not allowed* to make a choice; a control system always led people towards accepting jobs with lower pay.

Section III provides a description of the 2007–2008 reform of the financing of Swedish unemployment insurance. In this example, the state wanted to achieve a specific goal (lower wages for unskilled workers). The state could not legislate directly: setting wages is a task for the social partners. Instead, the state chose an indirect way of legislating, by creating a system in which high wages for unskilled workers would become so costly for the members of the unemployment funds that the trade unions would adapt by lowering wages in occupations with high unemployment.

In this case, the state *allowed* the trade unions to decide their strategy on wages for unskilled workers. The funding for unemployment insurance became more like private insurance, in the sense that the unemployment funds needed to extract fees from their members that reflected the individual funds' costs for unemployment. If they chose a strategy resulting in an increase in 'their' unemployment rate, the cost of unemployment insurance would increase for their members, in much the same way as insurance costs rise for a private industry if it becomes more accident-prone. However, no control system was in place, beyond the market pricing of the unemployment risk, for punishing trade unions for making the wrong choice.

Section IV includes a description of the Swedish pension system. It begins with the general development of the first Swedish retirement pension, and ends with the current pension system. One important goal in the current pension system was that it should promote later retirement. The state did not dare to legislate directly by raising the pensionable age. Instead, the same goal was to be achieved by introducing the lifetime principle, in which each year of work contributed to a higher pension and gave persons the right to postpone retirement, with actuarially adapted pensions rewarding a delayed pension and making early retirement costly. Employment protection was also extended to 67 years.

The new pension system is built partly on the same principles as private capital insurance for old age, and partly in a way that appears to the individual as a type of bank savings. Using one's own money was supposed to make persons retire later. However, there was no control system, outside this market pricing of taking early retirement, for punishing persons who made the wrong choice.

Both reforms failed in the sense that they did not achieve the specific goals described above. The important actors did not behave in the manner expected by the government. These problems are discussed in section V. When the state relies on market forces to achieve something indirectly, special problems arise.

II. UNEMPLOYMENT INSURANCE IN SWEDEN: BENEFIT LEVELS AND CEILING

The current Swedish unemployment insurance was introduced in 1997, and is divided into two parts. The first part is basic mandatory insurance, giving anyone who has worked full time for a year before being unemployed 1,600 SEK (176 euros) per week. There is also a second, voluntary system. By joining an unemployment insurance fund and paying contributions for at least one year before unemployment (in addition to the work requirement), the person receives 80 per cent of his or her previous pay, up to a ceiling of 3,400 SEK (374 euros) per week. At first glance, this system would appear to be dominated by the Protection of Established Position pole.

In 1997, the ceiling was 2,900 SEK (319 euros) per week. This amount was stipulated in the Employment Insurance Ordinance.[2] The government considered

[2] SFS (1997:835) s 4.

that there ought to be some sort of indexation[3] of this amount, but no index has ever been put in place.

In 2001, the ceiling was raised for the first 100 days of unemployment, to 3,400 SEK (374 euros) per week. In 2002, the ceiling was once again raised, to 3,650 SEK (402 euros) per week for the first 100 days and 3,400 SEK (374 euros) per week for the following weeks. In the government bill, the Social Democratic head of department wrote:

> It is difficult to find evidence suggesting that taxes and labour law are of consequence for 'structural unemployment', which is used as a measurement of how well the labour market works. In two areas, however, most economic experts are in agreement: the organisation of wage formation and the organisation of unemployment insurance are important for the functioning of the labour market ... The government intends to follow up on and evaluate the effects of this reform before any further changes are made. The functioning of the labour market must be taken into account. It is also important to retain the character of unemployment insurance as an insurance form based on the income replacement principle. (author's translation)[4]

If a person is unemployed and turns down a new job with pay equal to previous earnings, he or she will lose 20 per cent of his or her income, since unemployment insurance covers only up to 80 per cent of the previous income. The person is thus faced with a cost (a economic incentive to find a job). However, if the pay for the new job is 80 per cent of the previous pay, then there is no immediate cost involved in turning down the job. A ceiling that provides a benefit income for an unemployed person equal to the income for a person who is employed but with low pay, is thus problematic.

On the other hand, the income replacement principle and the need to protect established positions constitute a strongly held normative value. A person with a decent income may own a house and have a large mortgage. The idea that this income should be protected at the level necessary to keep the house is a strongly held value. The actual amount set as a ceiling reflects a balance between those two opposites.

In 2006, the Alliance (four centre-right parties) took over government in Sweden. The higher level of unemployment benefit during the first 100 days was abolished and the ceiling was not raised in line with inflation. Today, after years of minor erosion due to inflation and wage improvements, the ceiling for unemployment benefit is well below the minimum wages in collective agreements, and for unskilled full-time workers only a small minority do not reach the ceiling. Thus, for full-time workers, everybody with income-related benefit will have virtually the same unemployment benefit. For these persons, there is no longer a significant element of protection of established position in unemployment insurance.

[3] Government bill 1996/97:107, 90.

[4] Government bill 1999/2000:139, 24 and 34.

This is an example of a pragmatic balancing of normative values with the aim of upholding the social norm inherent in the social insurance system. All agree that unemployment insurance should only be for persons who are involuntarily unemployed. All Swedish social insurance includes a large element of control. The Swedish Public Employment Service supervises the unemployed and makes them seek vacant positions. The bylaws of the Inspection for Unemployment Insurance say that a person is entitled to refuse a job if the pay is less than 90 per cent of that person's benefit, and the Unemployment Insurance Act says that the pay must be in line with collective agreements,[5] which today is the only rule of any significance.

Politicians may agree or disagree on the appropriate level of compensation, and in Sweden they strongly disagree on the appropriate ceiling,[6] but they do agree that to uphold the system, there is a need to have a mix of economic incentives and control. The balance is tilted toward the Market-Functional pattern and Just Distribution under the current government, but this would move significantly towards Protection of Established Position, should the Social Democrats return to power.

However, all the major political parties agree on the appropriate social norm for the individual's behaviour in the system. They all agree on the norm that says that an unemployed person must take a new job at lower pay than the previous job, even if their benefit is equal to the pay. This is thus an example of the state directly setting the norms within the social security system. The particular problems arising when people are given the opportunity to act against the social norm if they pay the market price for it, do not occur in this example. There is, and always has been, a control system for inducing people to accept jobs with less pay.

III. INFLUENCING WAGE FORMATION INDIRECTLY THROUGH CHANGES IN UNEMPLOYMENT INSURANCE

A. Collective Bargaining and Wage Formation in Sweden

Besides unemployment insurance, wage formation is the second obviously important factor for the level of unemployment. Calculating minimum wages in Sweden is difficult, with over 300 central collective agreements, each having many minimum wage levels (related to age, years of experience, and so on). In 2005, Skedinger examined seven major collective agreements, and concluded that minimum wages were generally 60–70 per cent of median wages, and in some

[5] IAFFS 2004:3, s 15 and Act (1997:238) on Unemployment Insurance, s.11 point 2.

[6] The main opposition party, the Social Democratic Party, wants to raise the ceiling to a level that gives 80 per cent of wage earners 80 per cent of their actual income as benefit. See www.socialdemokraterna.se/Var-politik/Var-politik-A-till-O/A-kassan.

areas, such as hotels and restaurants, the minimum wage affected one-third of all workers; this is a high figure in an international comparison.[7]

The Government White Paper 2011:11 presented statistics on wages and education in Sweden. For persons educated to primary education level only, the average wage in 2007 was slightly more than 20,000 SEK (2,200 euros) per month, and approximately 67 per cent of these persons were in employment. The next grouping was of persons educated to secondary vocational level. Their average wage was almost the same, but their likelihood of being employed had risen to 87 per cent.[8]

These figures were interpreted as suggesting that high minimum wages made employers choose not to hire persons with primary education only, thus making them unemployed. The current government believes that lower wages for workers with the least education would decrease unemployment.

Since 1938, non-intervention regarding collective wage negotiations has been a guiding principle in the Swedish labour market. Only once (in 1971) has the state exercised its legislative powers to stop industrial action (strikes) and settle the wage conditions through special legislation.[9] Sweden has never had state minimum wages or state mechanisms for extending collective agreements beyond the persons directly or indirectly bound by the agreement itself. All major political parties agree that wage levels should be set within the framework of central collective agreements.

The government is of the opinion that the setting of wages is a problem to be solved by the social partners. Collective agreements are preferable to legislation, because mutual understanding creates legitimacy and stability regarding the agreements. The role of the state is only to provide the basic framework.[10] Thus, without violating a central element of the Swedish industrial relations model, the state can neither encourage employers to take a tough stance on minimum wages nor promise them support in the event of a strike.

Swedish blue-collar trade unions have (since the Second World War) always striven for high minimum wages and towards equalisation between occupations with high pay and those with lower pay. This is known as solidarity wage setting, and is sometimes applied at great cost. The large Swedish clothing industry was greatly downsized in the 1960s and 1970s. The trade unions accepted the argument that it was better to take temporary unemployment and work towards new jobs with normal Swedish wages, rather than to fight the closures of companies with low wages. The same applies today, when companies close plants and move production to countries with lower wages. Swedish trade unions do not criticise management for working to enhance profits. Instead, they accept globalisation,

[7] P Skedinger, 'Hur höga är minimilönerna?' (2005) 18 *IFAU* 33.

[8] Government White Paper 2011:11, 41.

[9] C Lundh, *Spelets regler—institutioner och lönebildning på den svenska arbetsmarknaden* (Stockholm, SNS Förlag, 2002) 254.

[10] Government bill 2011/12:1, *Bilaga 3 arbetsmarknad och arbetsliv*, 91.

and often argue that low-paying jobs should leave Sweden and be replaced by jobs with better pay.

From the Second World War to the mid-1970s, employers and trade unions were in agreement on central wage negotiations and solidarity wage setting. However, this has now evolved into a highly political question, and today employers are strongly against solidarity wage setting.[11]

Solidarity wage setting and unemployment insurance are linked to each other. If an industry pays wages that are too low, unemployment will be accepted as a price worth paying if wage demands make the industry unprofitable and thus force it to leave the market. Through labour market measures, such as further training, workers will be prepared for work in industries with better pay. However, the government did not believe labour market measures to be the answer for the workers least likely to be employed. The government, and employers, demanded wage cuts for unskilled workers, but were not able to intervene directly.

B. 2007 and 2008 Reform of the Financing of Unemployment Insurance

In Sweden, trade unions organise and operate most of the unemployment funds.[12] The system is heavily subsidised by the state. Many people believe that this system (the Ghent system) is a large contributory factor behind the high rate of Swedish unionisation.[13] For the average worker, membership of an unemployment fund and membership of a trade union have traditionally been mentally linked. Some unions do not allow membership without concurrent membership of their unemployment fund. However, it is always possible to be a member of the relevant unemployment fund, even if one is not affiliated with the trade union in question.

This reform was conducted in two steps, in 2007 and 2008. First, unemployment insurance and trade union membership became more expensive with the abolition of tax deductions of 40 per cent for unemployment insurance and 25 per cent for trade union membership. Before the reform, the state financed 90 per cent of unemployment fund costs. The system was constructed in such a way that the rate of unemployment in the fund became irrelevant. For unions with high unemployment, the replacement level on the margin was 100 per cent of direct expenses. That was changed. In the second step, the replacement rate was lowered to 70 per cent, and high unemployment came to be very costly for the funds as of 1 July 2008.

[11] Lundh, *Spelets regler,* above n 9, 187–94 and 223–85.

[12] Traditionally, trade or professional unions have operated all funds. In 1998, the state created Alfakassan, as a politically independent unemployment insurance fund, accepting members regardless of their profession. This fund, however, has only 73,000 members. Alfakassan, *Yearly Report 2010*, 9.

[13] See, eg, J Lind, 'A Nordic Saga? The Ghent System and Trade Unions' (2007) 15(1) *International Journal of Employment Studies* 49.

The government gave two motives for this reform.

> [1] If unemployment is expensive for the members of the unemployment fund, the fund will become more diligent in controlling the persons receiving benefit, to stop fraudulent claims ... [2] Because there is a connection between individual trade unions and individual unemployment funds, the unions will have incentives to act in a manner that does not raise the unemployment level of 'its' unemployment fund. (author's translation)[14]

Note particularly the second motive. The important decision, when a trade union can act in a way that enhances employment, is in central collective agreement negotiations regarding wages and other benefits. The trade unions with the highest unemployment rates can ask for the lowest wage increases, especially regarding minimum wages. When the reform was completed in July 2008, the central collective agreement had already been agreed on for the period 2007–2010.[15]

The unemployment fund for hotel and restaurant workers was forced to raise its membership fees by 333 SEK per month, to 430 SEK per month, which over a year amounts to 5,160 SEK (570 euros). The maximum gain from membership in the voluntary unemployment fund is 60,000 SEK (6,700 euros) a year. This is the difference between the basic flat rate mandatory insurance and the ceiling in the voluntary insurance scheme, based on the principle of income replacement.[16] Examining these figures, it is natural that persons in a sector in which they perceive their individual risk of unemployment to be low, may well decide not to purchase this insurance. Furthermore, young people in their first jobs, moving into their first rented apartment and living on their own, may also rationally decide not to insure themselves. If they do become involuntarily unemployed, there will be no one else in their household to support them, and if without personal wealth or other saleable possessions, they will be eligible for municipal social aid, and perhaps even housing benefit, which could be used to top up the basic flat rate unemployment benefit. A single parent working part-time will also often be in a similar situation, whereby it is perfectly rational to spend these 570 euros on other goods and services than on unemployment insurance. Housing benefit and municipal social aid may provide almost the same protection.

On the other hand, it is much harder to envisage a situation in which a white-collar worker would rationally not sign up for unemployment insurance. Their unemployment funds nowadays almost always have fees under 200 SEK (22 euros) per month, and many such workers pay as little as 90 SEK (10 euros) a

[14] Government bill 2006/07:15, 33ff.

[15] A Kjellberg, *Växande skillnader i a-kassan—ökad social polarisering*, Studies in Social Policy, Industrial Relations, Working Life and Mobility, Research Report 2010:2 (Sociologiska institutionen vid Lunds Universitet, updated 7 February 2012) 23 ff.

[16] This calculation leaves out the fact that benefits for long-term unemployment are also related to the person being insured, and that sick persons are often asked to change jobs and may need this benefit. However, probably not all the consequences of choosing not to insure oneself are visible to the average worker.

month.[17] In relation to their higher pay, this appears affordable, and should they abstain from income insurance, they would rarely be eligible for municipal social aid, either because they own a dwelling that is worth more than their mortgage (or they have other forms of personal wealth), or because they have a spouse with an income high enough to support them both.

This new system has led to a rapid decline in both union membership and unemployment fund membership for blue-collar unions. During the years 2007 and 2009, the unemployment fund for hotel and restaurant workers lost almost one-third of its members, as did the trade union itself.[18] The organisation rate dropped from 52 to 36 per cent.

Union density for private-sector, blue-collar workers fell by 10 per cent in the period 2007–2010, while falling only by 2 per cent for white-collar workers.[19] Membership of unemployment funds fell for blue-collar workers by 15 per cent in the same period.[20] The decline of union membership and unemployment insurance were both concentrated among those unions that most needed to raise their fees. When the fees increased, many workers thought hard about whether they could afford both memberships. Some dropped both, while others just dropped the one they considered the least useful.[21] Thus, for many people, the mental link between trade union membership and membership of an unemployment fund has been broken.

C. Trade Union Response to the New Financial Incentives

In 2010, there was a large round of collective bargaining, negotiations having started in 2009. Due to the economic crisis, the average wage increase was small, which was to be expected. The unemployment reform seemed to be having no effect at all. The blue-collar trade unions fought for the principle of solidarity wage setting in the same way as before, and in this they were successful. Trade unions in sectors with low wages received above-average pay increases, regardless of the unemployment rate. The low-pay trade union most affected, the Hotel and Restaurant Workers Union, behaved in exactly the same way as the least affected low-pay union, the Municipal Workers Union. Wage increases for

[17] A Kjellberg, 'The Decline in Swedish Union Density Since 2007' (2011) 1(1) *Nordic Journal of Working Life Studies* 75 ff. (He gives a table of selected funds and their fees.)

[18] Kjellberg, *Växande skillnader i a-kassan*, above n 15, 15.

[19] Kjellberg, 'The Decline in Swedish Union Density', above n 17, 80.

[20] It is difficult to compare this figure to that for white-collar workers, because workers with an academic degree can often choose between the unemployment fund for academics and the white-collar funds, and many switched to the cheapest alternative (the academic's fund increased by 5 per cent and the white-collar funds decreased by 11 per cent).

[21] Kjellberg, 'The Decline in Swedish Union Density', above n 17, 83 ff. See also A Kjellberg, 'The Swedish Ghent System and Trade Unions Under Pressure' (2009) 15(3–4) *Transfer* 487.

blue-collar workers were determined by pay levels only, and not by the level of unemployment.[22]

D. Analysis of the Market-Functionalism of the Finance Reform

Why was this reform such a failure? The financial incentives in the reform of the financing of unemployment insurance were designed to make trade unions with high unemployment hold back their pay demands. For a long time however, these unions have believed in solidarity wage setting, even if this principle is costly in terms of unemployment.[23] Along with many other blue-collar trade unions, the Hotel and Restaurant Workers Union genuinely believes that if their employers provide work that has such low productivity that it can be done only at low pay levels, then these jobs should disappear. In the long run, it is better for their members to become unemployed and then later be re-employed in another sector.

If the problem is not the job, but the worker, then the same reasoning applies. If the worker is unproductive, for example due to lack of secondary vocational training, then unemployment (and vocational training provided by the state during the unemployment period) followed by re-employment is better than lower pay.

This view of what is good for their members in the long run is so strongly held that even a trade union that has lost one-third of its members, both in the union and in the unemployment fund, still adheres to this view. This reform has thus utterly failed to achieve its purpose.

In a market, people and organisations make choices. When a state creates financial incentives in order to steer people towards certain choices, this works well enough when the preferences of the people and the government are similar. However, if these preferences are in utter opposition, then the people (in this case the trade unions) may well pay the market price in order to uphold their convictions (preferences).

The salient difference between this example and the example of the ceiling on unemployment benefits is thus that, with regard to the financing reform, there was no control system, outside this market pricing of the unemployment risk, for punishing trade unions for making the wrong choice. There was no direction from society on the level of social norm setting.

[22] Kjellberg, 'The Decline in Swedish Union Density', above n 17, 91.

[23] Lundh, *Spelets regler*, above n 9, 187–94 and 223–85. It is the employers that drive the movement toward flexible local wage setting. LO (the national Swedish confederation of blue-collar trade unions) works toward coordinated wage negotiations and solidarity between stronger and weaker groups of workers in the 2012 wage negotiations. See www.lo.se/home/lo/home.nsf/unidView/E501F3A44E7198FBC12578FB004EEEFF/$file/Gemensamma_krav_avtal2012.pdf (2012-02-01).

IV. THE PENSION EXAMPLE

A. Pension Systems and Pensionable Age in Sweden

Sweden put in place its first comprehensive state pension system in 1913. Almost everyone of working age had to make a contribution of 3–13 SEK per year, depending on income. This money was placed in a fund, in which each person had his or her individual account. Pensions were paid out when the person reached the age of 67, and were used to fund a lifetime monthly sum according to actuarial principles. For men, this would be 30 per cent of the money paid in (plus interest), and 24 per cent for women. Statistically, men had higher mortality rates.

Pensions were low, and assuming a person paid the maximum amount for 50 years at 0 per cent real interest, then that person would have received 195 SEK per year as old-age pension.[24] This figure should be compared to the normal pay for unskilled manual labour in full employment, which was 600 SEK per year.

Of all of the persons reaching 67 years of age, 80 per cent were unable to work. Only 20 per cent were healthy enough to choose between work and leisure. If they opted for leisure, then they would have had to pay the full price themselves. Their old-age pension was paid with their own money and would not provide much income.

There was also a pension supplement paid out by the state. The maximum amount for a man was 150 SEK per year (140 SEK for a woman). This supplement could be awarded to any person permanently unable to work and above 15 years of age. This was an invalidity pension, and a part of the reform much more expensive compared to the old-age pension.

The disabled person could earn up 50 SEK without the invalidity pension being affected. Higher incomes[25] would result in 50 per cent deductions in the invalidity benefit. Persons earning 350 SEK would thus receive no benefit. The usual thing for a 67-year-old to do would thus be to have both the old-age pension and apply for the supplement. The example of 50 years of full payments at no real interest would have resulted in an old-age pension of 195 SEK and a supplement of 77 SEK (old-age pension was regarded as a form of income). In 1933, after the system had been operational for 19 years, the average level of old-age pensions was 34 SEK for men and 11 SEK for women, annually.[26] By that time the supplement had been raised to 225 SEK for men (210 for women).[27] For ordinary people, the old-age pension was only a tiny supplement to a means-tested invalidity insurance system.

Looking at the first pension system, we see that it was clearly based on the principle of Just Distribution. It was mainly designed to make it possible for people

[24] 13 x 50 x 30% = 195 SEK. The figure is lower for women.

[25] For personal wealth, eg owning a farm, the authorities calculated a capital gain from the asset.

[26] Government bill 1935:217, 21.

[27] The increase was made in 1921.

to survive when they became permanently sick. A healthy shoemaker reaching 67 years of age was supposed to take out the miniscule old-age pension and then supplement that income by continuing to make and repair shoes. Only when permanently unable to work could he or she receive the state supplement, and that supplement was necessary to be able to survive on pension alone.

There was no absolute right to retirement at 67 years, if a right is defined as corresponding to a duty for someone else to help realise that right. The only thing that happened at 67 was that people got access to money they themselves had been forced to save in their individual accounts. It is worth noting that the old-age pension itself was quite uncontroversial, while the supplement to persons unable to work was very controversial.

A proper right to retirement was introduced with the 1935 Pension Act.[28] Pension was divided into two parts, a basic amount given to all who had paid their contributions, and an additional amount awarded in relation to fees paid in. The basic amount was 70 SEK, plus a supplement of 250–450 SEK per year, depending on the cost level of the municipality. The additional amount was 10 per cent of the fees paid in to the individual account (much less than the amount that would have been derived from an actuarial calculation). The supplement was reduced if the elderly person had an income of more than 100 SEK. In this system, a person (healthy or disabled) could choose to retire at 67 and receive a minimum pension of 320 SEK a year from the taxpayers, plus the small additional amount related to the savings in the person's individual account.

The pension levels were still very low. The majority of those aged 67 or older worked (or had other income) to supplement their pensions. The new increased levels were designed to make ordinary pensions high enough to avoid the need for poverty relief. The government admitted, however, that even with these new levels there would still be cases in which pensioners who had worked and paid contributions all their lives would still need to rely on local welfare.[29]

This pension system was significantly improved in 1946.[30] The new levels were 1,000 SEK for single persons and 1,600 for couples in low-cost municipalities.[31] These sums were paid out regardless of personal wealth or income.[32] The sums were set to be reasonable in relation to the lowest wage levels on the labour

[28] SFS 1935:434.

[29] Government bill 1935:217, 33. There were legal possibilities for the municipalities to supplement pensions more generally, without assessing the individual's personal situation as thoroughly as for poverty relief. In 1943, 3.8 per cent of old-age pensioners received such 'dignified' municipal aid, while 13.6 per cent required poverty relief. Government bill 1946:220, 107. The Swedish social security legislation based on the normative pattern of just distribution is still constructed around low basic benefits and supplements, relating eg to housing costs. See Thomas Erhag, Chapter 12.

[30] SFS 1946:431. The 1946 Pension Act came into force on 1 January 1948.

[31] Pension Act, s 4.

[32] Supplements for persons living in municipalities with higher costs were, however, tested against income and wealth.

market,[33] which were low. A family with children living on these sums would also need poverty relief, but a pensioner would not normally need to support any other person. The general idea was no longer simply to avoid poverty. Comparisons between working people and retired people are based on a normative idea that says that retired people too should be able to increase their standard of living above the maintenance level, if working people are able to do so.

The 1946 pensions system was almost exclusively based on the normative pattern of Just Distribution. The link between payment and pension was totally abolished. In reality, these contributions had such a marginal effect on pensions both in the 1913 and the 1935 systems that it was not deemed to be worth the administrative effort to continue with them. In its place, the state created a voluntary pension supplement system, whereby benefits were awarded in relation to contributions.

The minister for social affairs at the time, Gustaf Möller, was a very controversial person within the Social Democrat Party. He wanted to create social security systems based on the principle of Just Distribution and universal coverage, his goal being to eliminate poverty. The debate over social security was a fierce one. The 1946 pension reform was Möller's last important victory, but his final battle concerned sickness insurance. He could not persuade his party and was obliged to leave his post in 1951.[34] From that moment on, the principle of income replacement became an important part of the Swedish state social security systems.[35] Its application to pensions came in 1960, after lengthy political debate that included a referendum, and was called the ATP system.[36]

The ATP system consisted of a basic pension equal for all, and a mandatory supplementary pension. This supplementary pension was based on a points system. A person received points in relation to taxable income. For those with 30 years of contributions,[37] the best 15 years were used to calculate an average, and the supplementary pension would be 60 per cent of this average. Along with the basic pension, the system was meant to give a retired person two-thirds of the person's previous income. The pension age remained at 67 and the basic pension could not be taken out before that age. However, points in the supplementary

[33] Government bill 1946:220, 110: 8.6 per cent of the population declared an income between 600 and 1,000 SEK per year. However, the government believed many of them also to have undeclared incomes.

[34] In 1951, the Congress of LO (the national blue-collar workers federation) unanimously decided to back a national sickness insurance coordinated with the work injury insurance system, and thus based on the income replacement principle. See PG Edebalk, *Välfärdsstaten träder fram: Svensk socialförsäkring 1884–1955* (Lund, Arkiv Förlag, 1996) 165. This trade union founded the Social Democratic Party and the two organizations describe themselves as the two legs of the labour movement.

[35] Edebalk, *Välfärdsstaten träder fram*, above n 34, 165.

[36] N Eliasson, *Protection of Accrued Pension Rights: an Inquiry into Reforms of Statutory and Occupational Pension Schemes in a German, Norwegian and Swedish Context* (Lund, Juristförlaget i Lund, 2001) 124. SFS 1959 no 291 Act on Supplementary Earnings Based Pension.

[37] Twenty years in the beginning to be gradually increased to 30 years; Government bill 1959: 100, 43.

system could be earned only up to age 65. Older persons were not really regarded as being of proper working age.[38] The pensionable age was 67, but supplementary pensions could be taken out between 63 and 70. The pension was reduced or increased according to fixed rates, at levels close to actuarial rates. Making the pensionable age flexible was an immensely important addition. It was no longer taboo for the state to design a system that helped healthy people to retire early.

Flexible pensionable ages had been discussed before, but it was assumed that the working population's desire to retire was so strong that any flexible system would tend to lower the real pensionable age towards the lowest permitted age, even if the pension was reduced according to actuarial principles. Persons who had taken early retirement on such terms would then at 67 be likely to be in need of other public support.[39] In 1960, it was only the supplementary pension that could be taken out in advance, and it would take many years before people had earned enough points to be eligible for pensions that would permit early retirement. In 1976, the pensionable age was lowered to 65. Along with this reform, individuals were allowed to voluntarily receive this pension from the age of 60. The preparatory works emphasise that individuals age differently, and should be free to choose their pensionable age, from 60 to 70 years.[40] Those who chose to retire early paid by having their pensions reduced by 0.5 per cent per month.[41] However, the social insurance system was in other ways designed to help persons who, for instance, could work only part-time, through special part-time pension rules, and the possibility to take out half their pension and draw unemployment benefit for the rest of the time.

Since 1974, Swedish workers have had fairly strong employment protection through the Employment Protection Act. For an employee at the age of 67, an employer had the right under section 33 to terminate employment with no need for just cause. This age limit persisted even when the pensionable age was lowered to 65 in 1976. Retiring at 65 was perceived as a right for the employee, but not compulsory. However, many collective agreements stipulated a duty for the employee to retire at 65, and in 1982, the legal age limit was lowered to 65 years, as a way of adapting the law to what was actually common practice in collective agreements.[42] The preparatory works express the pensionable age as both a right and a *duty* to retire.

In 1990, the first persons appeared who had 30 qualification years and were thus fully qualified in the new system. It was obvious that the new system was

[38] Government bill 1959:100, 58. The ages 16–65 were in Swedish labelled 'den egentliga förvärvstiden'.

[39] Government White Paper 1955:32, 112 ff. The pensionable age for civil servants differed. A vast majority chose to retire at the earliest possible opportunity, and the lower the pensionable age, the larger the majority that chose the earliest possible opportunity. The inquiry cautioned, however, against making general assumptions based on civil servants.

[40] Government bill 1975:97, 45; National Social Insurance Act, ch 12, ss 1–2.

[41] National Social Insurance Act, ch 12, s 2.

[42] Government bill 1981/82:71, 104 ff.

going to be very expensive for the state. It was built as a pay-as-you-go system,[43] and each person was guaranteed a pension based on a fixed sum, the average of the best 15 years of income. As people started to live longer, pensions had to be paid out for longer periods, and the ratio between pensioners and people of working age increased. The state had to decide between lowering pensions, raising the pensionable age, or raising taxes. Even at this point it was obvious that raising the pensionable age must be a part of the solution.[44] Section 33 of the Employment Protection Act was changed in 1991, raising the age level of employment protection to 67 years.[45]

Finding a good balance between raising taxes, lowering pension levels and raising the retirement age all took a long time. In 1998, Sweden was able to introduce a new pension system agreed upon by all the major parties in Parliament.

The new pension system is financed by an income tax of 18.5 per cent.[46] Of this sum, 16 per cent goes into a pay-as-you-go system called income pension. In such systems, nothing is saved. Each year, pensions for the elderly are paid for by contributions paid in by younger people in the same year. The amount each individual pays in is registered, and the figure is updated annually with regard to the national income development index. When people take out their pension, they have a right to their share of future collective funds. Thus, a person who has SEK 2 million in his account will have twice as much as those with only 1 million. In this system, the state cannot lose money. If the ratio of pensioners to persons of working age should rise, pensions will be reduced each year to accommodate this. In this way, pensions automatically adjust annually to compensate for persons living longer, or for other demographic problems.

The remaining 2.5 per cent goes into an individual account called premium pension. The individual can choose to invest this money in funds that invest in stocks or in bonds. When the person retires, this money can be used to buy a monthly pension. The amount depends on how much has been paid in and on how successful the investments made by the fund have been. One important principle in both of these systems is the lifetime principle. People continue to add to their account throughout their lifetimes. There is no point at which extra work does not result in extra pension.

There is also a guarantee pension given to those who do not receive enough through the ordinary system. The right to guarantee pension is earned by living in Sweden above the age of 24 and below the age of 65, and 40 years is required for the full pension.[47] Guarantee pension can be taken out at 65 and is financed

[43] There was some funding, but it was too small to keep the system going.

[44] Government White Paper 1989:101.

[45] Act (1990:1357) on changing the Employment Protection Act (1982:80).

[46] Part of it is paid by the employer and part by the individual.

[47] Social Insurance Code (2010:110), ch. 67, arts 25 and 11–12. Only under certain conditions can the years between 16 and 24 count.

through ordinary taxes. In this system, it is the benefit level that is determined, not the cost to the state.

Collective agreements cover 90 per cent of the Swedish labour market. These agreements vary, but they usually require the employer to pay around 4.5 per cent of the employee's pay into a pension fund.[48] These pension systems usually define the contribution, not the benefit. Sometimes, employees can choose the investment fund for part of the money, with the rest going into a fund operated by the social partners.

The whole point of the new state pension system was to create a system that balanced itself. If average life expectancy rose, pensions would automatically get smaller (as has happened). Each year, new calculations are made based on changes of average lifespan. In the government bill, the government assumes that if average lifespan increases, the increase will consist of healthy years and that most people will choose to put some more of those healthy years into working.[49] The introduction of this new pension system was thus assumed to raise the real pensionable age. Christensen described it in the following words:

> The new system rewards people who work long hours, for many years, in jobs valued highly by the market, ie exactly the same values as apply in the market wage system and in private insurance. (author's translation)[50]

However, only a very small number of persons chose to postpone their pension to after the age of 65. In 2001, the government again looked at labour legislation and the rule that permitted employers to dismiss workers at 67. The pensionable age in section 33 of the Employment Act was a semi-mandatory rule, and collective agreements are allowed to deviate from it. When the age level was raised, the semi-mandatory structure was defended, because there may be legitimate reasons, eg safety reasons, for accepting collective agreements that give the employer the right to terminate employment earlier. Labour market reasons (more employment for the young) were not, in principle, acceptable. Nor was the idea that the employer should pay a price (for instance obligations to supplement the state pension) in return for the freedom to dismiss older workers. The social partners were expected to remove the obligation for the worker to accept retirement at 65 (or earlier) from collective agreements, unless there were very good reasons for such a rule,[51] but this did not happen. Collective agreements kept the retirement age at 65, and this applied to the majority of workers in Sweden.[52] A new section was inserted, stating that a worker had the right to employment protection up to

[48] LO (the national confederation of blue-collar workers) made it a priority to raise the level of pension towards that of white-collar workers. In 2012 they reached 4.5 per cent, up from 4.3 per cent in 2011.

[49] Government bill 1997/98:151, 621.

[50] A Christensen, 'Normativa grundmönster i pensionssystemen' in *Lovens liv, till Jørgen Dalberg-Larssen på 60-årdagen* (Copenhagen, Jurist og Økonomforbundets Forlag, 2000) 178.

[51] Government bill 1990/1991:25, 33–35.

[52] Government bill 2000/01:78, 15

age 67, regardless of collective agreements.[53] Since the end of 2002, all Swedish workers have had the right to employment protection up to age 67.

The government once again emphasises the construction of the new pension system. Because each year counts, it is important for all workers to be able to choose to work to 67. The state foresees an increased life expectancy, resulting in lower pensions. The preparatory work makes a point of stating that no one is forced to work longer than this. It is an individual freedom to choose additional years of work instead of lower pensions.[54]

B. Development of the Pensionable Age after the Reforms

With the new pension system, the state had constructed a system that made it financially more rewarding for the individual to delay retirement and more costly to retire early. This was mainly due to the new lifetime principle. Employment protection had been extended for some to 67 years by 1991, and to all workers at the end of 2002. Furthermore, as people started to live longer, the state pension had been continuously decreasing in relation to previous income. All of these three factors could reasonably have been expected to make people choose later retirement. There is no legal development I am aware of that has been expected to make people choose to retire earlier. Still, people use the flexibility more often to take early retirement compared to later. Part of the explanation may be that older people today are wealthier than before, even though state pensions are lower.[55]

Figure 9.1[56] describes the distribution by age of persons receiving old-age pension in Sweden in the years 2003 and 2009. Old-age pension refers to the income pension based on the pay-as-you-go system and the pre-funded premium pension. Persons receiving guarantee pension are not included here, because this pension can only be claimed from age 65 at the earliest.

[53] SFS 2001:298. The new rule came into force in September 2001, but age limits in existing collective agreements remained in place until the end of 2002.

[54] Government bill 2000/01:78, 25 ff.

[55] One important factor is the greatly improved pensions in collective agreements covering 90 per cent of the Swedish workforce. People retiring today have smaller state pensions compared to previous generations, but their total pension can be higher. Another important factor is that older persons also tend to have private wealth, often in the form of a house with little or no mortgage. Such factors partly explain why people feel they can afford to take early retirement. See Government Inquiry 2011:42, 9–11. With regard to income, the average 66-year-old newly retired person was 34 per cent better off compared to the average retired person (61).

[56] If the graph in Figure 9.1 is compared to a graph of the number of persons who left the labour market completely, the same pattern appears. At the age of 60 (when it is not possible to take out state pension), 25 per cent will have left the labour market, with social security, municipal financial aid, or private insurance or wealth being what such people live on. For the ages 61 to 64, this number increases by 5–8 per cent each year, reaching 53 per cent at age 64. It then jumps suddenly to 83 per cent at age 65. It increases by 3 per cent to 86 per cent and 89 per cent for the ages 66 and 67, after which it flattens out. (The Swedish labour force survey made by Statistics Sweden AKU 2009, the definition of leaving the labour market being that the person works or seeks employment less than 1 hour per week).

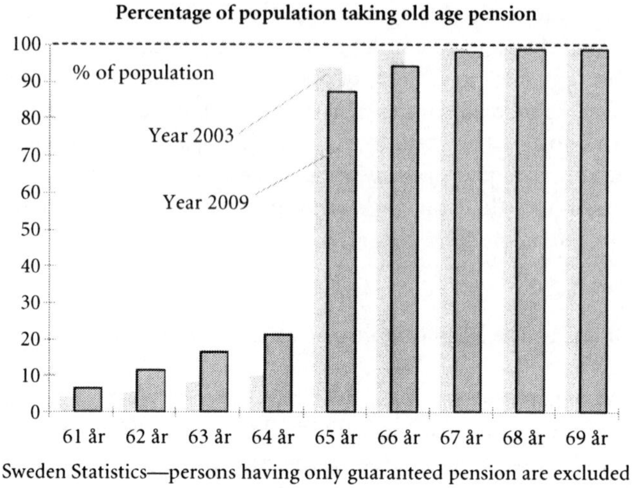

Figure 9.1: Percentage of Swedish population taking old-age pension*

Source: Swedish Pensions Agency, *Pensionsåldern 2011*, 22 (author's translation).
* Persons having only guaranteed pension are excluded.

The persons depicted above are thus free to take their pension at any age, but they must pay for their decision with a reduced pension if they retire early, or they will be well compensated if they delay their retirement. What stands out is that most people still choose to claim their pension at 65, a pattern that cannot be produced by individuals acting rationally on a market. Each person is different; some have expensive hobbies and no savings and would choose to delay. Others like hiking or other inexpensive activities, and do not need a large pension. Some have savings, and so on.

Individuals making rational decisions would have produced a curved pattern that could be explained. There is absolutely no logical reason to believe that for the majority of individuals, the optimal balance is to claim their pension at 65. This suggests that people do not retire at 65 because they deliberately choose to do so, but rather that they work until this age because they believe it to be their duty to do so (if they would rather retire early), or that it is their duty to retire at that age (if they would rather work longer). Retiring at 65 seems to be a social norm. People follow it because others expect them to do so, and as good citizens they want to do what is expected of them.

It is easy to see how this norm developed. Since 1976, the right to retire at the taxpayer's expense has been set at 65. The right to unemployment insurance also ceases at that age, and the right to sickness insurance is restricted.[57] Though

[57] Social Insurance Code 2010:110, ch 27, s 36 and Act (1997:238) on Unemployment Insurance, s 22.

employment protection has applied up to age 67 since 1991, it was only by the end of 2002 that all workers enjoyed this protection. Before then, most workers had a lower age limit, usually 65, when collective agreements stipulated an obligation to accept termination of employment.

The persons claiming pension before or after the age of 65 are probably the most individualistic—those who dare to disobey norms that are not formally binding. Looking at the year 2003: it is not surprising that very few persons claimed their pension after 65. At that point, the 2001 change that made collective agreements with a pensionable age lower than 67 illegal came into force, and it takes time for such changes to sink in. In 2009, the number of persons claiming pension at 66 multiplied (albeit from a small base). However, the number of persons claiming pension after 67 did not change significantly. The most plausible explanation for this is that persons who employers wished to dismiss, and had previously been allowed to dismiss at 65, could now remain in work until age 67. If this pattern had changed due to improved health or an increased preference for working longer, it would have affected the ages above 67 as well.

Looking at the number of persons claiming pension before age 65, we see an increase in all ages, and this is larger than the increase of persons delaying pension until after 65. The age at which persons are actually taking out state pension is thus going down in Sweden.[58] How is this possible?

The new Swedish pension system was constructed to be fair and market-functional. It was designed to create the largest possible correlation between the individual's input and the benefits he or she receives. In the context of an ageing population and thus diminishing pensions, if the pension age stayed at 65, people would be expected rationally to choose to work longer. Is it only a coincidence that the flexibility within the state pension system is used more to retire early than to delay retiring? Might Sweden have accidentally constructed a new pension system that contributes to a reduced actual pension age?

C. Analysis of Market-Functionalism in the Pension Reform

If society creates markets, then society also in principle abstains from defining social norms. In the market, individuals are allowed to satisfy their preferences as far as their financial resources permit. The exceptions to this general rule are those areas that are legislated, ie the sex trade, discrimination, and so on.

[58] It is very hard to isolate the importance of the state pension system. Real pensionable age looks different if it is measured in terms of persons working in the labour market. It has become harder to claim long-term sickness benefit (early retirement), and some collective agreements providing pension rights before the age of 65 have rescinded those rights, for instance, the right of some municipal workers to retire at 63. Some persons claiming a state pension before the age of 65 in 2009 may have had a chance to take early retirement or pension from a collective agreement if they had retired in 2003. Compare Swedish Pensions Agency, *Pensionsåldern 2011*, 16 ff and Swedish Pensions Agency, *Arbetslivets längd 2011*, 18.

The old ATP system was designed around a social norm. The state guaranteed each person a pension of around 60–67 per cent of their previous earnings. It took quite a few years to achieve this level. Anna Christensen called this hybrid between actuarial pensions and the replacement of lost earnings *accumulated entitlements*, and described it as a normative pattern in its own right.[59] In such a system, each individual feels that the pension is paid out by society and according to its rules. Therefore, a norm such as not taking retirement before 65 can evolve and become permanent. This was a pension system based on normative rules relating to the pensionable age as decided by society.

I believe that the new system creates another mental framework around pensions. Each year, every worker receives a bright orange envelope from the Swedish Pensions Agency. This contains information about how much money has been paid into the income pension system, how much the previously earned money has grown according to the income development index, and finally, how much the pension would be worth when retiring at different ages. The same applies to the funded system, but this amount changes according to how well the fund has managed its money.

There is a lot of discussion regarding both the pension system and this annual information. During a recession, less money gets paid into the system and pensions are lowered. When this occurs, the discussion revolves around whether or not the state should guarantee pension levels. Many people feel insecure about having their pensions re-evaluated each year according to economic developments. This is also evident in regard to the funded system. If share values drop, the riskiest funds may lose a lot of value, and people end up feeling cheated—they feel they were forced to play the market with their pension. So far, each time this has been up for discussion, the politicians have stood firmly by the system and tried to explain why market logic is good for society at large.

I believe that each time the new pension system is defended and explained, citizens are trained to view pensions in a new light. Each year, the bright orange envelope provides each worker with a figure in SEK for their income pension. They know that this is *exactly* the amount they have paid into the system, plus any increase determined by the state for each year, which could be viewed as a form of interest. In the pre-funded premium pension, the amount in SEK represents money paid in by them and profits from investments made with their money. In their minds, the income pension behaves like a bank account and the premium pension behaves like a fund. When a person retires today, they feel they are taking out the money they put into the pension system bank and fund. They thus feel that they have paid for their pension with their own money. This feeling arises even though the balance of the income pension account is a fictional amount,

[59] A Christensen, 'Normative Patterns and the Normative Field: a Post-Liberal View on Law' in T Wilhelmsson and S Hurri (eds), *From Dissonance to Sense: Welfare State Expectations, Privatisation and Private Law* (Aldershot, Ashgate, 1999) 97.

used only to illustrate the relative value of accrued pension rights between individuals.[60]

If a person has lived within the new system for 40 years and has adapted to the logic of all these yearly envelopes, that person would then at age 61 make a conscious decision: retire now and get some pension, or retire later and get more pension. People might rationally calculate how much they will need for the rest of their lives and then retire as soon as this point is reached. If the system gives them a pension that is exactly matched to their lifetime contributions and expected remaining lifetime, then no one should have any moral objections if their preference is to retire early rather than buy a new luxury car. Calculating lifetime earnings exactly creates a normative frame, wherein taking early retirement is a consumer decision just like any other.

The old ATP system also gave rights attributed to the individual, but not in a way that prompted comparison with a bank account. A worker could not in advance know the value of each pension point. It might be completely worthless if that person already had 30 years of pension contributions and the year in question was not one of the best 15.[61] In the old ATP system, the pensionable age could be raised. If the pensionable age was raised to 66 and a person retiring at 65 pays the price of a 6 per cent lower pension (0.5 per cent per month of early retirement), the normative message is clear, ie you should keep working until age 66, and this would probably have been quite an effective reform. Seeing one's pension reduced because of having gone against a clearly defined norm involves some sort of punishment. I believe that this difference is very important. Looking at the cost of taking early retirement, there is no great difference between the old and the new pension system: it was costly in the old pension system as well. A loss of 0.5 per cent for each month is not much different when compared to the actuarially correct figures[62] in the new system, yet normatively it is very different.

If a person checks the balance of a bank account to decide whether or not to withdraw money to renovate the kitchen, or to go on holiday, there is no element of solidarity involved. People feel entitled to use the money in their accounts in a selfish way. I believe Sweden is sitting on a normative time bomb here. It is likely that Sweden will try to raise the pensionable age in the future.[63] This may become complicated. A person looking at a pension account and realising that he or she could retire at 65 (or even 61), but is stopped from doing so because the state is

[60] Compare Eliasson, *Protection of Accrued Pension Rights*, above n 36, 164.

[61] Ibid 128.

[62] See www.pensionsmyndigheten.se/4615.html. The Swedish Pensions Agency stated, in a press release dated 14 December 2011, that delaying taking out pension or taking out pension early normally affects the amount by 7–8 per cent a year, ie around 0.6 per cent per month.

[63] Pensionsåldersutredningen (the Government Inquiry on Pensionable Age Committee Directive 2011:34) is currently investigating all age limits with regard to pension. Raising the limit where a person may have other social security than a pension, and raising the age limit for employment protection will mostly be seen as improvements for the person concerned. However, forcing people to take out their pension later is likely to be very unpopular. Preliminary conclusions are expected soon, and the final report will be released in 2013.

blocking access to the savings account until the person reaches a greater age, will become very angry. Because people regard the money in their pension accounts as their own, they will feel cheated, and because delaying their pensions will result in them getting more pension, this then seems paternalistic. Why should a person be required to work to 67 instead of 65, and consequently get 15 per cent more pension? It is offensive to think that the state knows better than the individual which choice will provide the most utility for that person. The benefit to society at large is not visible within the framework of the pension system.

For those persons not receiving the guarantee pension, the only age limit the state can change in the new pension system is the rule allowing persons to claim pension from age 61. In the new system, the state cannot make decisions in the income pension and premium pension systems that create an impression that 66 or any other age is the normal age to retire. By creating a market-based system, this becomes the choice of the individual.

Society is unequal: differences in health are one reason why this is so. A system such as the Swedish one, ie a system based on the lifetime principle and creating an impression of citizens saving for their own pensions, is adequate only if society decides that there is no need to ask for solidarity from those lucky enough to be healthy in old age. The Swedish legislator has always promoted solidarity through taxes and social security. However, the legislator saw no need to promote solidarity by asking healthy people to work longer, even though they would prefer to live on their pensions. The reason for this was that the legislator thought that the income earned was enough to make persons want to work longer, as long as the pension system was based on the lifetime principle and actuarially correct rewards for delaying retirement.

The market-functionalism of the pension reform is thus of the same type as that of the financing of unemployment. There is no control system, outside this market pricing of taking early retirement, for punishing people for making the wrong choice. There is no direction from society regarding the level of social norm setting.

V. COMMON LESSON LEARNED FROM THE TWO EXAMPLES

Markets are excellent when the quest is to find a way to enable people to satisfy their own preferences using their own resources, but they are not so good if the state wants people or organisations to make specific choices. If the state can honestly say that it is neutral in regard to whether the trade unions should choose to decrease minimum wages in collective agreements or accept higher unemployment and all the consequences arising from it, then the design of the Swedish unemployment reform of 2007 and 2008 is a good example of market-functionalism. However, if the state considers one outcome to be good (lowering wages in collective agreements) and the other to be bad (allowing unemployment to rise, and accepting the drop in membership of unemployment insurance funds and trade unions), then creating a market that allows that choice to be made is a bad idea.

Two different views can be taken on whether or not reduced wages for low-skilled workers are good or bad, but the Swedish unemployment reform has so far utterly failed to achieve such a goal, and the reform has come at a very high cost. The Swedish government made a huge error when predicting the preferences of the trade unions, and the reform failed. The Swedish labour market is so particular, that it is difficult to imagine a similar story unfolding in any other Member States.[64]

If there is a demographic time bomb in Europe and the long-term solution must be to delay retirement, then it is a bad idea to ask people if they prefer money or early retirement. Society should only create a market in which such a choice can be made if it genuinely believes that both choices are easily accommodated, but this is not the case. It is important that people choose to work longer. The Swedish state created this market believing that this was the choice people would make, but it seems to have got the preferences of individuals all wrong. People seem to abstain from buying into early retirement because they think that it is morally wrong to do so. When told that they are free to choose, as long as they pay the price, they then tend to choose early retirement over delayed retirement.

It is easy here to see other European countries making the same mistake. A word often used in EU documents is flexibility, meaning that the individual need not retire at a certain age, but should instead be given a choice. Along with this choice, incentives to make the right choice are often mentioned. Flexibility should reward those who chose later retirement.[65] The discussion about workers also puts emphasis on the right to work, and the need to have high-quality jobs for older people.[66] It is relatively easy to extend employment protection to higher ages and to legislate against age discrimination. With regard to people who are young enough to feel that they should work, measures promoting active participation will probably be acceptable. Here, EU documents suggest changes that would allow fewer people to live on sickness benefits and early retirement before reaching the pensionable age.[67] Such benefits are given to people who cannot work at the moment, but may be able to do so if provided with a suitable job and support.

[64] Compare L Scruggs, 'The Ghent System and Union Membership in Europe' (2002) 55(2) *Political Research Quarterly* 286, Only four countries have real Ghent systems, defined as insurance systems based on voluntary unemployment insurance, mainly operated by trade union funds and with large subsidies from the state (Iceland, Finland, Denmark and Sweden). Belgium has a hybrid system that is sometimes counted as a real Ghent system. If a similar story should unfold in other Member States, these countries are the only possible alternatives.

[65] See, eg, Commission Staff Document on Ex Ante Evaluation, accompanying document to the decision of the European Parliament and of the Council on the year of active ageing, COM(2010)462, 5.

[66] Ibid.

[67] Communication from the Commission to the European Parliament, the Council, the European Economic and Social Committee and the Committee of the Regions, Dealing with the impact of an ageing population in the EU, COM(2009)180 final ('2009 Ageing Report').

However, it is quite another thing to ask a healthy person to delay retirement. The will (preference) for leisure time seems to be a preference not to be confronted directly.

So far, the experience in Sweden is that for persons above the pension age, such reforms have only a marginal effect. It is very difficult to increase the obligation to work. Official EU documents seem to be as wary as Swedish politicians are, when increasing mandatory retirement ages is suggested. Working longer is described as a way of meeting the preferences of the elderly. An elderly person not in work is described as a form of social exclusion.

The Swedish pension reform has succeeded in making the pension system affordable for the state. One goal of the reform has clearly been achieved. However, the other goal—to promote an increase in the real pension age—has not been reached. Flexibility is not the answer to this problem, and increased employment protection, though beneficial, is not very potent, since few people choose to use the protection to work longer.

Markets (however cleverly designed) cannot convince trade unions of the merits of combating unemployment through wage cuts. Nor can markets convince a 62-year-old healthy individual, who has saved what he or she deems enough in individual pension accounts, to work longer. In order to achieve this, society needs to address the social norm directly.

The average, healthy 62-year-old needs to work longer because the state needs the tax on the earned income to fund public spending. Solidarity ought to be important when deciding on retirement, yet there is absolutely no solidarity involved in the framework of the pension system. Instead, pension accounts are presented as a form of individual wealth. The stronger the perception becomes of pension accounts as a form of individual wealth, the more difficult it becomes to ask for solidarity from individuals.

Sweden needs ways of strengthening the duty aspect of the social norm of later retirement, and perhaps other countries in the European Union need to do so as well. If market forces are allowed to have the same influence over social security insurance systems as over private insurance, the state will lose the possibility to address the duty side of this and other social norms. The state's ability to steer society through social norms is damaged if people perceive them not as social norms, but as market preferences.

10

Parenthood Meets Market-Functionalism: Parental Rights in the Labour Market and the Importance of the Gender Dimension

JENNY JULÉN VOTINIUS

I. INTRODUCTION

THE IDEA THAT it should be possible to balance working life with the responsibilities of parenthood has been strongly put forward for many years throughout the European Union. Commonly used policies to facilitate the situation for working parents include different financial benefits, easy access to public child care, and labour market regulation that pays special attention to the working parent's situation. This labour market regulation on parenthood is the focus of this chapter. The primary aim is to discuss the normative conflict that can be identified between, on the one hand, the ideals that lie behind labour regulation intended to promote and support parenthood; and on the other hand, the ideal of market efficiency that characterises not only the modern labour market, but also, to a great extent, modern labour law. Over the years, I have devoted considerable time to the study of this normative conflict from different perspectives, both in my thesis and in several of my other scientific publications; still, I have never before addressed it in relation to the theory of law as normative patterns in a normative field.[1] This is the purpose of this chapter.

[1] J Julén Votinius, 'Troublesome Transformation' in M Rönnmar (ed), *Labour Law: Fundamental Rights and Social Europe*, Swedish Studies in European Law vol 4 (Oxford, Hart, 2011); J Julén Votinius, 'Missgynnande i fråga om ekonomiska förmåner som en nödvändig följd av föräldraledighet' (2010/11) 3 *Juridisk Tidskrift*, 620; J Julén Votinius, 'Normative Perceptions Twisting the Law' in A Numhauser Henning and M Rönnmar (eds), *Fifteen Years with the Norma Research Programme, Anniversary Volume* (Lund, Lund University, 2010); J Julén Votinius, 'Normkonflikter i regleringen om arbetstagares föräldraskap' (2008) 4 *Retfaerd* 123, 102–30; J Julén Votinius, *Föräldrar i arbete. En könskritisk undersökning av småbarnsföräldrars arbetsrättsliga ställning (Parents at Work: a Gender-Critical Study on the Position of Parents of Young Children in Labour Law)* (Stockholm/Göteborg, Makadam, 2007); J Julén Votinius, 'On the Gendered Norm of Standard Employment in a Changing Labour

The legal rules designed to protect the working parent are based on the principle that it should be possible to reconcile paid work with parenthood. But when the legal rules for working parents are applied in working life, these rules are also understood in terms of arguments and practices which support the employer's market-oriented interests rather than parental interests. An important assumption for these arguments and practices is that the employee's parenthood-related commitments should *not* encroach on the job. Even if this approach to employees' parenthood is contrary to the stance taken in the specific rules on parental rights, this approach is actually supported in labour law. Apart from the specific rules for working parents, labour market regulations generally do not acknowledge the fact that an employee may also be a parent. This can be described as a normative conflict, or incoherence, affecting the judicial sphere: deviating norms and values encroach upon the rules on parenthood and weaken their position. As a result of this conflict, and despite the sometimes fairly strongly formulated protection of parental rights, in practice these specific rules in labour law concerning employees' parenthood have a relatively weak normative position—not only in working life but also in labour law.

The crucial matter for the following discussion is thus the underlying values that affect the application and impact of the rules. In this regard, the relationship of particular interest is the one between the regulations that apply specifically to employees with parental responsibility and the more general labour law framework. In cases where the values that form the basis of the general labour law rules differ from the values that form the basis for the special rules for parents, the legal position of the parenthood-related rules is weakened and their effect is limited. In practice, this means that the general labour law rules allow the employer to act in a manner which prevents employees from exercising the rights they enjoy under the special rules for parents, or which at least reduces employees' propensity to exercise these rights. A more extensive exploration of the parental rules' weak position must also necessarily acknowledge gender-related perceptions of employees and of parents. Such perceptions exist in society and in the everyday life, but they are also expressed in, and influence, the law and the legal arguments. Perceptions of gender are highly relevant for the conceptual basis underlying the current regulations, and for the application of law. This is especially true when it comes to rules designed to balance demands for parental rights in the labour market against demands for market efficiency.

This chapter is based on an analysis of EU law, as implemented in Swedish national law. In the national legal contexts within the European Union, considerable

Market' in J Fudge and R Owens (eds) *Precarious Work, Women, and the New Economy* (Oxford, Hart, 2006) 265–82; J Julén, 'Hired with Children: on the Reconciliation of Parenthood and Working Life' in *Normative Development in the Welfare State: Legal Studies of Employment, Family and Social Security within the Norma Research Programme*, Norma 2003:2 (Lund, 2003); J Julén, 'A Blessing or a Ban? About the Discrimination of Pregnant Job Seekers' in A Numhauser-Henning (ed), *Legal Perspectives on Equal Treatment and Non-discrimination* (The Hague, Kluwer, 2001).

differences exist with respect to regulations designed to support working parents, both in terms of the existence or extent of such regulations, and in terms of how the legislation is designed. Because it provides for extensive support and protection for working parents, the Swedish legislative system is particularly well suited for an exploration of normative tensions surrounding the parental rules in labour law, and affecting the interpretation and application of these rules.

The chapter is structured in the following manner. Section II provides a brief presentation of the theory of law as normative patterns in a normative field. In Section III, different aspects of this theory are discussed in more detail, with particular emphasis on the theory's potential as a heuristic tool. Section IV introduces two conflicting ideals in the area of parental labour rights: the ideal of protection of parental needs and responsibilities, and the ideal of market efficiency. Furthermore, these ideals are related to concepts that are developed or used within the theory of law as normative patterns in a normative field. Following the approach outlined in section IV, section V will introduce the rules on parenthood in EU labour law, and position these rules in the field of tension that arises between the conflicting values identified previously. Using Sweden as the primary national example, section VI discusses the expression and character of this normative conflict in a legal system that strongly supports the idea that it should be possible to reconcile work and parenthood, and in which working parents are granted extensive rights. Section VII is a comparative reflection on what hitherto has emerged on how the balance is struck between the protection of parental needs and the interest of market efficiency in EU and Swedish labour law, respectively. These findings are discussed in relation to the terminology in the theory of law as normative patterns in a normative field. With the aim to increase understanding of the complex interaction of values that negatively affect the efficiency of the regulation designed to protect working parents, section VIII will discuss and present an analysis of findings from the previous sections, in the gendered context to which they belong. Here, the theory of law as normative patterns in a normative field, applied as a set of heuristic principles, will be used as one of the tools.

II. ON THE THEORY OF LAW AS NORMATIVE PATTERNS IN A NORMATIVE FIELD

The theory of law as normative patterns in a normative field is based on an understanding that much of the content of legal rules is a legal codification of moral practices and fundamental values that have emerged in society, and that are the basis for the organisation of communities and establishment of relationships between people.[2] The notion of normative patterns is used to describe the

[2] A Christensen, 'Skydd för etablerad position—Ett normativt grundmönster' (1996) 4 *Tidskrift for Rettsvitenskap* 527.

idea that closely related moral practices and fundamental values form moral and conceptual patterns. Through legislation, legal interpretation and jurisprudence, these patterns also manifest themselves in the content of the law.[3] Some patterns, which reflect social ideas about what is just and how social relations should be shaped, are more constant in history and thus more established than others. In the theory of law as normative patterns in a normative field, these are called *Basic Normative Patterns*. Since the basic normative patterns do not form a system or hierarchy, and since there is no definitive way to determine which pattern ultimately should be given priority, conflicts continuously arise between the patterns.[4] In a normative field (that is, in a more or less defined area of law) the basic patterns serve as poles, with the ability to attract or repel the legal regulation.[5] Thus, it is in the tension between different basic normative patterns that legal rules emerge and get their content.

Within the framework of the theory of law as normative patterns in a normative field, mainly three basic normative patterns have been highlighted. The pattern *Protection of Established Position* expresses the idea that a person who has earned a certain position should not be deprived of that position without a cause. Legal rules that have been designed close to this pattern are, for example, rules on employment protection and security of tenure, and the principle that benefits should be calculated in relation to lost earnings, which is central in social security law.[6] The *Market-Functional* pattern supports the market economy. This pattern includes the freedom of contract, the right to property and the freedom of trade.[7] Finally, the pattern of *Just Distribution* expresses the idea that distribution or redistribution is to take place, based upon some material principle of justice. In connection with this pattern, we find rules and principles on distribution according to need or according to performance, but also rules on equal distribution.[8]

III. HEURISTIC ASPECTS OF THE THEORY OF LAW AS NORMATIVE PATTERNS IN A NORMATIVE FIELD

Even though I have not applied the theory of law as normative patterns in a normative field in my previous work, my research can be described as being based on

[3] A Christensen, *Hemrätt i hyreshuset. En rättsvetenskaplig studie av bostadshyresgästens besittningsskydd* (Stockholm, Juristförlaget, 1994) 4.

[4] Christensen, 'Skydd för etablerad position', above n 2, 530.

[5] Christensen, *Hemrätt i hyreshuset*, above n 3; A Christensen, 'Normative Patterns and the Normative Field: a Post-Liberal View on Law' in T Wilhelmsson and S Hurri (eds), *From Dissonance to Sense: Welfare State Expectations, Privatisation and Private Law* (Aldershot, Ashgate, 1998) 8ff.

[6] Christensen, *Hemrätt i hyreshuset*, above n 3; A Christensen 'Protection of the Established Position: a Basic Normative Pattern' in (2000) 40 *Scandinavian Studies in Law, Legal Theory* 285; A Christensen, 'Normativa grundmönster i socialrätten' (1997) 78 *Retfaerd* 73.

[7] Cf P Norberg, 'Non-Discrimination as a Social and Free Market Value' in A Numhauser-Henning (ed), *Legal Perspectives on Equal Treatment and Non-discrimination* (The Hauge, Kluwer, 2001).

[8] Christensen, 'Normativa grundmönster i socialrätten', above n 6.

an approach that shares some fundamental premises with this theory, and with other closely related theories. Thus, it is true to say that the way that Professor Anna Christensen, who formulated this theory, and I perceive and explain legal and social features forms part of different branches of the same community of thought.

As is usually the case with contributions of certain originality, the theory of law as normative patterns in a normative field has sometimes provoked criticism of varying content and value. By its very nature the theory of law as normative patterns in a normative field is an open theory, and thus has an inherent flexibility. Such open theories are sometimes accused of failing to meet the necessary requirements to form a theory. This approach rests on the conviction that a network of ideas must meet strict formal requirements in order to be called theory. Basically, according to this conviction, such a network of ideas must form an organised structure of thoughts, in which the constituent concepts are precisely defined, the different concepts relate to each other in a clear and unambiguous manner, and so on. This strict definition of how a theory should be constructed can be said to be well suited for explanatory models in the natural sciences, and for systems in formal logic and mathematics. However, when it comes to models of thinking about law and its relation to the surrounding community, this strict view of what constitutes a theory is much more problematic. History provides us with numerous examples of attempts to create social theories according to this recipe—and their limited success. A well-known example is that of Leibniz, who among everything else was a mathematician and a legal scholar. Some centuries ago, he took on the challenge of including the social sciences in a mathematically characterised structure, which was built on a few simple concepts.[9] His theory worked in mathematics, and possibly also in philosophy, but was hardly applicable in the fields of law and social science. Social phenomena are too complex, and too dependent on interpretations, to form the basis for intricate and scholastic theoretical systems. Therefore, such systems lack any greater explanatory value in the social sphere.

Within the field of theory of science, extensive discussions have taken place about the similarities and differences between the theories of natural and social sciences.[10] I do not aspire to add to that discussion here. A question more interesting than that of what a scientific practice is called is the question of whether and how the practice fulfils its purpose. In my opinion, one prominent feature of the theory of law as normative patterns in a normative field is its ability to function as

[9] GV Leibniz, *Nova methodus discendae docendaeque jurisprudentiae (A New Method for Learning and Teaching Law)* (1667). Cf JH Wigmore, 'Nova Methodus Discendae Docendaeque Jurisprudentiae' (1917) 8 *Harvard Law Review* 30, 812–29; E Cassirer, *The Philosophy of the Enlightenment* (Princeton, NJ, Princeton University Press 2009) 28 ff and 236 ff; S Strömholm, *A Short History of Legal Thinking in the West* (Stockholm, Norstedt, 1985) 179; MH Hoeflich, 'Law and Geometry: Legal Science from Leibniz to Langdell' (1986) 30 *American Journal of Legal History* 95; R Berkowitz, *The Gift of Science: Leibniz and the Modern Legal Tradition* (Cambridge, MA, Harvard University Press, 2005).

[10] Cf S Gordon, *The History and Philosophy of Social Science* (Routledge, London, 1991) 589–668.

an effective heuristic principle; that is, as a starting point to look for and be able to find legal and social phenomena. This is a feature of the theory that deserves to be highlighted, and that I would say has not received sufficient attention. The theory of law as normative patterns in a normative field has been used and applied by many researchers, mainly for the purpose of describing the internal structure of the law in relation to underlying societal structures. To this end, the theory has been used to distinguish and compare the basic ideas and general underlying value structures that have been shaped in a similar way in different legal systems and in various areas of law. Researchers have used previously identified normative patterns in these studies, such as Protection of Established Position, or of the Market-Functional pattern, to conduct detailed studies of certain legal phenomena and for analysis of how different legal systems can be positioned in relation to each other in a normative field. The theory of law as normative patterns in a normative field is very well suited for this purpose.

However, the theory of law as normative patterns in a normative field is just as useful for more dynamic applications. The idea of describing the law in terms of normative conflicts contains a dynamic element. This dynamic component of the theory cannot serve only as a methodological basis for a treatment of the law in relation to normative conflicts that are already identified. It also serves as a tool for discovering normative patterns and conflicts that have previously been overlooked, or that at least have not been attributed sufficient importance. This is what I mean when I talk about using the theory as heuristic principle. With this application, it is not about deriving conclusions from an already complete system of thought, thus working from top to bottom and confirming the validity of the theory; instead, it is about finding and developing new knowledge or discovering new aspects of what is known. In this context, this means to identify new normative patterns. Here, the procedure is that the exploration begins from the bottom, in the particular, and works its way upwards in order to identify general principles and structures. It is exactly this approach which appears, by the way, to be one of the key points of departure in Christensen's way of thinking about law and about jurisprudence as a whole. Computers, she says, are stupid not because they are machines, but because they operate in complete hierarchical systems and lack the human capacity to connect scattered particularities into general patterns.[11] Seen from its heuristic aspect, the theory of law as normative patterns in a normative field can also be used as a tool by researchers who do not embrace the theory as a whole. Thus, the theory of law as normative patterns in a normative field contributes to the methodological developments within the community of thought in which it is included.

In this chapter I will show how key ideas in my research on parental rules and labour law could be formulated in relation to the theory of law as normative patterns in a normative field, thus supporting at least the central theses of this theory.

[11] Christensen, 'Normativa grundmönster i socialrätten', above n 6, 69.

I will initially apply an approach in which the tension between the values behind the specific rules protecting working parents and the values of labour market efficiency are discussed in relation to the conflict between two of the basic patterns in a normative field: the pattern called Protection of Established Position and the Market-Functional pattern. In addition, the theory of law as normative patterns in a normative field will be applied to my research, and will be used as a methodological tool to look for, develop and explain other ideas that have a normative impact in the field to which labour law rules on parenthood belong. The theory will be used in this more dynamic way in order to integrate the gender aspects in the analysis; these gender aspects are manifested in the area of labour law in an obvious way, especially in matters of employment and parenthood.

IV. ESSENTIAL VALUES BEHIND LABOUR LAW RULES FOR WORKING PARENTS

There is a clear contradiction between the demands of working life and the demands of parenthood, and this contradiction is the point of departure for the legislative discourse on the reconciliation of paid work and parenthood. The contradiction between paid work and parenthood is largely a product of the modern industrial society. A need to combine work with parental responsibilities emerged in the new order of production that evolved from the industrialisation process during the latter half of the nineteenth century and the early twentieth century. An implication of this order of production was that paid activities in production are clearly separated from domestic chores. Unpaid housework, including child care, still had to be done. But in the industrial society, domestic work must be combined with work outside the home, since this is how households earn their living.[12] With the emergence of industrial society, the employment relationship became a key element in order of production. In the employment relationship, the employer represents a commercial interest in maximising efficiency and competitiveness of the business, while many employees need to be able to engage in parenting without being hindered by their work situation, or even be favourably treated due to their parental responsibility.

This fact—that the employee's parental interest is difficult to reconcile with the employer's market-oriented interest—is the very essence of the normative conflict that characterises the question of the suitable and feasible in reconciling work and parenthood. In order to facilitate the analysis, the arguments, social practices and rules that apply in this conflict can be divided into two normative categories, which represent different sets of values. At the core of the labour law regulations aimed at protecting parenthood is the value of *work-family balance*. In fact, an

[12] JW Scott and LA Tilly, 'Women's Work and the Family in Nineteenth-Century Europe' (1975) 17 *Comparative Studies in Society and History* 36.

increase of the possibilities to combine work and parenthood is the very *raison d'être* of these rules.

But in working life, the rules about parenthood can thus also be understood in the light of arguments, practices and rules that support employer's market-oriented interest over parental interest. This approach means that the employee's parenting duties should *not* interfere with work. Within this normative category, the value of the employee's *work life commitment* is of central importance. This normative category is also an important part of the cognitive context that makes the male employee the benchmark and standard in the workplace, and as is evident in many studies, also in labour law.[13] The fact that the male employee is allowed in this way to constitute the ideal employee is something that contributes to the undermining of the protection of parenthood in labour law rules, since men are typically not expected to interrupt paid employment in order to care for young children. The tensions that surround parenthood rules are clearly visible only when these rules are considered as part of the broader labour law context. It is only then that the market-oriented arguments and practices referred to here as work life commitment come into their full strength. Christensen notes that 'Women cannot work or at least ought to be free from work in connection with delivery [of a child]. According to the normative pattern of modern labour relationships, wages cease too.'[14] This is indeed true, but it does not tell the whole truth. In the modern labour relationship, the consequences for those who are away from work to care for their children many times imply far more intrusive actions than just the suspension of wages. Such actions are sometimes explicitly allowed in general labour law regulations. And when they are prohibited, they can sometimes still be impossible to prevent in practice, because the law is designed in a way that does not allow for effective protection.

In Sweden, the value of work-family balance and the ideals that are associated with this value have been put forward quite aggressively for many years by politicians, unions, and other participants in the public debate. Also on the EU level, issues related to the reconciliation of paid work and parenthood have at times been attributed relatively great significance in the political discourse. This has resulted in the fact that today it is not particularly accepted to talk about employees' parenthood as a problem in the workplace and in working life. However, in the working life context, it does not appear necessary to describe parenthood as

[13] The Swedish historian Anita Göransson describes 'the male metal worker, who in theory and practice was the archetype of the true proletarian, who set the standard for the blue-collar worker and who became the hero of the labour movement', A Göransson, 'Bröd och rosor: lönearbete och kvinnliga strategier' (1987) 1 *Historisk tidskrift*, 114. For a discussion on the male norm in the US labour market, see J Williams, *Unbending Gender: Why Family and Work Conflict and What To Do About It* (Oxford, Oxford University Press, 2001). Within the EU context, Fenwick and Hervey discuss perceptions of the employee as constantly available and without parental duties, H Fenwick and TK Hervey, 'Sex Equality in the Single Market: New Directions for the European Court of Justice' (1995) 32 *Common Market Law Review* 443.

[14] Christensen, 'Normative Patterns and the Normative Field', above n 5, 12.

something problematic, in order for it to be considered as such. The employee's need for room to manage the care responsibilities that come with parenthood has never been established as a completely obvious claim in working life. This is true even though labour law rules on parenthood contain fairly detailed instructions about the fact that work should be reconcilable with parenthood, as well as instructions on how to achieve this. The less-than-accepted status of parenthood in relation to work exists even though some employers provide their employees with parenthood-related benefits that go beyond legal requirements. Compared to the very strong command in working life about the value of work life commitment, the values that meet the parenthood-related needs of employees are weakly anchored in employer practices and in the consciousness of employees. Employers often expect the employee to be more adaptable and available to meet business needs than is possible for those who are primarily responsible for the family's children. Many employees with small children have the greatest understanding for these expectations, and the result is that they see themselves as someone who causes problems in the workplace when they ask to exercise their parenthood-related rights.[15] In other words, the ideas and arguments behind the normative category work life commitment are so influential that parenthood-related needs are perceived as a source of problems in the workplace, without this necessarily having to be said out loud in the public debate.

In the following two sections, the influence and dominance of the normative values work-family balance and work life commitment will be discussed in relation to parental rules in EU labour law and in relation to the Swedish Parental Leave Act. The EU rules on pregnancy and maternity leave, and the Swedish Parental Leave Act define the group of employees who, according to the respective legal systems, should be allowed to claim the value of work-family balance and thus, to a certain extent, deviate from the value of work life commitment. The value of work life commitment is essential for the organisation of working life, but it does not stop at serving as an organisational principle. As we will see, it also has important legal implications. In fact, the value of work life commitment is a fundamental point of departure for most general labour law regulations. This fact is central for understanding how the content of parental rules is interpreted, and for how the legal position of the working parents of young children is perceived.

V. WORKING PARENTS IN EU LABOUR LAW

The ambition to establish a labour market within the European Union which allows for parenthood is manifested, inter alia, in various policy documents, in the

[15] This also applies in a country like Sweden, where the social acceptance of parental leave is comparatively broad. See, eg, the Equal Opportunities Ombudsman's *Report on Parenthood* (1999) 10, and C Kugelberg, 'Jämställdhetsideal och könsdiskriminering. Unga människor möter arbetslivet' (2004) 10(2) *Arbetsmarknad & Arbetsliv* 105.

European Employment Strategy, in the Community Action Programmes on equal opportunities for men and women, in the Pregnant Workers Directive (which is currently under revision) and in the newly revised Parental Leave Directive.[16] Although there have been many progressive elements in the legislative debates and in the non-binding legal documents, the actual achievements in terms of legal rules that support enforcement of the idea that working life and parenthood should be reconciled are limited.[17] Ever since labour legislation in this area began to emerge within EU law, emphasis in the binding legislative documents has been on the protection of pregnant women against discrimination and occupational health risks, rather than on the right to parental leave and on the protection of working parents against detrimental treatment due to their parenthood responsibilities. The fact that the law has developed in this way clearly illustrates that the normative field to which the labour law regulations on parenthood belong also is imbued with gendered norms and beliefs, in relation to both employees and parents. Many scholars have pointed out that the view of the mother as the main, or even sole, person responsible for care of children has been very persistent in the binding EU documents and in the case law.[18]

[16] Europe 2020, *A Strategy for Smart, Sustainable and Inclusive Growth*, COM(2010)2020 final, 19; *Strategy for Equality between Women and Men 2010–2015*, COM(2010)0491 final; *Reconciliation of Work and Family Life in the Context of Demographic Change* 11841/11 SOC 584, adopted 17 June 2011 by the Employment, Social Policy, Health and Consumer Affairs Council (EPSCO); Council Directive 92/85/EEC of 19 October 1992 on the introduction of measures to encourage improvements in the safety and health at work of pregnant workers and workers who have recently given birth or are breastfeeding ('Pregnant Workers Directive') [1992] OJ L348/1.7; Directive 2010/18/EU implementing the revised Framework Agreement on parental leave concluded by Businesseurope, UEAPME, CEEP and ETUC and repealing Directive 96/34/EC ('Parental Leave Directive') [2010] OJ L68.

[17] As early as in 1974, the Council drew attention to the need for measures for employees who want to combine family responsibilities with gainful employment: Council Resolution of 21 January 1974 concerning a social action programme, EGT C13/74, 1. Cf Ekosok's statement in EGT C286/75, 8–9, and action programmes for equal opportunities COM(81)758 final; COM(85)801 final; Council Resolution of 21 May 1991, EGT C142/91, 1; Council Decision of 22 December 1995, EGT L335/95, 37; Council Decision of 20 December 2000, EGT L017, 19 January 2001, 22–29. See also Resolution of the Council and of the Representatives of the Governments of the Member States of 6 December 1994, EGT C368/94, 3, and Council Decision 2000/228/EEG of 13 March 2000, EGT L72, 21 March 2000, 15, as well as Resolution of the Council of 29 June 2000, EGT C218, 5.

[18] Cf Petra Foubert: 'In soft law measures, the EC institutions often set themselves up as proponents of genuine sex equality in both the private and the public spheres. However, thus far, there seems to be no translation of this idea into enforceable legal measures. That fact in itself already limits the field of action for the Court of Justice'. P Foubert, *The Legal Protection of the Pregnant Worker in the European Community: Sex Equality, Thoughts of Social and Economic Policy and Comparative Leaps to the United States of America* (The Hague, Kluwer Law International, 2002) 214. Cf J Shaw, 'Pregnancy Discrimination in Sex Discrimination' (1991) 16 *European Law Review* 313; S Fredman, 'A Difference with Distinction: Pregnancy and Parenthood Reassessed' (1994) 110 *Law Quarterly Review* 106; C Boch, 'Official: During Pregnancy, Females are Pregnant' (1998) 23 *European Law Review* 488; K Lundström, *Jämlikhet mellan kvinnor och män i EG-rätten. En feministisk analys* (Uppsala, Iustus förlag, 1999) 244 ff; C McGlynn, 'Ideologies of Motherhood in European Community Sex Equality Law' (2000) 6 *European Law Journal* 39; E Caracciolo di Torella, "Maternity and Equal Treatment" (1998) 23 *European Law Review* 165; E Caracciolo di Torella and A Masselot, 'Pregnancy, Maternity and the Organisation of Family Life: an Attempt to Classify the Case Law of the Court of Justice' (2001) 26 *European Law Review* 239.

In EU labour law, the rules on pregnancy and motherhood can be found in the Pregnant Workers Directive and the Equal Treatment Directive.[19] The Pregnant Workers Directive guarantees women a continuous period of maternity leave, before and/or after childbirth. Maternity leave must comprise *at least* 14 weeks, but the Member States are allowed to choose to have longer periods of maternity leave.[20] There is no upper limit on how long the leave can be.[21] Immediately before or after delivery, at least two weeks of maternity leave must be mandatory, which means that the woman should *not be permitted* to work for these two weeks.[22] This provision, too, is a minimum requirement, and thus it is permissible for the Member States to provide for longer periods of compulsory leave.

In addition, pregnant and breastfeeding employees are entitled to leave of absence from work that poses health risks, if the employer cannot move the employee to another job, as well as leave of absence to undergo antenatal examinations. Leave for antenatal examinations must be granted without loss of pay.[23] For the other forms of leave, the Directive does not contain the same unconditional provisions in terms of salary or other compensation. Thus, in connection with absence from work that involves health risks, as well as in cases of transfer from this kind of work, the employee will normally either keep her employment benefits or be entitled to an adequate allowance. But in these cases, the Directive allows the Member States to require that the employee meet certain conditions for entitlement to this pay or allowance. If the Member State makes the entitlement to compensation conditional upon the employee's having been employed for certain period of time before the expected date of delivery, the specified period must not exceed 12 months.[24]

The same qualification requirements may be imposed in relation to the right to compensation during maternity leave. In both cases, the Directive states that the allowance must be adequate, but it is only in connection with the allowance during maternity leave that this adequate level is defined. During maternity leave, the allowance should be at least equivalent to the compensation which the employee

[19] Directive 2006/54/EC of the European Parliament and of the Council of 5 July 2006 on the implementation of the principle of equal opportunities and equal treatment of men and women in matters of employment and occupation (recast) ('Equal Treatment Directive').

[20] Pregnant Workers Directive, Art 8. The Directive is currently under revision and the period of maternity leave is expected to be extended.

[21] The fact that EU law does not impose any upper limit on how long a period of leave the Member States may reserve for female employees and call maternity leave, has been especially emphasized by the CJEU in Case 184/83 *Ulrich Hofmann v Barmer Ersatzkasse* [1984] ECR 3047, para 25; Case C-136/95 *Caisse nationale d'assurance vieillesse des travailleurs salaries (CNAVTS) v Évelyne Thibault* [1998] ECR I-2011, para 30; and Case C-284/02 *Land Brandenburg v Ursula Sass* [2004] ECR I-11143, para 44. The Member States may also decide for themselves how the leave is to be divided between the time before and the time after the delivery; see Maternity Directive, Art 8, 'at least 14 weeks allocated before and/or after confinement in accordance with national legislation and/or practice', and Case C-411/96 *Margaret Boyle v Equal Opportunities Commission* [1998] ECR I-6401, para 49 ff.

[22] Pregnant Workers Directive, Art 8.

[23] Ibid Art 9.

[24] Ibid Art 11.

concerned would receive in the event of sick leave, *unless* there is a ceiling for the maternity leave allowance laid down under national legislation.[25] In addition, during maternity leave, the employee must enjoy the protection of all other rights connected with her employment contract.

Through its numerous references to national law and practice, the Pregnant Workers Directive allows Member States to both maintain and introduce rules that deviate from the Directive.[26] Such rules may limit the effectiveness of the protection provided by the Directive, but they can also go beyond the level of protection of the Directive. To the extent that maternity protection consists of compulsory leave, the woman is prevented from working. Compulsory leave is the same as prohibition to work, and the Directive specifies no upper limit for the duration of such prohibition periods that Member States may maintain. Even though the rules prohibiting work here have the good intention to ensure women's right to leave, such rules may also have less favourable consequences, as the women who can and want to work are prevented from doing so. Such mandatory rules could mean diminished opportunities for women to rule over their own lives, economic loss, and a risk of having a deteriorated position in the labour market. To the extent that maternity protection consists of rights that the pregnant woman or new mother is free to exercise, such as non-compulsory leave, the rules do not restrict women's freedom of action; on the contrary, such rules increase the opportunities for women to combine gainful employment with parenthood.

The reconciliation of work and parenthood is affected not only by the right to parental leave, but is also largely dependent on the extent to which legal rules assure the employee protection against unfair treatment in the form of dismissal or deterioration in employment conditions. The Pregnant Workers Directive also provides special rules in this area. During the period from the beginning of pregnancy to the end of maternity leave, the employment may not, as a rule, be terminated.[27] The Directive does not completely exclude the possibility to dismiss

[25] Case C-342/93 *Gillespie and others v Northern Health and Social Services Board and others* [1996] ECR I-475; Case C-66/96 *Handels- og Kontorsfunktionærernes Forbund i Danmark representing Berit Høj Pedersen v Fællesforeningen for Danmarks Brugsforeninger representerande Kvickly Skive* [1998] ECR I-7327, para 49.

[26] Cf C McGlynn, 'Reclaiming a Feminist Vision: the Reconciliation of Paid Work and Family Life in European Union Law and Policy' (2001) 7 *Columbia Journal of European Law* 242, and Foubert, *The Legal Protection of the Pregnant Worker*, above n 18, 107 ff.

[27] Pregnant Workers Directive, Arts 11 and 10. A breastfeeding employee is thus not covered by any particular employment protection from the end of the period of maternity leave. The question of who should be included in the category 'pregnant worker' according to the Maternity Directive was raised in Case C-506/06 *Sabine Mayr v Konditorei Gerhard Flöckner OHG* [2008] ECR I-01017. The question that was subject to the CJEU's preliminary ruling in this case was as follows: 'Is a worker, who undergoes in vitro fertilisation, a "pregnant worker" within the meaning of the first part of Article 2(a) of [Directive 92/85] if, at the time at which she was given notice of dismissal, the woman's ova had already been fertilised with the sperm cells of her partner and "in vitro" embryos thus existed, but they had not yet been implanted within her?' The Court answered this question in the negative, but found that the Equal Treatment Directive instead could be applicable in a case like this, provided that the *in vitro* fertilisation treatment is at an adequately advanced stage.

a pregnant employee or an employee on maternity leave, but this must be done only in exceptional cases which are not connected with the woman's condition, and which are permitted under national legislation and practice.[28] Furthermore, in such exceptional cases, the employer who wants to dismiss an employee who is covered by the Directive must provide a detailed, written justification citing duly substantiated grounds for this action.[29]

However, the most essential rules of EU law concerning the protection against dismissal and unfair treatment during pregnancy and maternity leave are not those of the Pregnant Workers Directive. Instead, the protection is guaranteed mainly by the prohibition against sex discrimination in the Equal Treatment Directive and the case law that has developed around this Directive.[30] In 1990, for the first time, the European Court of Justice (CJEU) held that a refusal to hire on the basis that the job applicant is pregnant must be regarded as an expression of direct sex discrimination.[31] Over the years, this principle has since been consolidated and developed in a fairly large number of cases relating to unfair treatment with regard to access to employment, recruitment, protection of employment, and termination of employment contracts.[32] Apart from conditions of pay, in relation to which the case law has been developed on the basis of the Equal Pay Directive, the CJEU has consequently adhered to the principle that detrimental treatment on the grounds of pregnancy or maternity leave constitutes direct discrimination on the grounds of sex.[33] Since 2002 this case law has also been codified, in part, in the Equal Treatment

[28] Cf Case C-109/00 *Tele Danmark v Handels- og Kontorfunktionærernes Forbund, representing Marianne Brandt-Nielsen* [2001] ECR I-6993 and Case C-438/99 *Maria Luisa Jiménez Melgar v Ayuntamiento de Los Barrios* [2001] ECR I-6915.

[29] Pregnant Workers Directive, Art 10(2).

[30] Equal Treatment Directive, Arts 2(2)(c) and 14, formerly Art 2(7) in Directive 2002/73/EC of the European Parliament and of the Council of 23 September 2002 amending Council Directive 76/207/EEC on the implementation of the principle of equal treatment for men and women as regards access to employment, vocational training and promotion, and working conditions [2002] OJ L269/15.

[31] Case C-177/88 *Elisabeth Johanna Pacifica Dekker v Stitching Vormingscentrum voor Jong Volwassenen (VJV-centrum) Plus* [1990] ECR I-3941.

[32] See, among many cases, Case C-177/88 *Elisabeth Johanna Pacifica Dekker v Stitching Vormingscentrum voor Jong Volwassenen (VJV-centrum) Plus* [1990] ECR I-3941, para 12; Case C-207/98 *Silke-Karin Mahlburg v Land Mecklenburg-Vorpommern* [2000] ECR I-00549, para 29; Case C-109/00 *Tele Danmark v Handels- og Kontorfunktionærernes Forbund, representing Marianne Brandt-Nielsen* [2001] ECR I-6993, para 28; Case C-438/99 *Maria Luisa Jiménez Melgar v Ayuntamiento de Los Barrios* [2001] ECR I-6915, para 44; Case C-342/93 *Gillespie and others* [1996] ECR I-475, para 22; Case C-136/95 *Caisse nationale d'assurance vieillesse des travailleurs salaries (CNAVTS) v Évelyne Thibault* [1998] ECR I-2011, paras 29 and 32; Case C-147/02 *Alabaster* [2004] ECR I-3127, para 47; and Case C-284/02 *Land Brandenburg v Ursula Sass* [2004] ECR I-11143, para 36.

[33] Directive 75/117/EEC on equal pay for men and women [1975] OJ L045/19. This Directive, along with Directive 76/207/EEC on equal treatment for men and women as regards access to employment, vocational training and promotion, and working conditions [1976] OJ L039/40, Directive 86/378/EEC on equal treatment for men and women in occupational social security schemes [1986] OJ L225/40 and Directive 97/80/EC on the burden of proof in cases of discrimination based on sex [1998] OJ L14/6, is now replaced by the Equal Treatment Directive. In the case law concerning pay, the CJEU has taken the firm position that a woman on maternity leave is in a situation so unique that she cannot and should not be compared with anyone else. Since comparison is a necessary prerequisite in determining wage discrimination, this implies that in principle, a woman on maternity leave can never have any success

Directive, which states that any less favourable treatment of a woman related to pregnancy is categorised as discrimination within the meaning of the Directive.[34]

The categorisation of pregnancy and maternity discrimination as direct discrimination means that pregnant employees and employees on maternity leave are granted a very high level of protection against detrimental treatment. The high level of protection, along with the fact that the right to leave according to the Pregnant Workers Directive is combined with a right to financial benefits, shows that the EU rules on pregnancy and maternity are far more influenced by the value of work-family balance than of the value work life commitment.

The situation is quite different when it comes to the EU law on parental leave, which gives both men and women the right to leave when they become parents. Despite what one might expect of rules on leave from work, these rules are clearly influenced by the value of work life commitment—the idea that the needs and expectations of working life must take precedence over the needs of family life. Certainly, the Parental Leave Directive includes a right to parental leave, but in many respects the right to leave must be adaptable to the needs of the employer. Thus, the employer must be allowed to postpone the granting of parental leave for justifiable reasons related to the operation of the organisation.[35] Moreover, Member States may authorise special arrangements to meet the operational and organisational requirements of small undertakings, which may be particularly sensitive to the interference that can result during parental leave.[36] Since small businesses employ a significant proportion of EU employees, the possibility of such restrictions means that the right to parental leave could be limited for a substantial number of persons.[37] Furthermore, the Directive does not require Member States to grant any right to compensation along with the right to parental leave. This means that in practice the possibilities to use the right to leave are very limited for most employees.[38] Since 2010, the Parental Leave Directive, just like the EU rules on pregnancy and maternity, contains provisions on protection against unfair treatment or dismissal arising from the employee's request for or exercise of the right to parental leave.[39] However, no protection is provided in the

in claiming that she has been subject to wage discrimination: Case C-342/93 *Gillespie and others v Northern Health and Social Services Board and others* [1996] ECR I-475; Case C-218/98 *Oumar Dabo Abdoulaye and others v Régie Nationale des Usines Renault SA* [1999] ECR I-5723; and Case C-220/02 *Osterreichischer Gewerkschaftsbund, Gewerkschaft der Privatangestellten v Wirtschaftskammer Osterreich* [2004] ECR 1-5907. See also Foubert, *The Legal Protection of the Pregnant Worker*, above n 18.

[34] Equal Treatment Directive, Arts 2(2)(c) and 14.

[35] Parental Leave Directive and Framework Agreement, Part II, 3, s 1c.

[36] Parental Leave Directive and Framework Agreement, Part II, 3, s 1d.

[37] The Directive does not specify how small a company should be to belong to the group of small undertakings.

[38] Also, the Pregnant Workers Directive allows the Member States to impose qualification requirements for entitlement to compensation. But whereas EU law requires Member States to have compensation arrangements for employees on maternity leave, there are no such requirements for employees who are on parental leave. Cf the Pregnant Workers Directive, Art 11.

[39] Parental Leave Directive and Framework Agreement, Part II, 5, s 4.

Directive itself. It is the Member States who, on their own or through delegation to the social partners, must take necessary measures in accordance with national law, collective agreements or practice. This solution leaves a certain margin for the Member States to limit the scope of protection in national legislation.

The many limitations that surround the rights that are granted to working parents at the Union level have a clear impact when the EU labour law on parenthood, taken as a whole, is placed in the normative field where the rules belong. Altogether, EU regulation on working parents is influenced by and supports the value of work life commitment substantially more than that of work-family balance. Even though the rules on pregnancy and maternity can be of great importance for the protection of the employee's parental rights in the individual case, upon closer examination these rules do not challenge in any significant way the hegemonic position that the values of work life commitment enjoy in labour law. This is partly because the truly strong employment protection provided by these rules does not cover all employees, but only the female portion of the workforce, and partly because the strong protection is applicable only for a very short, initial period of time in the employee's parenthood. After maternity leave, women are in the same legal position as men, and in this situation the value of work life commitment is explicitly predominant. The parenthood of men, just like the parenthood of women after the expiry of the maternity leave, is in principle only protected to the extent that the Member State has determined.[40] Apart from the protection granted to women in connection with pregnancy and maternity leave, the EU legal rules do not provide employees with any significant possibilities to combine paid work with the caring tasks of parenthood. When the period of maternity leave has expired, the value of work life commitment is almost unreservedly respected as a superior norm in the very few EU rules on parenthood that are still applicable: after an initial short period, working life does not have to tolerate in any significant way the employee's need to care for their child.

VI. WORKING PARENTS IN SWEDISH LABOUR LAW

Unlike EU law, the Swedish rules on employees' parenting is based on a very clear ambition to create real opportunities for employees to combine work with parenthood. Thus, the legislator's express intention has been to design rules that expressly support the value of work-family balance, and consequently to restrain claims based on the value of work life commitment. This has been achieved mainly through the introduction of extensive rules on the right to leave (and on the corresponding rights to parental benefits), as well as policies and legislative

[40] Equal Treatment Directive, Art 2(7) is a specific rule to protect men against unfavourable treatment when they are on leave to take care of their children. However, this rule applies only in Member States which have introduced a special right to paternity leave. The Directive emphasises that it is up to the Member State to determine whether such a right should exist at all in the national legislation.

measures aimed at creating a more equal sharing of parental leave between men and women.

In Sweden, parental benefit is payable for 13 months for each child, with an amount equal to the employee's sickness benefit. In addition, parental benefit is paid at a low, flat-rate level for another three months.[41] Parents are entitled to receive half of the leave days with parental benefit, but most of the days can be transferred to the other parent. However, two months of parental leave on the sickness benefit level is reserved for each parent, and thus as a rule cannot be transferred.[42] Parental benefits can be paid until the child turns eight years old or finishes the first school year.[43]

Since the early 2000s, in order to increase further the possibilities to combine work and parenthood, attention has been paid to the need to strengthen protection against unfavourable treatment on the grounds of parental leave. In 2006, this discussion resulted in the introduction of a stricter prohibition on unfavourable treatment in the Parental Leave Act. This clause protects both employees and job seekers, and it covers virtually all situations in which a person might experience less favourable treatment in working life.[44] The prohibition, which is applicable as soon as the less favourable treatment has a connection with the employee's parental leave, is designed in principle to ensure for workers on parental leave the same high level of protection against deterioration of working conditions as the protection that is ensured during pregnancy and maternity leave.[45]

However, the protection against less favourable treatment due to parental leave is limited by an important exemption rule, according to which detrimental treatment of workers on parental leave can be justified in certain cases. The exemption rule is applicable if the employer can show that the less favourable treatment is a 'necessary consequence' of the parental leave. For example, an employee who wants to be on leave on a part-time basis must, in some special cases, accept being transferred for the duration of the leave, if this is necessary for the organisation in the workplace.[46] The employee subjected to such a permitted transfer must also accept that shift premiums or supplements for unsocial working hours will be

[41] Social Security Code, ch 12, ss 35–41. The recipient of parental allowance always has the right to take parental leave. But employees are also entitled to take time off to care for their children during time when they choose not to receive parental benefit: first, in any extent during the first 18 months of the child's life, secondly, as reduced working hours until the child has reached the age of eight years, Parental Leave Act (1995:584), ss 5 and 7. Reduced working hours means that the employee works 75 per cent of a full-time position and is on leave the rest of the time.

[42] Social Security Code, ch 12, s 17. One parent may use all the leave in cases where the parent has sole custody, in cases where the other parent due to illness or disability cannot care for the child, and in cases where the other parent is not covered by the Swedish social insurance for parental allowance.

[43] Social Security Code, ch 12, s 13.

[44] Parental Leave Act, s 16.

[45] Government bill 2005/06:185, 76, Ds 2005:15, 91.

[46] Government White Paper 2005:15, 108 ff. A need for such temporary reassignment may arise if the employee normally works in shifts, since in production activities carried out in shifts, the agreed working hours are the basis for the organisation.

lost as a result of the transfer.[47] A deterioration that is a necessary consequence of the parental leave could also be that when recruiting or promoting, the employer bypasses the best qualified person for reasons relating to that person's parental leave, for example, in cases where the employer is not able to hire a replacement, the period of temporary employment is very short, or because the employment must start immediately.[48]

The starting point in the preparatory works is that the exemption rule is to be interpreted in a restrictive way.[49] Nevertheless, the examples set out in the preparatory works show that, in fact, there are many circumstances in which less favourable treatment may be justified by reverting to the fact that such treatment is a necessary consequence of the parental leave. This becomes even more obvious in the definition given in the preparatory works of when less favourable treatment is to be regarded as a 'necessary consequence' of the parental leave.[50] According to this definition, less favourable treatment is permitted as a necessary consequence in cases where the employee on parental leave would otherwise be 'particularly favoured in relation to other employees in a way that could be perceived as unfair towards these employees, or otherwise appear as unreasonable or obviously unjustified'.[51] There are thus two circumstances in which the employer may treat an employee less favourably in regard to his or her parental leave. The first concerns a situation where it could be perceived as unfair towards another employee to treat the employee on parental leave as if he or she had been working. The second concerns a situation where it appears to be generally unreasonable or obviously unjustified to treat the employee on parental leave as if he or she had been working. In contrast to the strict prohibition against discrimination due to pregnancy and maternity leave in EU law, the Swedish rules on prohibition against less favourable treatment due to parental leave in an individual case can be set aside by referring to perceptions of fairness, and to what demands can be regarded as reasonable and justified in terms of the employee in question.[52]

The declarations in the preparatory works regarding the situations in which the prohibition of unfavourable treatment on grounds of parental leave will not apply are interesting, since they provide a current picture of the legislator's position on the question of how working life should be reconciled with parenthood, and

[47] Ibid 108 ff.

[48] Government bill 2005/06:185, 87; Government White Paper 2005:15, 107–8.

[49] Government bill 2005/06:185, 87.

[50] For a detailed discussion on this theme, see Votinius, *Föräldrar i arbete*, above n 1, 274 ff.

[51] Government bill 2005/06:185, 87.

[52] So far, the exemption rule has been referred to in three cases from the Swedish Labour Court: AD 2009 no 13, AD 2009 no 15 and AD 2009 no 45. The first two cases concerned the employee's right to certain financial benefits (gratuity and pension contribution, respectively) during periods of parental leave. The Labour Court found that the exemption rule was applicable in these cases, and that consequently the employer was allowed to withdraw the benefits in question from employees on parental leave. The third case concerned a non-financial benefit, or the right of an employee to participate in an intermediate course shortly before the beginning of parental leave. In this case, the Labour Court found that the exemption rule was not applicable.

what an employer must accept in relation to employees' parental leave. Thus, these declarations say something about the extent to which the value of work-family balance should be allowed to encroach upon the working life domain, where the value of work life commitment has a completely hegemonic position. It shows that the actual position of the value of work-family balance in Swedish labour law today is not quite as strong and independent as it may appear when looking at the parental rules; rather, its impact on the legal rules is adjusted to the demands of working life and the labour market.

VII. A TRANSLATION TO THE MODEL OF NORMATIVE PATTERNS

To sum up so far, the operative field of the labour law rules on parenthood could be described as a field characterised by the tensions that exist between the values of work-family balance and the value of work life commitment. As the two conflicting values of work-family balance and the value of work life commitment clearly affect the content and application of the legal rules, it is correct to describe them as having normative impact on the law. Pursuant to the theory of law as normative patterns in a normative field, these two values can be said to belong to two separate and opposite poles in the normative field of parental rights in labour law. As the values of work-family balance emphasise the conservative right to protection of employment and employment conditions, work-family balance could, according to the terminology of this theory, be said to represent the normative basic pattern Protection of Established Position, while the opposite, market-oriented, value of work life commitment belongs to the Market-Functional pattern.[53]

In the previous discussion, we have seen that the Swedish rules provide employees with the right to a substantial period of paid leave when they become parents. That is not the case in the EU regulation, where the right to leave is more limited and not associated to any greater extent with the right to compensation. As regards the capacity of the legislation to enable employees to care for and spend time with their children without having to give up their position in the labour market, the Swedish rules are far more powerful than the EU legal regulation. Thus, in this respect, the Swedish rules are more oriented towards the value of work-family balance than is the case with the EU rules. With the theory of law as normative patterns in a normative field, this could be described as follows: in the normative field where parental rules belong, the Swedish rules on parental leave are closer to the normative pole Protection of Established Position, and further away from the Market-Functional pole. However, as regards the protection of employment and employment conditions, the EU rules on maternity leave and pregnancy have a much more stringent wording than the Swedish parental leave legislation.[54] Thus,

[53] Christensen, 'Normative Patterns and the Normative Field', above n 5.

[54] I here ignore the protection of employment that can be obtained by interpreting the EU law into the Swedish law.

in terms of employment protection, it is the EU legal rules, and not the Swedish rules, that correspond best to the value of work-family balance. With the theory of law as normative patterns in a normative field, it is in this respect that the EU rules are closest to the pole of Protection of Established Position. This could be interpreted to mean that the Swedish and EU labour rules give employees about more or less equal room for managing their parenthood in relation to work, even though this is done in slightly different ways.

It could also mean, in other words, that the Swedish and EU legal rules are situated at approximately the same position in the tension between the normative poles Protection of Established Position and the Market-Functional pattern. But anyone who is familiar with the two regulatory systems, even if only briefly, knows that this is not true. Swedish labour law provides employees with a much larger space for their parenting than does EU law. Thus, for an analysis of the normative field to which the parental rules belong, it does not seem to be sufficient to position the two sets of rules in the tension between the values of work life commitment and work-family balance, which are included in the Market-Functional pattern and the basic pattern of Protection of Established Position, respectively. Such a description lacks an important dimension; or, in the theory of basic normative patterns, it seems as if all the basic patterns in this normative field are not yet identified.

In cases like this, the heuristic (dynamic) aspect of the theory of law as normative patterns in a normative field may have an important function. A fundamental basis of this theory is that it can detect and visualise phenomena in a sphere, using a bottom-up approach intended to identify individual rules and principles that seem to attract each other and form a context—a pattern. In connection with the identification of these patterns, it is also possible to distinguish their underlying normative beliefs, values and ideals, which are also rooted in social practices. Through the application of such a heuristic approach, I have found that in the description and analysis of the normative field surrounding employees' parenthood, where we have already identified work-family balance and work life commitment, there is a pressing need to introduce a gender dimension; that is, a dimension that involves different perceptions of man and woman as parents and employees.[55] It is only when this gender dimension is taken into account that it becomes possible to perceive the Swedish and EU legal regulatory regimes' actual positions in the normative field.[56]

[55] There is extensive research that addresses issues of gender and gender perceptions in working life. See, eg, RM Kanter, *Men and Women of the Corporation* (New York, Basic Books, 1977); S Walby, *Patriarchy at Work: Patriarchal and Capitalist Relations in Employment* (Cambridge, Polity Press/Basil Blackwell, 1986); J Acker, 'Hierarchies, Jobs, Bodies: a Theory of Gendered Organizations' (1990) 4 *Gender and Society* 2, 139–58; J Acker, "Gendering Organizational Theory" in A Mills and P Tancred (eds), *Gendering Organizational Analysis* (London, Sage, 1992); C Cockburn, *In the Way of Women: Men's Resistance to Sex Equality in Organizations* (London, Macmillan, 1991).

[56] The fact that the theory of normative patterns does not treat gender as a separate analytical category has been criticised. Cf, eg, S Fransson, *Lönediskriminering. En arbetsrättslig studie av könsdiskriminerande löneskillnader och konflikten mellan kollektivavtal och lag* (Uppsala, Iustus, 2000) 50.

VIII. THE MISSING DIMENSION

As we have seen, the EU regulations that specifically apply to employees with parental responsibility are mainly concentrated on the pregnancy, and to the maternity leave which, in the context of EU law, is almost regarded as an extension of the pregnancy. The clear focus on pregnancy and maternity in the binding EU legal rules is not uncontroversial within the European Union. Thus, many non-binding documents call for a legal development in support of increased gender equality in matters of employment and parenthood. The need to facilitate the balancing of family life and working life for both men and women has been emphasised over and over throughout the past decades, in central soft law and in policy documents on employment and gender equality in the European Union.[57]

Nevertheless, the fact remains that it is motherhood (or rather the motherhood of the pregnant, newly delivered and breastfeeding woman) that is the primary object of protection under EU law. Although EU law also provides rules on parental leave, the real and powerful protection for the employee is the one that applies during pregnancy and maternity leave, and this protection covers only female employees. In the EU legal context, the emphasis on women's parenthood is not only justified by arguments about women's needs for physical recovery, but also with arguments about the special relationship between a woman and her child.[58] The description of women's parenthood as something different and more worthy of protection than the parenthood of men has been manifested in the case law of the ECJ and has thus been formalised into a legal norm. The meaning of this legal norm is that women, in their capacity of being women, already have a special capacity to care for and create special relationships with their children; the relationship between the woman and the child can be disrupted if the woman is engaged in paid work, and therefore this requires special rules that enable women's care work. This legal norm also means that such special rules cannot be required for men, since there is no special relationship between men and their children, and since the relationship that nevertheless exists will not be disturbed by a man's engagement in gainful employment.

[57] Out of a vast amount of documents I choose to mention only a few examples here. Thus, the Employment Guidelines 2000 stated that 'Policies on career breaks, parental leave and part-time work, as well as flexible working arrangements which serve the interests of both employers and employees, are of particular importance to women and men', and that 'An equal sharing of family responsibilities is crucial in this respect'. In 2000, the Council also adopted a Resolution on balanced participation of men and women in family and working life (2000/C218/02). See also *A Better Work-Life Balance: Stronger Support for Reconciling Professional, Private and Family Life*, COM(2008)635 final. In the Strategy for Equality between Women and Men 2010–2015, COM(2010)491 final, one of the European Commission's key actions for the period is to assess remaining gaps in entitlement to paternity leave and the options for addressing them.

[58] Case 163/82 *Commission v Italy* [1983] ECR 3273, para 16; Case 184/83 *Ulrich Hofmann v Barmer Ersatzkasse* [1984] ECR 3047, para 25; Case 312/86, *Commission v France* [1988] ECR 6315, paras 13 and 14; Case T-51/98 *Ann Ruth Burrill and Alberto Noriega v Commission* [1999] ECR II-1059, para 48; Case C-284/02 *Land Brandenburg v Ursula Sass* [2004] ECR I-11143, paras 52–53.

While the EU legal regulation on employees' parenthood focuses primarily on pregnancy and maternity leave, as we have seen, most of the Swedish labour law on parenthood concerns parental leave—the leave for child care that is granted to both male and female employees.[59] Indeed, an equal division of the parental care responsibilities is not always the obvious starting point in the context where these rules are interpreted and applied. In addition, in Sweden there is a structural resistance to the idea of parenting involving both the father and mother in equal measure. This resistance is expressed, inter alia, in the fact that women still take the greater share of the parental leave, and that women are far more likely than men to suffer deterioration in their working situation as a result of having children, or even just because they are expected to have children at some point in the future. This, however, does not change the fact that the Swedish rules on the parenthood of workers are designed to promote an equal distribution of the care responsibilities that come with parenthood. Under Swedish law, the primary object of protection is not the pregnant woman, but the working parent.

Behind the binding EU labour law rules, which in many respects are based on a belief that the caring tasks of parenthood are primarily the responsibility of women, there is a complementary approach to woman and man. According to this approach, a woman's main responsibilities lie within the domestic sphere, while men should be the main breadwinners and have their area of responsibility in the public sphere, including working life.[60] The Swedish rules, which in the last 40 years have emphasised shared parental responsibilities, are instead based on an equality approach to man and woman. According to this approach, both parents are expected to have joint responsibility for the actual care of the children, as well as for the support of the family.[61] In the clash between the complementary and the equality-based approach to man and woman, a conflict arises, which in relation to questions about the reconciliation of working life and parenthood can be said to involve the two values *shared parental responsibilities*, and the *uniqueness of motherhood.*

On one level, this conflict is about the gender division of the care work which is generated in the home when a child has been born. But the conflict also has an effect on the extent to which labour law requires that working life should accommodate employees' parenthood. In a system where the regulation is designed to encourage shared parental responsibilities, it is naturally important that working life is

[59] Swedish law also protects workers during pregnancy, but until quite recently, the pregnant woman's position in Swedish labour law was rather weak. The trend towards stronger employment protection for pregnant women is largely due to the fact that Sweden, as a Member State of the European Union, is obliged to comply with the EU regulations, including EU law which prohibits discrimination related to pregnancy.

[60] See Clarissa Kugelberg, 'Jämställdhetsideal och könsdiskriminering—unga människor möter arbetslivet' (2004) 10(2) *Arbetsmarknad och arbetsliv*, 102; Kari Melby *et al*, *The Nordic Model of Marriage and the Welfare State*, Nord 2000:27 (Copenhagen, 2000).

[61] The equality-based approach is reflected not least in the preparatory works; cf, eg, Government bill 2000/01:44, 22; Government bill 2005/06:185, 74.

organised in a way that is truly compatible with parenthood, since both parents are presumed to engage both in the care of children and in gainful employment. Legislation designed to support the value of shared parental responsibilities will therefore also have a reinforcing effect on the value of work-family balance.

The reconciliation of working life and parenthood is not as important in a system that mainly protects the parenthood of one of the parents: the mother. In such a system, the other parent, the father, is not expected to engage in the care of children to any great extent, but instead primarily pursue gainful employment. An approach which focuses primarily on women's parenthood may on the contrary operate in the opposite direction. Thus, the value of the uniqueness of motherhood tends to strengthen the positions of the value of work life commitment.

The fact that domestic life is organised in accordance with an ideal of the mother as the main person responsible for the care of children is an important, if not necessary, prerequisite for an organisation of working life that is based on an ideal of work life commitment. If the traditional gender division of labour were completely abandoned in homes, so that men and women in all families actually took an equal share of the care of the children, it would be very difficult to maintain an ideal in working life, in which the employee's parenthood-related commitments would not encroach on the job. This way, the values of the uniqueness of motherhood and work life commitment interact to maintain systems that not only consolidate the positioning of women in homes, and of men in working life, but that also spare working life from demands for the accommodation of working parents.

In order to transfer this analysis of the gender dimension of parental rules to the model that is the basis for the theory of law as normative patterns in a normative field, we can say that initially, the value of shared parental responsibilities can be attributed to the pattern Just Distribution. This pattern has been described as encompassing different models for distribution: equal distribution, distribution in accordance with need, in accordance with seniority, etc.[62] In previous research applying the theory of law as normative patterns in a normative field, the pattern of Just Distribution has mainly been identified in studies on the organisation of the distribution of benefits and goods.[63] But the concept of just distribution could just as well be used to describe the distribution of responsibilities, such as parental

[62] Christensen, 'Normative Patterns and the Normative Field', above n 5, 7. The principle of Just Distribution regarding pay and pension benefits for men and women has been discussed in A Christensen, 'Den EG-rättsliga likhetsprincipen versus den europeiska enförsörjarfamiljen' in U Bernitz, S Gustavsson and Lars Oxenheim (eds), *Europaperspektiv. Årsbok för Europaforskning inom ekonomi, juridik och statskunskap* (Uppsala, Santérus, 1999) 13–40.

[63] The pattern Just Distribution is discussed, inter alia, in A Numhauser-Henning, 'Freedom of Movement and Transfer of Social Security Rights, Pension Rights and the EC Coordination Rules on Applicable Legislation in the Light of Migration and Labour-Market Developments' in R Blanpain (ed), *Collective Bargaining, Discrimination Social Security and European Integration* (The Hague, Kluwer Law International, 2003).

care responsibilities. Seen from this perspective, the ideal of shared parental responsibilities fits in very well with the basic pattern of Just Distribution.

Perhaps more controversially, regarding the value of the uniqueness of motherhood, I argue that the normative perceptions that divide man and woman into different categories fulfil the criterion for being treated as a normative basic pattern. According to the theory of law as normative patterns in a normative field, basic normative patterns represent enduring legitimate normative conceptions in society, which are confirmed within the framework of law by legislators and courts. They reflect, and codify, social normative conceptions and practices aimed at making long-lasting human relationships and sustainable societies possible.[64] And if anything corresponds to precisely this description, it is the idea that men are of one kind and women of another. This does not mean that notions of gender look the same always and everywhere. Nor does it mean that notions of gender cannot be criticised or questioned. What it does mean is that notions of gender permeate society and act as organisational principles in a variety of areas, and that in this capacity they serve as common agreements on how people should live together.[65] It also means that beliefs about the differences between men and women are embedded in law, and that they affect the design and application of legal rules.

Consequently, on the basis of the analysis of the normative field where the rules on working parents belong, I propose here the introduction of *Gender Difference* as an additional normative basic pattern. The further implications of this additional pattern remain to be explored, as do other important questions that emerge from or relate to the analysis in this chapter. One such important question is whether the market-functional values and interests in the labour market must necessarily operate contrary to the interests of working parents, or if the matter can be understood in a different way. Another set of questions arises from the fact that in many respects, in both the labour market and family life, traditional organisational principles have been abandoned or have at least lost their dominant position. New and flexible forms of employment in recent decades have become as established as permanent employment, and family constellations that differ from the composition of the nuclear family are commonplace. This raises questions about the possible effects of this trend for the relationship between the

[64] Christensen, 'Skydd för etablerad position', above n 2, 565; A Numhauser-Henning, 'Introduction' in A Numhauser-Henning and M Rönnmar, *Fifteen Years with the Norma Research Programme* (Lund, Norma Research Programme, Faculty of Law, Lund University, 2010) 18 ff; H Hydén, *Normvetenskap* (Lund, Sociologiska Institutionen, 2002) 241 ff.

[65] I here refer to a few examples out of the abundance of scientific publications in this field: S Harding, *The Science Question in Feminism* (Milton Keynes, Open University Press, 1986); J Wallach Scott, *Gender and the Politics of History* (New York, Columbia University Press, 1988); K. O'Donovan, *Sexual Divisions in Law* (London, Weidenfeld & Nicolson, 1985); C Pateman, *The Disorder of Women: Democracy, Feminism, and Political Theory* (Stanford, Stanford University Press, 1989); S Benhabib, *Situating the Self: Gender, Community and Postmodernism in Contemporary Ethics* (Cambridge, Polity Press, 1992).

values that operate in the normative setting in which the regulations on working parents receive their form and content.

Here, I shall confine myself to the final conclusion that, inspired by the heuristic aspect of the theory of law as normative patterns in a normative field, it is possible to use an analysis of the rules in any legal field as a basis for identifying normative patterns that reflect perceptions and ideals that are deeply rooted in society and that affect the content of law. A really good theory does not stop at contributing to the more practical side of research. It goes much further than that—it inspires and encourages intellectual freedom, creativity and innovation. The theory of law as normative patterns in a normative field is just precisely a theory.

Part V

Just Distribution and Normative Development

11

Flexicurity and Labour Law: Labour Market Segmentation, Precarious Work and Just Distribution

JUDY FUDGE

I. INTRODUCTION

FLEXICURITY IS THE European Union's response to how to address the profound changes in the labour market that have accompanied the growth of the European internal market, deepening and expanding globalisation, and the deployment of new technologies. Yet despite the fact that it is the dominant approach to labour market regulation within the European Union, flexicurity's precise meaning or content is contentious; the emphasis tends to oscillate from flexibility to security depending on the specific EU institution or actor endorsing it.[1]

Labour law is a central component of the flexicurity approach, and the key concern of 'modern' European labour law is to address labour segmentation. My goal in this chapter is to probe the relationship between flexicurity, labour law and labour law market segmentation, focusing on women workers in precarious work in particular. To do so, I use the theoretical framework developed by Anna Christensen and Ann Numhauser-Henning under the umbrella of the Norma Research Programme (Norma).[2] Norma's interdisciplinary approach places legal norms and institutions in their social contexts; it is also historical and comparative, as it seeks to understand the relationship between social change and legal developments. Much of the focus of Norma's research has been the 'altered conditions for the functioning of the labour market and their significance for labour law and labour market policy'.[3] Thus, it is ideally suited to studying flexicurity.[4]

[1] L Burroni and M Keune 'Flexicurity: a Conceptual Critique' (2011) 17 *European Journal of Industrial Relations* 75.

[2] A Numhauser-Henning and M Rönnmar (eds), *Fifteen Years with the Norma Research Programme* (Lund, Norma Research Programme, Faculty of Law, Lund University, 2010).

[3] A Numhauser-Henning, 'Introduction' in A Numhauser-Henning and M Rönnmar (eds), *Fifteen Years with the Norma Research Programme* (Lund, Norma Research Programme, Faculty of Law, Lund University, 2010) 15.

[4] See the essays in the collection edited by Numhauser-Henning and Rönnmar, *Fifteen Years with the Norma Research Programme*, above n 2.

Using this theoretical framework, I conceptualise flexicurity as a normative field, of which labour law is a central element, in order to determine whether the normative patterns of market functioning, protection of established positions, and just redistribution has been realigned within modern EU labour law. I will begin by outlining the key components of Norma's theoretical framework that I will use to assess the European Union's flexicurity approach. Once I have sketched this conceptual framework, I will use it to examine the development of the EU's commitment to flexicurity, beginning with the atypical work Directives in the late 1990s through to statements in the Europe 2020 Strategy, focusing on the relationship between flexicurity and modernising labour law. In section IV, I will concentrate upon a key theme in EU labour law, which is regulating atypical forms of employment that are located at the margins of labour law. I suggest that the strategy of increasing 'flexibility at the margins'—the loosening of restrictions on such non-standard or atypical contracts as part-time, fixed-term and through-agency work—runs the risk of reinforcing segmented labour markets, especially labour markets that are segmented on a gender basis. In the conclusion, I reflect on whether, and, if so, the extent to which the normative field of flexicurity has disrupted traditional normative patterns in labour law.

II. NORMATIVE PATTERNS, NORMATIVE FIELDS AND SOCIAL CHANGE

In an attempt to explain the rise of social regulation in the wake of the expansion of the liberal market order, Anna Christensen developed the theory of law as normative patterns in a normative field to account for the post-liberal legal order.[5] She claimed that all societies have ideas about what is just and how social relations should be shaped, and that these ideas become embedded in normative patterns. She used the term 'pattern' to capture the combination of social practice, reality and the ideal, and she identified three basic normative patterns—Market-Functional, Protection of Established Position and Just Distribution—that prevailed under the welfare state. According to Christensen, these normative patterns are not organised hierarchically; they conflict and shift in a normative field, which refers to areas of law that correspond to social life, such as labour law and social security law.[6] She illustrated how normative patterns function as 'magnetic poles seeking to attract legal rules' through an examination of social security law in Europe, and she provided a nuanced and subtle account of how normative patterns have changed position over 50 years.[7]

[5] A Christensen, 'Normative Patterns and the Normative Field: a Post Liberal View on Law' in T Wilhelmsson and S Hurri (eds), *From Dissonance to Sense: Welfare State Expectations, Privatisation and Private Law* (Aldershot, Ashgate, 1999).

[6] Ibid.

[7] Ibid.

Christensen sought to combine an attention to law as 'normative patterns in a normative field' with an appreciation of the relationship between the legal system and the structure of society and conditions of economic production.[8] Ann Numhauser-Henning has elaborated upon the external component of this theoretical framework and she explained that normative patterns 'reflect normative practices functional to society and human relationships'.[9] Changes in the 'conditions of production' explain the movements 'in the normative field, which can thus also be pictured as a functional field'.[10]

The concept of a normative field is particularly useful in the context of the European Union, which is a multilevel governance structure in which Member States retain sovereignty over social policy. It is helpful to think of flexicurity as a project to create a new normative field, rather than as a discourse, which I see as more akin to a normative pattern. The benefit of this approach is that it not only emphasises the extent to which flexicurity challenges existing policy domains, such as the separation of employment policy from social security, it also allows for multiple normative patterns, or discourses, that can conflict and combine in new ways. It takes seriously the claim that flexicurity is an attempt to create a new method of regulating the labour market that transcends the traditional dichotomy between flexibility and security in employment relations. Yet, it also appreciates that there are a variety of normative patterns, not all of which align. Seeing flexicurity as a normative field constructed by actors and institutions through a range of processes allows us to appreciate the conflicts between normative patterns and differences in power relations that help to explain specific positions and understandings.

III. FLEXICURITY AND LABOUR LAW

A. Introduction

The flexicurity policy agenda needs to be placed in the broader economic and political context of Social Europe.[11] It is the outcome of the interactions of, and power relations between, key European institutions, such as the Commission, Council, Parliament, European Court of Justice (CJEU), Member States and social partners, and it is given effect by a range of legal processes, which include Directives, the Open Method of Coordination, social dialogue, and the use of European social funds.

[8] Ibid.

[9] Numhauser-Henning, 'Introduction', above n 3, 18.

[10] Ibid.

[11] For a discussion of the history of flexicurity in the European Union see N Countouris, *The Changing Law of the Employment Relationship: Comparative Analysis in the European Context* (Aldershot, Ashgate, 2007) ch 6; J Kenner, 'New Frontiers in EU Labour Law: from Flexicurity to Flex-Security' in M Dougan, *Fifty Years of European Treaties* (Oxford, Hart, 2009) 279; M Rönnmar, 'Flexicurity, Labour Law and the Notion of Equal Treatment' in M Rönnmar (ed), *Labour Law: Fundamental Rights and Social Europe* (Oxford/Portland, Hart, 2011) 153.

The Single European Act, which came into force on 1 July 1987, added new momentum to European integration and the completion of the internal market. It was fundamental to securing a constitutional priority for economic freedoms and subjecting social rights to challenges; it also shifted power to employers.[12] In response to the expansion and harmonisation of the internal market, explicit Treaty competences over social policy were also expanded and the Community adopted a Charter on the Fundamental Rights of Workers (1989) as a counterbalance. Health and safety standards were harmonised in the Single European Act, the Maastricht Treaty included a wide range of social policy areas that were formally integrated into the Employment Chapter of the 1997 Amsterdam Treaty, and the 2001 Nice Treaty provided for further possibilities for Member State cooperation on social policy.[13] These changes, especially 'the institutionalisation of EU-level social dialogue and the extension of powers to make labour law directives', resulted in a considerable amount of legislative activity in the area of employment policy from 1993 to 2002.[14]

B. Atypical Work Directives

For the purpose of understanding the genealogy of the labour law component of the flexicurity agenda, the Part-Time Work Directive and the Fixed-term Work Directive are crucial.[15] Although the term 'flexicurity' does not appear in either Directive, both explicitly refer to flexibility and security.[16] Moreover, they are specifically designed to address the labour market segmentation associated with different atypical forms of contract. Atypical employment contracts differ from the standard employment contract, which is a full-time, year-round and ongoing employment relationship with a single employer, which has been the fulcrum of employment legislation and social security.[17] Although the precise form of the standard employment relationship took different shapes, and the extent to, and ways in which, it was institutionalised differed in specific national contexts, its

[12] F Scharpf, 'Negative Integration and Positive Integration in the Political Economy of European Welfare States' in G Marks *et al* (eds), *Governance in the European Union* (London, Sage,1996).

[13] M Keune, 'EU Enlargement and Social Standards: Exporting the European Social Model?' in J Orbie and L Tortell (eds), *The European Union and the Social Dimension of Globalization* (London, Routledge, 2009) 46.

[14] S Deakin and R Rogowski, 'Reflexive Labour Law, Capabilities and the Future of Social Europe' in R Rogowski *et al* (eds), *Transforming European Employment Policy: Labour Market Transitions and the Promotion of Capability* (Cheltenham, Edward Elgar, 2012).

[15] Countouris, *The Changing Law of the Employment Relationship*, above n 11, ch 6; Council Directive 97/81 of 15 December 1997 concerning the framework agreement on part-time working [1997] OJ L14/9 ('Part-time Work Directive'); Council Directive 99/70 of 28 June 1999 concerning the framework agreement on fixed-term work [1999] OJ L175/43 ('Fixed-term Work Directive').

[16] Countouris, *The Changing Law of the Employment Relationship*, above n 11, 211.

[17] G Bosch, 'Towards a New Standard Employment Relationship in Western Europe' (2004) 42 *British Journal of Industrial Relations* 618.

function across industrialised capitalist counties was the same.[18] Historically, it 'incorporated a degree of regularity and durability in employment relationships, protected workers from socially unacceptable practices and working conditions, established rights and obligations, and provided a core of social stability to underpin economic growth'.[19] It also rested on a specific gender order; it provided security for male workers and an economically dependent female housewife and children.[20] Women workers have traditionally been, and continue to be, over-represented in atypical working arrangements, especially part-time and casual work, that are lower paid than, and lack the social and employment benefits and job protection associated with, standard employment contracts.[21] The atypical work Directives are designed 'to redress the risk of precariouness through measures designed to improve the quality of non-standard jobs'.[22]

The Part-time Work and Fixed-term Work Directives can be seen as pro-typical flexicurity labour laws both in form and content since they exemplify the flexicurity policy agenda's regulatory techniques and normative patterns. They fall between soft law and hard law measures, and are adaptable to the distinct social models of the Member States. Both Directives are products of the social dialogue procedure and, thus, depart from the 'classic' Community method of law-making.[23] They give legal effect to the social partners' agreements, and they provide principles and standards, with the details to be filled in by Member States.[24] They also provide a great deal of flexibility to Member States and to social partners about how to implement the standards and to exclude groups of workers from their coverage.[25] The flexibility provided in these two atypical work Directives allows for 'vertical dissonance' between EU legislation and the appearance of formal compliance by Member States.[26]

[18] LF Vosko, *Managing the Margins: Gender, Citizenship, and the International Regulation of Precarious Employment* (Oxford, Oxford University Press, 2010) 3–6.

[19] G Rodgers, 'Precarious Work in Western Europe: the State of the Debate' in G Rodgers and JJ Rodgers (eds), *Precarious Jobs in Labor Market Regulation: the Growth of Atypical Employment in Western Europe* (Geneva, ILO, 1989) 1.

[20] J Fudge, 'Labour as a "Fictive Commodity" Radically Reconceptualizing Labour Law' in G Davidov and B Langille (eds), *The Idea of Labour Law* (Oxford, Oxford University Press, 2011) 120.

[21] D Ashiagbor, 'EU Employment Policies and Precarious Work' in J Fudge and R Owens (eds), *Precarious Work, Women, and the New Economy: the Challenge to Legal Norms* (Oxford, Hart, 2006) 77; Vosko, *Managing the Margins*, above n 18.

[22] M Bell, 'Between Flexicurity and Fundamental Social Rights: the EU Directives on Atypical Work' (2012) 37 *EL Rev.* 33.

[23] In this classic method the European Commission has the sole right of initiative, the European Parliament has an increasingly important voice, the Council of Ministers takes the final decision, and the resulting Community hard law is enforced by the CJEU.

[24] M Jeffery, 'Not Really Going to Work? Of the Directive on Part-time Work, "Atypical Work" and Attempts to Regulate it' (1998) 27 *Industrial Law Journal* 193.

[25] Ibid; J Murray, 'Normalising Temporary Work: the Proposed Directive on Fixed-Term Work' (1999) 28 *Industrial Law Journal* 269.

[26] C Kilpatrick and M Freedland, 'The United Kingdom: How is EU Governance Transformative?' in S Sciarra, P Davies and M Freedland (eds), *Employment Policy and the Regulation of Part-time Work in the European Union: a Comparative Analysis* (Cambridge, Cambridge University Press, 2004) 299–357, at 356. An example of this flexibility in the Fixed-term Work Directive is the decision to

The Part-Time Work Directive established a template for the other Directives on different forms of atypical work by combining the principle of non-discrimination as the basis for social protection with an emphasis on flexibility both in procedures and norms.[27] The notion of a comparable full-time or permanent worker was introduced as a means of defining part-time and fixed-term workers, respectively, and the principle of non-discrimination (actually a ban on less favourable treatment unless justified on objective grounds) was introduced, as was recourse to the principle of *pro rata temporis*, which provides employment-related benefits and protection in proportion to the length of time worked. The aims of the Part-time Directive are: (1) to provide for the removal of discrimination against part-time workers and to improve the quality of part-time work; (2) to facilitate the development of part-time work on a voluntary basis; and (3) to contribute to the flexible organisation of working time in a manner which takes into account the needs of employers and workers. In contrast to the Part-time Work Directive, the Fixed-term Work Directive does not emphasise promoting this form of atypical work.[28] Instead, its goal is to improve the quality of fixed-term work by ensuring the principle of non-discrimination and to establish a framework to prevent abuse arising from the use of successive fixed-term employment contracts or relationships.[29] Significantly, the fixed-term Directive specifically excluded fixed-term workers placed in a user firm by a temporary employment agency, a form of atypical work that was not the subject of a Directive until 2008.[30]

The emphasis on non-discrimination as the approach to regulating atypical workers owes a great deal to sex equality law, which is not surprising given the fact that the Equal Treatment Directive was used to improve the terms and conditions of employment of the women who historically have filled the ranks of atypical workers.[31] This regulatory approach simultaneously evokes the market-enhancing notion of fair competition and resonates with fundamental social rights endorsed by the European Union.[32] In this way, 'the equal treatment formula' was:

> ideally suited to broker a Social Dialogue agreement that satisfied opposite and in principle conflicting needs. Employers would be able to foster and strengthen change in working practices, trade unions would have improved working conditions for atypical

leave it to each Member State to determine 'the conditions under which fixed-term contracts shall be regarded as successive'.

[27] J Murray, 'Normalising Temporary Work', above n 25; S Sciarra, *Is Flexicurity a European Policy?*, URGE Working Paper 4 (2008),

[28] JMurray, 'Normalising Temporary Work', above n 25, 269–75.

[29] See the Fixed-term Work Directive, above n 15.

[30] Ibid, Annex Preamble, para. 4.

[31] Dir 76/207/EEC of 9 February 1976. A Numhauser-Henning, 'EU Equality Law: Comprehensive and Truly Transformative' in M Rönnmar (ed), *Labour Law: Fundamental Rights and Social Europe* (Oxford/Portland, Hart, 2011) 113.

[32] Bell, 'Between Flexicurity and Fundamental Social Rights', above n 22, 45.

workers while reducing any temptation to a race to the bottom and the EC institutions were laying down a 'floor of rights' in this area while promoting their job creation.[33]

The broader, more ideological, effect of the EU Directives has been to demarginalise part-time and fixed-term work,[34] a process more akin to recognising that these types of employment contracts are a regular and legitimate component of the labour market that should be facilitated, rather than with providing traditional forms of worker protection.[35] The European Commission has embraced this approach to regulation, which it refers to as providing flexible and reliable contracts.[36] However, the nomenclature of atypical contracts has continued to prevail despite the rapid expansion of these types of working arrangements.

C. Lisbon Employment Strategy

In 2000, the Lisbon European Council set a new strategic goal:

> to become the most competitive and dynamic knowledge-based economy in the world capable of sustainable economic growth with more and better jobs and greater social cohesion.[37]

This goal was distilled into the three objectives of full employment, quality and productivity at work, and social cohesion and inclusion, and a target employment rate of 70 per cent was set.[38]

The means of achieving the Lisbon European Employment Strategy was through the Open Method of Coordination (OMC), which is a regulatory technique modelled on the method of governance used to ensure that Member State's economic policies conformed to the requirements of the economic and monetary union. It is a 'soft law' technique for coordination, and it combines an 'intergovernmental approach dominated by the Council and the Commission, political monitoring at the highest level, clear procedures and iterative processes'.[39] The elaboration and implementation of employment policy revolves around the setting of guidelines, benchmarks and indicators at the European level, their translation into national

[33] Countouris, *The Changing Law of the Employment Relationship*, above n 11, 209.

[34] P Davies and M Freedland, 'The Role of EU Employment Law and Policy in the De-marginalization of Part-time Work: a Study in the Interaction between EU Regulation and Member State Regulation' in S Sciarra, P Davies and M Freedland (eds), *Employment Policy and the Regulation of Part-time Work in the European Union: a Comparative Analysis* (Cambridge, Cambridge University Press, 2004) 77.

[35] Ibid.

[36] Communication from the Commission to the European Parliament, the Council, the European Economic and Social Committee and the Committee of the Regions, Towards common principles of flexicurity: more and better jobs through flexibility and security, COM(2007)359 final (27 June 2007).

[37] D Ashiagbor, *The European Employment Strategy: Labour Market Regulation and New Governance* (Oxford, Oxford University Press, 2005) 139 quoting the Presidency conclusions.

[38] Ibid 130–40.

[39] C Barnard, *EC Employment Law*, 3rd edn (Oxford, Oxford University Press, 2006) 20, references omitted.

policies, and the periodic monitoring of such implementation, mostly by means of peer review and surveillance by EU institutions.[40] Member States are obliged to report annually on the principal measures taken to implement employment policy in light of the Union's broad economic policy and the employment guidelines.[41] Moreover, the structural funds of the European Union, 'play a key part in the implementation of the Employment Strategy'[42] because they can be used by the European Union to finance active labour market polices in the Member States.[43] However, the ability of the European Union to steer employment policy is limited by the small size of the European Social Fund (ESF) budget.[44]

Lisbon was an important moment for the European Union; it marked a political willingness to prioritise the '"European social model" by means of "activating" the welfare state and modernizing social protection'.[45] It also exemplified the change in social policy 'from employment protection (giving rights to those already in work) to employment creation (getting those out of work into employment)'.[46] The Lisbon Strategy was renewed in 2005, and this renewal led to modifications to the OMC and the governance structure.[47] The centre of gravity for employment policy at the European Commission and Council shifted from labour and social policy actors to ones responsible for economic and financial affairs.[48] The relaunch focused on 'growth, jobs (in numerical terms) and budget stability'.[49] It also led to the adoption in 2007 by the European Union of a set of common principles for flexicurity to guide employment policy and social security in 2007.

D. Flexicurity: an Emerging Policy Agenda

The term 'flexicurity' was initially used to describe the successful combination of flexibility and security in the Dutch and Danish labour market policies in the 1990s.[50] Although very different (the Dutch approach was to promote atypical employment while at the same time providing these workers with employment and social security benefits comparable to workers in standard employment, whereas

[40] Ashiagbor, *The European Employment Strategy*, above n 37; S Velluti, *New Governance and the European Employment Strategy* (London, Routledge, 2010).

[41] The reports, initially called National Action Plans, were renamed National Programme Reviews.

[42] Ashiagbor, *The European Employment Strategy*, above n 37, 195.

[43] Ibid 196.

[44] C Kilpatrick, 'New EU Employment Governance and Constitutionalism' in G de Burca and J Scott (eds), *Law and New Governance in the EU and the US* (Oxford, Hart, 2006) 123.

[45] Ashiagbor, 'EU Employment Policies and Precarious Work', above n 21, 85.

[46] Barnard, *EC Employment Law*, above n 39, 27.

[47] Changes to the OMC are discussed in Sciarra, *Is Flexicurity a European Policy?*, above n 27, 2–4; Deakin and Rogowski, 'Reflexive Labour Law', above n 14, 11–12; Velluti, *New Governance and the European Employment Strategy*, above n 40, 163–65.

[48] T Weishaupt and K Lack, 'The European Employment Strategy: Assessing the Status Quo' (2011) 7 *German Policy Studies* 9.

[49] Velluti, *New Governance and the European Employment Strategy*, above n 40, 23.

[50] Keune, 'EU Enlargement and Social Standards', above n 13, 94.

the Danish model encouraged flexible standard employment contracts combined with high unemployment benefits and active labour market policies), each country reduced unemployment rates and increased employment rates.[51] In an influential article, Ton Wilthagen and Frank Tros elaborated on the concept of flexicurity as a new approach to regulating employment and labour markets.[52] They identified two key components of flexicurity:

> Flexicurity is (1) a degree of job, employment, income and 'combination' security that facilitates the labour market careers and biographies of workers with a relatively weak position and allows for enduring and high quality labour market participation and social inclusion, while at the same time providing (2) a degree of numerical (both external and internal), functional and wage flexibility that allows for labour markets' (and individual companies') timely and adequate adjustment to changing conditions in order to maintain and enhance competitiveness and productivity.[53]

What flexicurity offered was an approach that did not see flexibility and security as trade-offs but, instead, as compliments. It was designed to overcome some of the limits of the deregulation discourse that was so closely aligned to flexibility and, from the outset, its target was combating labour market segmentation.

Flexicurity moved from being a topic of academic discussion to becoming a prominent policy concept within the European Employment Strategy.[54] In 2006, in the *Green Paper on Modernizing Labour Law to Meet the Challenges of the 21st Century*, the European Commission looked at the 'role labour law might play in advancing a "flexicurity" agenda'.[55] While the Commission did not spell out the elements of its flexibility agenda, it identified 'the need for the adaption of employment legislation to promote flexibility combined with employment security and reduce labour market segmentation'.[56] Moreover, the Commission also noted that changes to labour law were not enough; other policy components of flexicurity included:

> life-long learning enabling people to keep pace with new skill needs; active labour market policies encouraging unemployed or inactive people to have a new chance in the labour market; and more flexible social security rules catering for the needs of those switching between jobs or temporarily leaving the labour market.[57]

[51] Ibid.

[52] T Wilthagen and F Tros, 'The Concept of "Flexicurity": a New Approach to Regulating Employment and Labour Markets' (2004) 10(2) *Transfer* 166.

[53] Ibid 6. They developed a matrix of different types of flexicurity and different types of security in order to help to identify the specific trade-offs and interconnections between different combinations of different types of flexibility and security. The matrix consists of 'four forms of flexibility …—external-numerical, internal-numerical, functional flexibility and flexible pay—and four forms of security—job security, employment security, income security (or social security) and "combination security", which refers to "the security of a worker of being able to combine his or her job with other—notably private—responsibilities and commitments"' (ibid 7).

[54] T Wilthagen, 'Mapping out Flexicurity Pathways in the European Union' (2008), available at http://ssrn.com/abstract=1187252; Keune, 'EU Enlargement and Social Standards', above n 13, 95.

[55] European Commission, *Green Paper on Modernizing Labour Law to Meet the Challenges of the 21st Century*, COM(2006)708 final (Brussels, 22 November 2006) 4.

[56] Ibid 3.

[57] Ibid 4.

In the Green Paper, the Commission identified the general tendency in the reform of national employment protection legislation as:

> increasing flexibility 'on the margins', ie introducing more flexible forms of employment with lesser protection against dismissal to promote the entry of newcomers and disadvantaged jobseekers to the labour market and to allow those who wanted to have more choice over their employment. The outcome has given rise to increasingly segmented labour markets.[58]

By contrast, at the EU level, research, political and legislative action has focused on 'establishing how new more flexible forms of work might be combined with minimum social rights for all workers'.[59] The Commission was particularly concerned about the gender dimension of the segmentation,[60] and considered 'stringent employment protection legislation' to worsen the 'prospects of women, youths and older workers'.[61] According to this view, labour market segmentation was regarded as a consequence of the protection of workers with standard employment contracts.

Although the Commission emphasised the need for security, the Green Paper 'introduced, for the first time, a deregulatory emphasis in [its] stance on the development of national labour law system'.[62] Moreover, it focused almost exclusively on individual, and not collective, labour law and did not mention the Supiot Report, which promoted an innovative approach to balancing flexibility and security via the concept of labour force membership.[63]

In June 2007, the European Expert Group, which was appointed by the Commission and included Wilthagen as rapporteur, released its Report.[64] Eschewing a one-size-fits-all strategy, the Report identified four ideal-type situations of labour market failure corresponding to which it mapped out four pathways to flexicurity from which Member States could choose. It also identified four components of flexicurity: flexible and reliable contractual arrangements; comprehensive lifelong learning strategies; effective active labour market policies; and modern social security.[65] The Report described flexicurity as:

> a policy strategy to enhance, at the same time and in a deliberate way, the flexibility of labour markets, work organisations and employment relations, on the one hand, and security—employment security and social security—on the other. Its objective is to combine employment and income security with flexible labour markets, work organisation and labour relations. The key principles that underpin a flexicurity strategy are

[58] Ibid 5.

[59] Ibid 6.

[60] Ibid 9.

[61] Ibid 8.

[62] Deakin and Rogowski, 'Reflexive Labour Law, above n 14, 12.

[63] Ibid; S Sciarra, 'EU Commission Green Paper "Modernising Labour Law to Meet the Challenges of the 21st Century"' (2007) 36 *Industrial Law Journal* 375.

[64] European Expert Group on Flexicurity, *Flexicurity Pathways: Turning Hurdles into Stepping Stones* (June 2007).

[65] Ibid 5.

> that flexibility and security should not be seen as opposites, but can be made mutually supportive.[66]

Flexicurity is not a single policy nor an integrated theory or set of independent policy prescriptions; it is political and strategic concept that can be used to induce legal and policy innovation that can take the shape of a variety of different policies.[67] It is what Peter Auer and Bernard Gazier describe as a policy agenda, which is:

> a deliberate intervention aimed at transforming existing systems of reference in a given field and pointing them in a new direction. [Policy agendas] provide a form of cognitive evidence using concepts, values and evaluations. They are developed by experts and policymakers and are refined through debate; they appear in a pluralistic context because they are diverse and perhaps compete against each other.[68]

In the field of labour market and social policy, Auer and Gazier contrast flexicurity with three other policy agendas that vie for hegemony: flexibility, transitional labour markets and capabilities.[69] They explain that although policy agendas are not generally binding, they can promote convergence by setting targets and by developing recommendations.[70]

Flexicurity is a policy agenda that blurs the borders between the distinct social systems of employment protection and social security by making employability, and not job protection, the favoured form of social protection.[71] It is an attempt to reconfigure a new normative field. It requires a fundamental reconceptualisation of the role of social policy:

> the old social protection offered by Western welfare states was based on what kind of social security would be offered to workers seeking to 'decommodify' their labour and under what conditions. The new forms of protection have focused more on securing and maintaining their 'commodification'.[72]

The relationship between labour law and activation policies is central to the flexicurity agenda,[73] which deploys a range of, largely proceduralist, legal techniques to achieve labour law's new objectives.[74] A key development has been the:

[66] Ibid 11.

[67] P Auer and B Gazier, *Flexicurity as a Policy Agenda*, CESifo DICE Report 2 (2008) 4. Sciarra describes flexicurity as a methodology or a group of policies rather than a single policy, see above n 27.

[68] Auer and Gazier, *Flexicurity as a Policy Agenda*, above n 67, 4.

[69] Ibid 4–6. See also Deakin and Rogowski, 'Reflexive Labour Law', above n 14, on the difference between the flexicurity and capabilities approaches to labour market reform.

[70] Auer and Gazier, *Flexicurity as a Policy Agenda*, above n 67, 4.

[71] T Wilthagen, *Flexicurity: a New Paradigm for Labour Market Policy Reform?*, WZB Discussion Paper FS I (Berlin, 1998) 98–202.

[72] J Lewis and A Plomien, '"Flexicurity" as a Policy Strategy: the Implications for Gender Equality' (2009) 38 *Economy and Society* 438 (references omitted).

[73] C Crouch, 'Beyond the Flexibility/Security Trade-off: Reconciling Confident Consumers with Insecure Workers' (2012) 50 *British Journal of Industrial Relations* 11.

[74] R Rogowski, 'Governance of the European Social Model: the Case of Flexicurity' (March/April 2008) *Intereconomics* 87.

> introduction of 'reflexive regulation', or legally induced 'voluntary' regulation to induce reductions in standards of protection, matching attempts in collective bargaining for derogations from sector standards by company-level negotiations.[75]

The European Expert Group's Report identified combating labour market segmentation between standard employment contracts and atypical or non-standard contracts as the first pathway to flexicurity. The concern was that casual work, agency work and false self-employment were not providing stepping stones to better jobs and that these kinds of contracts received insufficient protection and labour law coverage. The Report recommended integrating atypical or non-standard employment contracts more fully into labour law, collective agreements, social security and lifelong learning, and considered making standard employment more attractive to firms.[76] This idea draws on the approach developed in the Part-time and Fixed-term Work Directives, which is to bring non-standard employment relationships 'fully into labour law and to make them equal to standard employment through the pro rata temporis principle'.[77] The low initial costs of non-standard contracts would be retained in order to facilitate the entry of outsiders into the labour force. Remarkably, however, the Experts Report made no explicit reference to gender equality, despite the fact that only a few months earlier the Commission released a report on *Equality between Women and Men*, in which it warned that flexicurity policies 'should avoid stressing the "flexibility" aspects for women [mainly in the form of atypical contracts] and the "security" aspects for men'.[78]

In its 26 June 2007 Communication, Towards common principles of flexicurity: more and better jobs through flexibility and security, the European Commission identified the need for an 'integrated flexicurity approach' that 'requires policies that address simultaneously the flexibility of labour markets, work organization and labour relations, and security—employment and social security'.[79] It also announced that it and the Member States had reached a consensus on an integrated approach to flexicurity based upon four policy components: flexible and reliable contractual arrangements; comprehensive lifelong learning strategies; effective active labour market policies; and modern social security.[80] The Commission implemented the policy agenda by developing a list of eight common principles

[75] Crouch, 'Beyond the Flexibility/Security Trade-off' above n 73, 11.

[76] European Expert Group Report, above n 64, 23.

[77] However, the European Expert Group Report noted that pension schemes should not be based on *pro rata* principles as this would disfavour part-time workers and that social security benefits should also be made accessible to workers on non-standard contracts. Ibid 28.

[78] European Commission, Report from the Commission to the Council, the European Parliament, the European Economic and Social Committee and the Committee of the Regions on Equality between Women and Men, COM(2002)49 final (Brussels, 2007) para 3.1, as quoted in Lewis and Plomien, '"Flexicurity" as a Policy Strategy', above n 72, 440.

[79] European Commission, Towards common principles of flexicurity, above n 36, 4.

[80] Ibid 5.

of flexicurity, and adopting ends, means, targets and indicators, and integrating them all into a strategic approach.[81]

The Commission's flexicurity Communication generated a great deal of activity at the EU level. Different EU institutions, as well as the social partners and Member States, had different interpretations of, or gave different weights to, the flexicurity agenda's objectives. The Commission, for example, had a deregulatory emphasis when it came to employment protection legislation.[82] It advocated promoting:

> flexibility through low levels of dismissal protection as well as the normalization of non-standard contracts, while security is largely limited to employment security to be fostered through lifelong learning and active labour market policies.[83]

The atypical work Directives exemplified the European Union's approach to normalising non-standard contracts by providing for non-discrimination or parity of treatment with standard employment relationships. The European Commission not only simultaneously emphasised the normative patterns of Market-Functioning and Just Distribution, it brought these two seemingly opposed discourses into realignment by reinterpreting the latter. Just Distribution was no longer concerned exclusively with the relations between workers and employers but, rather, between those workers who had standard employment contracts and those who did not and either had atypical contracts or were unemployed. Protection of Established Position had little normative weight; in fact, it was seen as contributing to the problem of labour market segmentation, which was to be addressed by the reconceived idea of Just Distribution. Implicit in the Commission's agenda was the assumption that flexicurity would contribute to gender equality. But instead of specifying how equality would be cultivated, the Commission appears to have assumed that greater labour force participation of women would lead to greater equality. The problem is that this assumption ignores the different obligations and responsibilities of women when it comes to unpaid care work, a difference that the Commission acknowledged in its equality documents, but not in the mainstream flexicurity agenda.[84]

However, not all of the EU institutions agreed with the particular reading of flexicurity provided by the Commission. In its report to the European Parliament proposing a resolution on the flexicurity principles, the Committee on Employment and Social Affairs explained that the definition of flexicurity in the Commission's *Green Paper on Modernizing Labour Law* was too narrow and not adequately policy-oriented.[85] It called for the provision of a core of rights, which would include, inter alia, freedom of association, protection against dismissal, and social benefits such

[81] Auer and Gazier, 'Flexicurity as a Policy Agenda', above n 67, 14.

[82] Deakin and Rogowski, 'Reflexive Labour Law', above n 14.

[83] Keune, 'EU Enlargement and Social Standards', above n 13, 96.

[84] Lewis and Plomien, '"Flexicurity" as a Policy Strategy', above n 72, 440.

[85] European Parliament, *Report on Common Principles of Flexicurity*, 2007/2209(INI) (Brussels, Committee on Employment and Social Affairs, 15 November 2007) Explanatory Statement, para 6.

as pensions and unemployment benefits, regardless of an employee's specific employment status.[86] Just Distribution and Protection of Established Position were paramount for this Parliamentary Committee. However, the Committee on Economic and Monetary Affairs tended to side with the Commission's deregulation approach and emphasised the importance of the Market-Functional pattern; it regretted 'rigid national employment protection laws'.[87]

The European Parliament endorsed an expansive conception of Just Distribution that encompassed relations between employers and workers, between workers in standard contracts and those in non-standard arrangements, and between women and men. It opposed the European Commission's call for indicators for 'strictness of employment protection', proposing instead a limited set of qualitative indicators on the quality of work.[88] It called for the extension of a core set of rights, including equal treatment, health and safety, freedom of association, collective bargaining, collective action, training and acquired rights, to all forms of contract, not just standard ones. It also advocated for protection against the recurring accumulation of atypical contracts.[89] Moreover, the Parliament expressed particular concern that the Commission was not sufficiently attentive to gender inequality, especially the unequal distribution of unpaid work.[90] It urged the Commission to promote gender equality, drawing attention to the lack of public child care facilities as a central problem for European workers.[91]

The division of opinion amongst the European institutions over the mix of different normative patterns reflects a division between the social partners. BusinessEurope promoted flexible labour law and a variety of employment contracts.[92] By contrast:

> the European Trade Union Congress identifie[d] the prevalence of precarious employment and excessive flexibility as key problems and puts forward the improvement of the quality of jobs as a key objective.[93]

On 14 December 2007, the European Council validated eight principles of flexicurity, and called on Member States to take these into account in drawing up and implementing 'national flexicurity pathways'.[94] Although the flexicurity principles endorsed by the Council were fairly similar to those proposed by the European Commission, there were some significant differences in emphasis. The Council

[86] Ibid, Motion, para 25.

[87] Ibid, Opinion of the Committee on Economic and Monetary Affairs (6 November 2007) for the Committee on Employment and Social Affairs, para 4.

[88] European Parliament Resolution of 29 November 2007 on common principles of flexicurity, 2007/2209(INI), para 11.

[89] Ibid 29.

[90] Ibid 45.

[91] Ibid par. 7.

[92] Keune, 'EU Enlargement and Social Standards', above n 13, 98.

[93] Ibid 98.

[94] Council of the European Union, Council Conclusions: Towards Common Principles of Flexicurity, adopted on 5/6 December 2007.

dropped the references to flexibility in dismissals contained in the Commission's initial principles,[95] and security was expanded to included stepping stones for those people 'at the margins of the labour market' to move into 'legally secure employment'.[96] At the Council's request, the Commission launched a 'Mission for Flexicurity', which aimed:

> to promote the implementation of flexicurity in different national contexts by raising the profile of the flexicurity approach and its common principles and by helping the relevant labour market actors to take ownership of the process.[97]

In 2009, the European Council adopted conclusions on 'flexicurity in times of crisis', which endorsed the flexicurity principles as key elements of Member State responses to the global crisis.[98] The Council emphasised that the 'commitment and active involvement of all stakeholders through social dialogue and collective bargaining is an essential prerequisite for an effective implementation of flexicurity principles'.[99] It also stressed the need to enhance and improve 'activation measures and providing adequate income support and access to quality services to people who are hit by the impacts of the crisis', although it took pains to note that social protection should be in line with 'the sustainability of public finances'.[100]

The following year, in its evaluation of the 2010 Lisbon Strategy, the European Commission identified the 'success of the Flexicurity concept' as representing 'the ability of Lisbon to stimulate and frame policy debates and generate mutually acceptable solutions'.[101] However, the problem was that Member States had not begun to fully implement the agenda. According to the Commission, most labour law reforms 'tended to focus on easing labour market regulation for new entrants to facilitate more contractual diversity', whereas what was needed was 'the reform of legislation on existing contracts'.[102] It emphasised reducing employment protection for existing employment contracts, and advocated 'ensuring transitions between types of contracts and opportunities to progress'.[103]

The Commission also identified shortcomings in the principal governance instruments of the revamped Lisbon governance structure that undermined their effectiveness in policy learning and implementation. The Integrated Guidelines and National Review Programmes were criticised as too broad and not sufficiently

[95] Ibid Principle 4, at 5. Contrast it with European Commission, Towards common principles of flexicurity, above n 36, Principle 5, at 9.

[96] Council Conclusions, above n 94, 5.

[97] Council Secretariat, *Report by the "Flexicurity" Mission*, 17047l1/08REV 1(en) (Brussels, 12 December 2008).

[98] Council of the European Union, Council Conclusions on Flexicurity in Times of Crisis, 294th Employment, Social Policy, Health and Consumer Affairs Council Meeting, Luxembourg, 8 June 2009.

[99] Ibid 3.

[100] Ibid 4.

[101] Lisbon Strategy Evaluation Document, Commission Staff Working Document, SEC(2010)114 final (Brussels, 2 February 2010) 3.

[102] Ibid 16.

[103] Ibid 16.

action-focused.[104] Country specific recommendations were too often vague and adopted a single-strand approach. The lack of a 'transparent and robust evaluation framework' undermined their acceptance in some Member States, where they 'remained low profile policy advice'.[105] Nor did the OMC escape criticism; according to the Report, 'evidence suggests that ... most Member States have used the OMC as a reporting device rather than one of policy development'.[106] The problem was that these instruments were too soft.

E. Europe 2020

In March 2010, the European Commission issued a Communication that advocated replacing the failed Lisbon strategy with Europe 2020, which would become the key over-arching strategy for the European Union for the next 10-year period. The Europe 2020 strategy established a new governance process, the European Semester, which was designed to provide for stronger economic governance and coordination at the EU level. After the financial crisis, the goal was to give the Commission a greater role in guiding Member State budgets.[107] It also established three key priorities (smart growth, sustainable growth, inclusive growth), set five targets (including a 75 per cent employment rate), and provided for seven flagship programmes, including a Flagship Agenda for New Skills and Jobs.[108] Flexicurity is a centrepiece of this agenda, and the Commission stressed the importance of moving to the second phase of the flexicurity agenda, during which Member States are to 'implement their national pathways for flexicurity'.[109] The role of labour ministers in this agenda was also enhanced.[110]

The European Council endorsed Europe 2020, and in October adopted the Commission's guidelines for employment policies of the Member States.[111] Flexicurity is the key approach to achieving Guideline 7: 'Increasing labour market participation and reducing structural unemployment'.[112] The elaboration to the Guideline emphasised the need to combat 'segmentation, inactivity and gender inequality',[113] and Member States were called upon 'to step up social dialogue and tackle labour market segmentation with measures addressing precarious

[104] Ibid 20.
[105] Ibid 21.
[106] Ibid.
[107] Weishaupt and Lack, 'The European Employment Strategy', above n 48.
[108] Communication from the Commission, Europe 2020: A strategy for smart, sustainable and inclusive growth, COM(2010)2020 (Brussels, 3 March 2010) 16–17.
[109] Ibid 17.
[110] Weishaupt and Lack, 'The European Employment Strategy', above n 48.
[111] Council Decision of 21 October 2010 on guidelines for the employment policies of the Member States, 2010/707/EU [2010] OJ L308/46.
[112] Annex 7, 508/49.
[113] Ibid.

employment, underemployment and undeclared work'.[114] The Guideline stressed the quality of jobs and the need to provide social security for people on fixed-term contracts or self-employed. Work-life policies are coupled with affordable care and the reorganisation of paid work as a means of improving the employment rate of women.[115] This renewed emphasis on better job quality and working conditions is a prominent theme of the European Commission's Flagship Agenda for New Skills and Jobs.[116]

However, this emphasis on job quality and gender equality does not fit well with the Commission's technique for addressing labour market segmentation, which is to reduce:

> the existing divisions between those holding temporary and permanent contracts by extending the use of open-ended contractual arrangements, with a sufficiently long probation period and a gradual increase of protection rights.[117]

The stress on 'a sufficiently long probation' suggests that parity between workers employed on different types of contracts is likely to be achieved by reducing the protection associated with open-ended contracts.

IV. LABOUR LAW, LABOUR MARKET SEGMENTATION AND PRECARIOUS WORK

The European Parliament's concern with the relationship between atypical contracts and precarious employment, especially the precarious employment of women on very atypical contracts, helps to explain the emphasis on the quality of flexible forms of employment in Europe 2020.[118] In the Flagship Agenda for New Skills and Jobs, the European Commission agreed to the Parliament's request that it review the effectiveness of the EU Directives on part-time work and fixed-term contracts and their impact on female participation in employment and equal pay in 2012.[119]

In February 2010, the Parliamentary Committee on Employment and Social Affairs released a report on 'atypical contracts, secured professional paths, flexicurity and new forms of social dialogue'.[120] Its central theme was the need for protection of strong employment and labour rights and it called for solid labour laws for all kinds of employment based on a clear institutional framework. A key

[114] Ibid.

[115] Ibid.

[116] Communication from the Commission, An Agenda for new skills and jobs: a European contribution towards full employment, COM(2010)682 final (Strasbourg, 23 November 2010).

[117] Ibid 5.

[118] European Parliament Resolution of 19 October 2010 on precarious women workers, 2010/2018 (INI).

[119] Ibid 16.

[120] Committee on Employment and Social Affairs, *Atypical Contracts, Secured Professional Paths, Flexicurity and New Forms of Social Dialogue* [2011] OJ C351 E/06.

concern was that workers on very atypical contracts (those contracts that deviated the most from standard employment contracts) were falling between the cracks of labour law and social policy. Deploring the Council's and Commission's narrow approach to flexicurity, the Report called for security for flexible work in terms of job protection and rights.[121] In the explanatory statement, the rapporteur also suggested that there was:

> an important gender dimension to the debate on atypical work, as men are disproportionately represented in standard employment relationships and increasing numbers of women in the labour force work under atypical conditions.[122]

A month before the European Commission issued its Communication on the new skills and jobs agenda, the European Parliament adopted a resolution pointing out 'the gendered nature of precarious employment' and the need to ensure that non-standard work does not become precarious work.[123] It urged the Council and Commission 'to identify the characteristics of precarious employment in the guidelines of the Member States' employment policies and in the new gender equality strategy'.[124] The Parliament also expressed disappointment with the Directives on atypical work, and called upon the Commission and Members States to take further legislative measures 'introducing binding minimum social standards and granting all employees equal access to social services and benefits'.[125]

The Parliament's concern with atypical and precarious work was informed by mounting evidence that much of the non-standard and flexible work, such as part-time, fixed term and temporary agency work, promoted by EU institutions is precarious in that the resulting jobs are unstable, provide low wages and insecure income, and do not confer access to social protection.[126] While not all forms of employment that deviate from the standard employment relationship are precarious, there is a clear relationship between the form of the employment arrangement and the precarious nature of the job.[127] The 2006 *Green Paper on Modernizing Labour Law* noted that there was evidence of some detrimental effects associated

[121] Ibid para 46.

[122] Ibid 17.

[123] European Parliament Resolution, above n 118, which was forwarded to the European Commission, Council and Member States

[124] Ibid 2.

[125] Ibid 6.

[126] J Fudge and R Owens (eds), *Precarious Women, Work and the New Economy: the Challenge to Legal Norms* (Oxford, Hart, 2006); LF Vosko, M MacDonald and I Campbell (eds), *Gender and the Contours of Precarious Employment* (London, Routledge, 2009); Vosko, *Managing the Margins*, above n 18.

[127] Operationalising the concept of precariousness is difficult because of its multidimensional nature and different approaches use different indicators. See M Laparra, JC Barbier, I Darmon, C Frade, L Frey, R Lindley and K Vogler-Ludwig, *Managing Labour Market Risks in Europe: Policy Implications*, ESOPE Project, Fifth Framework Programme (DG Research, 2004); A Tangian, *Is Flexible Work Precarious? A Study Based on the 4th European Survey of Working Conditions 2005*, Diskussionpapier 153 (Düsseldorf, Hans Bokerler Stiftung, 2007) 37, available at www.boeckler.de/pdf/p_wsi_diskp_153_e.pdf.

with the increasing diversity of working arrangements, and identified the risk that part of the workforce could get 'trapped in a succession of short-term, low quality jobs with inadequate social protection leaving them in a vulnerable position'.[128] Exploratory analyses of the 2005 European survey of working conditions have concluded that the more flexible (or atypical) employment is, the more precarious it is.[129] In general, non-standard forms of employment tend to be associated with lower rates of pay and have lower social security coverage.[130] Moreover, women tend to be over-represented in precarious work.[131]

Instead of providing specific protections and benefits for workers on a full range of atypical contracts in order to combat precariousness, as was noted in the preceding section, the European Union's strategy has been to use the principles of non-discrimination and equal treatment to target specific forms of atypical work for regulation. However, atypical workers Directives, which include the Temporary Agency Work Directive 2008/104/EC that was adopted in 2008, apply these principles in a diluted form. Under the Part-time Work Directive and the Fixed-Term Work Directive a complaint of unfavourable treatment must relate solely to the nature of the contract. Thus, unlike the approach generally adopted in EU anti-discrimination legislation, only direct and not indirect discrimination is prohibited.[132] Moreover, these Directives also permit discrimination between standard workers, on the one hand, and part-time and fixed-term workers, on the other, if the grounds for the discriminatory treatment can be objectively justified.[133] For example, in defining what constitutes comparable full-time work under the Part-time Work Directive, 'due regard' may be given to 'other considerations which may include seniority and qualifications/skills'.[134] Since women's parenting responsibilities take a toll on their ability to accumulate seniority, and skill is gender-saturated and highly correlated with sex segregation and hierarchies that disadvantage women, these considerations are likely to make it difficult for part-time women workers to find comparable full-time workers.[135] The Part-time Work and Fixed-term Work Directives are an uneasy amalgam of a commitment to the principle of non-discrimination while simultaneously providing

[128] European Commission Green Paper, above n 55, 20.

[129] European Foundation for the Improvement of Living and Working Conditions, *Flexible Forms of Work: Very 'Atypical' Contractual Arrangements* (March 2010).

[130] Ibid.

[131] See references cited above n 126; Vosko, *Managing the Margins*, above n 18, 132, 144–46.

[132] Rönnmar, 'Flexicurity, Labour Law', above n 11, 170.

[133] Jeffery, 'Not Really Going to Work?', above n 24, 196; Vosko, *Managing the Margins*, above n 18, 136; A Numhauser-Henning, 'Fixed Term Work in Nordic Labour Law' (2002) 18(4) *International Journal of Comparative Labour Law and Industrial Relations* 429; Case C-586/10 *Kücük*, CJEU, Judgment of 26 January 2012.

[134] Jeffery, 'Not Really Going to Work?', above n 24, 196. However, as Bell, 'Between Flexicurity and Fundamental Social Rights, above n. 22, 39 notes, the CJEU has given a narrow interpretation to what constitutes an objective justification for discrimination.

[135] N Busby, *A Right to Care? Unpaid Care Work in European Employment Law* (Oxford, Oxford University Press, 2011) ch 3.

employers with enough flexibility to 'maintain practices that disadvantage' atypical workers.[136]

Unlike the first two atypical work Directives, the 2008 Temporary Agency Work Directive does not adopt the language of non-discrimination, and instead uses the term 'equal treatment'.[137] While it is not clear how much turns on the specific terminology, the material scope of this Directive is much narrower than that of its predecessors. The Temporary Agency Work Directive restricts the principle of equal treatment to basic working and employment conditions, a restriction not found in the other atypical work Directives.[138] Moreover, it allows for collective agreements to depart from the principle of equal treatment so long as the overall protection of temporary agency workers is respected, whereas the two earlier Directives only permit more favourable provisions to be adopted by the social partners.[139] The Temporary Agency Work Directive also allows the social partners at the Member State level to include a qualifying period for equal treatment, subject to the caveat that the Member States take measures to prevent the misuse of such arrangements.[140] However, unlike the Fixed-term Work Directive there is no requirement for Member States to establish conditions under which the temporary agency work is to be transformed into an open-ended contract with the user.[141]

A major limitation of all the atypical work Directives is their limited material scope. None provide for non-discrimination (or equal treatment) when it comes to statutory social security entitlements. Member States are solely responsible for the provision of social security protection. Moreover, the Part-time Work Directive permits derogations from occupational-based social security when it comes to casual workers. The limited material scope of the Directives clearly illustrates the conflict between the two aims of improving security for workers and enhancing employers' flexibility.[142]

Even more fundamentally, it is not obvious that a non-discrimination approach, especially one that hinges on the principle of comparability, can ensure the quality of atypical jobs. The problem is that an atypical worker must find a comparator in an ongoing employment relationship in order to make a claim and the European Court of Justice has taken a very narrow and formal approach to the issue of comparators. In *Wippel*, the CJEU ruled that full-time workers who had fixed hours

[136] Bell, 'Between Flexicurity and Fundamental Social Rights', above n 22, 37.

[137] See Directive 2008/104/EC ('Temporary Agency Work Directive').

[138] However, as Bell, 'Between Flexicurity and Fundamental Social Rights, above n 22, 37 notes, this restriction in the material scope of the Temporary Agency Work Directive is balanced by the absence of the possibility of providing an objective justification for differences of treatment with respect to basic working conditions. He also shows how the CJEU has given a broad interpretation to the material scope of the Directive.

[139] Temporary Agency Work Directive, Art 5(3).

[140] Ibid Arts 5(4) and 45(5).

[141] Vosko, *Managing the Margins*, above n 18, 155.

[142] I Bleijenberg, J de Bruijn and J Bussemaker, 'European Social Citizenship and Gender: the Part-time Work Directive' (2004) 10 *European Journal of Industrial Relation* 319.

and who could not refuse work did not have the 'same type of contract' as a part-time worker who was employed in the same establishment on a casual (zero hour) basis and, as a result of this difference, they were not comparable workers.[143] The paradox of this approach is that the more precarious the worker's contract the less likely she is to be able to rely upon the Directives in order to improve her working and employment conditions.[144]

In many instances the comparability principle and non-discrimination approach makes little sense as a basis to improve or protect the quality of work of workers employed in atypical contracts. For example, fixed-term workers do not simply need permanent workers' benefits on a *pro rata temporis* basis; instead, what they need is:

> a fully-fledged scheme of portability of entitlements, which recognizes all relevant working experience (even if undertaken with different employers and with breaks in between) for the whole range of conditions of employment and employment rights governing the work in question.[145]

Modeling fixed-term work on permanent employment does not address the distinctive problems associated with fixed-term work.[146] Moreover, none of the atypical work Directives ensure that workers on contracts that deviate from the standard will earn a living wage. As Nicole Busby points out, 'in practical terms, the part-time worker who finds herself employed in a sector which is generally low paid has no redress as long as her pay is set at a similarly low rate as that of her full-time comparator'.[147] The need to find a comparator with a standard worker instead of providing substantive rights to workers in precarious employment arrangements means that the atypical work Directives do not directly address the problem of low quality, bad jobs.

The atypical work Directives are perfectly compatible with a hierarchy of employment protection that is linked to the form of the employment contract, which, in turn, reinforces labour market segmentation. The comparability standard ignores the possibility that the terms and conditions of the standard or norm (the full-time workers) upon which atypical workers' entitlement is based might be in decline. In the long run, parity can be achieved by harmonising wages and working conditions down.

The EU approach to regulating atypical work is premised upon a specific diagnosis of the cause of labour market segmentation in general and the gendered nature of that segmentation in particular. While the simple relationship between

[143] Case 313/02 *Nicole Wippel v Peek & Cloppenburg GmbH & Co. kG* [2004] ECR 1-09483. See the discussion in Rönnmar, 'Flexicurity, Labour Law and the Notion of Equal Treatment', above n 11, 171.

[144] D McCann, *Regulating Flexible Work* (Oxford, Oxford University Press, 2008) 178–80; Bell, 'Between Flexicurity and Fundamental Social Rights', above n 22, 41.

[145] Murray, 'Normalising Temporary Work', above n 25, 274.

[146] Vosko, *Managing the Margins*, above n 18, 152–56, makes similar arguments regarding the Temporary Agency Work Directive.

[147] Busby, *A Right to Care?*, above n 135, 122.

deregulation of labour markets and increased employment has been called into question, Jill Rubery notes that there is a twist to the argument about the disadvantages of labour market regulation that is accepted as conventional wisdom.[148] The twist she identifies is that regulation, especially employment protection legislation, 'while it may not harm the overall levels of employment, it may still harm employment prospects for disadvantaged social groups'.[149] From this flexibility-oriented perspective, labour market deregulation is seen as contributing to gender equality.

The emphasis on labour law as creating labour market segmentation is a prominent theme in the European Union's flexicurity agenda. While the Commission assumes strict employment legislation to have limited effects on total unemployment, it claims that such legislation:

> can have a negative impact on groups that are most likely to face problems of entry into the labour market, such as young people, women, older workers and the long-term unemployed.[150]

In respect to the causes of labour market segmentation, the flexicurity agenda is indistinguishable from a flexibility agenda for labour law. Flexicurity shares another distinctive feature of the 'labour market flexibility debate', which is, according to Rubery, that it considers inequalities to be the product of workers-workers conflicts rather than capital-labour conflicts'.[151]

The problem with this approach to the causes of labour market segmentation is that it is simplistic and it ignores other contributing factors. Labour market segmentation literature and feminist history suggest that divisions in the labour force and labour market segmentation emerge out of struggles between labour and capital. Although it is possible that employment segmentation and gender divisions are an 'outcome, intended or unintended, of employment regulation', their origins are 'found in efforts to regulate an exploitative labour market'.[152] From this perspective, the solution is not to abolish employment regulation in order to combat gender segmentation, but instead to consider what types of regulations and institutions are the most effective at cultivating equality within the labour market. According to Rubery:

> regulation may act to intensify insider/outsider divisions but forms of regulation can equally be used to create more inclusive labour markets by extending the scope of protection to job sectors such as service sectors or to nonstandard contracts where women may be overrepresented.[153]

[148] J Rubery, 'Towards a Gendering of the Labour Market Regulation Debate' (2011) 35 *Cambridge Journal of Economics* 1104.
[149] Ibid.
[150] European Commission, Towards common principles for flexicurity, above n 36, 6.
[151] Rubery, 'Towards a Gendering of the Labour Market Regulation Debate', above n 148.
[152] Ibid 1121.
[153] Ibid 1105.

The labour law pathway of the flexicurity agenda tends to ignore the demand side and 'systemic and structural blockages to equal opportunities, whether due to direct discrimination or to the working of indirect mechanisms'.[154] While the flexicurity agenda endorses the principle of equality between men and women and the European Union is committed to equal pay,[155] very few of the Commission's flexicurity policy documents deal with the structural barriers confronted by women—their responsibility for unpaid care work—that make them flexible workers.[156] The Part-Time Work Directive, for example:

> guarantees equal access to the European labour market for workers with care-giving tasks, without, however, guaranteeing them a minimum of social welfare. Thus, the EU recognizes workers' need to combine a job with domestic responsibilities, but leaves the financial and practical consequences of the combination to the individual.[157]

The failure to integrate the labour law pathway of the flexicurity agenda within a broad family policy agenda means that the unequal division of socially necessary, but unpaid, care and provisioning work is ignored. The problem is that women's traditional and continuing disproportionate responsibility for unpaid care work not only creates a barrier to women's employment, it also reinforces gender stereotypes when it comes to women's occupations and careers, which, in turn, undermine women's economic and employment equality.[158] The flexicurity agenda does not address this vicious circle because it does not challenge the unequal and gendered division of responsibility for care work.

V. CONCLUSION

Different normative patterns compete for dominance in the flexicurity agenda. Flexicurity has a deep affinity with the Market-Functional pattern since promoting flexible and well-functioning labour markets is the policy agenda's fundamental objective. As Ann Numhauser-Henning explains, demands for 'flexibility and market adjustment' have entailed:

> an increase in part-time work, fixed-term work and temporary agency work and other unstable employment relationships—and a decrease in the group of workers offered permanent, relatively secure, traditional employment. These developments impose strains on labour law, in that they engender demands for the deregulation of traditional

[154] J Jenson, 'Writing Women Out, Folding Gender In: the European Union "Modernises" Social Policy' (2008) 15 *Social Politics* 149.

[155] European Commission, Towards common principles for flexicurity, above n 36, 9.

[156] Lewis and Plomien, '"Flexicurity" as a Policy Strategy', above n 72, 453; Busby, *A Right to Care?*, above n 135.

[157] I Bleijenberg, J de Bruijn and J Bussemaker, 'European Social Citizenship and Gender', above n 142, 324.

[158] Åsa Löfström, 'Gender Equality, Economic Growth and Employment', available at www.se2009.eu/polopoly_fs/1.17994!menu/standard/file/EUstudie_sidvis.pdf.

> employment protection, and for conditions conducive to more flexible modes of employment—more lately expressed in the EU flexicurity strategy.[159]

Nonetheless, Just Distribution is a strong competing norm since it is flexicurity's commitment to social protection that distinguishes it as a policy agenda from flexibility, which focuses exclusively on the market as the only legitimate norm of distribution.

However, while Just Distribution is still a vibrant normative pattern, it no longer means what it did under the welfare state. Instead of being simply defined as worker protection, today social justice is defined as 'employability'. This change in the pattern of Just Distribution also reflects a shift in the source of conflict that labour law is designed to mediate. Under flexicurity, the key concern of labour law is to address labour market segmentation. Labour market segmentation, and not the inequality of power between employers and workers, is seen as the key distributive conflict under the flexicurity agenda. The emphasis on flexible contract arrangements is part of the Market-Functional pattern, and it tends to go hand in hand with policies aimed at deregulating the labour market and reducing worker protection. It also minimises the commitment to the Protection of Established Position.

There is, however, a countervailing, albeit weaker, normative pattern of Just Distribution regarding atypical employment contracts, which emphasises social protection and equality. This pattern would reduce the asymmetry between standard employment relationships and non-standard employment relationships by integrating the latter more fully into labour law, collective agreements, social security and lifelong learning.[160] The priority given to good quality jobs in the European Commission's Flagship Agenda on New Skill and Jobs also reinforces an interpretation of Just Distribution that emphasises social protection and equality.

A structuralist analysis helps to explain the bias in the flexicurity agenda towards the normative pattern of market flexibility and away from that of social protection and equality. 'In the context of the "flexicurity" debate', Samantha Velluti reports 'national governments have used the OMC in a rather unbalanced way favouring flexibility measures to the disadvantage of the security of the workers'.[161] The broader context of economic integration and monetary union, especially the economic guidelines and the Stability and Growth Pact, place limits on the extent to which Member States can finance modern social security, lifelong learning and child care. The CJEU has also demonstrated a 'deregulatory bias' regarding labour law in its 'emerging free movement jurisprudence'.[162] Although the case law from the Court interpreting the atypical work Directives opens the

[159] Numhauser-Henning, 'Introduction', above n 3, 16.

[160] European Expert Group Report, above n 64, 23.

[161] Velluti, *New Governance and the European Employment Strategy*, above n 40, 236; Rogowski, 'Governance of the European Social Model', above n 74, 41 also notes that the Barroso Commission has tended to downplay social protection in its conception of flexicurity.

[162] Deakin and Rogowski, 'Reflexive Labour Law', above n 14, 25.

door to a reading that is consonant with fundamental social rights and not simply flexibility, this opening has been very narrow.[163] The accession of Member States with wages, costs and social entitlements that were not aligned with those of existing members contributes to creating the conditions for a race to the bottom for wages and labour standards.[164] The financial crisis and the European Union's governance reforms (the Euro Pact Plus) have tipped the balance in Europe further towards downward harmonisation and towards deregulation of employment protection.[165] The tilt in the OMC process to national civil servants and away from national Parliaments is also a factor contributing to the dominance of the market-functioning discourse.[166]

In this political and economic climate it is unlikely that Member States will be willing to experiment by implementing employment laws and policies designed to improve the quality of atypical work. This is not to claim that there is an inherent economic or political logic to the flexicurity agenda and the OMC; the mechanism of soft law or selective coordination could promote social protection and solidarity. Instead, the claim is that the OMC does not promote social protection and solidarity because the process is embedded in a specific economic agenda that emphasises deregulation and a governance structure at the European Union that provides limited protection for social rights from downward harmonisation.

It is an open question the extent to, and ways in, which the European Union's flexicurity policy agenda will influence labour laws in Member States. Part-time, fixed-term and other forms of non-standard work on the margins of the labour market have the potential to operate as bridges into the labour market and facilitate labour market participation. However, they can also function as traps that confine their incumbents to precarious work. It all depends upon the broader institutional and political structure in which flexicurity policies are embedded, and the willingness of Member States to tackle the gendered division of domestic labour. The challenge for labour law is to develop a new standard employment contract, with new social rights and social obligations, and not simply to adapt atypical work arrangements to the old model.[167]

[163] Bell, 'Between Flexicurity and Fundamental Social Rights', above n 22, 47. However, contrast the Rönnmar, 'Flexicurity, Labour Law and the Notion of Equal Treatment', above n 11, 171 and Busby, *A Right to Care?*, above n 135, 121.

[164] C Woolfson, *Precarious Work, Regulation, and Labour Standards in Times of Crisis*, Themes on Migration and Ethnic Studies 34 (REMESO, Institute for Research on Migration, Ethnicity and Society, 2010).

[165] C Barnard, 'The Financial Crisis and the Euro Plus Pact: a Labour Lawyer's Perspective' (2012) 41 *Industrial Law Journal* 98.

[166] Velluti, *New Governance and the European Employment Strategy*, above n 40, 237 and Sciarra, *Is Flexicurity a European Policy?*, above n 27, 2.

[167] G Schmid, 'Non-standard Employment in Europe: Its Development and Consequences for the European Employment Strategy' (2011) 7 *German Policy Studies* 203.

12

Changing Normative Patterns in Statutory Old-Age Pensions

Reflections on Developments Due to Pension Reform and EU Citizenship

THOMAS ERHAG

I. INTRODUCTION

IN AN ARTICLE published in *Retfaerd* in 1997,[1] Anna Christensen described economic and labour market development and its effect on European social security systems. The essence of the article is that there was an obvious normative shift in social security, from just distribution and ensuring a basic income level for every citizen, towards protection of accrued or acquired rights and a more market-oriented normative basis. It was important for Anna Christensen to stress the relationship between social security and the market, as these two phenomena will constantly affect each other, for example by limiting how social insurance can be designed without interfering with the over-arching structure of wage labour on the open market.

During the 1990s, development of Swedish pension insurance came to a halt and a period of reforms started, not only in Sweden but in all the Nordic countries, as well as in EU Member States. Christensen described Swedish social security as moving in the normative field, from an emphasis on basic protection and hence Just Distribution, towards acquired rights and the normative pole of Market-Function. According to Christensen, this would prove to make the social situation for persons outside the labour market increasingly difficult.

This chapter will focus on this normative shift—and illustrate it with examples from the Swedish pension reform, and the free movement of persons. Reference will be made to the strengthened right in EU law to free movement for persons,

[1] A Christensen, 'Normativa grundmönster i socialrätten' (1997) 78 *Retfaerd* 20.

even those not pursuing an economic activity, and their right to basic social protection. The chapter will, in this context, discuss the normative changes of basic protection in old-age and invalidity insurance for persons lacking earning capacity as a result of invalidity or old age.

II. NORMATIVE PATTERNS IN PENSIONS

In a later article written in collaboration with Mattias Malmstedt,[2] Anna Christensen described the national rules on social security as based on two different normative patterns. These two patterns correspond to the distinction made between 'contributory' and 'non-contributory' benefits. The first pattern is based upon employment and contributions as the normative base for social security benefits, and signifies, in its pure form, that contributions paid correspond to the risk insured. This is what is usually known as the principle of equivalence or the principle of insurance. An example for old-age pension is that this is calculated in relation to contributions paid and the number of contributory years. The pension is 'earned' by employment and contributions, and when due, is regarded as an acquired right of the same kind as a private right. The pattern is built upon commutative justice and is closely related to the basic principles of private law.

The other pattern is redistributive and based on solidarity within the national community. The 'solidaristic' community is framed by the nation-state. The criterion for entitlement is legal residence within that state's territory. Typical examples in pensions are tax-financed basic pensions or guaranteed minimum levels of income support, and means-tested income supplements. Christensen called these *solidarity benefits.*

These solidaristic and closed communities function well enough as long as there are no substantial movements across existing borders. It is when people begin to move that problems arise. Old borders become obstacles to free movement within a larger area. The European Union, the internal market, and the principle of free movement for persons have forced the Member States to give up their old national right of refusing entry and residence to migrants.

However, the Member States have retained the right to deny residence to persons without sufficient means to support themselves in the new host country. These rules are found in the Directive 2004/38, laying down the conditions under which a Member State may deny an EU citizen the right to stay in the country. Member States may set up proportional demands for sufficient economic means and sickness insurance coverage.

However, it is not entirely clear how efficient this EU legislation actually is, and the question of its compatibility with the TFEU Articles on EU Citizenship is still

[2] A Christensen and M Malmstedt, 'Lex loci laboris versus Lex loci domicilii: an Inquiry into the Normative Foundations of European Social Security Law' (2000) 2(1) *European Journal of Social Security* 69.

under development.[3] Movement across old national borders also causes the old frontiers of solidarity, previously regarded as self-evident, to appear in a new normative light as a violation of a new principle of equality, where all who belong to a *greater* community are treated equally.[4] The European Court of Justice (CJEU) has also underlined that there must be a certain degree of solidarity between the EU Member States and all EU citizens.[5]

An important part of national sovereignty in contemporary society serves to prevent non-nationals from entering and taking up residence in a country not their own. However, it is apparent that this sovereignty has changed its appearance.

III. FIRST, A LOOK BACK AT EARLY SWEDISH PENSION LEGISLATION

The German Bismarckian reform plans for social security were discussed in the Swedish Parliament as early as 1882.[6] Two years later, a proposal by an MP resulted in a public investigation into the need for introducing accident and pension insurance for workers. No reform was enacted, but there was obvious political interest in the 'social' aspect and in the ongoing reform programme in Germany.[7] However, the invalidity and pension insurance that was introduced differed substantially from the German model as introduced by Bismarck.

The law introduced in 1913 regulated a combined invalidity and pension insurance financed by employee contributions. As a complement, however, a tax-financed additional pension was also introduced. This insurance was the world's first universal social insurance, covering the entire population and not only workers, as was the case in Germany. The purpose of the Swedish reform was to provide support for elderly and invalid members of society, who due to an incapacity for work could not support themselves. This kind of social protection was to be more secure and less stigmatising than that offered by '*fattigvården*', the institutions for the poor or other individuals.[8] An incapacity for work was presumed from the age of 67.[9] The insurance protection was thus based on the need for income and was not in relation to earlier income, a development in contradiction with

[3] E Spaventa, 'The Impact of Articles 12, 18, 39 and 43 of the EC Treaty on the Coordination of Social Security Systems' in Y Jorens, *50 Years of Social Security Coordination: Past, Present, Future*, European Commission, Directorate-General for Employment, Social Affairs and Equal Opportunities Unit E.3.—Luxembourg: Office for Official Publications of the European Communities (2009); M Coucheir and M Sakslin (eds), *The Relationship and Interaction between the Coordination Regulations and Directive 2004/38/EC*, Think Tank Report 2008 (trESS, 2008), available at www.tress-network.org.

[4] Christensen and Malmstedt, 'Lex loci laboris versus Lex loci domicilii', above n 2.

[5] See on this issue S Giubbioni, *A Certain Degree of Solidarity: Free Movement of Persons and Access to Social Protection in the Case-law of the European Court of Justice*, URGE Working Paper 3 (2008).

[6] Protokoll i andra kammaren 1882:29.

[7] PG Edebalk, 'Bismarck och de första tyska socialförsäkringarna (2003) 4 *Socialvetenskaplig tidskrift* 357.

[8] Proposition 1913 no 126, *Förslag till lag om allmän pensionsförsäkring*.

[9] F Schmidt, *Allmänna och privata pensioner* (Stockholm, PA Norstedt och söner, 1974) 9 ff.

the Bismarckian solution. The reason for this was to be found in the structure of Swedish society; emigration and urbanisation had left the country with a relatively elderly population, especially in rural areas, creating a heavy burden on local poverty-fighting initiatives (*fattigvården*).[10]

This means that the normative pattern of Just Distribution, ie the securing of a basic income level for all, already appeared in the first Swedish pension (invalidity and old-age) social insurance. The introduction of obligatory short-term sickness insurance was not thought to be relevant, since there were already sufficient alternatives provided by trade unions and other private providers.[11] Obligatory sickness insurance was not fully implemented until 1955.

The pension system from 1913 was reformed in 1935.[12] The basic structure was retained, with a contribution-based pension combined with a supplement. The contribution-based pension consisted, in the one part, of a nominal basic pension, and in the other, an amount relative to the amount of contributions paid in.

Unlike the 1913 pension, the calculation of the contributory part was equal for both men and women. The supplement of 250 SEK was need-related, and the amount of supplementary pension was reduced by 70 per cent of any annual earnings over 100 SEK. A new feature of the 1935 pension compared to the system from 1913 was the level of ambition as well as the cost. The legislator can be said to have departed from the dependency on private insurance as a model for the contribution-based pension. This principle was followed in the 1946 reform. Old-age pension would now be paid out irrespective of earlier income. In addition, various supplements could now be awarded in specific situations (eg spouse supplement, widow's pension). Rationality was one of the major reasons.[13]

In almost all European countries, the basic pension related to need has been developed with a supplementary pension scheme related to earlier income and years of insurance, meaning that the system is based on accrued rights. However, it is important to note that there is a great difference between public pension insurance and private insurance. Public insurance is not normally constructed as actuarial insurance. It contains various redistributional effects based on social policy, and may, for example, promote parental leave, cover periods of unemployment, sickness or studies etc, as well as employ a ceiling for the level of income protected, with no corresponding ceiling for contributions.[14]

In the 1950s and 1960s, the debate on pensions and the issue of public responsibility for ensuring a sufficient level for pensions reached a new dimension. The basic pension was to be developed in value and related to a consumer price index.

[10] Edebalk, 'Bismarck och de första tyska socialförsäkringarna', above n 6, 359; Schmidt, *Allmänna och privata pensioner*, above n 8, 10 ff.

[11] Edebalk, 'Bismarck och de första tyska socialförsäkringarna', above n 6, 358.

[12] Proposition 1935 no 217.

[13] Proposition 1946 no 220, 19.

[14] T Erhag, *Fri rörlighet och finansiering av social trygghet* (Stockholm, Santérus, 2002).

Along with certain means-tested supplements, it was to provide a just income level for all insured persons in Sweden for whom the risk of invalidity or old age had materialised. The system combined a flat-rate universal benefit (*folkpension*) with an earnings-related supplement (ATP). Note that the *folkpension* constituted fundamental income support for both rich and poor, and was paid out to any person who was insured, resident in Sweden, and who met the criteria of old age or a more-or-less permanent incapacity for work. There was no qualification period, meaning that a person insured in Sweden and who was either an invalid or at a pensionable age, received a basic pension. ATP, a defined benefit system, provided for additional income-related protection.

The Swedish pension system was further developed as a universal system until the end of the 1990s, with a high level of ambition concerning both personal scope and the level of income protection. However, there was one group of persons experiencing difficulties on the labour market: older workers. Persons who were laid off in relation to structural changes were not finding new employment. Various labour law initiatives attempted to strengthen their position on the labour market, but to no great effect.

During the same period we see an increasing inflow to invalidity insurance, which in the 1990s was a part of the pension system as a pre-retirement pension. The construction of Swedish invalidity insurance was such, and to a large extent still is, that acquired pension rights are paid out before a person reaches the legal retirement age of 65, on condition that the person has a lasting reduced capacity for work. The insured person can then use the period between pre-retirement and the age of 65 as the basis for the calculation of the right to old-age pension.

In order to enable this group of older persons to receive benefit from the pension system, the legislator needed to widen the scope of the invalidity concept that formed a precondition for the right to this benefit. Hence, the concept of incapacity for work in invalidity insurance was made relative to the situation on the labour market. Persons reaching the age of 60, not being able to find a job, could thus receive a pension instead. The concept of incapacity for work moved from being a medical invalidity concept towards being a labour market-oriented concept.[15]

This system was then shaken up by the economic crisis in the early 1990s. Large budget deficits made it necessary to cut public expenditure in social security systems. The normative impact of this crisis was apparent in pension insurance. One obvious impact from a normative perspective was that it was made more difficult to enter all branches of the social insurance programme; the criteria for receiving benefits were changed and the level of benefits was lowered.

The invalidity concept needed to be changed into a more medically-oriented concept, removing the former references to age and labour markets. The method for assessing incapacity has also changed, from the requirement of '*varaktig*' (lasting)

15 L Vahlne-Westerhäll, *Den starka statens fall* (Stockholm, Norstedts, 2002) 264 ff.

incapacity to '*bestående*' (more-or-less permanent) incapacity. A prescribed method for medically assessing this includes shifting the prognosis from 'at least one year of incapacity' to 'incapacity for the foreseeable future'. The intention is obvious: people should stay in the labour market, but the result is not always convincing and legislative changes have not managed to stop the inflow to invalidity insurance.

Reform of old-age insurance is, however, a little more complicated, as it must take into account that the contents of the individual right to pension being changed are part of a pension right already acquired. Thus, the established position of the individual has to be changed. However, in the early 1990s, all the political parties in the Swedish Parliament, with one exception, agreed to reform the Swedish pension system. The question here, however, is what happened to *Just Distribution* during and after the Swedish pension reform?

IV. JUST DISTRIBUTION IN THE NEW SWEDISH PENSION SYSTEM

Christensen noted that the largest normative difference after the Swedish pension reform was the strengthening of the relationship between contributions and benefits—the insurance principle. The principle of acquired rights was thus strengthened and there was less room for redistribution. However, the new pension system also has expressions for the normative pattern of Just Distribution.

During this same period in the 1990s, Sweden applied for membership in the European Union, and the pension system was to be coordinated within the framework of EU Regulation 1408/71. This also proved to be a normative challenge.

The guarantee pension is the benefit that is perhaps the clearest expression of just distribution in the new system. Guarantee benefit, or guarantee pension, is available from the age of 65. This is an inflation-indexed supplement with a specified maximum, to the total benefit provided by the two earnings-related schemes.

This marks a fundamental shift compared to the old system, in which the *folkpension* was the symbolic basis of the pension system and paid out an equal amount to all insured persons. The condition for insurance was residence. The residence-based guarantee pension is financed by general taxation revenue. Along with a means-tested housing supplement, this will normally be sufficient to meet the subsistence norm, as expressed in social service legislation, Social Services Act (2001:453).

Since the guarantee pension is pro-rated in regard to years of residence, with 40 years required for the full amount, it is possible that immigrants working late in life, including Swedes returning from a life abroad, may fall under the subsistence norm and require social assistance provided by local authorities. In terms of Just Distribution, this perhaps somewhat surprisingly brings us back to the 1913 pension reform, in which the idea was to ensure Just Distribution equal to all at a state level, and not put pressure on local means-tested benefits.

The benefit guaranteeing that persons over 65 should not need to apply for social security is maintenance support for the elderly. This benefit guarantees a decent standard of living, even if one receives little or no pension or other means of income.

In other words, maintenance support for the elderly is available if other retirement benefits prove insufficient. All other benefits to which the person is entitled must be claimed before qualifying for maintenance support. Such benefits include old-age and guarantee pension, as well as the housing supplement for pensioners, and the special housing supplement.

This means that in relation to the old pension system, Just Distribution is, as a normative pattern, a clear basis of the pension system. However, the normative shift of the new pension system has placed this pattern under certain constraints and it is not as strong as before. In order to qualify for benefits, an insured person must fulfil technical prerequisites. In addition, means testing is used more extensively, and consequently the expression of Just Distribution in pension insurance is very closely related to social assistance.

V. JUST DISTRIBUTION AND COORDINATION OF PENSION BENEFITS

A. Effects of EU Law

I will now turn to describing changes in statutory pension law due to the effects of EU law, with a specific focus on Just Distribution. A first important change was already made during the preparatory stage for EU membership. As relevant EU law contains a principle of exportability of pension benefits (Article 10 of Regulation 1408/71 and Article 7 of Regulation 883/2004), a person who had been insured/resident in Sweden for a short period of time, and had thus qualified for a basic pension (*folkpension*), could export the full right to this benefit.

This would not, however, be possible according to domestic Swedish law, as the right to and payment of *folkpension* was linked to a residence criterion. However, EU law of course waives this residence criterion, and hence Just Distribution was expanded to the whole of Europe, based on an 'acquired rights' perspective. This perspective and expression of another normative pattern was not really present in the design of this Swedish benefit. The solution was to pro-rate the benefit with regard to years of residence. For a full basic pension, 40 years of residence are now required.[16]

As for the right to *folkpension*, today's guarantee pension is pro-rated with regard to years of residence, with 40 years needed for the full amount. It is possible that immigrants in late working life may, as mentioned above, still fall under the subsistence norm and require social assistance from local authorities.

[16] Social Security Code, ch. 67, s 25.

In order to fill this 'gap', maintenance support for the elderly was introduced. This benefit is a part of social security legislation, although it has the explicit intention of being a state initiative to relieve municipalities from the burden of increased pressure on social security schemes.[17] It is a residence-based benefit, and is also listed as a special non-contributory benefit in Regulation 883/2004 (Article 70, Annex X), and as such is not to be exported.

B. Free Movement for All and Equal Treatment

The basic principle of Directive 2004/38 is that EU citizens should be able to enjoy freedom of movement, in more or less the same way as when nationals of a Member State change their residence within their home state. For the right of residence in the territory of another Member State for a period of up to three months, the host Member State can demand no conditions or formalities other than the requirement to hold a valid identity card or passport. However, in Article 14 of Directive 2004/38, a precondition for residence is established by stating that the person must not become an unreasonable burden on the social security system of the host Member State.

For those not economically active, the Directive requires (as was the case in the replaced Directives 90/364, 90/365 and 93/96) that the person in question has sufficient resources for themselves and their family members, so as not to become a burden on the social security system of the host Member State during their period of residence, and also that they have comprehensive sickness insurance in the host Member State (Article 7(1)(b)–(c)). This means that the right to residence is without conditions for those who are economically active, but that there are conditions attached for other categories of person. The burden requirement is further developed in Article 14, where retaining the right of residence is made conditional on the person not becoming an unreasonable burden on the social assistance system of the host state. Unfortunately, the word 'unreasonable' was missed in the Swedish translation, a mistake that was also repeated when implementing the Directive in the Swedish Aliens Act.

When the right to residence is made permanent after five years, the requirements on sickness insurance cover and sufficient means can no longer be upheld. The right to equal treatment is an important feature of the Directive (Article 24). All persons being legally resident in a Member State with the support of the Directive must be treated the same as the citizens of the host state in the areas covered by the TFEU. Important exceptions to this rule are also mentioned in Article 24. Such an exception must, however, be clearly expressed in national law and be designed in conformity with the general principles of EU law. Sweden has

[17] Proposition 2000/01:136, 13 ff.

not introduced such explicit exceptions, eg in relation to access to social assistance and social services.

This room for exceptions to the principle of equal treatment in relation to social benefit is motivated with reference to the need for Member States to be able to control such costs, but also to be able to hinder so-called social tourism. These interests are also acknowledged by the CJEU as mandatory requirements motivating limits to the free movement of persons.[18]

C. Just Distribution and Equal Treatment of Migrants

In relation to the widening of the material scope for the free movement of persons to actually include all persons in the European Union, and not only those economically active, it has been remarked that this will put particular pressure on the Nordic states, with their residence-based solidarity benefits.[19] Case law from the CJEU on the EU Citizenship and free movement Articles of the TFEU, as well as the subsequent adoption of Directive 2004/38 on free movement for persons, has meant a strengthened right to free movement and equal treatment for all EU citizens, also in relation to social security benefits.[20] Directive 2004/38 was adopted on the same day as Regulation 883/2004, also expanding the coordination system to all EU citizens covered by national social security law.[21]

As mentioned above, Directive 2004/38 does not allow Member States to refuse entry and residence to citizens from other EU Member States, unless certain conditions are met.

The Member States have thus retained the right to deny residence to persons without sufficient means to support themselves in the host country. This is expressed in the Preamble to the Directive: in cases where beneficiaries of the right of residence do not become an *unreasonable burden* on the social security system

[18] See, eg, the judgment in Case C-209/03 *Bidar* [2005] ECR I-2119, para 56: 'On this point, it must be observed that, although the Member States must, in the organisation and application of their social assistance systems, show a certain degree of financial solidarity with nationals of other Member States (see *Grzelczyk*, paragraph 44), it is permissible for a Member State to ensure that the grant of assistance to cover the maintenance costs of students from other Member States does not become an unreasonable burden which could have consequences for the overall level of assistance which may be granted by that State'.

[19] Y Jorens and F van Overmeieren, 'General Principles of Coordination in Regulation 883/2004' (2009) 11(1–2) *European Journal of Social Security* 54; H Verschueren, 'European (Internal) Migration Law as an Instrument for Defining the Boundaries of National Solidarity Systems' (2007) *European Journal of Migration and Law* 342; S Giubboni, 'Free Movement of Persons and European Solidarity' (2007) 13(3) *European Law Journal* 360.

[20] See, eg, Spaventa, 'The Impact of Articles 12, 18, 39 and 43 of the EC Treaty', above n 3.

[21] Directive 2004/38/EC of the European Parliament and of the Council of 29 April 2004 on the right of citizens of the Union and their family members to move and reside freely within the territory of the Member States, amending Regulation (EEC) 1612/68 and repealing Directives 64/221/EEC, 68/360/EEC, 72/194/EEC, 73/148/EEC, 75/34/EEC, 75/35/EEC, 90/364/EEC, 90/365/EEC and 93/96/EEC.

of the host Member State, they should not be expelled. Furthermore, expulsion measures should not be the automatic consequence of recourse to the social security system. The host Member State must assess whether the situation of having insufficient means is a case of temporary difficulties, or of a more permanent nature. In assessing this, it must take into account the length of residence, the personal circumstances, and the amount of aid already granted, in order to ascertain whether or not the beneficiary has become an unreasonable burden on the state's social security system, before proceeding to expel this person.

These rules of the Directive have been implemented in the Swedish Aliens Act (Utlänningslagen), chapter 3a. However, in Sweden, both the requirement in the Directive for sickness insurance cover and sufficient resources are to some extent covered by social insurance, eg as is the case for pensioners. The purpose of maintenance support for the elderly is thus to provide a decent standard of living for any pensioner resident in Sweden, especially if that person has not gained enough pension rights in Sweden or any other country.

The meaning of the EU legislation is that an EU citizen prima facie has the right of entry and the right of residence in the host country, as well as a right to equal treatment in all aspects, in that country. This right of residence and to equal treatment is, however, conditional, as expressed in recital 16 of Directive 2004/38:

> As long as the beneficiaries of the right of residence do not become an unreasonable burden on the social assistance system of the host Member State they should not be expelled.

However, this EU legislation means that in a legal system such as the Swedish one, there will be a need to develop mechanisms in social law that are apt to compel the insurance administration to make decisions on the 'legal' status of EU citizens. This has proved to be difficult. In addition, it is difficult to judge whether national tax-financed solidarity benefits are a part of what in the Directive is referred to as 'social assistance'. If not, equal treatment in relation to the solidarity benefits of the host state can in fact be used to fulfil the demand for legal residence described in the Directive, since these national benefits are intended to provide for a decent income level and standard of living.

VI. CAN ACCESS TO HOST STATE BENEFITS BE SUFFICIENT RESOURCES?

When judging whether or not a person possesses sufficient resources, the CJEU has stated that there is no requirement as to the origin of these resources.[22] The question then is whether the social security benefits for which the person is eligible in the host country can count as resources that can be used in order to claim free movement and the right of residence under Directive 2004/38. In relation to this issue, it should also be remembered that the CJEU has stated that provisions

[22] Case C-200/02 *Zhu och Chen* [2003] ECR I-9925.

laying down a fundamental principle, such as that of the free movement of persons, must be interpreted broadly.[23]

Access to benefits and sickness insurance cover seems to provide for a basis in EU law for equal treatment in the host country, also in relation to residence-based benefits. Regulation 883/2004 makes it possible for old-age and sickness benefits to be made available in the host state, at the expense of the competent state. This is the case, for example, for pensioners, cross-border workers and their family members, and for the family members of economically active persons. But will this right to equal treatment also extend to benefits paid at the expense of the host country, and can Article 4 of Regulation 883/2004 be used for these purposes when the choice-of-law rules of section II of the Regulation indicate the host state as the competent state for the economically non-active person taking up residence?

Such an interpretation would mean, for example, that a pensioner would have equal access to all the benefits under the legislation of the host state, and could also use these benefits to meet the conditions of Directive 2004/38 concerning sufficient resources and sickness insurance cover. The opposite interpretation would mean that if the relevant benefit was considered part of the social security system of the host state in the meaning of this concept under the Directive, the same person would risk his or her right of residence as defined in chapter 3a of the Swedish Aliens Act, which implemented Directive 2004/38.

This question relates to the relationship between Regulation 883/2004 and Directive 2004/38, insofar as the Regulation can be considered as *lex specialis* in relation to the Directive; we have legal grounds for stating that residence in the Regulation should be understood separately and not be dependent on the demands for legal residence under Directive 2004/38. There are, however, no references in either Regulation 883/2004 or Regulation 987/2009 as to whether a person, in fulfilling the residence requirement under those Regulations, must be legally resident according to the Directive. The EU legislator could, of course, have expressed this if this indeed was the original intention. The situation is unclear and it seems likely that the CJEU will need to address the question of the connection between these two instruments of secondary law.[24]

The Swedish social security administration has stated, with reference to paragraph 17a of the Preamble to Regulation 883/2004:

> Once the legislation of a Member State becomes applicable to a person under Title II of this Regulation, the conditions for affiliation and entitlement to benefits should be defined by the legislation of the competent Member State while respecting Community law.

[23] Ibid paras 30–31.

[24] See further M Coucheir and M Sakslin (eds), *The relationship and interaction between the coordination Regulations and Directive 2004/38/EC, Think Tank Report 2008*, Training and Reporting on European Social Security Project DG EMPL/E/3—VC/2007/0188 (Ghent 2008).

Thus, the Swedish requirement on a residence permit or right of residence under Directive 2004/38, in order to be considered as resident under Swedish law, should also be upheld in relation to the residence requirement of Regulation 883/2004. In practice this means that the fulfilment of the conditions for legal residence under the Directive is a condition for being considered as resident under the Swedish Code of Social Security. Consequently, however, this means that since the residence concept in Regulation 883/2004 (Article 11 of 987/2009) is broader than that of Swedish law, some persons for whom Sweden would be considered as their competent state would still not be eligible for Swedish benefits, since they would not fulfil the residence requirement. This conclusion has little or no support in the wording of the Regulation.

It would be even more difficult to argue that the Swedish demand for legal residence and right of residence under the Directive is a precondition for fulfilling the residence criterion in Swedish law in relation to maintenance support for the elderly. This hybrid benefit is classified as a non-contributory benefit according to Article 70 of Regulation 883/2004; it is not exportable and must under all circumstances be paid only by the state of residence. Being an Annex X benefit, it is available solely to persons habitually resident in Sweden according to the Regulation, even though there is no reference to Directive 2004/38. The person must, of course, also fulfil the other conditions to be eligible for the benefit. However, for a pensioner on a small pension or no pension at all, it would be possible to meet the requirement on sufficient resources by relying on Swedish benefits.

One example of this, at least in part, was recently seen in a judgment from the Swedish Migration Court of Appeals.[25] The case concerned a Polish citizen and pensioner who moved to Sweden, where her two adult children lived and worked. After registering as a resident in Sweden, she applied for and was granted maintenance support for the elderly, as well as a housing supplement, by the social insurance administration. This was fairly unproblematic, as both benefits are social insurance benefits granted on the objective basis of residence to those pensioners who cannot support themselves. However, the question arose of whether this granting of a special non-contributory social security benefit, as falling within the scope of Regulation 883/2004, would deprive the person of the right to residence according to the implemented Directive 2004/38? The question thus was whether the residence-based benefit providing for Just Distribution was awarded to a person outside the scope of the solidarity expressed in Swedish law, due to the permissible limits to this solidarity made possible under Directive 2004/38. Was the Polish pensioner, as a recipient of the residence-based benefit maintenance support for the elderly, in fact becoming an unreasonable burden on the social assistance system of the host Member State of Sweden, according to Articles 7(b) and 14 of Directive 2004/38, as implemented in Swedish law?

[25] MÖD 2011:19.

The Migration Court came to the conclusion (without asking the CJEU for a preliminary ruling) that since the Swedish benefit was not awarded according to the Swedish Social Services Act, but according to the Code of Social Security, the benefit could not be considered social assistance. Swedish preparatory works also support this line of interpretation.[26] Accordingly, the Polish pensioner could not be considered an unreasonable burden on social assistance, the right of residence could be upheld and the fear of expulsion could be dismissed.

From a Swedish perspective, this outcome is not surprising, but it does show not only how EU law has broadened the possible scope of benefits aimed at providing for Just Distribution in a national context; it also illustrates that this is a sign that social security law in residence-based systems can be used as leverage in actually meeting or exceeding the criteria of Directive 2004/38. Benefits in the host state, or in the new residence state, can be claimed in relation to meeting the requirements in respect of both sickness insurance and basic income protection, thus meeting the criteria for legal residence.

VII. CONCLUSIONS

One problem for European social security systems is that there are an increasing number of persons in need of a secured income. Two of the reasons for this are the ageing population, and the problem of keeping people in the labour market. From the Swedish perspective, this pressure on social security has meant that there has been a need for reform and thus changes in social security law. The reformed Swedish pension system is designed to cope with this increasing inflow of beneficiaries, a result of an ageing population. From a normative perspective, this means that there was a shift in how insurance, equality and securement of basic income were expressed through the pension system. We can still see, however, that the new system reflects the same normative patterns as the old system, ie there is an emphasis on guaranteeing an income level with income-related benefits, combined with the need to secure the right to a basic pension income for those residing in Sweden. As regards normative patterns, the pattern of Just Distribution is still an important feature of the Swedish pension system. According to Christensen, the need for securing basic income has grown, although the normative pattern of Just Distribution has not been strengthened in pension reform. Instead, there has been a movement towards an increased emphasis on earnings-related benefits, acquired rights and market-function.[27]

These legal constructs, the benefits based on the pattern of Just Distribution, are by their nature residence-based and limited to a specific territory. The limit of this solidarity is decided by the status of residence and the degree of

[26] T Erhag, 'Uppehållsrätt i socialförsäkringen' in *Festskrift to Lotta Vahlne Westerhäll* (Stockholm, Santérus förlag, 2011).

[27] Christensen, 'Normativa grundmönster i socialrätten', above n 1.

integration. During the 1990s and the Swedish pension reform there were also legal adjustments made in relation to coping with EU law and the fear of the uncontrolled export of benefits. The introduction of pro rata calculation in relation to residence-based guarantee pension was a clear expression of a fear of outflowing pension rights. This export was not possible earlier through the mechanism of upholding residence criteria, which after EU membership was seen as being potentially discriminatory.

This change, however, created a gap in the intended protection of Just Distribution in the pension scheme, as incoming persons without sufficient pension might need basic income protection upon arrival in Sweden. This need was no longer met by the residence-based guarantee pension. The legislator thus created a new expression of Just Distribution in the Swedish pension system, and we now see an increased emphasis on means-tested, social assistance-type benefits also in pension legislation. This functions as a final safety net for pensioners, no matter what their origin.

In this chapter, I have shown that the application of these benefits poses a challenge, especially in relation to an increased right to free movement for all EU citizens, even for those not economically active. The changes made by Regulation 883/2004 and Directive 2004/38 thus created a movement in the normative pattern of Just Distribution.

The new Regulation 883/2004, with its widened personal scope and extensive definition of residence, together with a strengthened right of residence and equal treatment also in relation to social benefits, has now put some pressure on Swedish law. For economically active persons, there is hardly any possibility of upholding the residence criteria.

For the economically non-active, there are such possibilities, but the assessment of the right of residence and the understanding and interpretation of lawful residence, which are distributed over various administrative bodies, as well as the varying demands in different kinds of legislation, have made the handling of the right of residence under the implemented Directive 2004/38 very difficult for Swedish administrative authorities. In addition, it is very difficult for a migrant to predict the outcome of the interpretation of lawful residence by the various national authorities, such as those for migration, taxes and social security. When arriving in a country with residence-based social security, this is of utmost importance. A gap in the understanding of residence in EU law and national law might otherwise mean the loss of benefits, as well as the right of residence. One basic demand for the application of Swedish residence criteria in social security law is to make these clear and precise, and possible to predict in advance. This demand has also been expressed by the CJEU in the *Collins* judgment.[28]

There is an obvious risk of mixing the understanding of residence under national law with the understanding of residence under EU law and Regulation

[28] Case C-138/02 *Collins* [2004] ECR I-2773, para 72.

883/2004. A comparison would seem to imply that the concept of residence is broader in EU law than in Swedish law, and under such circumstances there must be room for giving precedence to the broader interpretation. An example is provided by the fact that the demand for lawful residence under Directive 2004/38 is expressed neither in Regulation 883/2004, nor in Swedish social security legislation. There are attempts currently in progress to clarify this in relation to other Swedish legislation (Folkbokföringslagen/Law on National Registration). Similar clarification would also be welcome in social security law. However, the Swedish legislator cannot have an impact on the relationship between Regulation 883/2004 and Directive 2004/38. It is not clear whether residence according to the Regulation presumes lawful residence under Directive 2004/38. Nothing in the Regulation indicates this.

For Swedish residence-based social security, this means that the demand for lawful residence vaguely expressed in the preparatory works of the Swedish Social Security Code can hardly be upheld in relation to the residence-based benefit of maintenance support for the elderly. This benefit is also a special non-contributory benefit, available solely to persons having their habitual residence in Sweden, under Regulation 883/2004, Article 70. For a pensioner migrating to Sweden, with little or perhaps no pension to export to Sweden, it would thus seem possible to fulfil the requirement on sufficient resources (Article 7(1)(b) of Directive 2004/38) by relying on a benefit in the host country of Sweden. The same argument applies to the right to health care. If a person is registered as resident in Sweden under national registration law, that formal status is the single requirement for full health care coverage under Swedish law.

If this line of argumentation is accepted, the result will be remarkable. The conditions for the rights to free movement and residence in other EU Member States, having sufficient resources and having comprehensive sickness insurance cover, would then be covered by access to benefits in the host state—Swedish benefits. There might be possibilities to overcome this, through careful changes in Swedish law. However, from the perspective of equal treatment and Just Distribution, it is apparent that this situation forces us to rethink the purpose and normative foundations of social security law.

Or, as Anna Christensen expressed it:

> Movement across old national borders also causes the old frontiers of solidarity, previously regarded as self-evident, to appear in a new normative light as a violation of a new principle of equality, where all who belong to a *greater* community are treated in an equal manner.[29]

[29] Christensen and Malmstedt, 'Lex loci laboris versus Lex loci domicilii', above n 2.

13

Normative Patterns in the Context of Divorce in Sweden

EVA RYRSTEDT

I. INTRODUCTION

FAMILY LAW, AND primarily marital law, is a part of the legislative system that has deep roots in how people think and feel about the formation of the family. It is also strongly connected to tradition.[1] These are probably the most prominent reasons for the difficulty in harmonising the legislation of different nations. Another aspect of this difficulty is of course the construction of the rules that enable, for example, the individual's independence, such as the rules constituting the welfare state or the rules on equality of men and women. These rules provide the basis for the necessity and the possibility for constructing different marital rules.

Harmonisation of family law has been debated throughout the last century in the Nordic countries, and this fact makes clear just how difficult such a prospect is(!) The Nordic countries are fairly similar regarding their views on the individual's independence, the participation of men and women in the workplace, and how the welfare state is construed. Nevertheless, and despite the actual efforts made (principally during the twentieth century), the similarities in family law are strong, but so are the dissimilarities(!)[2]

However, it is not only harmonisation within the Nordic countries that has been the subject of debate, but also harmonisation in Europe. A group under the name of the Commission on European Family Law (CEFL) was founded in 2001, and since then has been investigating whether a harmonisation of family law within Europe would be possible. Their work has, inter alia, resulted in two sets of principles: Principles of European Family Law regarding Divorce and

[1] Compare E Ryrstedt, *Bodelning och bostad; ekonomisk självständighet eller gemenskap* (Lund, Juristförlaget, 1998) 383 and *Äktenskapsbalk. Förslag av familjelagssakkunniga*, SOU 1981:85, 97–100.

[2] See further for harmonisation in Sweden, E Ryrstedt,'Ett strategiskt förhållningssätt till harmonisering' (2005) *Svensk Juristtidning* 851. See also E Ryrstedt, 'Anmälan' av Katharina Boele-Woelki *et al*, *Principles of European Family Law, regarding Divorce and Maintenance Between Former Spouses* (Intersentia, 2004)170; Katharina Boele-Woelki *et al*, *Principles of European Family Law, regarding Parental Responsibility* (Intersentia, 2007) 331; (2011) 3 *Juridisk Tidskrift* 748.

Maintenance between Former Spouses, and Principles of European Family Law regarding Parental Responsibilities.[3] In constructing these principles, the CEFL has attempted to maintain consistency regarding which concepts to use in the legislation—without, however, ensuring that the various countries interpret the concepts in the same way. Particularly in cases where the content of a concept is dependent on interpretation, this proves to be an intricate and difficult affair.[4]

Throughout the Nordic countries, marital regulations are based on the shared notion of economic independence, but at the same time on the ongoing marriage as a community.[5] This view of economic independence is particularly significant when the marriage ends in a divorce. Today, maintenance between former spouses is an exception and very rare in both Sweden and the other Nordic countries, but this is not the case in most other European countries. The welfare state has thus transferred the previous marital responsibility onto the state.[6]

These notions of economic independence after the dissolution of a marriage, and thus the 'clean break' principle[7] in the case of divorce, are a powerful part of today's society in Sweden and the other Nordic countries. One of the reasons that a harmonisation with other European countries regarding the economic consequences of divorce law may be difficult to achieve is the aforesaid strong hold on people's minds compared to the notions of dependency governing the situation after the dissolution of a marriage in other countries. However, as the rights of individuals seem to increase in strength throughout Europe, the normative perspective of harmonisation of family law is important in conforming the legislation to these strong views on individuality and independence.

Thus, the basis for the 'clean break' principle in Swedish divorce law is an interesting matter for debate. With a starting point in the normative patterns (discussed further in the next section) of 'Community', 'Economic Independence', 'Established Position' and 'Just Distribution', which have formed the Swedish law on marriage and divorce, this chapter aims to discuss the possible effects of the Swedish 'clean break' principle after a divorce, meaning the ability to end the marriage and thereby terminate the obligations between the former spouses (the obligation to pay maintenance for children is not included, however).[8] The

[3] By Katharina Boele-Woelki, Frédérique Ferrand, Cristina Beilfuss Gonzáles, Maarit Jänterä-Jareborg, Nigel Lowe, Dieter Martiny and Walter Pintens.

[4] Compare Ryrstedt, 'Anmälan', above n 2, 760–61.

[5] Ibid 762. See further Ryrstedt, *Bodelning och boskap*, above n 1, 17–22 and 29–55. For marriage as based on unity and community, compare and contrast A Agell, 'Familjestabiliteten i Sverige: ett rättsligt perspektiv' (1992) *Kungliga Vitterhets Historie och Antikvitetsakademiens årsbok* 132 and A Agell, 'Individ, familj, stat: om värderingar i familjerättslagstiftningen under 1900-talet' (1984) *Svensk Juristtidning* 715.

[6] Compare regarding Sweden, Ryrstedt, 'Anmälan' above n 2, 762.

[7] See further for this concept S Harris-Short and J Miles, *Family Law: Text, Cases and Materials* (Oxford, Oxford University Press, 2007) 547–48. It has been said that the notion is easy to fulfil, where there is enough capital to meet the parties' claims.

[8] The way the notion is used, eg, in England includes child maintenance, Harris-Short and Miles, *Family Law*, above n 7, 547–48.

'clean break' principle as such has an impact both on the ongoing marriage, the situation arising in connection with the dissolution of the marriage, and the situation after the dissolution of the marriage; primarily on furthering equality in the working lives of spouses and ex-spouses, whether of the same sex or not. Another important aspect of the access to divorce is the possibility for an individual to reconstruct a family, for example through remarriage.

II. TENSION BETWEEN NORMATIVE PATTERNS AND A STRANGE MIX OF RULES

From a legislative point of view, marriage in Sweden is a strange mix of rules. Few other areas of the law are so clearly based on the evolution of society, as taken in the broad sense of culture, religion, industrial development, and perhaps most of all, the views on different gender roles, both within the family and in society.

This rather diverse mix of rules in marriage legislation is especially evident in the case of the legislation on divorce. These rules are of great interest, since, originating in society as they do, they greatly affect the situation for ex-spouses after the dissolution of their marriage. At the same they possibly also enhance the spousal perception of independence, based on the financial regulation existing between the spouses. These rules are dependent on life within the former marriage, just as life within the marriage is dependent on the rules; but also on the way the individual man or woman is perceived in Sweden.

The different notions governing the rules on marital law relate to the theory of law as normative patterns in a normative field, as developed by Anna Christensen. The common trait of these patterns is the tension between them. These patterns are active within a normative field,[9] the interest in this chapter being divorce law. As expressed by Christensen, these normative patterns are deeply rooted, meaning they are decisive for how people think and act in everyday life; but they are also decisive for legal developments.[10]

Discussing different normative patterns in the normative field of any part of marital law, however, can hardly occur without including the concept of status. As Christensen stresses, the process has gone from status to contract in developing modern society.[11] In older times, an individual's status in society determined his

[9] A Christensen, 'Skydd för etablerad position—ett normativt grundmönster' (1996) 4 *Tidsskrift for Rettsvitenskap* 527. For more on normative patterns see, eg, A Christensen, 'Polycentricity and Normative Patterns' in H Petersen and H Zahle (eds), *Legal Polycentricity: Consequences of Pluralism in Law* (Aldershot, Ashgate, 1995).

[10] A Christensen, *Hemrätt i Hyreshuset* (Stockholm, Juristförlaget, 1994) 2.

[11] Christensen, 'Skydd för etablerad position', above n 9, 530. See also H Sumner Maine, *Ancient Law: Its Connection with the Early History of Society, and its Relation to Modern Ideas*, 11th edn (London, John Murray, 1887) 304–6, and M Weber, *Wirtschaft und Gesellschaft: Grundriß der verstehenden Soziologie*, 5th edn (J Winckelmann (ed), Tübingen, Mohr, 1972) 401–3 and 426. Cp also PS Atiyah, *The Rise and Fall of Freedom of Contract* (Oxford, Oxford University Press, 1979) 259.

or her social relations.[12] Thus, the theory of interest here—Christensen's theory on normative basic patterns—does relate to the theory of the development of society going from status to contract, as developed mainly by Max Weber.[13] The kinship between Christensen's normative theory and the model of societal development from status to contract is evident.[14] The notions of community, following the status within the family as opposed to individuality and contract, involve an embedded conflict between individual ownership and the rules on marital property and its division.[15]

Status, however, cannot be understood in the original way in a marriage of today. Instead, the concept of status must be interpreted in the context of modern society. The remaining feature, and the most important one for the relationship to be viewed as a status relationship, would appear to be the coherent normative relations of the married couple. Even if a marriage of today entails both duties and rights (not the case in archaic marriages),[16] there still do not appear to be many legitimate separate interests, since these must give way to the best interests of the married couple.

Though certain grounds for divorce were acknowledged in Sweden as early as the sixteenth century, the fundamental idea was to permit divorce only in extreme cases, in order to uphold the stability of the family,[17] which in turn laid the foundations for marriage being perceived as a lifelong union. The fact that this view[18] still prevails is another indicator of today's ongoing marriage taking the form of a status relationship, as a relationship such as the one stressed by Christensen is, in essence, indissoluble.[19] Though nowadays the perception of marriage as always being lifelong is a fiction, that fiction still upholds the status relationship. Since the constitution of a marriage today is founded on a contract that includes components such as independence, varying interests and the right to terminate the contract, the status relationship can never gain the penetrating power it had in earlier times. However, the contract, being based on free will, can still be termed a status contract—meaning a change in the legal circumstances for the individual in the manner described by Weber,[20] entailing eg the right of inheritance.[21]

[12] Christensen, 'Skydd för etablerad position', above n 9, 530.

[13] See further M Weber, *Ekonomi och samhälle: förståelsesociologins grunder del 2* (Lund, Argos, 1985).

[14] A Christensen, *Normative Development within the Social Dimension*, Norma 1996:1 (Lund, 1996) 7.

[15] Ryrstedt, *Bodelning och bostad*, above n 1, 15.

[16] See further A Christensen, 'Konflikt eller harmoni: två normativa strukturer' in Sällskapet för politisk filosofi (ed), *Rättigheter, Politisk filosofi* (Stehag, 1988) 42.

[17] Christensen, 'Skydd för etablerad position', above n 9, 560.

[18] As can be seen eg in the preparatory work preceding the new Marriage Code in 1988, SOU 1981:85, 100.

[19] See for a further explication on different types of interests within a contract, Christensen, 'Konflikt eller harmoni', above n 16, 42.

[20] Compare. Weber, *Ekonomi och samhälle*, above n 13, 198.

[21] Ibid 196.

Throughout history, notions of community between spouses have been very strong in marital law in Sweden, and this is still the case. This is evident in the legislation governing the perception of the ongoing marriage.

Even if time has led to more contract elements within marriages,[22] due perhaps primarily to the shift towards greater independence for women, marriage is still perceived as a unit, in both personal and economic matters. The expressions of this unit in the 1920 Swedish Marriage Code, where the unit was characterised by responsibility for each other and for the children, and where the spouses were presumed to cooperate,[23] are in principle just as evident in today's legislation as they were nearly 100 years ago.

The tension in the normative structure is especially evident within marriage; the individual's economic independence is the basis for certain parts of the rules, while the community within the marriage is strong.[24] Perhaps the most prominent feature of community in the ongoing marriage, however, is the notion of the rights of both spouses to the same standard of living.

This feature was not part of the law until the 1920 Marriage Code, simply because previously there was no need for such legislation. In those days, the status relationship of marriage entailed the family's whole way of living. It was thus the abandonment of the patriarchal views on marriage, and the developing views on men and women as being independent individuals that resulted in the necessity of regulating their community.[25] The continuing strong position of community within marriage is demonstrated by the persistence of the rules on maintenance within marriage.

Aside from the notion of a spouse entering a marriage of his or her own free will, the development of marital legislation over the last 100 years has been determined by the dissolution of the marriage now being based solely on a spouse's decision to end the marriage. This development means that the contract has been further cemented. The spouses are also even more independent in relation to each other, since they are viewed as autonomous individuals.[26]

However, contrary to this development, the notion of community still remains. Each of the spouses may terminate the contract of marriage itself, but they cannot obviate the consequences of the notion of community in the marriage.

Another consequence of the community within the marriage is thus the demand for division of property between the parties upon the dissolution of the marriage. Such a division is based on fairness (often founded on a general need from a social perspective), and the normative pattern of Just Distribution thus deals with distributing and redistributing values.[27] At the same time, however,

[22] Ryrstedt, *Bodelning och bostad*, above n 1, 30.
[23] Familj och äktenskap I, SOU 1972:41, s 109.
[24] Ryrstedt, *Bodelning och bostad*, above n 1, 34.
[25] Ibid 41.
[26] Compare Christensen, 'Konflikt eller harmoni', above n 16, 42.
[27] See Christensen, 'Skydd för etablerad position', above n 9, 528 for Just Distribution as a normative pattern and for an identification and description of it.

ideas of individuality have developed and more recently become stronger. This means that the tensions between notions of such a community and the ideas of individuality can be found in most rules in contemporary Swedish matrimonial law. Like the normative practice, changes in society determine the strength of these patterns.[28] The patterns of individual ownership and economic independence, however, are also closely related to the Market-Functional pattern, as identified and described by Christensen. This is an important pattern for many normative relations in society. Herein, the free contract is entailed, which also can be considered as a normative pattern in its own right, as it appears in other contexts and in a more basic sense.[29]

III. FEATURES OF INTEREST IN MARITAL LAW

As stated in the above, a new Marriage Code was introduced in Sweden in 1920. It consisted of some rather liberal rules, a fact best demonstrated by many of these rules still being in force(!)

In examining some of these rules, we find that one of the main ones is the right for spouses to live at the same standard within the marriage. This originates from a regulation stating that both spouses must contribute whatever he or she is able to during the marriage. If the one requires more, then the other must lend his or her support.[30] This usually works out successfully (more or less) as long as the two parties are married. In a marriage where one of the spouses is a high earner and the other is not, the spouses' internal affairs are usually arranged in a manner acceptable to both. Though formal means exist to force the higher earner to pay the other more (via maintenance within the marriage even though the spouses are still living together), in most cases, such a line of action would lead to a divorce and is seldom adopted.

Nevertheless, these rules still form the basis for the way spouses should cohabit within the marriage. However, contradictory to this basis for the marriage, each spouse owns his or her own property and has his or her own debts within the marriage.[31] This being said, it must still be stressed that spouses may of course co-own a property, just as other persons may do. Each spouse would then own his or her own share of that property. Superimposed on these rules are the rules on marriage property and separate property. Spousal property is marriage property as the main rule, which means that the net value is usually divided into two equal parts after dissolution of the marriage. There are several ways for property

[28] Ryrstedt, *Bodelning och bostad*, above n 1, 18.

[29] Christensen, 'Skydd för etablerad position', above n 9, 529–31. Compare also A Numhauser-Henning, *Rätten till fäderneslandet, Om jordförvärvslagen och dess funktioner mot bakgrund av jordbrukets utveckling i det svenska samhället* (Lund, Juristförlaget i Lund, 1988) 151; A Numhauser-Henning, *Den neoliberala arbetsrätten: exemplet Chile* (Lund, Juristförlaget i Lund, 1996) 144.

[30] See for rules on maintenance during the marriage Marriage Code (Äktenskapsbalk (1987:230)), ch 6, ss 1–6.

[31] Marriage Code, ch 1, s 3.

to become separate property, however.[32] Separate property will not normally be part of the division between spouses in the event of a divorce.[33] The main ways for property to become separate is by spouses entering into a nuptial agreement, or when a third party gives away possession with the condition that the received property be separate, as may also occur in a will.[34]

At the time when the new Marriage Code was being introduced, divorce was still a rather unusual concept, but it evolved rapidly, due to the emerging view on marriage as a voluntary union, and divorce soon became fairly easy to obtain. Nevertheless, it was 1973 before the final step was taken to accord divorce the status of a right for each spouse. The Swedish legislation was then amended in accordance with societal development and the echo of individuality permeating it. Since then, the wish of one spouse to divorce the other is all it takes—the mere wish is sufficient and the decision is respected.[35]

During the first part of the twentieth century, in the environment of a very low divorce rate, the need to provide maintenance to a former spouse after a divorce was finalised, was taken as self-evident. Christensen demonstrates this accepted need as an outcome of the normative pattern of Established Position.[36] As the right to divorce developed, maintenance to a former spouse underwent changes in accordance with that development and with developments in society, meaning that women too had greater opportunities to support themselves. Even though the courts became more and more reluctant to award maintenance to a former spouse, possibly due to the rather ambiguous structure of the law, it did not take long before a new and clear attitude towards maintenance after divorce was spelled out in the law. The law was amended in 1978, the primary rule being that spouses should support themselves independently after a divorce. Even though there are a few exceptions to the main rule, these are not commonly used, mainly perhaps because of a condition in the *traveaux préparatoires*, which states that to be awarded maintenance, the need for it must have arisen as a direct result of the marriage itself,[37] which was subsequently also established in a case from the Supreme Court.[38] Another important part of the legislation on maintenance after divorce is that where a spouse *is* awarded maintenance, this is normally only a basic amount, ie the spouse does not normally have the right to continue living at the same standard as before, or at the same standard at which the other spouse lives after the divorce.[39]

[32] See further ibid ch 7, ss 1–3.

[33] See further ibid ch 10, s 1.

[34] See further ibid ch 7, ss 1–3.

[35] See further ibid ch 5.

[36] Christensen, 'Skydd för etablerad position', above n 9, 562.

[37] *Underhåll till barn och frånskilda, mm,* Prop. 1978/79:12, 139. See also *Underhåll till barn och frånskilda*, SOU 1977:37, 109.

[38] NJA 1998, 238.

[39] Compare SOU 1972:41, 113; A Agell, *Underhåll till barn och make?* 4th edn (Uppsala, Iustus, 1988) 118; A Agell and M Brattström, *Äktenskap, Samboende, Partnerskap*, 5th edn (Uppsala, Iustus, 2011) 69; L Tottie and Ö Teleman, *Äktenskapsbalken; En kommentar*, 2nd edn (Stockholm, Norstedts juridik, 2010) 133.

IV. EFFECTS OF THE RIGHT TO DIVORCE

A. Marriage: Contract and Status Relationship?

A marriage today in Sweden is both a contract-based concept and a status relationship.[40] The contract-based components are fairly evident insofar as what constitutes the ongoing marriage, ie the entering into the marriage and the ending of it.[41]

It could thus be said that marriage is a contract that includes a certain right to terminate. However, the effects of a termination indicate that this is a something more than the mere termination of a contract, since marriage is supposed to be a lifelong union. This notion is an important aspect of the ongoing marriage as a status relationship. The very foundation of a marriage is community or unity. This is demonstrated, for example, by the right of each spouse to live at the same economic standard within the marriage, notwithstanding that the spouses might only possess separate assets. Legally, this responsibility each spouse has towards the other is non-optional, even if it is, of course, possible for consenting spouses simply to disregard it. At the same time, however, the patterns of economic independence or individual ownership are prominent in the ownership as such, this being the basis for the rules stipulating that each spouse owns his or her own property.

The basic normative patterns of Community and Economic Independence or individual ownership thus seem to be in constant conflict with each other during the marriage, but also at the point of the dissolution of the marriage.[42] As stated above, the oldest and still clear concept of community is still evident in most of the rules that apply during a marriage, but is also what constitutes the basis for the division of property when a marriage is dissolved in Sweden. In being the cause of the legislation on how property should be divided between spouses (or rather former spouses), the normative pattern of Just Distribution makes an appearance. Notwithstanding these two patterns working towards the same goal, being an equal division of the spouses' net assets as the main rule, today the normative patterns of Economic Independence or individual ownership are in some ways gaining ground, perhaps most clearly seen in the main principle of each spouse being economically independent after a divorce, thus meaning that no maintenance should normally be awarded.

B. Co-aligning 'Just Distribution' and the 'Clean Break' Principle

That divorce has become the right of both spouses means that no one can be forced to stay in a marriage. However, the dissolution of a marriage—the

[40] Compare Ryrstedt, *Bodelning och bostad*, above n 1, 39, 383.
[41] Ibid 39.
[42] See, eg, ibid 15, 35, 120, 173.

terminating of the contract—does still entail certain effects; it creates various economic consequences. These effects have the same basis as the marriage itself, meaning primarily the normative pattern of Community. This unity, as perceived by both society and the law, characterises the ongoing marriage and results in the prevalence of the normative pattern of Just Distribution. Due to both of these normative patterns, divorce in Sweden is, as a rule, followed by a division of assets, as discussed above.[43]

The principle of a 'clean break', however, is also hailed. As stated above, the most important part of the 'clean break' principle is this: the primary rule regarding maintenance is that it should not be awarded to a former spouse. Former spouses are presumed capable of supporting themselves. Furthermore, and adding to the notion of independent ex-spouses, a child's need for maintenance is not calculated by taking into account that the parent with whom the child lives might not be able to work as much as he or she would like, or at least might not be able to pursue a career in the same manner as if he or she were not the parent providing the primary care for the child. However, in the child maintenance calculation, it is possible to include to some extent the fact that a residential parent's earning capacity is affected by the care of at least a *young* child.[44]

Maintenance between former spouses has been extremely rare in Sweden for about as long as divorce has been construed as a right. This is due to several factors, such as the desire for spouses to be able to truly end the contract-based concept that the entering into and ending of a marriage is perceived as. One prerequisite for such legislation is, of course, equality, not only between men and women as groups, but also, and more importantly, between the spouses in a marriage[45] (be they heterosexuals or homosexuals). Equality between men and women might not be the focal point any longer, but rather the equality between individuals taking on different family roles.

What makes the 'clean break' principle possible to maintain in Sweden, however, is the equal division of all spousal assets as the main rule. As an outcome of the community within the marriage, the division of all assets will put each spouse on the same economic footing for life after the marriage, apart from each spouse's own income. Thus, the 'clean break' principle is also a result of the patterns of Community and Just Distribution. However, here these two patterns are supported by the pattern of Economic Independence or individual ownership. Individuality is a vein permeating all of today's society, and is an important part of marriage, in struggle, conflict and finally, co-existence with the pattern of Community.

[43] Compare ibid 31.

[44] See, eg, NJA 1977, 748; NJA 1981, 1215; NJA 1982, 133; but compare and contrast NJA 1990, 697, where the Supreme Court did not find a reduction of the working hours a reason to affect child maintenance.

[45] Compare Prop. 1978/79:12, 139 and SOU 1977:37, 109.

One of the requisites for enabling such legislation is, of course, the fact that Sweden is a state based on social welfare, which goes back to an individualised view of its citizens. Once more, the basic patterns of Economic Independence or individual ownership need to be highlighted.

Thus, the 'clean break' principle does not mean that there are not any financial consequences. On the contrary, as discussed above, one very important consequence of the dissolution of marriage is the equal division of all property. Even if this principle can be avoided, for example through a nuptial agreement, usually it is not. Instead, the equal division principle seems to be a vital and well-accepted notion in society, which is a little surprising since ownership within the marriage is founded on the pattern of individual ownership or economic independence, where each spouse owns his or her assets individually.

Furthermore, this division is conducted once and for all, usually with no lingering after-effects from the marriage. Thus, it does not conflict with the 'clean break' principle.

So why then does this basic normative pattern of Just Distribution enjoy such a strong standing in Sweden? As stated previously, the pattern of Community is a very important normative pattern within marriage law, and has a close connection to the status relationship that the ongoing marriage so obviously is (at least in the 'new' forms it has taken). The equal division of spousal assets that generally follows the cessation of community is conducted with fairness as the starting point; this may be said to be based on a general need where a 'weaker' spouse needs protection, and always in the perspective of the pattern of Economic Independence or individual ownership.

Furthermore, the interaction of these different patterns and the tension between them form the reason why the equal division of property following the cessation of a marriage does not exist totally separately from the rules on maintenance between ex-spouses. On the contrary, in cases where an equal division does not occur, due, for example, to a nuptial agreement, it is possible for the economically 'weaker' spouse instead to be awarded maintenance in a 'one-off' payment(!)[46]

The opposition between the normative patterns of Community and Economic Independence or individual ownership and the constant conflict these patterns exhibit is clearest when it comes to the situation after a marriage has been dissolved. Though the conflict between the different normative patterns does sometimes render the legislation a strange mix of 'old and new', it has also been seen to further the ongoing development of gender equality between spouses. It cannot be disregarded that the normative pattern of community in a marriage forms the basis for the actual economic equality throughout its duration.[47] On the other hand, it is the normative pattern of Economic Independence or individual

[46] See Prop. 1986/87:1, 190 and 194. Compare also Ryrstedt, *Bodelning och boskap*, above n 1, 169–70.

[47] Compare Ryrstedt, *Bodelning och boskap*, above n 1, 389 and 401.

ownership that forms the basis for equality between men and women after the dissolution of a marriage.[48]

C. Effects on the Ongoing Marriage

The basic normative patterns of Community in concordance with Economic Independence or individual ownership have, as discussed above, led to both a just distribution of assets—an equal division—as well as to the primary rule of no maintenance. These two economic consequences of divorce are what form the 'clean break' principle, which has evolved out of legislation and practice.

A 'clean break' means a definitive termination of the relationship between the spouses. First and foremost, it is a prerequisite that the marriage be a contract so as to allow termination. In turn, the right to terminate all consequences of the marriage is a result of the existing gender equality between spouses as bearers of different family roles, and thus naturally mirrors this equality.[49]

Legislation and case law that promote a 'clean break' thus clearly presuppose gender equality between spouses, but may, of course, at the same time further such a development. Gender equality between spouses is most often seen as the ability of each spouse to support himself or herself, and often means that both spouses work outside the home.

Gender equality as the basis for, but also the outcome of a 'clean break' between spouses, is primarily based on the part of the 'clean break' principle emanating from the cardinal rule of no maintenance. Looking solely at the prospect of Just Distribution in connection with divorce, this might not affect, nor be affected by gender equality in the same way, and thus not affect how spouses actually live together during the marriage. If there were to be an effect, this would mean rather that a spouse might find it less important to work outside the home, since the assets have still been divided equally.

However, though this may be the case, the division stems from the pattern of community and may be moderated by the spouses knowledge that a divorce will mean a 'clean break' and will thus enhance the incentive for both to work and pursue a career. It thus seems evident that the composition of rules constituting the 'clean break' principle does not work on its own, nor can the rules be analysed in this manner.

D. Reshaping of Families

Having to pay maintenance to a former spouse can, of course, be very demanding, and in some respects may even be detrimental. Apart from the actual economic

[48] See further ibid 389–90.

[49] Compare Prop. 1978/79:12, 139. See also SOU 1977:37, 109.

burden, it may also prohibit various life choices, for example, career changes that, at least for a while, may entail less income.[50] Another important limitation making maintenance payments may entail. is that the spouse making the payments may have difficulties in marrying again (or forming other new family constellations). Even if the liable ex-spouse forms new family ties, he or she might be limited regarding the possible extent of the new family; for example, this might affect decisions on how many children will be born into the new family.

Even for the spouse receiving the maintenance, this situation may prove detrimental.[51] In addition to thwarting the quest to further gender equality aspects in general, it may put a stop to incentives to enhance a further career for this spouse, who is generally perceived as the weaker party and in need of economic protection. This can result in a former spouse remaining in a more economically disadvantageous situation than might otherwise be the case, because of receiving maintenance. This might not even be a conscious choice, which makes the institution of maintenance to a former spouse even more debatable. The awarding of maintenance might thus keep the recipient spouse in poverty, or at least in a worse economic situation than might otherwise be the case, without being aware of the consequences of his or her actions in connection with the maintenance.[52]

The 'clean break' principle thus entails another very important feature: it enables remarriage or other ways of reshaping the family. The perception of remarriage and cohabitation as positive and important features seems to emanate from a deeply rooted view of the nuclear family as the foundation of society. This view of the nuclear family appears to exist with no relation to the family having to be the original, biologically founded family. Instead, the clear value of this family type seems to be connected with the labelling itself, so this may also include a reconstructed or reshaped family.

The legislator's views on the importance of these new nuclear families are evident, for example, by facilitating the 'new' family to take precedence over the 'old' one. In Sweden, a parent needs to pay maintenance for a child only if he or she has the necessary means. When assessing if this is the case, a new spouse to be provided for, as well as children with whom the parent lives and provides for, are all taken into consideration, along with what the parent himself or herself requires, all this before determining whether there is anything over for the child that no longer lives with this parent.[53] Enabling such legislation are yet again the provisions of the social welfare system, which in this case provide a public support scheme, normally guaranteeing a child living with only one of its parents a certain amount as public support, though this support is coupled to a certain onus on repayment.[54]

[50] Compare SOU 1977:37, 109.
[51] Compare ibid.
[52] Compare Ur fattigdomsfällan, SOU 2001:24, regarding benefits.
[53] Children and Parents' Code (Föräldrabalken (1949:381)), ch 7, ss 1–6.
[54] Social Insurance Code (Socialförsäkringsbalk (2010:110)), chs 17–19.

Furthermore (and restating the importance of the reshaped nuclear family), a step-parent has subsidiary maintenance obligations towards a step-child living in the family. This new parent must step in and, together with the other parent, ensure that this child lives under the same economic conditions as the adults in the family. The importance of having someone economically responsible for the children is thus stressed by the legislator, as is the new family being validated as being as important as the old one.[55]

Finding a way to enhance gender equality and concurrently safeguard the interests of weaker parties, especially when considering that marriage is both contract-based and a status relationship, is difficult. Independence for both spouses, especially in the context of a possible divorce, is, however, important to achieve. Unless the goal of independent spouses is achieved, the right to divorce (especially for men) will exist as a right on paper only. Marriage being partly a status relationship quite naturally does involve some kind of division of assets as its outcome. At the same time, such a division has the advantage of providing an equal economic footing as a starting point for the 'after life' following divorce.

However, Just distribution does not seem to play a large role in the context of the old family, other than being part of the 'clean break' principle. The 'clean break' principle does provide for a total cessation of economic responsibilities between the former spouses, and, due to the equal division, a possibility for both former spouses to start new lives and families on an equal economic footing, regardless of whether or not this entails new partners.

V. CONCLUDING REMARKS

When discussing harmonisation, it is of course important to stress the differences between Sweden in particular, and the Nordic countries in general, from many other European countries. In many of these countries, the individual does not appear to be as autonomous as in Sweden—at least not yet. Those differences seem to be the primary root of the difficulties in attaining a goal such as harmonisation. The fact that the Nordic countries have now striven to reach this goal for nearly a century without succeeding is evidence of just how difficult it is in such a field—in family law, and perhaps most of all in divorce law. However beneficial such a harmonisation in Europe may prove in many other areas, the difficulties and the underlying reasons for the differences in this particular area need to be acknowledged.

When looking at the CEFL principles regarding divorce, we see that these principles include economic self-reliance for each spouse as the main principle after a divorce. However, economic maintenance with the aim of preventing injustice is possible, and the CEFL stresses the importance of the societal structure regarding

[55] Children and Parents' Code, ch 7, s 5.

the issue of maintenance.[56] This brings up the discussion of the importance of underlying structures, and of course the benefit of harmonisation if a concept or a regulation may be used not only in different ways in different nations, but is also presupposed right from the beginning to be used in these different ways. Such a harmonisation is in danger of being a harmonisation in name only. This might mean that the harmonisation may be to no avail, and may even be counter-productive. Having legislation whose wording is the same throughout the European Union, but which is interpreted differently in the different Member States, will confuse the application of the law. This may lead in turn to higher costs for both the courts and the inhabitants in the respective Member State. In addition, access to justice may also be jeopardised.

Instead, promoting an understanding of each Member State's respective national law would be important in facilitating the movement of the citizens of the European Union. The natural starting point would then be the conceptual framework, and making sure that the understanding of the different concept within the legal area here, marital law, is uniform.

Nevertheless, Nordic development in divorce law has set a precedent before, and may well do so again. The most important indicator for such a scenario is the development towards a more individual view in Europe and thus the growing status of economic independence in concordance with marital community, as described in this chapter. Such a development started in the Nordic countries nearly a century ago and since then has evolved into the current system. In the rest of Europe, this view on individuality has been an ongoing development, although it started later than in the Nordic region and seems to be developing at a slower rate. With the increasing movement within the European Union, it is probable that the impact of the notion of individuality may evolve faster than previous changes. In this case, the harmonisation of marital law may become a viable option.

[56] Ryrstedt, 'Anmälan', above n 2, 762.

Index